Historic Hiking Trails

Historic Hiking Trails

*A Directory of Over 900 Routes
with Awards Available to Hikers*

STEVE RAJTAR

McFarland & Company, Inc., Publishers

Jefferson, North Carolina, and London

Library of Congress Cataloguing-in-Publication Data

Rajtar, Steve, 1951–
    Historic hiking trails : a directory of over 900 routes with awards
available to hikers / Steve Rajtar.
      p.   cm.
    Includes index.
    ISBN 0-7864-1196-1 (softcover : 50# alkaline paper) ∞
    1. Trails—United States—States—Directories. 2. Hiking—
United States—States—Guidebooks. 3. Trails—United States—
States—Guidebooks. 4. United States—Guidebooks. I. Title.
GV199.4.R35 2002
917.304'929—dc21   2002003337

British Library cataloguing data are available

Manufactured in the United States of America

Cover photograph: Members of the Florida Trail Association hiking on a
spur of the Florida National Scenic Trail
Background map ©2002 Photospin

McFarland & Company, Inc., Publishers
  Box 611, Jefferson, North Carolina 28640
    www.mcfarlandpub.com

ACKNOWLEDGMENTS

This book describes hundreds of trails and provides an easy way to get in touch with the individuals who maintain them and provide detailed hike plans, plus the patches, medals and other items that are available. The countless hours that have been spent by the men and women, many of them in their teens, in establishing and continuing these trails, is greatly appreciated.

My job in writing this book was greatly facilitated because of the earlier compilations assembled by Ken Humphreys and the other members of Troop 343 in Memphis, and Richard Shields of *The Carolina Trader*. I'd also like to thank Rich Gagnon who was relentless in his seeking out information on trails that had incorrectly been assumed as terminated, and Frederick J. Oppliger who hiked about 150 of the trails I set up and made some very important corrections and improvements.

Thanks also to Carol Rodkey, who took the cover photo while we were on the Paisley Historical Trail.

Last, but most importantly, I want to thank my wife, Gayle, and my children, Jason and Kelly, who hiked many of these trails with me, sometimes against their will. They made it far more enjoyable to actually traverse the routes and make suggestions to the respective sponsors for improvements, so that the trails listed herein could be recommended to you.

CONTENTS

PREFACE

For too many of us, "History" was a subject in school that involved memorization of faceless dead people and dates of events that we had difficulty relating to. There was no obvious relevance to our lives. As a result, many adults and children want little to do with History.

That is unfortunate, because things that happened before give us a better understanding of how we arrived at this point in our society's evolution. It's fascinating to compare how primitive (or how modern) our ancestors appear to us in hindsight. Experiencing, not memorizing, History can be a fun and valuable activity.

For that reason, hundreds of historic trails have been established to make available to the general public information about the history of the areas in which they are located. While walking by the sites of actual historical events (rather then reading about them), one can get a feel of the times and people who helped form our country and communities. By walking the routes taken by early settlers, one can better imagine the hardships the pioneers faced. By walking the many battlegrounds, one can see how the armies conducted their campaigns, an activity far more valuable and interesting than rote memorization of casualty statistics and dates.

Most of the trails listed in this book are sponsored in some fashion by members of youth organizations, often because hiking is one of their major activities. Despite those relationships, nearly all of the trails and the listed awards are available to everyone, being located in our cities and public parklands. Even if you are not interested in patches and medals, a walk along the hike route while reading the written hike plan provided by the sponsor can provide a much better appreciation for the history of the area, superior to what you can get from a textbook.

INTRODUCTION

What Is a Historic Trail?

The broad category of "historic trails" includes a variety of walking, biking, driving and canoeing routes, the completion of which generally entitle the participants to awards of some sort. They are sponsored by youth groups, historical societies, community or commercial groups, and vary in length, terrain, and degree of historical import. Each trail fits into one or more of the following categories:

1. "Historic" Trail

The use of the word "historic," strictly speaking, implies that the trail route itself played some significant role in history. One example is the Trail of Tears, along which 18,000 Cherokees were forced against their will to walk from their homes in Alabama, Georgia and Tennessee to reservations in Oklahoma. Retracing their footsteps along that trail gives the hiker a feel for the hardships they suffered along the way.

2. "Historical" Trail

A trail designated as "historical" should be one which takes the hiker by or into buildings or sites which have some relationship to a significant person or event, but which itself is not a route which figured in history. An example of this type is the Historical Battlefield Trail at Chickamauga National Battlefield Park, where the hiker will see numerous statues, plaques, buildings and battle sites, but the foot trail itself lacks any historic importance.

3. Nature or Scenic Trails

These trails have been selected, not solely because of ties with history, but also because of the wildlife or scenery available along the route that can be viewed along with the historical sites. Often, plants or other items are labelled for the hikers' edification. Many of these are found at youth camps or public parks.

4. Recreational Trails

This type of trail is established for the long-distance hiker as well as the history buff. Even if it may pass along a historic route or include historical sites, its primary purpose is to give the outdoor enthusiast an established route to walk for health and enjoyment. A popular example of this type of trail is the 2135-mile Appalachian Trail.

The distinctions among these categories are generally not important to most people. Many "historic" hikes are misnamed "historical," and vice-versa, and only the hypertechnical historian is likely to care. The important factors are the established routes and the awards available upon their completion. In this book, any trail with these qualities is a "historic trail."

Sponsors of Historic Trails

The ways historic trails are created and maintained are as varied as the types of trails which exist. Many were laid out as community service projects, with the maintenance of records and the trails themselves taken over by various groups. But for these individuals' personal efforts, there would be no such trails showing hikers the way to these historical locations.

Some trails are sponsored by historical associations involved with the preservation of the history of a local area. They are often established in connection with a local historical museum, which usually lies along the hiking route. These trails generally emphasize the locale's culture and architecture through the years, as well as specific events and individual people.

A large number of trails, generally those outside of urban areas, would exist regardless of the awards program. A local organization interested in promoting use of the route will often develop a patch or other souvenir for the trail, which often runs through a battlefield or park.

A few trails, generally the longer, recreational trails, are sponsored by organizations whose major purpose is the maintenance of the physical aspects of the trails themselves. Often, awards are available for hiking a specific number of miles along the trail, rather than requiring the entire trail to be hiked.

Alternate Means of Transportation

Some of the described trails specifically allow bicycles, cars or canoes as alternatives to hiking on foot. Some prohibit these, but most trail brochures are silent on this point.

In this book, some trails are described as "appropriate" for bicycling. That only means that the terrain may be traversed on bicycles with reasonable effort. Whether completing the trail by bicycle entitles the individual to the awards is a different question, best asked when you request a copy of the trail brochure from the sponsor.

Explanation of Entries

Although most of the trail sponsors have provided complete information for this book, there are some trails for which such information is not available. There are other trails which used to exist, but no longer are maintained or no longer offer awards for their completion. These trails are listed at the end of each state. Some may perhaps be revived in the future, but at present they are "history" themselves.

Most of the trail descriptions have an entry for "sites." What is shown is a representative sampling of what can be seen along the route. The actual hike plan may contain descriptions of over a hundred sites of interest.

Keep in mind that this information will change from time to time, without advance notice. Prices will likely increase as trail sponsors use up their stock of awards and have to order new ones. Even if you have a brochure for a trail you wish to hike, unless it is very recent it is advisable to contact the sponsor to make sure that nothing important has changed. A phone call or letter can save an unnecessary surprise that can disappoint your group.

ALABAMA

Chinnabee Silent Trail

Location: Talladega National Forest near Talladega, AL. *Theme:* Nature. *Sponsor:* Talladega Chamber of Commerce, P.O. Drawer A, Talladega, AL 35160, (205) 362-9075; or U.S. Department of Agriculture, Forest Service, Talladega Ranger District, 1001 North St., Talladega, AL 35160-2503, (205) 362-2909.

Length: 6 miles (straight). *Route:* The trail begins at the Lake Chinnabee parking area (FS 600) and goes to the Pinhoti Trail. *Terrain:* Mountains, valleys and ridges. *Cycling:* Not permitted. *Awards:* Patch $4.00. *Submit:* No requirement. *Register:* Not required

Desoto Scout Trail

Location: Comer Scout Reservation, Mentone, AL. *Theme:* Various historical events, including a portion of the Trail of Tears. *Sponsor:* Choccolocco Council, BSA, 4110 McClellan Blvd., Anniston, AL 36201-2132, (205) 237-1777.

Length: 16 miles (straight). *Route:* The trail begins at DeSoto Falls and proceeds south through Camp Cloudmont, Comer Scout Reservation, and DeSoto State Park to end at Edna Hill Church. *Terrain:* Varied, rugged along portion of the Little River. *Cycling:* Not recommended. *Awards:* Medal $3.50; Patch $3.00; Coffee Mug $3.50. *Submit:* Group leader's certification of completion. *Register:* Not required. *Sites:* DeSoto Falls, Billys Ford, Lake Howard, Little River, Hartline Ford, Branner's Ridge, Lookout Mountain, Shelter Rock, Edna Hill Church.

Florence Alabama Historical Trail

Location: Florence, AL. *Theme:* Local history. *Sponsor:* BSA Troop 217, 80 Valley View Dr., Tuscumbia, AL 35674.

Length: 7 miles (loop). *Route:* The trail begins in MacFarland Bottom Park on the Tennessee River, heads north through the center of town, and returns to the start. *Terrain:* City streets. *Cycling:* Appropriate. *Awards:* Patch $3.50. *Submit:* Completed 15-item questionnaire. *Register:* Not required. *Sites:* First Presbyterian Church, O'Neal Bridge, Indian Mound, Wilson Park, W.C. Handy Home Museum, Pope's Tavern, Wesleyan Hall, Rogers Hall.

Horseshoe Bend National Military Park Trails

Location: Horseshoe Bend National Military Park, Daviston, AL. *Theme:* Nature and military park. *Sponsor:* Tukabatchee Area Council, BSA, 3067 Carter Hill Rd., P.O. Box 11106, Montgomery, AL 36111, (334) 262-2697 or fax (334) 834-6521.

Length: Horseshoe Bend Battlefield Trail—2.8 miles (loop). Horseshoe Bend Ecology Trail—2.1 miles (loop). *Route:* Both trails are located within the park. *Terrain:* Woods paths and paved roads. *Cycling:* Check first with the rangers for permission. *Awards:* 2 Patches $3.00 each. *Submit:* No requirement. *Register:* Not required.

Odum Scout Trail

Location: Talladega National Forest near Talladega, AL. *Theme:* Nature. *Sponsor:* Talladega Chamber of Commerce, City Hall

Building, P.O. Drawer A, Talladega, AL 35160, (205) 362-9075.

Length: 10.1 miles (straight). *Route:* The trail begins at the microwave towers atop Cheaha Mountain, then winds along the mountain west to High Falls, then to the old rock quarry near Pyriton. *Terrain:* Mountains and ridges. *Cycling:* Not recommended. *Awards:* Patch $2.75. *Submit:* Group leader's certification of completion. *Register:* Not required. *Sites:* Cheaha Mountain High Falls.

Pinhoti Trail

Location: Talladega National Forest near Heflin, AL. *Theme:* Recreation. *Sponsor:* Mrs. Lucille Morgan, Cleburn County Library, P.O. Box 428, Heflin, AL 36264.

Length: 62.8 miles (straight). *Route:* The trail endpoints are FR 600 near Friendship in the southwest, and Coleman Lake at FR 500-4 in the northeast. *Terrain:* Mountains, valleys and ridges. *Cycling:* Not recommended. *Awards:* Patch $3.00. *Submit:* No requirement. *Register:* Not required. *Sites:* Clairmont Gap, Patterson Gap, Adams Gap, Horseblock Mountain, Pine Mountain, Highrock Lake.

River Mont Cave Historic Trail

Location: Bridgeport, AL. *Theme:* Strategic Civil War area and ancient cave. *Sponsor:* Corky Coffman, 102 Carl Maynor Ln., Bridgeport, AL 35740, (256) 495-2667.

Length: 12 miles (straight). *Route:* The trail begins on the shore of the Tennessee River east of Bridgeport, follows roads through the city to Summerhouse Mountain, then up and over the mountain to Russell Cave National Monument. *Terrain:* Easy city and rural roads, steep switchbacks up and down Summerhouse Mountain. *Cycling:* Only possible on the first half and on top of the mountain. *Awards:* Medal $7.00; Patch $5.00; Hat pin $3.00. *Submit:* Group leader's certification of completion, stamped by ranger at Russell Cave. *Register:* Necessary to arrange for representative to take you to the starting point. *Sites:* Battery Hill, Split Rock, Kilpatrick Row, Russell Cave.

Tannehill Scout Trail

Location: Tannehill Historical State Park, McCalla, AL. *Theme:* Route of iron products from furnace to Confederate arsenal.

Sponsor: Tannehill Historical State Park, Rt. 1, Box 124, 12632 Confederate Pkwy., McCalla, AL 35111, (205) 477-6571.

Length: 12.6 miles (straight). *Route:* The trail begins at the base camp near Edd Farley Field, then proceeds to furnace, past slave and pioneer cemeteries, and ends at Chababa River. *Terrain:* Easy woods path. *Cycling:* Possible. *Awards:* Patch $2.50. *Submit:* No requirement. *Register:* Advance registration required to qualify for awards. *Sites:* Old Peanut House, Oglesby's Orchard, Marchant House, Oglesby House Site, Garden of Inspiration, Slave Cemetery, Old Ford, Stage Ford, Old Four Corners, Roger's Place, Double Team Hill, Hall's Sawmill Ford, Williams Home Site, Gray Hill School, Shady Grove Church, Pioneer Cemetery, Stone Stage House, Harmon House Site, Boothe Ford.

Tuscumbia Historical Trek

Location: Tuscumbia, AL. *Theme:* Historical places and people, including Helen Keller. *Sponsor:* BSA Troop 217, 80 Valley View Dr., Tuscumbia, AL 35674.

Length: 2 miles (loop). *Route:* The trail begins in Spring Park within the city, goes north on Main St., south on Water St., and back to the start. *Terrain:* City streets. *Cycling:* Appropriate. *Awards:* Patch $2.50. *Submit:* Completed 24-item questionnaire. *Register:* Not required. *Sites:* Colbert County Courthouse, Big Spring, Commercial Row, Post Office, Helen Keller Public Library, Stagecoach Stop, Railroad Depot, Ivy Green, Winston Home.

USS Alabama Historical Trail

Location: Mobile, AL. *Theme:* Local historical places and events. *Sponsor:* USS Alabama Historical Trail, Inc., 5860 College Pkwy., Mobile, AL 36613, (334) 675-7037.

Length: 11 miles (loop). *Route:* The trail begins at Fort Conde, follows Government St. and nearby streets westward, and returns to the start. *Terrain:* City streets. *Cycling:* Appropriate. *Awards:* Medal $5.00; Patch $4.00. *Submit:* Completed 12-item questionnaire. *Register:* As you arrive at Fort Conde. *Sites:* Fort Conde, Phoenix Fire Station, Washington Square, Magnolia Cemetery, Barton Academy, Lott Tapia House, Duffee Oak City Hall, Boyington Oak, Semmes Statue, Bishop Portier College,

Spanish Plaza, Twelve Oaks First Baptist Church, Oakleigh Mansion, Ketchum Mansion, Catholic Basilica, City of Mobile Museum, Church Street Cemetery, Semmes House, Calef-Staples Cottage, Matthews House, Shepard Home, Murphy High School, A.M.E. Zion Church, Carlen House, Government Street Methodist Church, Trinity Episcopal Church.

Other Alabama Awards

U.S.S. Alabama Overnight Award—Spend a night aboard a battleship, visit other water and aircraft. Patch included in overnight price. Bat-

tleship Memorial Park, P.O. Box 65, Mobile, AL 36601, (334) 433-2703.

Formerly Sponsored Trails

Big Spring Historical Trail
Chief Pushmataha Trail
Discovery Trail
Historic Montgomery Trail
Horseshoe Bend Historic Trail
Maxwell Historical Trail
Space Walk Scenic Trail
Thunderbird Scout Trail
Warpath Ridge Trail

ALASKA

Chilkoot Trail

Location: Near Skagway, AK. *Theme:* Historic route followed by hopeful gold prospectors in Gold Rush of 1898. *Sponsor:* Klondike Gold Rush National Historical Park, P.O. Box 517, Skagway, AK 99840, (907) 983-2921.
Length: 33 miles (straight). *Route:* The trail begins at the ghost town of Dyea, 9 miles from Skagway. It proceeds up to the pass summit, where hikers cross into Canada, then to Whitehorse, Yukon Territory. *Terrain:* Extremely rugged. *Cycling:* Not recommended. *Awards:* No "official" award, but patches and T-shirts for the trail are available at the sporting goods store in Skagway. *Submit:* No requirements. *Register:* At visitors center at the Klondike Gold Rush National Historical Park at 2nd Ave. and Broadway in Skagway. *Sites:* Chilkoot Pass, Dyea Ruins, Slide Cemetery, Finnigan's Point, Canyon City, Sheep Camp, The Scales, Lindeman Lake, Lake Bennett.

Iditarod Historic Trail

Location: Chugach National Forest between Anchorage and Seward, AK. *Theme:* Historic route through Johnson Pass. *Sponsor:* Western Alaska Council, BSA, 3117 Patterson St., Anchorage, AK 99504-4041, (907) 337-9547.

Length: 23 miles (straight). *Route:* The trail begins at approximately 101 Seward Hwy., then heads through Johnson Pass and rejoins the highway. *Terrain:* Rugged, with snow often present in the pass until late June. *Cycling:* Not recommended. *Awards:* Medal $5.00. *Submit:* Group leader's certification of completion. *Register:* At least 3 weeks in advance. *Sites:* Johnson Pass.

Iditarod National Historic Trail

Location: Seward to Nome, AK. *Theme:* Route taken by dogsled team taking diphtheria serum to Nome during a 1925 epidemic. *Sponsor:* Seward Iditarod Trail Blazers, Inc., P.O. Box 1923, Seward, AK 99664 (volunteer group for the Seward segment).
Length: Main Seward-Nome route is 926 miles (total trail network exceeds 2300 miles). *Route:* The trail begins on Fourth Ave. in Seward and heads north and west, passing through Girdwood, Eklutna, Knik, Susitna, Skwetna, Rainy Pass, Rohn River Roadhouse, Pioneer Roadhouse, Big River, Takotna, Moore Creek, Iditarod, Dishkakat, Kaltag, Unalakleet, Golovin, and Nome. There is also a "Northern Route". *Terrain:* Varies from city street to mountains, valleys, and tundra. *Cycling:* Portions are used for mountain biking. *Awards:* Patch $5.00.

Submit: No requirement. *Register:* Not required. *Sites:* Hoben Park.

Sitka Historic Trail

Location: Sitka, AK. *Theme:* Battle of Sitka and totem poles. *Sponsor:* National Park Service, Sitka National Historical Park, P.O. Box 738, Sitka, AK 99835, (907) 747-6281, Peter_Gorman@nps.gov.

Length: 1.75 miles (loop). *Route:* The trail winds through the park on both sides of the Indian River. *Terrain:* Walking paths. *Cycling:* Not appropriate. *Awards:* T-shirt $4.00. *Submit:* Shirts are available for purchase in the Visitor Center. *Register:* Not required. *Sites:* Russian Memorial, Tlingit Fort Site, 1804 Battleground, Merrill Rock, Sitka Sound, Indian River.

ARIZONA

Blue Primitive Area Trails

Location: Blue Range Primitive Area, east central AZ. *Theme:* Recreation. *Sponsor:* Grand Canyon Council, BSA, 2200 E. Cedar, Suite 12, Flagstaff, AZ 86001-1984, (520) 774-0685.

Length: Bear Mountain Trail—32 miles (straight). Blue River Trail—42 miles (straight). Horse Ridge Trail—22 miles (loop). Pueblo Park Trail—33 miles (straight). Strayhorse Creek Trail—29 miles (loop). *Routes:* The Horse Ridge Trail begins and ends on SR 666 one-half mile southwest of its junction with FR 567 by Beaverhead Lodge, and includes a stopover at Blue River. The Bear Mountain Trail begins at Trailhead #38 and ends near where Grant Creek crosses a highway. The Strayhorse Creek Trail begins and ends at Rose Peak off SR 666. The Blue River Trail starts at Hannigan's Meadow, follows an old wagon route, and ends where the San Francisco River meets FR 212. The Pueblo Park Trail begins at Burnt Corral south of Strayhorse at the junction of SR 666 and FR 587, and ends where Pueblo Creek meets FR 232 at the Forest Park Campground. *Terrain:* Rugged. *Cycling:* Not recommended. *Awards:* Neckerchief & Patch $5.00; 6 Segments $1.00 each. *Submit:* Group leader's certification of completion. *Register:* Not required.

Bradshaw Trails

Location: Prescott, AZ. *Theme:* Recreation. *Sponsor:* Grand Canyon Council, BSA, 2200 E. Cedar, Suite 12, Flagstaff, AZ 86001-1984, (520) 774-0685.

Length: 6 to 15 miles each. *Routes:* Bradshaw Trail—Starts on Senator Hwy. 3 miles west of Palace Station, and follows Water Shed Trail to Prescott (15 miles). Granite Mountain Trail—Starts at Iron Springs and goes to top of Granite Mountain and back (11 mile loop). Maverick Ridge Trail—Starts at junction of Senator Hwy. and road to Davis Dunkirk Mine and ends at Lower Wolf Creek Campground (6 miles). Mingus Mountain Trail—Starts at intersection of FT 102 and narrow gauge railroad, up the north side of Woodchute Mountain (8.5 miles). Sierra Prieta Trail—Starts at Prescott Pines Resort and ends at Highland Pines (11 miles). *Terrain:* Rugged. *Cycling:* Not recommended. *Awards:* Main Patch $2.50; 5 Segments $1.00 each. *Submit:* Group leader's certification of completion. *Register:* Not required

Butterfield Stage Route Trail

Location: Maricopa Mountains, south of Phoenix, AZ. *Theme:* Portion of trail used by Butterfield Stage on route from Tipton, MO, to San Francisco, CA. *Sponsor:* Theodore Roosevelt Council, BSA, 2969 N. Greenfield Rd., Phoenix, AZ 85016-7715, (602) 955-7747.

Length: 5.75 miles (straight). *Route:* The trail begins north of Maricopa, AZ, and is reached by taking the paved road (which turns to dirt later) heading toward Gila Bend, and following the signs from there. *Terrain:* Dirt path. *Cycling:* Possible. *Awards:* Patch. *Submit:* No requirement. *Register:* Not required

Catalina Challenge Trail

Location: Santa Catalina Mountains near
Tucson, AZ. *Theme:* Recreation. *Sponsor:*
Catalina Council, BSA, 5049 E. Broadway,
Tucson, AZ 87511, (520) 750-0385.

Length: 50 miles (straight). *Route:* The
trail begins at Oracle, AZ, and follows the
Oracle Ridge Trail, Wilderness of Rocks Trail,
Aspen Trail, Palisades Trail, Lower Bear
Canyon Trail, and ends at Sabino Visitors'
Center. *Terrain:* Rugged. *Cycling:* Not
recommended. *Awards:* Patch. *Submit:* No
requirement. *Register:* Not required

Chiricahua Crest Trail

Location: Santa Catalina Mountains near
Tucson, AZ. *Theme:* Recreation. *Sponsor:*
Catalina Council, BSA, 5049 E. Broadway,
Tucson, AZ 87511, (520) 750-0385.

Length: 30 miles (loop). *Route:* The trail
begins at Camp Victorio in Barfoot Park,
follows the crest of the Chiricahuas, down
Raspberry Ridge Trail, and into Rucker
Canyon. It then goes into Price Canyon and
returns to Camp Victorio. *Terrain:* Rugged.
Cycling: Not recommended. *Awards:* Patch.
Submit: No requirement. *Register:* Not
required

General Crook Trail

Location: Prescott, AZ. *Theme:* Follows
wagon route ordered built by General George
Crook in 1871. *Sponsor:* Grand Canyon
Council, BSA, 2200 E. Cedar, Suite 12, Flag-
staff, AZ 86001-1984, (520) 774-0685.

Length: 150 miles (straight). *Route:*
Segments: Fort Whipple to Fort Verde. Fort
Verde to General Springs. General Springs to
Cottonwood Wash. *Terrain:* Dirt path.
Cycling: Possible, but horseback is
recommended. *Awards:* Main Patch $2.50; 4
Segments $1.50 each; Medal for completing
all segments. *Submit:* Group leader's
certification of completion. *Register:* Not
required

Glen Canyon Trails

Location: Page, AZ, and Kanab, UT.
Theme: Recreation. *Sponsor:* Grand Canyon
Council, BSA, 2200 E. Cedar, Suite 12, Flag-
staff, AZ 86001-1984, (520) 774-0685.

Length: 25 to 78 miles each. *Routes:* Egypt
Trail—Trailhead is 10 miles down a dirt road
from Hole-In-the-Rock Road, then trail
drops to Escalante River, then to Coyote
Gulch (51 miles). Escalante Trail—Follows
Escalante Trail from Calf Creek to Coyote
Gulch (78 miles). Moki Trail—Start at Hall's
Crossing access road, go down Moki Canyon
to Lake Powell (30 miles). Moody Creek
Trail—From junction of dirt roads which go
to Moody and Silver Falls Creeks, hike to
Moody Creek, then along Escalante River,
then along Silver Falls Creek to the start (41
miles loop). Silver Falls Trail—Take the
Harris Wash Trailhead to the Escalante River,
then up Silver Falls Creek to the road
junction mentioned above (25 miles).
Terrain: Rugged. *Cycling:* Not
recommended. *Awards:* Main Patch $2.50; 6
Segments $1.00 each. *Submit:* Group leader's
certification of completion. *Register:* Not
required

Grand Canyon Trails

Location: Grand Canyon, AZ. *Theme:*
Recreation. *Sponsor:* Grand Canyon Council,
BSA, 2200 E. Cedar, Suite 12, Flag-staff, AZ
86001-1984, (520) 774-0685.

Length: Varies. *Routes:* Bass, Grandview,
Hance and Hermit Trails—South Rim to
Colorado River. Paria Canyon Trail—US 89
in Utah to Lee's Ferry, AZ (45 miles).
Primitive Trails—Either rim to Colorado
River. Rainbow Bridge Trail—Either Rainbow
Trail along west side of Navajo Mountain
starting at Rainbow Lodge, or Cameron Trail
starting near Navajo Mountain School and
going on the east and north sides of Navajo
Mountain. Rim-to-Rim-to-Rim Trail—Same
as Rim-to-Rim, with return (47 miles). Rim-
to-Rim Trail—From South Rim, take Bright
Angel Trail or South Kaibab Trail, then North
Kaibab Trail up Bright Angel Creek to North
Rim. Supai to River Trail—Mooney Falls to
Colorado River (12 miles). Thunder River
Trail—North Rim to Colorado River.
Terrain: Rugged. *Cycling:* Not recommended.
Awards: Main Patch $2.50; 11 Segments $1.00
each; Medal for completing 3 segments.
Submit: Group leader's certification of
completion. *Register:* At least 3 months in
advance (for permit to hike the Canyon)
Sites: Colorado River, Grand Canyon.

High Line Trail

Location: Tonto National Forest near
Phoenix, AZ. *Theme:* Access route built by
forest rangers. *Sponsor:* Grand Canyon
Council, BSA, 2200 E. Cedar, Suite 12, Flag-
staff, AZ 86001-1984, (520) 774-0685.

Length: 51 miles (straight). *Baker Butte Segment* 18 miles. *Fish Hatchery Segment* 17 miles. *Promontory Butte Segment* 16 miles. *Route:* The trail begins south of Pine, AZ, and parallels the General Crook Trail to Camp Geronimo, Washington Park, Tonto Creek and See Canyon, and ends near SR 260. *Terrain:* Rugged. *Cycling:* Not recommended. *Awards:* Patch. *Submit:* No requirement. *Register:* Not required. *Sites:* Milk Ranch Point, Washington Park, Zane Grey's Cabin, Trout Hatchery, See Canyon.

Ho-Ho-Kam Trail

Location: Santa Catalina Mountains near Tucson, AZ. *Theme:* Recreation. *Sponsor:* Catalina Council, BSA, 5049 E. Broadway, Tucson, AZ 87511, (520) 750-0385.

Length: 30 miles (loop). *Route:* The trail begins at Camp Lawton Boy Scout Camp and goes to the top of Mt. Bigelow, through Marshall Gulch, along Lemmon Creek and Sabino Creek, then along Palisades Trail, and back to the start. *Terrain:* Rugged. *Cycling:* Not recommended. *Awards:* Medal. *Submit:* No requirement. *Register:* Not required

Mt. Kimball Trail

Location: Catalina Mountains—25 miles NE of Tucson, AZ. *Theme:* Climbing. *Sponsor:* Catalina Council, BSA, 5049 East Blvd., Suite 200, Tucson, AZ 85711, (520) 750-0585 ext. 14.

Length: 12 miles. *Route:* The trail begins at the north end of Alverron Rd. at Finger Rock Canyon, and ends at the top of Mt. Kimball. *Terrain:* Steep and moderate incline. *Cycling:* Impossible. *Awards:* Medal $7.50. *Submit:* Patch request. *Register:* Not required. *Sites:* Catalina Mountains, Finger Rock Canyon, Mount Kimball.

Oak Creek-Sedona Rim Trails

Location: Cococino National Forest, Sedona, AZ. *Theme:* Recreation. *Sponsor:* Grand Canyon Council, BSA, 2200 E. Cedar, Suite 12, Flag-staff, AZ 86001-1984, (520) 774-0685.

Length: (distances in miles) Overnight Hikes: Dry Beaver Creek Trail (6-8), East Pocket Trail (a/k/a A.B. Young Trail) (5-7), Loy Trail (10), Mooney Trail (12-14), Wet Beaver Creek Trail (6-8), Wilson Mountain Trail (6-8). Day Hikes: Casner Canyon Trail

(4), Cookstove Trail (1.5), Dry Creek Trail (6), Harding Spring Trail (1.5), Jacks Canyon-Munds Mountain Trail (9-10), Soldier Pass Trail (4), Thomas Point Trail (2), Vultee Arch-Devil's Bridge Trail (5-6). (For the awards, a hiker must complete 1 hike from each group.) *Routes:* The Wilson Mountain Trail goes from Midgley Bridge to the top of the mountain and back. The East Pocket Trail goes from Bootlegger Campground to the East Pocket Knob fire lookout tower and back. The Wet Beaver Creek Trail goes from the Beaver Creek ranger station along Wet Beaver Creek to the rim above and back. The Dry Beaver Creek Trail begins 0.8 mile south of Wild Horse Mesa Dr. in Oak Creek and runs to Horse Mesa and back. The Loy Trail begins at Loy Butte at the edge of Hancock Ranch and runs to Secret Mountain Saddle and back. The Mooney Trail starts at Black Tank on Sycamore Pass Rd. and runs into Sycamore Canyon and back. The Harding Springs Trail begins and ends at Cove Spring Camp. The Cookstove Trail begins and ends at the water standpipe at the north end of Pine Flat Camp. The Thomas Point Trail follows FT #142. The Casner Canyon Trail begins at the notch across Oak Creek at milepost 376.9 on SR 89A. The Jack's Canyon-Munds Mountain Trail includes 6.5 miles in Jack's Canyon and a 2.5-miles climb up Munds Mountain. The Soldier Pass Trail begins and ends on SR 89A between Devil's Kitchen and Coffeepot Rock. The Vultee Arch-Devil's Bridge Trail is accessible from FR 152. The Dry Creek Trail begins and ends at the end of FR 152. *Terrain:* Rugged. *Cycling:* Not recommended. *Awards:* Patch $2.50; 14 Segments $1.00 each. *Submit:* Group leader's certification of completion. *Register:* Not required

San Francisco Peaks Trails

Location: North of Flagstaff, AZ. *Theme:* Recreation. *Sponsor:* Grand Canyon Council, BSA, 2200 E. Cedar, Suite 12, Flag-staff, AZ 86001-1984, (520) 774-0685.

Length: 6 different hikes of 4 to 9 miles each (any 3 required for award) with trailheads at Lockett Meadow and Snow Bowl. *Routes:* In addition, there are 3 other trails in this group: Crack-In-the-Rock Trail—18-mile guided loop trail to Wupatki National Monument. Mount Elden Segment—Any 10 non-repeating miles in

Mount Elden-Dry Lake Hills Trails System near Flagstaff. Sycamore Canyon Trail—Downstream through the canyon, starting at the Boy Scout Reservation and ending at the Verde River (44 miles). *Terrain:* Generally rugged. *Cycling:* Not recommended. *Awards:* Main Patch $2.50; 6 Segments $1.50 each. *Submit:* Group leader's certification of completion. *Register:* Only the Crack-In-the-Rock Trail requires advance registration

Senior Trail

Location: Santa Catalina Mountains near Tucson, AZ. *Theme:* Recreation. *Sponsor:* Catalina Council, BSA, 5049 E. Broadway, Tucson, AZ 87511, (520) 750-0385.
Length: 40 miles (approx.). *Route:* The trail begins at the parking lot at the end of the tram run in Upper Sabino Canyon, then proceeds to the top of Mt. Bigelow, Soldier Camp, Marshall Gulch, Lemmon Rock, Romero Saddle, and follows Esperero Canyon to Sabino Canyon Visitors' Center. *Terrain:* Rugged. *Cycling:* Not recommended. *Awards:* Medal. *Submit:* No requirement. *Register:* Not required

White Mountain Trails

Location: Apache-Sitgreaves National Forest near Phoenix, AZ. *Theme:* Recreation. *Sponsor:* Grand Canyon Council, BSA, 2200

E. Cedar, Suite 12, Flag-staff, AZ 86001-1984, (520) 774-0685.
Length: Bear Canyons Trail 26 miles (straight). East Eagle Creek Trail 22 miles (loop). Mount Baldy Trail 25 miles (loop). Rose Spring Trail 24 miles (loop). Squirrel Canyon Trail 20 miles (loop). *Routes:* Mount Baldy—Start at Greer, AZ, hike up Mount Baldy on either Trail 94 or 95 and hike down on the other. Squirrel Canyon—From FR 54, take Trail 34 through Squirrel Canyon to trail 45 and Honeymoon Camp-ground. Return by Trails 45 and 48 through Warren Canyon to Trail 34. East Eagle Creek—Start at Strayhorse Campground on FR 504, go south on FR 587 to Burnt Corral, then take Trails 33, 45, 27, 91 and 15 to Rose Peak and SR 666. Rose Spring—Start at FR 54 west of SR 666, and take Trails 54 and 45 to Rose Spring and return. Bear Canyons—Take FR 217 down the first Bear Canyon, up Hot Air Canyon, over Telephone Mesa and down the second Bear Canyon to Eagle Creek. *Terrain:* Rugged. *Cycling:* Not recommended (not allowed for award qualification). *Awards:* Main Patch $2.50; 5 Segments $1.00 each. *Submit:* Group leader's certification of completion. *Register:* Not required.

Formerly Sponsored Trail

Yuma Historic Trail

ARKANSAS

Arkansas Post National Memorial Trail

Location: Gillett, AR. *Theme:* First non-Indian settlement west of the Mississippi River. *Sponsor:* Quapaw Area Council, BSA, P.O. Box 3663, 3220 Cantrell Rd., Little Rock, AR 72203-3663, (501) 664-4780.
Length: 2 miles (loop). *Route:* The trail begins and ends at the Visitor Center, with a visit to the Post. *Terrain:* Walks and trails; wheelchair accessible. *Cycling:* Possible, but

check in advance for permission. *Awards:* Patch $1.25 (This and other trails sponsored by the same organization may be aggregated to qualify for the Arkansas 100 Miles Hiking Award, a patch for $6.00.). *Submit:* Completed questionnaire. *Register:* Upon arrival at the Post. *Sites:* Visitor Center, Arkansas Post.

Batesville Historical Trail

Location: Batesville, AR. *Theme:* History

of Batesville. *Sponsor:* Lones O'Daniel, 1695 Hill St., Batesville, AR 72501.

Length: 17.4 miles (loop). *Route:* The trail begins and ends at the building occupied by America's Flea Market on Main St. *Terrain:* City streets. *Cycling:* Appropriate. *Awards:* Patch. *Submit:* Completed 31-item questionnaire. *Register:* Not required. *Sites:* Courthouse, Hail Building, Barrett Store Building, County Library, Pioneer Cemetery, Garrott House, First Methodist Church, First Baptist Church, First Presbyterian Church, Lock and Dam, Old Bayou Bridge.

Bayou Meto Trail

Location: Jacksonville, AR. *Theme:* Early history of Jacksonville. *Sponsor:* Quapaw Area Council, BSA, 3220 Cantrell Rd., Little Rock, AR 72202-1847, (501) 664-4780.

Length: 5-10 miles. *Route:* The trail runs in and around Jacksonville, and by the Little Rock Air Force Base. *Terrain:* City streets. *Cycling:* Possible, but does not qualify for awards. *Awards:* Patch $1.50 (This and other trails sponsored by the same organization may be aggregated to qualify for the Arkansas 100 Miles Hiking Award, a patch for $6.00.). *Submit:* Completed answer card. *Register:* Advance registration required for map and answer card. *Sites:* Military Highway, Southwest Trail, Little Rock Air Force Base.

Burns Park Scout Hiking Trail

Location: North Little Rock, AR. *Theme:* Nature and history. *Sponsor:* Quapaw Area Council, BSA, 3220 Cantrell Rd., Little Rock, AR 72202-1847, (501) 664-4780.

Length: 5-10 miles. *Route:* The trail is within Burns Park, the second-largest city park in the U.S. *Terrain:* Woods, hills and valleys. *Cycling:* Not recommended. *Awards:* Medal; Patch (This and other trails sponsored by the same organization may be aggregated to qualify for the Arkansas 100 Miles Hiking Award, a patch for $6.00.). *Submit:* Completed answer booklet. *Register:* Advance registration required for map and answer booklet. *Sites:* White Oak Bayou.

Butterfield Hiking Trail

Location: West Fork, AR. *Theme:* Route of Butterfield Stage. *Sponsor:* Westark Area Council, BSA, Station A, P.O. Box 3156, Ft. Smith, AR 72913, (501) 782-7244.

Length: 14.5 miles. *Route:* The trail is within Devil's Den State Park. *Terrain:* Woods. *Cycling:* Not recommended. *Awards:* Medal $6.00; Patch $4.55. *Submit:* Group leader's certification of completion of hike and overnight camping. *Register:* Not required.

Esperanza Trail

Location: Mound City, AR. *Theme:* History and nature. *Sponsor:* Esperanza Trail Committee, P.O. Box 1368, West Memphis, AR 72301.

Length: 12 miles (straight). *Route:* The trail begins and ends at Mound City, mostly following the banks of Mound City Chute and Hopefield Chute. *Terrain:* Roads and forest. *Cycling:* Not recommended, and does not qualify for awards. *Awards:* Medal $3.00; Patch $1.50. *Submit:* Completed 16-item questionnaire. *Register:* Advance registration required. *Sites:* Lake Cayman, Indian Mounds, Old Levee, Sultana Steamboat, Military Road, Old River Landing, Hopefield Lake, Hopefield, Dueling Grounds, Fort Esperanza.

Helena Historical Trail

Location: Helena, AK. *Theme:* Local History. *Sponsor:* Gene Schieffler, 426 Plaza Blvd., P.O. Box 2309, West Helena, AK 72390-0309, (870) 572-2161.

Length: 10.0 miles (loop). *Route:* The trail begins and ends at the Delta Cultural Center and winds through downtown Helena. *Terrain:* City streets and river levee. *Cycling:* Appropriate. *Awards:* Patch $1.00. *Submit:* Completed 30-item questionnaire. *Register:* Not required. *Sites:* Keesee House, American Legion Hut, St. Mary's Cemetery, DeSoto Marker, Phillips County Courthouse, Moore-Tappan House.

Indian Heritage Award

Location: Toltec Mounds State Park near North Little Rock, AR. *Theme:* Archaeology. *Sponsor:* Quapaw Area Council, BSA, 3220 Cantrell Rd., Little Rock, AR 72202-1847, (501) 664-4780.

Length: 0.5 mile (loop). *Route:* The only hiking required is the Mound Lake Trail, which is completely within the park. *Terrain:* Easy path. *Cycling:* Not recommended. *Awards:* Patch $1.50 (This and other trails sponsored by the same organization may be aggregated to qualify for the Arkansas 100

Miles Hiking Award, a patch for $6.00.).
Submit: Certification of visit to
archaeological laboratory at the park and
knowledge of Arkansas archaeology. *Register:*
Not required. *Sites:* Archaeological
Laboratory, Toltec Mounds.

Lost Bridge Trail

Location: Beaver Lake, Garfield, AR.
Theme: Recreation and nature. *Sponsor:*
West Ark Area Council, BSA, P.O. Box 3156,
Ft. Smith, AR 72913, (501) 782-7244.
Length: 5.0 miles (loop). *Route:* The trail
begins and ends at the park entrance.
Terrain: Dirt and gravel roads. *Cycling:*
Possible. *Awards:* Patch. *Register:* Not
required. *Submit:* Completed questionnaire.
Sites: Old Homesite, Old Pond, Overlook,
Campaign Area.

Mt. Pinnacle Trek

Location: Near Little Rock, AR. *Theme:*
Peak climb. *Sponsor:* Quapaw Area Council,
BSA, P.O. Box 3663, 3220 Cantrell Rd., Little
Rock, AR 72203-3663, (501) 664-4780.
Length: 2 miles (loop). *Route:* The trail
begins at the base of Mt. Pinnacle, goes to the
top, and returns to the start. *Terrain:* Dirt
path. *Cycling:* Not recommended. *Awards:*
Patch $1.50 (This and other trails sponsored
by the same organization may be aggregated
to qualify for the Arkansas 100 Miles Hiking
Award, a patch for $6.00.). *Submit:* Group
leader's certification of completion of hike
and conservation project. *Register:* Not
required. *Sites:* Mt. Pinnacle (1,011').

Pea Ridge Battlefield Trail

Location: Pea Ridge National Military
Park, AR. *Theme:* Civil War battle—March,
1862. *Sponsor:* Eastern National Park and
Monument Association, Pea Ridge National
Military Park, Pea Ridge, AR 72751, (501)
451-8122.
Length: 10 miles (loop). *Route:* The trail
starts at the Visitor Center and circles most
of the park in a clockwise oval. *Terrain:*
Woods. *Cycling:* Not recommended. *Awards:*
Medal $9.00; Patch $3.50 (one each for Boy
Scouts and Girl Scouts). *Submit:* Completed
22-item workbook. *Register:* Upon arrival at
park. *Sites:* Elkhorn Tavern, General Curtis'
Headquarters Site, Confederate Artillery,
Federal Artillery, Winton Spring, Leetown
Site, Leetown Battlefield.

Petit Jean Trail

Location: Petit Jean State Park near
Morrilton, AR. *Theme:* Nature. *Sponsor:*
Quapaw Area Council, BSA, 3220 Cantrell
Rd., Little Rock, AR 72202-1847, (501) 664-
4780.
Length: 15 miles (loop). *Route:* The trail
begins and ends at the northwest corner of
the Pork Road Bridge crossing Cedar Creek.
Terrain: Rugged wooded path. *Cycling:* Not
recommended. *Awards:* Patch $4.00 (This
and other trails sponsored by the same
organization may be aggregated to qualify for
the Arkansas 100 Miles Hiking Award, a patch
for $6.00.). *Submit:* Completed answer card.
Register: Advance registration required to
obtain map and answer card. *Sites:* Cedar
Falls, Rock House, Petit Jean Mountain, Bear
Cave, Seven Hollow, Falls Overlook, Pioneer
Cabin.

Poison Springs Historical Trail

Location: Camden, AR. *Theme:* Battle of
Poison Springs. *Sponsor:* DeSoto Area
Council, BSA, 118 W. Peach St., El Dorado,
AR 71730, (870) 863-5166.
Length: 15 miles (straight). *Route:* The
endpoints are SR 4, southwest of Camden
(along Old Middle Washington Rd.), and SR
76 at battle ground area. *Terrain:* Rugged
hills. *Cycling:* Not recommended. *Awards:*
Medal; Patch. *Submit:* Group leader's
certification of completion. *Register:* Not
required. *Sites:* Old Stagecoach Road, Battle
Ground.

Quapaw Line Trail

Location: Little Rock, AR. *Theme:* History
of Little Rock. *Sponsor:* Quapaw Area
Council, BSA, 3220 Cantrell Rd., Little Rock,
AR 72202-1847, (501) 664-4780.
Length: 10 miles (loop). *Route:* The trail
begins and ends at the Museum of Science
and Natural History in McArthur Park.
Terrain: City streets. *Cycling:* Possible, but
does not qualify for awards. *Awards:* Patch
$2.25 (This and other trails sponsored by the
same organization may be aggregated to
qualify for the Arkansas 100 Miles Hiking
Award, a patch for $6.00.). *Submit:*
Completed answer card, stamped at museum.
Register: Advance registration required for
map and answer card. *Sites:* Park Museum, 3
Capitol Buildings, Quapaw Line Marker.

Sarasen Trail

Location: Pine Bluff, AR. *Theme:* Indian lore. *Sponsor:* Quapaw Area Council, BSA, 3220 Cantrell Rd., Little Rock, AR 72202-1847, (501) 664-4780.

Length: 10 miles. *Route:* The trail begins at the Pine Bluff Civic Center, and covers the hunting grounds of the Quapaw Indians. *Terrain:* Woodlands and city streets. *Cycling:* Not recommended. *Awards:* Patch $4.75 (This and other trails sponsored by the same organization may be aggregated to qualify for the Arkansas 100 Miles Hiking Award, a patch for $6.00.). *Submit:* Completed answer card. *Register:* Advance registration required for map and answer card. *Sites:* Pine Bluff Civic Center, Lake Pine Bluff, Arkansas River.

Formerly Sponsored Trails

Benton DeSoto Historic Trail
Brinkley Trail
Cub Zoo Trail
DeSoto Arkansas Trail
Hernando de Soto Commemorative Trail
Hot Springs Historical Trail
Jonesboro Trail
Ma'Kya Trail
Ozark Highlands Trail
Poteau Mountain Trail
Trail of Tears
White Rock Wilderness Trail

CALIFORNIA

American River Bike Trail

Location: Near the American River, Sacramento, CA. *Theme:* Recreation. *Sponsor:* Golden Empire Council, BSA, 251 Commerce Cir., Sacramento, CA 95815, (916) 758-9867.

Length: 50 miles (loop). *Route:* Contact sponsor for details. *Terrain:* Paved bike path. *Cycling:* Appropriate. *Awards:* Patch $2.50. *Submit:* No requirement. *Register:* Not required.

Broken Arrow Trail

Location: Camp Tahquitz, north of San Gorgonio Wilderness, CA. *Theme:* Recreation. *Sponsor:* Long Beach Area Council, BSA, P.O. Box 7338, Long Beach, CA 90807, (310) 427-0911.

Length: 20 miles (minimum). *Route:* The trail must begin from the trailhead at either Poopout Hill, Forsee Creek, or Angelus, include 3 nights in the backcountry, and climb Mt. San Gorgonio (11,502') and four additional peaks from the list below. *Terrain:* Rugged. *Cycling:* Not recommended. *Awards:* Medal. *Submit:* Group leader's certification of completion. *Register:* At Camp Tahquitz. *Sites (mountain peaks):* Jepson (11,201'), East San . Bernardino (10,691'), East Dobbs (10,510'), San Bernardino (10,624'), West Dobbs (10,454'), Anderson (10,864'), Zanhiser (10,156'), Shields (10,701'), Lake (10,156'), Alto Diablo (10,430'), South (10,830'), Tribe of Tahquitz (10,067'), Bighorn (11,105'), Big Charlton (10,815'), Grinnell (10,370'), Little Charlton (10,676')

Dinkey Lakes Loop Trail

Location: Camp Silver Fir, Sanger, CA. *Theme:* Recreation. *Sponsor:* Verdugo Hills Council, BSA, 1325 Grandview Ave., Glendale, CA 91201, (818) 351-8815.

Length: 5 nights (loop). *Route:* The trail begins and ends at Camp Silver Fir, and includes a climb of Dogtooth Peak and one of the Three Sisters. *Terrain:* Rugged. *Cycling:* Not recommended. *Awards:* Patch. *Submit:* Group leader's certification of completion of hike and conservation project. *Register:* Upon arrival at camp office.

Fages Trail

Location: El Cerrito, CA. *Theme:* Route traveled by first European expedition of record. *Sponsor:* Mt. Diablo Silverado Council, BSA, 600 Ellinwood Dr., Pleasant Hill, CA 94523, (510) 674-6100.

Length: 10.4 miles (loop). *Route:* The trail

begins and ends at Camp Herms. *Terrain:* Woods path, dirt roads. *Cycling:* Not recommended. *Awards:* Medal $5.00; Patch $2.25; First-time Segment $0.50; Repeater Segment n/c; Repeater Bear Pin $1.50; Jacket Patch $7.00. *Submit:* Group leader's certification of completion. *Register:* Advance registration required. *Sites:* Jewel Lake, Inspiration Point, Wildcat Creek, Wildcat Peak.

High Sierra Trail

Location: Southern CA. *Theme:* Scenic mountains. *Sponsor:* Los Angeles Area Council, BSA, 2333 Scout Way, Los Angeles, CA 90036, (213) 413-0575 or (213) 413-4300.

Length: Giant Forest-Miller King Trail 44 miles (straight), Miller King-Mt. Whitney Trail, 52 miles (straight). *Routes:* The Giant Forest-Miller King segment begins at Crescent Meadow and ends at Whitney Portal. The segment to Mt. Whitney continues to the mountain. *Terrain:* Steep mountain climbs. *Cycling:* Impossible. *Awards:* Patch $3.25; 2 segments $1.50 each. *Submit:* Group leader's certificate of completion. *Register:* At least two weeks in advance.

Los Padres Council Historic Trail

Location: Camp Roberts, San Miguel, CA. *Theme:* Local history. *Sponsor:* Los Padres Council, BSA, 4000 Modoc Rd., Santa Barbara, CA 93110-1807, (805) 967-0105.

Length: 14 miles (straight) plus short loop in San Luis Obispo. *Route:* The long portion of the trail begins at the intersection of Nacimiento Rd. and San Marcos Rd. and goes through Camp Roberts to end at the Mission San Miguel. *Terrain:* Roads. *Cycling:* Possible (but walking required for awards). *Awards:* Patch (for loop trail and tour of Mission San Miguel); Silver Bell Attachment for 14-mile trail; Medal planned. *Submit:* Completed 4-item questionnaire, stamped at missions. *Register:* Not required. *Sites:* Mission Plaza, Mission San Luis Obispo de Tolosa, Presbyterian Church, Judge Walter Murray Adobe, The Creamery, Dallidet Adobe, San Luis Obispo County Historical Museum, San Miguel Mission, Kundert Medical Building, Ramona Depot, Ah Louis Store, Sauer Adobes, Sinsheimer Brothers Store, Site of Casa Grande, Andrews Bank Building, Fremont Theater.

Manzana-Sisquoc-Manzana Loop

Location: San Rafael Wilderness, CA. *Theme:* Recreation. *Sponsor:* Los Padres Council, BSA, 4000 Modoc Rd., Santa Barbara, CA 93110, (805) 967-0105.

Length: 46 miles (loop). *Route:* The trail begins and ends at Nira in the Los Padres National Forest. *Terrain:* Rugged. *Cycling:* Not recommended. *Awards:* Patch $2.75. *Submit:* Group leader's certification of completion. *Register:* Not required. *Sites* (campgrounds along route): Coldwater, Abel, Manzana Schoolhouse, Cliff, Lonnie Davies, Mormon, White Ledge, Manzana, Happy Hunting Ground, Sycamore, Manzana Narrows, South Fork, Fish Creek, Nira.

Presidio Trail

Location: San Francisco, CA. *Theme:* History of Fort Mason and vicinity. *Sponsor:* Bay Area Council, BSA, East Bay Scout Shop, 2950 Merced St., San Leandro, CA 94577, (510) 357-0309.

Length: 7.3 miles. *Route:* The trail passes by the buildings comprising Fort Mason. *Terrain:* Sidewalks and paths. *Cycling:* Check with sponsor. *Awards:* Patch $3.00. *Submit:* Request for patches. *Register:* In advance.

The Redwoods Historical Trail

Location: Boulder Creek Scout Reservation, Boulder Creek, CA. *Theme:* Redwoods trees and the logging industry. *Sponsor:* Boulder Creek Scout Reservation, 14586 Bear Creek Rd., P.O. Box 263, Boulder Creek, CA 95006, (408) 338-3636.

Length: 5 miles (loop). *Route:* The trail begins across the road from the ranger's residence, loops through most of the reservation, and returns to the start, stopping at 18 stations dealing with the logging industry. *Terrain:* Woods and unimproved roads. *Cycling:* Not recommended. *Awards:* Patch. *Submit:* Completed 15-item questionnaire. *Register:* In advance with ranger. *Sites:* Mt. Radin, Mt. McDonald, Skid Road, Fritch Creek, Lumber Mill Ruins, Tanner's Shack.

Sacramento Historic Trail

Location: Sacramento, CA. *Theme:* Route of road cut through woods by John Sutter in 1839. *Sponsor:* Golden Empire Council, BSA, 251 Commerce Cir., Sacramento, CA 95815, (916) 929-1417.

Length: 5 miles (loop). *Route:* The trail begins at Sutter's Fort State Historic Park, heads west to Old Sacramento on the Sacramento River, and returns to the start. *Terrain:* City streets. *Cycling:* Appropriate. *Awards:* Patch $2.50. *Submit:* Group leader's certification of completion. *Register:* Not required. *Sites:* State Indian Museum, Sutter's Fort, Crocker Art Gallery, State Capitol, Pony Express Monument, Lady Adams Building, Delta King, Eagle Theatre, Central Pacific Railroad Passenger Station, Wells Fargo Museum, Big Four Building, Sacramento History Museum, California State, Railroad Museum, Towe Ford Museum, Governor's Mansion, The Globe.

Sacramento Historic Train Trail

Location: Sacramento, CA. *Theme:* Route of first railroad in the West. *Sponsor:* Golden Empire Council, BSA, 251 Commerce Cir., Sacramento, CA 95815, (916) 929-1417.

Length: 2.25 miles (loop). *Route:* Begin at the California State Railroad Museum at 125 I St. and walk 1.75 miles to the Light Rail at the 13th St. Station. Ride the train 9 miles east to the Butterfield Station, then back to the 13th St. Station and an additional 1.2 miles to the St. Rose of Lima Park on the K St. Mall. Walk the remaining 0.5 mile to the beginning. *Terrain:* City streets. *Cycling:* Not permitted. *Awards:* Patch. *Submit:* Group leader's certificate of completion. *Register:* Not required. *Sites:* California State Railroad Museum, SVRR Station Plaque, Front Street Passenger Station, Butterfield Station, Goethe Park, Routier Station.

Tahquitz Trails Award

Location: Camp Tahquitz, north of San Gorgonio Wilderness, CA. *Theme:* Recreation. *Sponsor:* Long Beach Area Council, BSA, P.O. Box 7338, Long Beach, CA 90807, (310) 427-0911.

Length: Varies. *Route:* The trail must begin from the trailhead at either Poopout Hill, Forsee Creek, or Angelus, and include a night of camping. *Terrain:* Rugged. *Cycling:* Not recommended. *Awards:* Patch. *Submit:* Group leader's certification of completion. *Register:* At Camp Tahquitz. *Sites:* Mountain peaks listed under Broken Arrow Trail.

U.S. Mormon Battalion Trail

Location: Anza-Borrego Desert State Park, CA. *Theme:* History of Mormon Battalion in Mexican War. *Sponsor:* Desert Pacific Council, BSA, 1207 Upas St., P.O. Box 33366, San Diego, CA 92103, (619) 298-6121.

Length: 5 or 15 miles. *Route:* The actual route may vary, but it is suggested that it be in Box Canyon for the 5-mile route, or from the intersection of San Felipe Rd. and Montezuma Rd. southward to Palm Springs. *Terrain:* Dirt path, generally not marked. *Cycling:* Not recommended. *Awards:* 2 Patches. *Submit:* Group leader's certification of completion. *Register:* Not required. *Sites:* Mormon Battalion Memorial, Old Town, Mormon Battalion Visitor's Center, Sealey Stables, Hazard Museum.

Other California Hiking Awards

Advanced Backpacker Award—20 days of backpacking. Patch. Sponsored by Los Angeles Area Council, BSA, 2333 Scout Way, Los Angeles, CA 90026, (213) 413-4400.

Back Country Exploration Award—6 days of backpacking. Patch. Sponsored by Western Los Angeles County Council, BSA, P.O. Box 6030, 14140 Ventura Blvd., Sherman Oaks, CA 91413, (818) 784-4272.

Backpacker Award—9 days of backpacking. Patch. Sponsored by Los Angeles Area Council, BSA, 2333 Scout Way, Los Angeles, CA 90026, (213) 413-4400.

California State Park Award—Backpack in a California state park or along former California Riding and Hiking Trail. Patch. Sponsored by Los Angeles Area Council, BSA, 2333 Scout Way, Los Angeles, CA 90026, (213) 413-4400.

Camelback Trek—15- or 30-mile backpack along California Riding and Hiking Trail, trails in the Cuyamaca Rancho State Park, or trails in the Cleveland National Forest (except the Pacific Crest Trail). Main patch and additional 15- and 30-mile footprint patches. Sponsored by Desert Pacific Council, BSA, 1207 Upas St., P.O. Box 33366, San Diego, CA 92103, (619) 298-6121.

Condor Award—5 days of backpacking in Ventura County. Patch. Sponsored by Ventura County Council, BSA, 509 E. Daily Dr., Camarillo, CA 93010, (805) 482-8938.

Cross-Country Backpack Award—6 days of backpacking. Patch. Sponsored by Western Los Angeles County Council, BSA, P.O. Box 6030, 14140 Ventura Blvd., Sherman Oaks, CA 91413, (818) 784-4272.

DeAnza's Trail—Overnight backpack north of Borrego Springs. Patch. Sponsored by California Inland Empire Council, BSA, 1230 Indiana Ct., Redlands, CA 92374-2896, (909) 825-8844 or (909) 793-2463.

Desert Backpack—Backpack in Mojave or Sonaran Desert. Patch. Sponsored by Desert Pacific Council, BSA, 1207 Upas St., P.O. Box 33366, San Diego, CA 92103, (619) 298-6121.

Desolation Wilderness 50-Miler Award—Backpack from Loon Lake to Echo Lakes. Patch. Sponsored by Golden Empire Council, BSA, 251 Commerce Cir., Sacramento, CA 95815, (916) 929-1417.

El Camino Real Award—5- or 15-mile hike along El Camino Real, plus visits to missions and study of history. Patches. Sponsored by Desert Pacific Council, BSA, 1207 Upas St., P.O. Box 33366, San Diego, CA 92103, (619) 298-6121.

Far Western Adventure—6 days of backpacking in any back-country or wilderness other than the High Sierra. Patch. Sponsored by Los Padres Council, BSA, 4000 Modoc Rd., Santa Barbara, CA 93110, (805) 967-0105.

Firebird Trail—5-mile trail at Camp Helendale. Patch. Sponsored by California Inland Empire Council, BSA, 1230 Indiana Ct., Redlands, CA 92374-2896, (909) 825-8844 or (909) 793-2463.

Five Peaks Award—Climb 5 peaks in San Gorgonio Wilderness. Patch. Sponsored by San Gabriel Valley Council, BSA, 540 N. Rosemead Blvd., Pasadena, CA 91107, (818) 351-8815.

Folsom Lake 6x10 Trek—Completion of any 10-mile segment from a list of 6. Patch. Sponsored by Golden Empire Council, BSA, 251 Commerce Cir., Sacramento, CA 95815, (916) 929-1417.

14,495 Club Award—3-day backpack including climb of Mt. Whitney. Patch. Sponsored by Western Los Angeles County Council, BSA, P.O. Box 6030, 14140 Ventura Blvd., Sherman Oaks, CA 91413, (818) 784-4272.

Gabrielino Award—3 days of backpacking in San Gabrielino Mountains. Patch. Sponsored by Los Angeles Area Council, BSA, 2333 Scout Way, Los Angeles, CA 90026, (213) 413-4400.

Golden Arrowhead Award—6 days, 50 miles of backpacking. Patch. Sponsored by Western Los Angeles County Council, BSA, P.O. Box 6030, 14140 Ventura Blvd., Sherman Oaks, CA 91413, (818) 784-4272.

Golden Trout Award—6-day backpack from Quaking Aspen to Cottonwood Pass. Patch. Sponsored by Southern Sierra Council, BSA, 2417 M St., Bakersfield, CA 93301, (805) 325-9036.

High Adventure Backpack—7 days of backpacking in Sierra Nevada. Patch. Sponsored by Los Angeles Area Council, BSA, 2333 Scout Way, Los Angeles, CA 90026, (213) 413-4400.

High Adventure 1-Week Backpack—7-day backpack with at least 25 hours of hiking time. Patch. Sponsored by Los Angeles Area Council, BSA, 2333 Scout Way, Los Angeles, CA 90026, (213) 413-4400.

High Sierra Six Trek Award—Six 50-mile treks in six different areas of the High Sierra Nevada. Plaque. Sponsored by Desert Pacific Council, BSA, 1207 Upas St., P.O. Box 33366, San Diego, CA 92103, (619) 298-6121.

Inter-Council Long-Term Hiking Award—Cumulative time from long-term backpacks. Medal. Sponsored by Western Los Angeles County Council, BSA, P.O. Box 6030, 14140 Ventura Blvd., Sherman Oaks, CA 91413, (818) 784-4272.

John Muir Award—6-day backpack (with limitation on use of John Muir Trail). Patch. Sponsored by Los Angeles Area Council, BSA, 2333 Scout Way, Los Angeles, CA 90026, (213) 413-4400.

John Muir Trail—Completion of any of 6 designated backpack segments of 212-mile trail. Patch. Sponsored by Golden Empire Council, BSA, 251 Commerce Cir., Sacramento, CA 95815, (916) 929-1417.

Kern Plateau Award—6 days of backpacking on Kern Plateau. Patch. Sponsored by Southern Sierra Council, BSA, 2417 M St., Bakersfield, CA 93301, (661) 325-9036.

Kit Carson Trek—48-56-mile backpack from Echo Lakes to Camp Winton. Patch. Sponsored by Golden Empire Council, BSA, 251 Commerce Cir., Sacramento, CA 95815, (916) 929-1417.

Lazy Rat Award—20-mile float trip on a rubber raft or inner tube constructed raft. Patch. Sponsored by High Adventure Team, Desert Pacific Council, BSA, 1207 Upas St., San Diego, CA 92103, (619) 298-6121.

Los Padres Trails—2-day 12-mile hike in Los Padres National Forest. Patch. Sponsored by Los Padres Council, BSA, 4000 Modoc Rd., Santa Barbara, CA 93110, (805) 967-0105.

Marble Mountains/Trinity Alps

Backpacker Award—50-mile back-pack in Marble Mountains or Trinity Alps. Patch. Sponsored by Golden Empire Council, BSA, 251 Commerce Cir., Sacramento, CA 95815, (916) 929-1417.

Minarets Wilderness Award—3-day backpack in Minarets Wilderness. Patch. Sponsored by Orange County Council, BSA, 3590 Harbor Gateway N., Costa Mesa, CA 92704, (714) 546-4990

Mini-Peak Bagger Award—Climb 8 peaks from an approved list, not more than one per day. Patch. Sponsored by Los Angeles Area Council, BSA, 2333 Scout Way, Los Angeles, CA 90026, (213) 413-4400.

Monarch Trail—6-day 50-mile backpack in High Sierra Nevada. Patch. Sponsored by Southern Sierra Council, BSA, 2417 M St., Bakersfield, CA 93301, (661) 325-9036.

Mt. Baden-Powell Award—Climb Mt. Baden-Powell on day hike. Patch. Sponsored by California Inland Empire Council, BSA, 1230 Indiana Ct., Redlands, CA 92374-2896, (909) 825-8844 or (909) 793-2463.

Mt. Lassen 50-Mile Trek—53-mile backpack including Hat Creek Campground and Sulfur Works Campground. Patch. Sponsored by Golden Empire Council, BSA, 251 Commerce Cir., Sacramento, CA 95815, (916) 929-1417.

Mt. Pinos Award—Backpack to Observation Point on Mt. Pinos. Patch. Sponsored by Ventura County Council, BSA, 509 E. Daily Dr., Camarillo, CA 93010, (805) 482-8938.

Mt. Whitney Award—3-day backpack in Mt. Whitney Wilderness. Patch. Sponsored by Southern Sierra Council, BSA, 2417 M St., Bakersfield, CA 93301, (661) 325-9036.

National Forest Award—Overnight backpack in a national forest. Patch. Sponsored by Los Angeles Area Council, BSA, 2333 Scout Way, Los Angeles, CA 90026, (213) 413-4400.

National Park or National Monument Award—Overnight backpack in a national park or monument. Patch. Sponsored by Los Angeles Area Council, BSA, 2333 Scout Way, Los Angeles, CA 90026, (213) 413-4400.

Nine Peaks Honor Award—Day hike of Mt. San Jacinto, plus overnight backpack including climb of Mt. San Jacinto, plus these 9 peaks in this order: San Gorgonio, Jepson, Little Charleton, Charleton, Alta Diablo, Shields, Anderson, San Bernardino East and San Bernardino. Patch. Sponsored by

California Inland Empire Council, BSA, 1230 Indiana Ct., Redlands, CA 92374-2896, (909) 825-8844 or (909) 793-2463.

Old Baldy Peak Award—Climb Mt. San Antonio on day hike. Patch. Sponsored by Old Baldy Council, BSA, 1047 W. 6th St., Ontario, CA 91762, (909) 938-4534.

Pacific Crest Trail-Backpacking—15-mile backpack along Pacific Crest Trail, other than former California Riding and Hiking Trail in San Diego County or John Muir Trail in High Sierra Nevada. Main patch and 15-mile footprint patch. Sponsored by Desert Pacific Council, BSA, 1207 Upas St., P.O. Box 33366, San Diego, CA 92103, (619) 298-6121.

Pacific Crest Trail-Trail Building—12 hours of approved trail building along Pacific Crest Trail. Patch. Sponsored by Desert Pacific Council, BSA, 1207 Upas St., P.O. Box 33366, San Diego, CA 92103, (619) 298-6121.

Paiute Trail—6-day 55-mile backpack in Paiute Basin. Patch. Sponsored by Southern Sierra Council, BSA, 2417 M St., Bakersfield, CA 93301, (661) 325-9036.

Peak Bagger—Climb 5 peaks from an approved list. Patch. Sponsored by Los Angeles Area Council, BSA, 2333 Scout Way, Los Angeles, CA 90026, (213) 413-4400.

Pt. Reyes National Seashore Backpacker Award—10-mile overnight backpack at Pt. Reyes National Seashore. Patch. Sponsored by Golden Empire Council, BSA, 251 Commerce Cir., Sacramento, CA 95815, (916) 929-1417.

Powderhorn Award—7-day backpack of 65 miles. Patch. Sponsored by Western Los Angeles County Council, BSA, P.O. Box 6030, 14140 Ventura Blvd., Sherman Oaks, CA 91413, (818) 784-4272.

Puddleduck Award—Any backpack with 0.5" of rain in 48 hours. Patch. Sponsored by Los Padres Council, BSA, 4000 Modoc Rd., Santa Barbara, CA 93110, (805) 967-0105.

River Rat Award—20-mile canoe or kayak float trip on the Lower Colorado River between Hoover Dam and Imperial Dam. Patch. Sponsored by the High Adventure Team, Desert Pacific Council, BSA, 1207 Upas St., San Diego, CA 92103, (619) 298-6121.

San Bernardino Climb—Backpack including climb of San Bernardino Peak. Patch. Sponsored by California Inland Empire Council, BSA, 1230 Indiana Ct., Redlands, CA 92374-2896, (909) 825-8844 or (909) 793-2463.

San Gorgonio Climb—Backpack including climb of the following peaks: San Gorgonio,

Jepson, Charleton, or Anderson. Patch. Sponsored by Desert Pacific Council, BSA, 1207 Upas St., P.O. Box 33366, San Diego, CA 92103, (619) 298-6121.

San Jacinto Climb—Backpack including climb of one of the following peaks: San Jacinto, Jean, Folly, or Marian Mountain. Patch. Sponsored by Desert Pacific Council, BSA, 1207 Upas St., P.O. Box 33366, San Diego, CA 92103, (619) 298-6121.

Seven League Boot Award—Cumulative mileage from overnight backpacks. Patch. Sponsored by Orange County Council, BSA, 3590 Harbor Gateway N., Costa Mesa, CA 92704, (714) 546-4990.

Sierra High Adventure North and South Awards—6-day backpacks within designated areas. 2 Patches. Sponsored by Los Padres Council, BSA, 4000 Modoc Rd., Santa Barbara, CA 93110, (805) 967-0105.

Silver Bearpaw Award—6-day 50-mile backpack in Sequoia National Park. Patch. Sponsored by Western Los Angeles County Council, BSA, P.O. Box 6030, 14140 Ventura Blvd., Sherman Oaks, CA 91413, (818) 784-4272.

Silver Cloud Award—6-day 45-mile backpack in Sequoia National Park. Patch. Sponsored by Western Los Angeles County Council, BSA, P.O. Box 6030, 14140 Ventura Blvd., Sherman Oaks, CA 91413, (818) 784-4272.

Silver Fir Award—6-day backpack in Sequoia National Forest. Patch. Sponsored by Verdugo Hills Council, BSA, 1325 Grandview Ave., Glendale, CA 91201, (818) 351-8815.

Silver Knapsack Award—6-day 45-mile backpack in Sequoia National Forest. Patch. Sponsored by Western Los Angeles County Council, BSA, P.O. Box 6030, 14140 Ventura Blvd., Sherman Oaks, CA 91413, (818) 784-4272.

Silver Moccasins Award—6-day backpack. Patch. Sponsored by Los Angeles Area Council, BSA, 2333 Scout Way, Los Angeles, CA 90026, (213) 413-4400.

Tahoe Rim Trail—Completion of one or more sections of backpacking trail circling Lake Tahoe Basin. Patch. Sponsored by Golden Empire Council, BSA, 251 Commerce Cir., Sacramento, CA 95815, (916) 929-1417.

Tahoe-Yosemite Trail—Completion of any of 6 segments (12-71 miles) on a backpacking trek. Patch. Sponsored by Golden Empire Council, BSA, 251 Commerce Cir., Sacramento, CA 95815, (916) 929-1417.

3-Day Backpack—3-day backpack in backcountry or primitive area. Patch. Sponsored by Orange County Council, BSA, 3590 Harbor Gateway N., Costa Mesa, CA 92704, (714) 546-4990.

Topa Topa Award—Backpack to trail crest using either Middle Lion Camp, Thatcher School or Sisar Canyon trailhead. Patch. Sponsored by Ventura County Council, BSA, 509 E. Daily Dr., Camarillo, CA 93010, (805) 482-8938.

Training Hike—5-mile backpack in backcountry or wilderness. Patch. Sponsored by Los Angeles Area Council, BSA, 2333 Scout Way, Los Angeles, CA 90026, (213) 413-4400.

Tri-Trek Trail Backpacker Award—58-mile backpack between Camp Pabatsi, Glacial Trails Scout Reservation, and Sierra-Marin Scout Camp. Patch. Sponsored by Golden Empire Council, BSA, 251 Commerce Cir., Sacramento, CA 95815, (916) 929-1417.

Weekend Snow-Hiking Award—5-mile backpack in at least 2 inches of snow. Patch. Sponsored by Los Angeles Area Council, BSA, 2333 Scout Way, Los Angeles, CA 90026, (213) 413-4400.

Whitsett to Whitney Trail—90-mile backpack from Whitsett to Whitney. Patch. Sponsored by Western Los Angeles County Council, BSA, P.O. Box 6030, 14140 Ventura Blvd., Sherman Oaks, CA 91413, (818) 784-4272.

Yosemite High Sierra Trail—60-mile backpack from Yosemite Valley to Lake Merced, Vogelsang Lake, Tuolumne Meadows, Glen Aulen Falls, May Lake, and back to Yosemite Valley, or any other 50-mile trek in Yosemite National Park. Patch. Sponsored by Golden Empire Council, BSA, 251 Commerce Cir., Sacramento, CA 95815, (916) 929-1417.

Formerly Sponsored Trails

Border Field Trail
Colorado River Award
Domeland Wilderness Trail
Double Cone Trek
Explorer Mountaineering Backpack
Fort Ross Trail
Glacial Trek
Golden Eagle Trail
Golden Jubilee Trail
Keyhole Trek
McKie Rounds Hike
Portola Historical Trail

Rae Lakes Loop Trail
Rim of the World Trail
San Jac 50 Miler
Silliman Crest Backpack

Sugarloaf Valley Backpack Trip
Theodore Solomons Trail
Yosemite Trek

COLORADO

Barr Trail

Location: Manitou Springs, CO. *Theme:* Mountain Climbing. *Sponsor:* Pikes Peak Council, BSA, 525 E. Uintah, Colorado Springs, CO 80903, (719) 634-1584.

Length: 13.0 miles (straight). *Route:* The trail begins on Ruxton Ave. in Manitou Springs and leads to the top of Pikes Peak. *Terrain:* Steep climbing at altitudes from 7,000 to 14,000 feet. *Cycling:* Not possible. *Awards:* Patch $1.59. *Submit:* Request for patches. *Register:* Not required. *Sites:* Barr Camp Cabin, Snack Bar.

Falcon Trail

Location: USAF Academy, CO. *Theme:* Nature. *Sponsor:* Falcon Trail Coordinator, BSA Troop 78, U.S. Air Force Academy, P.O. Box 12, USAF Academy, CO 80840, (719) 472-3141.

Length: 12 miles (loop). *Route:* The trail begins immediately south of USAFA Building 5132 (Youth Center), circles much of the Academy grounds, and returns to the start. *Terrain:* Woods. *Cycling:* Not recommended. *Awards:* Patch $3.00. *Submit:* List of vegetation and wildlife species identified and description of conservation project

performed. *Register:* Upon arrival at Academy. *Sites:* Blodgett Peak, B-52 Exhibit, Falcon Stadium.

Gregg Boundary Trail

Location: Ben Delatour Scout Ranch, Livermore, CO. *Theme:* Recreation. *Sponsor:* Longs Peak Council, BSA, 2215 23rd Ave., P.O. Box 1166, Greeley, CO 80632-1166, (970) 330-6305.

Length: 15 miles (loop). *Route:* The trail begins and ends at the trail center in front of Coral Rock Lodge. *Terrain:* Jeep road, path with dense vegetation. *Cycling:* Not recommended. *Awards:* Patch. *Submit:* No requirement. *Register:* In advance. *Sites:* Elkhorn Creek, Lonetree Mountain.

Other Colorado Hiking Award

Old West Trails Hiking Award—Hike and study one of: Pony Express Trail, Oregon Trail, Mormon Trail, or Overland Trail. Medal $5.00. Sponsored by Longs Peak Council, BSA, 2215 23rd Ave., P.O. Box 1166, Greeley, CO 80631-1166, (970) 330-6305.

Formerly Sponsored Trail

Front Range Trails

CONNECTICUT

None

DELAWARE

Caesar Rodney Historic Trail

Location: Dover, DE. *Theme:* The life and times of Caesar Rodney, a signer of the Declaration of Independence. *Sponsor:* Del-Mar-Va Council, BSA, 801 Washington St., Wilmington, DE 19801-1597, (302) 652-3741.

Length: 11 miles (straight). *Route:* The trail begins at the site of Byfield, Rodney's ancestral home, goes north on SR 9, west on South Little Creek Rd., and winds through the streets of downtown Dover to end at the Delaware State Museum. *Terrain:* City streets and rural paved roads. *Cycling:* Appropriate. *Awards:* Medal $5.50; Patch $1.50. *Submit:* Completed 23-item questionnaire stamped by museum clerk. *Register:* Not required. *Sites:* Byfield, Kirk Building, Legislative Hall, Miller/Saulsbury House, Hall of Records, Old Christ Church, Kent County Court House, Old State House, Ridgely House, Governor's House, The Green, Sykes Building, Margaret M. O'Neill Visitor Center, Delaware State Museum, St. John River.

Other Delaware Hiking Award

Delaware State Park Trail Award—For completion of designated trails in 8 state parks within 1 year. Patch. Sponsored by DNREC—Trail Challenge, Division of Parks and Recreation, 89 Kings Hwy., P.O. Box 1401, Dover, DE 19903.

Formerly Sponsored Trail

New Castle Historic Trail

DISTRICT OF COLUMBIA

Lincoln Pilgrimage Trail

Location: Washington, DC. *Theme:* Places and events related to Abraham Lincoln. *Sponsor:* American Historical Trails, Inc., P.O. Box 769, Monroe, NC 28111-0769, (704) 289-1604, Carotrader@trellis.net.

Length: Route A—7.5 miles. Route B—11.5 miles (both routes end about 2 miles from the start). *Route:* The trail begins at Ford's Theatre, circles the White House, and heads east to end at the Capitol (Route A), or continues on from there to end at the Lincoln Memorial (Route B). *Terrain:* City streets. *Cycling:* Appropriate. *Awards:* Medal $6.00; Patch $2.25. *Submit:* Completed 50-item questionnaire. *Register:* Not required. *Sites:* Ford's Theatre, Petersen House, New York Avenue Presbyterian Church, Willard Hotel, Seward House Site, Epiphany Church, Dolly Madison House, Farragut Statue, Blair House, McPherson Statue, Franklin and Company, Renwick Gallery, Rawlins Statue, Winder Building, White House, Hancock Statue, Pension Building, Grand Army of the Republic Statue, Old City Hall, Library of Congress, National Portrait Gallery, Ericsson Statue, Tariff Commission Building, Judiciary Square, Peace Monument, Capitol, Lincoln Memorial.

National Capital Bicentennial Trail of Freedom

Location: Washington, DC. *Theme:* Revolutionary War era history. *Sponsor:* American Historical Trails, Inc., P.O. Box 769, Monroe, NC 28111-0769, (704) 289-1604, Carotrader@trellis.net.

Length: Route A—6.5 miles Route B—7.2 miles. Route C—9.5 miles (all routes end about 1 mile from the start). *Route:* The trail begins at the National Museum of American History, proceeds east to the Capitol, and west to end at the National Portrait Gallery (Route A) or Lafayette Park (Route B), or then south to the John Paul Jones Memorial (Route C). *Terrain:* City streets. *Cycling:*

Appropriate. *Awards:* Medal $6.00; National Patch $2.25; Washington Patch $2.25. *Submit:* Completed 75-item questionnaire. *Register:* Not required. *Sites:* Hale Statue, National Museum of American History, National Archives, Washington Townhouse Site, Capitol, National Portrait Gallery, Franklin Statue, John Marshall Park, Pulaski Statue, Liberty Bell Replica, Hamilton Statue, Kosciuszko Statue, Rochambeau Statue, Signers Island, Lafayette Statue, Von Steuben Statue, James Monroe House, John Paul Jones Statue.

National Capital Lincoln Trail

Location: Washington, DC. *Theme:* Places and events related to Abraham Lincoln. *Sponsor:* American Historical Trails, Inc., P.O. Box 769, Monroe, NC 28111-0769, (704) 289-1604, Carotrader@trellis.net.

Length: 8-11 miles (straight). *Route:* The trail begins at Ford's Theatre, and passes the White House and Lincoln Memorial before following Rock Creek Park and ending at the Battleground Cemetery at Georgia Ave. and Van Buren St. *Terrain:* City streets, footpath in Rock Creek Park. *Cycling:* Appropriate. *Awards:* Patch $2.00. *Submit:* Completed 5-item questionnaire. *Register:* Not required. *Sites:* Ford's Theatre, Scout Monument, Peterson House, Lincoln Memorial, Battleground Cemetery, New York Avenue

Presbyterian Church, National Zoo, Fort Stevens, National Museum of American History, White House.

The President's Trail

Location: Washington, DC. *Theme:* Places and events related to the presidents of the U.S. *Sponsor:* American Historical Trails, Inc., P.O. Box 769, Monroe, NC 28111-0769, (704) 289-1604, Carotrader@trellis.net.

Length: Route A—8 miles. Route B—9.5 miles. Route C—11 miles (all routes end 1 to 2 miles from the start). *Route:* The trail begins at the White House, goes east around the Capitol, then west to end at the Washington Monument (Route A), Jefferson Memorial (Route B), or the Lincoln Memorial (Route C). *Terrain:* City streets. *Cycling:* Appropriate. *Awards:* Medal $6.00; Patch $2.25. *Submit:* Completed 40-item questionnaire. *Register:* Not required. *Sites:* White House, Blair House, Jackson Statue, Octagon House, St. John's Church, Decatur House, Taylor-Cameron House, Commerce Department, National Portrait Gallery, Grant Statue, Franklin Roosevelt Marker, National Museum of American History, National Archives, Garfield Statue, Capitol, Supreme Court, Library of Congress, National Air & Space Museum, Washington Monument, Jefferson Memorial, Lincoln Memorial.

FLORIDA

Alachua Historical Trail

Location: Alachua and Newnansville, FL. *Theme:* Local history and architecture. *Sponsor:* Steve Rajtar, 1614 Bimini Dr., Orlando, FL 32806, (407) 894-7412, http://www.geocities.com/Yosemite/Rapids/8428, e-mail rajtar@aol.com.

Length: 5.4 miles (loop). *Route:* The trail begins near the Alachua City Hall, heads north through the ghost town of Newnansville, and then winds through Alachua to return to the beginning. *Terrain:* City streets. *Cycling:* Appropriate. *Awards:*

Patch $4.00. *Submit:* Patch order form. *Register:* Not required. *Sites:* Downing House, Newnansville Cemetery, Futch Furniture Store, Williams Store, Pierce Building, Bank of Alachua, Woman's Club, Farmers' Cooperative, First Presbyterian Church, Traxler House.

Altamonte Springs Historical Trail

Location: Altamonte Springs, FL. *Theme:* Local history and architecture. *Sponsor:* Steve Rajtar, 1614 Bimini Dr., Orlando, FL 32806, (407) 894-7412, http://www.geocities.

com/Yosemite/Rapids/8428, e-mail rajtar@
aol.com.

Length: 11.3 miles (loop). *Route:* The trail
begins and ends at Eastmonte Park, covering
Sanlando and areas near SR 436. *Terrain:*
City streets. *Cycling:* Appropriate. *Awards:*
Patch $4.00. *Submit:* Patch order form.
Register: Not required. *Sites:* St. Mary
Magdalene Catholic Church, Maltbie House,
Bundy House, Jasmine Theater, Nolan
House, Altamonte Chapel, Trovillion
Building, Kiegan Grocery Store, Rosenwald
School.

Altoona Historical Trail

Location: Altoona, FL. *Theme:* Local
history. *Sponsor:* Steve Rajtar, 1614 Bimini
Dr., Orlando, FL 32806 (407) 894-7412,
http://www.geocities.com/Yosemite/Rapids/8
428, e-mail rajtar@aol.com.

Length: 7.7 miles (loop). *Route:* The trail
begins at the McTureous Memorial and
covers sites between it and Pittman, along US
19. *Terrain:* Paved roads. *Cycling:*
Appropriate. *Awards:* Patch $4.00. *Submit:*
Patch order form. *Register:* Not required.
Sites: McTureous Memorial, First Baptist
Church, Carroll House, Altoona Station,
Altoona Cemetery, Altoona Elementary
School, Cameron-Graham Music Museum.

Andrew Jackson Historic Trail

Location: Munson, FL. *Theme:* Route
taken by Andrew Jackson from Tennessee to
Pensacola in 1814. *Sponsor:* John Steiger, 8100
Monticello Dr., Pensacola, FL 32514, (850)
477-0122; jsteiger@pcola.gulf.net.

Length: 22 miles (straight). *Route:* The
trail begins at Karick Lake and heads
westward to Juniper Creek, near Munson.
Terrain: Hills and woods. *Cycling:* Not
recommended. *Awards:* Medal $4.00; Patch
$2.50. *Submit:* No requirement. *Register:* Not
required. *Sites:* Peaden Family Cemetery,
Bear Lake, Blackwater River, Karick Lake.

Anona Historical Trail

Location: Largo, FL. *Theme:* Local history.
Sponsor: Steve Rajtar, 1614 Bimini Dr.,
Orlando, FL 32806, (407) 894-7412,
http://www.geocities.com/Yosemite/Rapids/8
428, e-mail rajtar@aol.com.

Length: 10.2 miles (loop). *Route:* The trail
begins and ends at John Bonner Nature Park,
and covers the area between the river and the
western side of Largo. *Terrain:* City streets.
Cycling: Appropriate. *Awards:* Patch $4.00.
Submit: Patch order form. *Register:* No
requirement. *Sites:* Anona Cemetery, Anona
United Methodist Church, Heritage Village, ,
Honey House, J.S. Hill Groves, Harris House,
Walsingham House.

Apopka Historical Trail

Location: Apopka, FL. *Theme:* Local
history and architecture. *Sponsor:* Steve
Rajtar, 1614 Bimini Dr., Orlando, FL 32806,
(407) 894-7412, http://www.geocities.com/
Yosemite/Rapids/8428, e-mail rajtar@aol.com.

Length: 8.2 miles (loop). *Route:* The trail
begins and ends at City Park, passes through
Edgewood and Greenwood Cemeteries, and
covers downtown. *Terrain:* City streets.
Cycling: Appropriate. *Awards:* Patch $4.00.
Submit: Patch order form. *Register:* Not
required. *Sites:* State Bank of Apopka, The
Lodge, Townsend's Plantation, Fern
Monument, First Presbyterian Church,
Edgewood Cemetery, First Baptist Church,
Fern City Sundries, St. Paul's A.M.E. Church,
City Hall.

Archer Historical Trail

Location: Archer, FL. *Theme:* Local history
and architecture. *Sponsor:* Steve Rajtar, 1614
Bimini Dr., Orlando, FL 32806, (407) 894-
7412, http://www.geocities.com/Yosemite/
Rapids/8428, e-mail rajtar@aol.com.

Length: 8.2 miles (loop). *Route:* The trail
starts in the middle of town, heads generally
north on University Ave. to the former site of
Cotton-Wood Plantation, then returns back
to town to wind through the streets and
return to the start. *Terrain:* City streets.
Cycling: Appropriate. *Awards:* Patch $4.00.
Submit: Patch order form. *Register:* Not
required. *Sites:* McDonald House, Bauknight
House, Bethlehem Presbyterian Church,
Quaker House, Maddox Foundry, Archer
Depot, Wood Store, Archer Baptist Church,
Neal House.

Astor Historical Trail

Location: Astor, Astor Park and Volusia, FL.
Theme: Local history. *Sponsor:* Steve Rajtar,
1614 Bimini Dr., Orlando, FL 32806, (407) 894-
7412, http://www.geocities.com/Yosemite/
Rapids/8428, e-mail rajtar@aol.com.

Length: 9.8 miles (loop). *Route:* The trail begins in Astor, heads east across the St. Johns River to visit Volusia, then heads west across the river to Astor Park, and then returns to the beginning. *Terrain:* City streets. *Cycling:* Appropriate. *Awards:* Patch $4.00. *Submit:* Patch order form. *Register:* Not required. *Sites:* First Baptist Church, Volusia Museum, Astor Bridge, Doss House, Astor-Astor Park Cemetery, Gustafson House.

Auburndale Historical Trail

Location: Auburndale, FL. *Theme:* Local history. *Sponsor:* Steve Rajtar, 1614 Bimini Dr., Orlando, FL 32806, (407) 894-7412, http://www.geocities.com/Yosemite/Rapids/8428, e-mail rajtar@aol.com.
Length: 4.1 miles (loop). *Route:* The trail begins in the city park across from the City Hall, loops south and east around the cemetery, then north along the shores of Lakes Ariana and Stella. *Terrain:* City streets. *Cycling:* Appropriate. *Awards:* Patch $4.00. *Submit:* Patch order form. *Register:* Not required. *Sites:* State Bank of Auburndale, Paul Smith Hotel, City Hall, Baynard House Museum, St. Alban's Episcopal Church, First Presbyterian Church, St. James A.M.E. Church, First Church of the Nazarene, Baynard House .

Babson Park Historical Trail

Location: Babson Park, FL. *Theme:* Local history. *Sponsor:* Steve Rajtar, 1614 Bimini Dr., Orlando, FL 32806, (407) 894-7412, http://www.geocities.com/Yosemite/Rapids/8428, e-mail rajtar@aol.com.
Length: 5.7 miles (loop). *Route:* The trail begins in the city park on Carson Ave., heads north on Scenic Hwy. past Webber College, then south and west near Crooked Lake, and northeast to return. *Terrain:* City streets. *Cycling:* Appropriate. *Awards:* Patch $4.00. *Submit:* Patch order form. *Register:* Not required. *Sites:* Babson Park Garage, First Christian Church of Babson Park, Audubon Center, Rogers Monument, Webber House.

Barberville Historical Trail

Location: Barberville and Emporia, FL. *Theme:* Local history. *Sponsor:* Steve Rajtar, 1614 Bimini Dr., Orlando, FL 32806, (407) 894-7412, http://www.geocities.com/Yosemite/Rapids/8428, e-mail rajtar@aol.com.

Length: 10.3 miles (loop). *Route:* The trail begins at the Pioneer Art Settlement, heads through it, through Barberville to the cemetery, northwest into Emporia, then back south to the start. *Terrain:* City streets. *Cycling:* Appropriate. *Awards:* Patch $4.00. *Submit:* Patch order form. *Register:* Not required. *Sites:* Purdom Cemetery, Underhill House, Black Bear Trail, Pioneer Art Settlement, Masonic Lodge, Oakdale Cemetery, Barberville Baptist Church, DeLong House, Emporia School, Felt House.

Barefoot Mailman Trail

Location: Palm Beach County, FL. *Theme:* Historic mail delivery route. *Sponsor:* South Florida Council, BSA, 15255 NW 82nd Ave., Miami Lakes, FL 33016, (305) 364-0020.
Length: 32.0 miles (straight)—2-day group backpack. *Route:* The trail begins in Pompano Beach and ends in South Point Park, South Beach, Miami. *Terrain:* Roads. *Cycling:* Not permitted. *Awards:* Patch. *Submit:* Purchase patches on day of annual hike. *Register:* Required; only open to members of South Florida Council, or by invitation. *Sites:* John Lloyd Park, Johnson Street Park, Hallandale Beach, South Point Park.

Bartow Historical Trail

Location: Bartow, FL. *Theme:* Local history and architecture. *Sponsor:* Steve Rajtar, 1614 Bimini Dr., Orlando, FL 32806, (407) 894-7412, http://www.geocities.com/Yosemite/Rapids/8428, e-mail rajtar@aol.com.
Length: 8.3 miles (loop). *Route:* The trail begins in the south part of town and heads south on Broadway Ave., loops around, then heads north on Broadway to the courthouse, passes the older homes on Church and Main Sts., and returns to the start. *Terrain:* City streets. *Cycling:* Appropriate. *Awards:* Patch $4.00. *Submit:* Patch order form. *Register:* Note required. *Sites:* County Courthouse, First Baptist Church, Schuck House, Holland House, Polk County Bank, Hughes Store, King House, President's House.

Bellamy Road Historical Trail

Location: Rural Alachua County, FL. *Theme:* Local history and architecture. *Sponsor:* Steve Rajtar, 1614 Bimini Dr., Orlando, FL 32806, (407) 894-7412, http://www.geocities.com/Yosemite/Rapids/8428, e-mail rajtar@aol.com.

Length: 11.3 miles (loop). *Route:* The trail follows the historic Bellamy Rd., and includes the settlement of Traxler. *Terrain:* City streets. *Cycling:* Appropriate. *Awards:* Patch $4.00. *Submit:* Patch order form. *Register:* Not required. *Sites:* F. Stephens House, J. Stephens House, Springhill Methodist Church, Hodges House, Traxler Commissary, Traxler House.

Belleview Historical Trail

Location: Belleview, FL. *Theme:* Local history. *Sponsor:* Steve Rajtar, 1614 Bimini Dr., Orlando, FL 32806, (407) 894-7412, http://www.geocities.com/Yosemite/Rapids/8428, e-mail rajtar@aol.com.

Length: 6.7 miles (loop). *Route:* The trail begins and end near Lake Lillian, and winds through the town. *Terrain:* City streets. *Cycling:* Appropriate. *Awards:* Patch $4.00. *Submit:* Patch order form. *Register:* Not required. *Sites:* Methodist Church, Roy Realty, St. Theresa Catholic Church, Masonic Hall, Pierce House, Ramah Missionary Baptist Church, Library.

Brooksville Historical Trail

Location: Brooksville, FL. *Theme:* Local history and architecture. *Sponsor:* Steve Rajtar, 1614 Bimini Dr., Orlando, FL 32806, (407) 894-7412, http://www.geocities.com/Yosemite/Rapids/8428, e-mail rajtar@aol.com.

Length: 7.0 miles (loop). *Route:* The trail begins and ends at McKethan Park, winding through town. *Terrain:* City streets. *Cycling:* Appropriate. *Awards:* Patch $4.00. *Submit:* Patch order form. *Register:* Not required. *Sites:* Lykes Memorial Library, Gwynn House, Rogers Christmas House, Tangerine Hotel, Roer House, Heritage Museum.

Bunnell Historical Trail

Location: Bunnell, FL. *Theme:* Local history and architecture. *Sponsor:* Steve Rajtar, 1614 Bimini Dr., Orlando, FL 32806, (407) 894-7412, http://www.geocities.com/Yosemite/Rapids/8428, e-mail rajtar@aol.com.

Length: 2.8 miles (loop). *Route:* The trail begins at the Bunnell State Bank building, heads northeast and east along Moody Blvd., heads west to Railroad St., and winds back to the start. *Terrain:* City streets. *Cycling:* Appropriate. *Awards:* Patch $4.00. *Submit:* Patch order form. *Register:* Not required. *Sites:* Pine Grove Inn, Hendricks House, Flagler County Courthouse, Deen House, Lambert House, Tribune Building, Bunnell Development Company, I. Moody House.

Bushnell Historical Trail

Location: Bushnell, FL. *Theme:* Local history and architecture. *Sponsor:* Steve Rajtar, 1614 Bimini Dr., Orlando, FL 32806, (407) 894-7412, http://www.geocities.com/Yosemite/Rapids/8428, e-mail rajtar@aol.com.

Length: 5.8 miles (loop). *Route:* The trail begins in downtown Bushnell, visits the Dade Battlefield Historic Memorial, then winds through town to the point of beginning. *Terrain:* City streets. *Cycling:* Appropriate. *Awards:* Patch $4.00. *Submit:* Patch order form. *Register:* Not required. *Sites:* Bilby House, Pierce Hotel, First Baptist Church, Towns House, Evergreen Cemetery, Texaco Station, Citizens Bank, Sumter County Courthouse, Masonic Lodge, Davis Building.

Campville-Windsor Historical Trail

Location: Campville and Windsor, FL. *Theme:* Local history and architecture. *Sponsor:* Steve Rajtar, 1614 Bimini Dr., Orlando, FL 32806, (407) 894-7412, http://www.geocities.com/Yosemite/Rapids/8428, e-mail rajtar@aol.com.

Length: 16.8 miles (loop). *Route:* The trail begins at the Owens-Illinois Park in Windsor, heads east to and loops through Campville, and returns west through Windsor to the point of beginning. *Terrain:* City streets. *Cycling:* Appropriate. *Awards:* Patch $4.00. *Submit:* Patch order form. *Register:* Not required. *Sites:* Parker House, Orange Creek Methodist Church, Kayton House, Canova House, Camp House, Providence Methodist Church, Torode House, Old Windsor Store, Double Pen House.

Cape Canaveral-Cocoa Beach Historical Trail

Location: Cape Canaveral and Cocoa Beach, FL. *Theme:* Local history. *Sponsor:* Steve Rajtar, 1614 Bimini Dr., Orlando, FL 32806, (407) 894-7412, http://www.geocities.com/Yosemite/Rapids/8428, e-mail rajtar@aol.com.

Length: 9.9 miles (straight). *Route:* The trail begins at the north end of Cape Canaveral, heads south on Atlantic Ave., winds through Cocoa Beach, and ends at the recreation complex at the west end of Cocoa Ave. *Terrain:* City streets. *Cycling:* Appropriate. *Awards:* Patch $4.00. *Submit:* Patch order form. *Register:* Not required. *Sites:* Starlite Motel, Cape Canaveral Lighthouse, Patrick Air Force Base, Cape Side Center, Storekeeper by the Sea, Alan Shepard Park, Propper Building, Ben Kori Building, Cape Canaveral Hospital, VFW Post.

Cedar Key Historical Trail

Location: Cedar Key, FL. *Theme:* Local history and architecture. *Sponsor:* Steve Rajtar, 1614 Bimini Dr., Orlando, FL 32806, (407) 894-7412, http://www.geocities.com/Yosemite/Rapids/8428, e-mail rajtar@aol.com.
Length: 5.8 miles (loop). *Route:* The trail begins in City Park, heads through the former railroad and fiber plant area, then winds through downtown and returns to the point of beginning. *Terrain:* City streets. *Cycling:* Appropriate. *Awards:* Patch $4.00. *Submit:* Patch order form. *Register:* Not required. *Sites:* Thomas Guest House, Block House, Cedar Key Cemetery, St. Clair Whitman National Museum, Christ Episcopal Church, Eagle Cedar Mill House, White House Annex, Lutterloh Building, Cedar Key State Bank.

Christmas Historical Trail

Location: Christmas, FL. *Theme:* Local history. *Sponsor:* Steve Rajtar, 1614 Bimini Dr., Orlando, FL 32806, (407) 894-7412, http://www.geocities.com/Yosemite/Rapids/8428, e-mail rajtar@aol.com.
Length: 7.2 miles (loop). *Route:* The trail begins at Fort Christmas Park, heads north to Christmas Creek, goes south to the Christmas community, and returns to the park. *Terrain:* Paved streets and dirt roads. *Cycling:* Appropriate. *Awards:* Patch $4.00. *Submit:* Patch order form. *Register:* Not required. *Sites:* Cracker House Replica, Christmas Cemetery, Fort Christmas Baptist Church, Tex Wheeler Studio, Pine Grove Missionary Baptist Church, Union School, Peace Garden, Old Post Office Museum, Savage Creek.

Citrus Park Historical Trail

Location: Citrus Park and Keystone Park, FL. *Theme:* Local history. *Sponsor:* Steve Rajtar, 1614 Bimini Dr., Orlando, FL 32806, (407) 894-7412, http://www.geocities.com/Yosemite/Rapids/8428, e-mail rajtar@aol.com.
Length: 10.1 miles (loop). *Route:* The trail begins near the baseball fields on Gunn Hwy., heads south to Spivey, north through downtown, further north near Keystone Park, then south back to the start. *Terrain:* City streets. *Cycling:* Appropriate. *Awards:* Patch $4.00. *Submit:* Patch order form. *Register:* Not required. *Sites:* Little Red Schoolhouse, Citrus Park School, Mobley House, Keystone United Methodist Church, Dey General Store, Keystone Service Station, Gunn Highway.

Clearwater Historical Trail

Location: Clearwater and Belleair, FL. *Theme:* Local history and architecture. *Sponsor:* Steve Rajtar, 1614 Bimini Dr., Orlando, FL 32806, (407) 894-7412, http://www.geocities.com/Yosemite/Rapids/8428, e-mail rajtar@aol.com.
Length: 10.1 miles (loop). *Route:* The trail begins in downtown Clearwater, loops south to the Belleview Biltmore Hotel, then returns to the point of beginning. *Terrain:* City streets. *Cycling:* Appropriate. *Awards:* Patch $4.00. *Submit:* Patch order form. *Register:* Not required. *Sites:* Plant-Ducros House, Bucknall House, McMullen House, South Ward School, Pinellas County Courthouse, Peace Memorial Presbyterian Church, Verona Inn, Fort Harrison Hotel, The Garden Seat.

Clermont Historical Trail

Location: Clermont, FL. *Theme:* Local history. *Sponsor:* Steve Rajtar, 1614 Bimini Dr., Orlando, FL 32806, (407) 894-7412, http://www.geocities.com/Yosemite/Rapids/8428, e-mail rajtar@aol.com.
Length: 8.7 miles (loop). *Route:* The trail begins in front of the library and covers most of the streets of Clermont. *Terrain:* City streets. *Cycling:* Appropriate. *Awards:* Patch $4.00. *Submit:* Patch order form. *Register:* No requirement. *Sites:* Hancock Building, St. Matthias Episcopal Church, Kern House, St. Mark's A.M.E. Church, Woman's Club, Lake Highlands Hotel, Clermont-Jenkins Civic Auditorium, Todd House.

Cocoa-Rockledge Historical Trail

Location: Cocoa and Rockledge, FL.
Theme: Local history. *Sponsor:* Steve Rajtar,
1614 Bimini Dr., Orlando, FL 32806, (407)
894-7412, http://www.geocities.com/
Yosemite/Rapids/8428, e-mail rajtar@aol.com.

Length: 8.0 miles (loop). *Route:* The trail
begins on King St. in Cocoa, heads south to
Rockledge, then returns north to wind
through historic Cocoa Village and return to
the start. *Terrain:* City streets. *Cycling:*
Appropriate. *Awards:* Patch $4.00. *Submit:*
Patch order form. *Register:* Not required.
Sites: St. Mark's Episcopal Church, Wuestoff
Hospital, Brevard County State Bank, St.
Mary's Church, Magruder-Waley House,
Brevard Hotel, Travis Hardware, Cannon
House, Harry T. Moore Center, Hicks House.

Crane Creek Historical Trail

Location: Melbourne, FL. *Theme:* Local
history. *Sponsor:* Steve Rajtar, 1614 Bimini
Dr., Orlando, FL 32806, (407) 894-7412,
http://www.geocities.com/Yosemite/Rapids/8
428, e-mail rajtar@aol.com.

Length: 9.1 miles (loop). *Route:* The trail
begins and ends at the Claude Edge Front
Street Park, and winds through downtown
Melbourne. *Terrain:* City streets. *Cycling:*
Appropriate. *Awards:* Patch $4.00. *Submit:*
Patch order form. *Register:* Not required.
Sites: Ruth Henegar School, Holy Trinity
Episcopal Church, Stone Middle School,
Goode House, Huggins Store, Melbourne
Hotel, Green Gables.

Crescent City Historical Trail

Location: Crescent City, FL. *Theme:* Local
history. *Sponsor:* Steve Rajtar, 1614 Bimini
Dr., Orlando, FL 32806, (407) 894-7412,
http://www.geocities.com/Yosemite/Rapids/8
428, e-mail rajtar@aol.com.

Length: 8.0 miles (loop). *Route:* The trail
begins on Summit St. between Edgewood
and Palmetto Aves., heads north to the
library, west and south along the edge of the
older part of town, then winds through
downtown to the start. *Terrain:* City streets.
Cycling: Appropriate. *Awards:* Patch $4.00.
Submit: Patch order form. *Register:* Not
required. *Sites:* Hubbard House, Morrow-
Sprague House, Church of the Holy
Comforter, Preston's Store, First Presbyterian
Church, Sprague House, First Baptist
Church, Woman's Club.

Cross Creek-Island Grove Historical Trail

Location: Cross Creek and Island Grove,
FL. *Theme:* Local history. *Sponsor:* Steve
Rajtar, 1614 Bimini Dr., Orlando, FL 32806,
(407) 894-7412, http://www.geocities.com/
Yosemite/Rapids/8428, e-mail rajtar@aol.
com.

Length: 11.2 miles (loop). *Route:* The trail
begins in Island Grove, goes northwest to
Cross Creek including the home of Marjorie
Kinnan Rawlings, and returns to the point of
beginning. *Terrain:* Rural paved roads.
Cycling: Appropriate. *Awards:* Patch $4.00.
Submit: Patch order form. *Register:* Not
required. *Sites:* Masonic Hall, Cason House,
Baker House, Evans House, Axline House,
Grove Trail, Du Pre House, Thomas House,
Baptist Church, Methodist Church.

Crystal River Historical Trail

Location: Crystal River, FL. *Theme:* Local
history. *Sponsor:* Steve Rajtar, 1614 Bimini
Dr., Orlando, FL 32806, (407) 894-7412,
http://www.geocities.com/Yosemite/Rapids/8
428, e-mail rajtar@aol.com.

Length: 9.0 miles (loop). *Route:* The trail
begins at the city park adjacent to the City
Hall on US 19, heads south and winds
through town, then goes north to the Indian
Mounds Museum, then returns. *Terrain:* City
streets. *Cycling:* Appropriate. *Awards:* Patch
$4.00. *Submit:* Patch order form. *Register:*
Not required. *Sites:* Crystal River Indian
Mounds Museum and State Park, First
Presbyterian Church, St. Ann's Episcopal
Church, First Baptist Church, Crystal River
Methodist Church, Seminole Club, Crystal
River Bank, Marine Museum.

Dade City Historical Trail

Location: Dade City, FL. *Theme:* Local
history and architecture. *Sponsor:* Steve Rajtar,
1614 Bimini Dr., Orlando, FL 32806, (407) 894-
7412, http://www.geocities.com/Yosemite/
Rapids/8428, e-mail rajtar@aol.com.

Length: 9.0 miles (loop). *Route:* The trail
begins at Price Park, winds through
downtown before heading north to
Whitehouse and the Pioneer Florida
Museum, then returns south to meander
through the rest of the residential and
commercial area, to return to the starting
point. *Terrain:* City streets. *Cycling:*

Appropriate. *Awards:* Patch $4.00. *Submit:*
Patch order form. *Register:* Not required.
Sites: Crescent Theatre, Cooper House,
Mount Zion A.M.E. Church, Telephone
Building, Porter House, Pasco High School,
American Legion Hall, Ross House, Gray
Moss Inn, Edwinola Hotel.

Davis Islands-Hyde Park Historical Trail

Location: Tampa, FL. *Theme:* Local history
and architecture. *Sponsor:* Steve Rajtar, 1614
Bimini Dr., Orlando, FL 32806, (407) 894-
7412, http://www.geocities.com/Yosemite/
Rapids/8428, e-mail rajtar@aol.com.
Length: 12.5 miles (loop). *Route:* The trail
begins by the old Florida Fairgrounds, passes
through the campus of the University of
Tampa, and heads southeast and circles
through Davis Islands, before heading west to
include the Hyde Park mansions before going
north to the point of beginning. *Terrain:*
City streets. *Cycling:* Appropriate. *Awards:*
Patch $4.00. *Submit:* Patch order form.
Register: Not required. *Sites:* Palmarin Hotel,
Palace of Florence, Knight Cottage, Davis
House, Pirate Ship, Tarpon Weighing Station,
Gorrie Elementary School, Leiman House,
Anderson House, Taliaferro House.

Daytona Beach Historical Trail

Location: Daytona Beach, FL. *Theme:*
Local history and architecture. *Sponsor:*
Steve Rajtar, 1614 Bimini Dr., Orlando, FL
32806, (407) 894-7412, http://www.geocities.
com/Yosemite/Rapids/8428, e-mail rajtar@
aol.com.
Length: 12.0 miles (loop). *Route:* The trail
begins on City Island, proceeds on the
mainland to and along Beach St., heads north
through the campus of Bethune-Cookman
College, and across the Halifax River to the
former town of Seabreeze. The trail
continues south on the barrier island to the
Memorial Bridge, re-crossing the river to the
starting point. *Terrain:* City streets. *Cycling:*
Appropriate. *Awards:* Patch $4.00. *Submit:*
Patch order form. *Register:* Not required.
Sites: Bandshell, Seabreeze United Church,
Bethune House, Merchant Bank Building,
Kress Building, Thompson House, St. Paul's
Catholic Church, Halifax River Yacht Club,
St. Mary's Episcopal Church.

DeBary Historical Trail

Location: DeBary, North Marion and Lake
Marion, FL. *Theme:* Local history. *Sponsor:*
Steve Rajtar, 1614 Bimini Dr., Orlando, FL
32806, (407) 894-7412, http://www.geocities.
com/Yosemite/Rapids/8428, e-mail rajtar@
aol.com.
Length: 10.9 miles (loop). *Route:* The trail
begins at the old US 17-92 bridge, loops
south through Lake Marion, then crosses the
St. Johns River north through North Marion
to DeBary, and then returns to the
beginning. *Terrain:* City streets. *Cycling:*
Appropriate. *Awards:* Patch $4.00. *Submit:*
Patch order form. *Register:* Not required.
Sites: Woodland Park Site, Lake Monroe
School, Valdez, Fort Florida Landing, Benson
Junction, DeBary Hall, Ox Brush Fiber
Company Site, Ferry Site.

DeLand Historical Trail

Location: DeLand, FL. *Theme:* Local
history and architecture. *Sponsor:* Steve
Rajtar, 1614 Bimini Dr., Orlando, FL 32806,
(407) 894-7412, http://www.geocities.com/
Yosemite/Rapids/8428, e-mail rajtar@aol.com.
Length: 11.7 miles (loop). *Route:* The trail
begins in the middle of downtown DeLand,
heads north and passes through the Stetson
University campus, heads west and then
south on Spring Garden Ave. past the Stetson
House, and continues east and north back to
the starting point. *Terrain:* City streets.
Cycling: Appropriate. *Awards:* Patch $4.00.
Submit: Patch order form. *Register:* Not
required. *Sites:* Fish Memorial Hospital,
Baker House, Putnam Inn, Stetson
University, Jackson House, Primitive Baptist
Church, St. Peter's Catholic Church,
Roberson House, DeLand House Museum,
Stetson House, Elizabeth Hall, Beaver
Quadrangle.

Deleon Springs Historical Trail

Location: Deleon Springs and Glenwood,
FL. *Theme:* Local history and architecture.
Sponsor: Steve Rajtar, 1614 Bimini Dr.,
Orlando, FL 32806, (407) 894-7412,
http://www.geocities.com/Yosemite/Rapids/8
428, e-mail rajtar@aol.com.
Length: 11.1 miles (loop). *Route:* The trail
begins near the entrance to the state park,
enters the park and passes by the sugar mill
and spring, then exits and heads through

downtown Deleon Springs before going south to Glenwood and returning north to the starting point. *Terrain:* City streets. *Cycling:* Appropriate. *Awards:* Patch $4.00. *Submit:* Patch order form. *Register:* Not required. *Sites:* Spring Garden Baptist Church, Glenwood House, Glenwood United Presbyterian Community Church, Spring Garden Ranch, Lake Woodruff, Mount Zion A.M.E. Church, South Farm, Booth House, Sugar Mill.

Downtown Tampa Historical Trail

Location: Tampa, FL. *Theme:* Local history and architecture. *Sponsor:* Steve Rajtar, 1614 Bimini Dr., Orlando, FL 32806, (407) 894-7412, http://www.geocities.com/Yosemite/Rapids/8428, e-mail rajtar@aol.com.

Length: 6.3 miles (loop). *Route:* The trail begins at the former site of Fort Brooke, winds through the central portion of Tampa, and returns to the beginning. *Terrain:* City streets. *Cycling:* Appropriate. *Awards:* Patch $4.00. *Submit:* Patch order form. *Register:* Not required. *Sites:* County Courthouse, Union Railroad Station, Oaklawn Cemetery, Kress Building, Sacred Heart Church, Tampa Theatre, Maas Brothers, Tibbetts' Corner, Floridan Hotel, First Paved Sidewalk.

Dunedin Historical Trail

Location: Dunedin, FL. *Theme:* Local history and architecture. *Sponsor:* Steve Rajtar, 1614 Bimini Dr., Orlando, FL 32806, (407) 894-7412, http://www.geocities.com/Yosemite/Rapids/8428, e-mail rajtar@aol.com.

Length: 10.6 miles (loop). *Route:* The trail begins and ends at Marina Park, looping through town. *Terrain:* City streets. *Cycling:* Appropriate. *Awards:* Patch $4.00. *Submit:* Patch order form. *Register:* Not required. *Sites:* Badeau House, Bouton House, Blatchley House, Caladesi Island, Andrews Memorial Chapel, Masonic Temple, Dunedin Cemetery, Mease Manor, Smith House, Mease Hospital.

Dunnellon Historical Trail

Location: Dunnellon, FL. *Theme:* Local history and architecture. *Sponsor:* Steve Rajtar, 1614 Bimini Dr., Orlando, FL 32806, (407) 894-7412, http://www.geocities.com/Yosemite/Rapids/8428, e-mail rajtar@aol.com.

Length: 7.7 miles (loop). *Route:* The trail begins at the Rainbow River tubing take-out point, heads west and winds through the town, and returns to the point of beginning. *Terrain:* City streets. *Cycling:* Appropriate. *Awards:* Patch $4.00. *Submit:* Patch order form. *Register:* Not required. *Sites:* Minnetrista, North House, First Baptist Church, Rosebank, Rockwell Cemetery, Bosewell House, Cocowitch House, Ohnmacht Building, Baskin House, Bank of Dunnellon.

Eatonville Historical Trail

Location: Eatonville, FL. *Theme:* Local history. *Sponsor:* Steve Rajtar, 1614 Bimini Dr., Orlando, FL 32806, (407) 894-7412, http://www.geocities.com/Yosemite/Rapids/8428, e-mail rajtar@aol.com.

Length: 5.0 miles (loop). *Route:* The trail begins across from the town hall, loops through nearly the entire town the length of Kennedy Blvd., and returns to the start. *Terrain:* City streets. *Cycling:* Appropriate. *Awards:* Patch $4.00. *Submit:* Patch order form. *Register:* Not required. *Sites:* Macedonia Missionary Baptist Church, Town Hall, Heroes' Night Club, St. Lawrence African Methodist Episcopal Church, Rainbow Club, Wymore Career Education Center, Zora Neale Hurston Monument, Zora Neale Hurston National Museum of Fine Arts, Eatonville Elementary School.

Eau Gallie Historical Trail

Location: Eau Gallie (Melbourne), Canova Beach and Satellite Beach, FL. *Theme:* Local history and architecture. *Sponsor:* Steve Rajtar, 1614 Bimini Dr., Orlando, FL 32806, (407) 894-7412, http://www.geocities.com/Yosemite/Rapids/8428, e-mail rajtar@aol.com.

Length: 4.2 miles (loop). *Route:* The trail begins near the intersection of Eau Gallie Blvd. and Highland Ave., heads north on Highland, east on McClendon St., and south on Pineapple Ave. to Eau Gallie Blvd., then follows the shore of the Eau Gallie River. It crosses the Indian River to Canova Beach, then passes through Satellite Beach and returns to its starting point. *Terrain:* City streets. *Cycling:* Appropriate. *Awards:* Patch $4.00. *Submit:* Patch order form. *Register:* Not required. *Sites:* Houston Cemetery, Sunny Point, Rossetter House, Sullivan

House, St. John's Episcopal Church, Hodgson House, Harbor City Hotel, Gleason House, Eau Gallie High School.

Egmont Key Historic Trail

Location: Egmont Key, off the coast of Tierra Verde, FL (near St. Petersburg and Ft. DeSoto). *Theme:* Historic fort and Coast Guard installation. *Sponsor:* Bruce W. Dietch, Troop 27, 4120 12th Ave. W., Bradenton, FL 34205, (941) 746-2053.

Length: 2 miles (loop). *Route:* The precise route varies because the ruins may be visited in any order, and the boat from the mainland may dock or anchor in more than one location. *Terrain:* Old brick roads. *Cycling:* Not recommended. *Awards:* Patch $3.00. *Submit:* Group leader's certification of completion of hike, overnight camping and conservation project. *Register:* Upon arrival on island; plus register in advance with sponsor to obtain award information. *Sites:* Ft. DeSoto, Lighthouse, Fort Dade Ruins.

Elfers Historical Trail

Location: New Port Richey, FL. *Theme:* Local history. *Sponsor:* Steve Rajtar, 1614 Bimini Dr., Orlando, FL 32806, (407) 894-7412, http://www.geocities.com/Yosemite/Rapids/8528, e-mail rajtar@aol.com.

Length: 7.9 miles (loop). *Route:* The trail begins and ends on Moog Rd., and heads north to wind through the southern part of New Port Richey. *Terrain:* City streets. *Cycling:* Appropriate. *Awards:* Patch $4.00. *Submit:* Patch order form. *Register:* Not required. *Sites:* Westside Baptist Church, Baker House, Our Lady Queen of Peace Catholic Church, St. Stephens' Episcopal Church, Butler House, Edenfield Store.

Enterprise Historical Trail

Location: Enterprise, FL. *Theme:* Local history. *Sponsor:* Steve Rajtar, 1614 Bimini Dr., Orlando, FL 32806, (407) 894-7412, http://www.geocities.com/Yosemite/Rapids/8428, e-mail rajtar@aol.com.

Length: 9.8 miles (loop). *Route:* The trail begins and ends at Mariners Cove Park, and includes Stone Island and downtown Enterprise. *Terrain:* City streets. *Cycling:* Appropriate. *Awards:* Patch $4.00. *Submit:* Patch order form. *Register:* Not required. *Sites:* All Saints' Episcopal Church, Courthouse Site, Enterprise School, Stone

Island, Fort Kingsbury Site, General Store Site, Bodine & McCarty Subdivision, Florida Methodist Children's Home, Old Enterprise Site.

Eustis Historical Trail

Location: Eustis, FL. *Theme:* Local history and architecture. *Sponsor:* Steve Rajtar, 1614 Bimini Dr., Orlando, FL 32806, (407) 894-7412, http://www.geocities.com/Yosemite/Rapids/8428, e-mail rajtar@aol.com.

Length: 9.2 miles (loop). *Route:* The trail begins and ends at Pendleton Park, and covers the streets of Eustis. *Terrain:* City streets. *Cycling:* Appropriate. *Awards:* Patch $4.00. *Submit:* Patch order form. *Register:* No requirement. *Sites:* Bartley Temple, Taylor House, Waterman Memorial Hospital, Greenwood Cemetery, The Palms, Ashmore House, St. Thomas Episcopal Church, Woman's Club, Clifford House, Palmer House.

Fellsmere Historical Trail

Location: Fellsmere, FL. *Theme:* Local history. *Sponsor:* Steve Rajtar, 1614 Bimini Dr., Orlando, FL 32806, (407) 894-7412, http://www.geocities.com/Yosemite/Rapids/8428, e-mail rajtar@aol.com.

Length: 4.2 miles (loop). *Route:* The trail begins at the municipal parking lot on Orange St., heads south to the city hall and school, east and north to the demonstration farm site, then south and west to the library and south to the point of beginning. *Terrain:* City streets. *Cycling:* Appropriate. *Awards:* Patch $4.00. *Submit:* Patch order form. *Register:* Not required. *Sites:* Fellsmere Estates Office, Fellsmere School, Broadway Inn, Bank Building, Marion Fell Library, Community Church, Fellsmere Historical Church, City Hall.

Floral City Historical Trail

Location: Floral City, FL. *Theme:* Local history and architecture. *Sponsor:* Steve Rajtar, 1614 Bimini Dr., Orlando, FL 32806, (407) 894-7412, http://www.geocities.com/Yosemite/Rapids/8428, e-mail rajtar@aol.com.

Length: 7.3 miles (loop). *Route:* The trail begins at Floral Park, heads north through town to the Hills of Rest Cemetery, follows Orange Ave. and other streets east to the old steamboat landing, crosses over the bridge to

Duval Island, then returns on streets and the Withlacoochee State Trail to the starting point. *Terrain:* City streets. *Cycling:* Appropriate. *Awards:* Patch $4.00. *Submit:* Patch order form. *Register:* Not required. *Sites:* Zimmerman House, Commercial Hotel, Canopy of Oaks, Orange State Canal, Steamboat Landing, Old Methodist Church, Crump House, Raulerson House, Formy-Duval House, Smoak Building.

Florida National Scenic Trail

Location: Stretches nearly the length of the state. *Theme:* Recreation. *Sponsor:* Florida Trail Association, Inc., P.O. Box 13708, Gainesville, FL 32604, (352) 378-8823, (800) 343-1882, fax (352) 378-4550.
Length: Over 1000 miles and growing (straight). *Route:* The endpoints are currently near Alabama and the Everglades National Park. *Terrain:* Varies. *Cycling:* Appropriate over only certain sections. *Awards:* Patch $3.00. *Submit:* No requirement. *Register:* Not required. *Sites:* Olustee Battlefield, Osceola National Forest, Ocala National Forest, Lake Okeechobee, Lake Kissimmee State Park, Cow Camp.

Forest City Historical Trail

Location: Altamonte Springs, FL. *Theme:* Local history. *Sponsor:* Steve Rajtar, 1614 Bimini Dr., Orlando, FL 32806, (407) 894-7412, http://www.geocities.com/Yosemite/Rapids/8428, e-mail rajtar@aol.com.
Length: 10.9 miles (loop). *Route:* The trail begins and ends at Merrill Park, and covers Altamont, Palm Springs, and Forest City. *Terrain:* City streets. *Cycling:* Appropriate. *Awards:* Patch $4.00. *Submit:* Patch order form. *Register:* Not required. *Sites:* Church of the Annunciation, Rolling Hills Golf Course, Sanlando Springs, Rolling Hills Moravian Church, Fosgate Plant Site.

Ft. Caroline Historic Trail

Location: Jacksonville, FL. *Theme:* Historic fort. *Sponsor:* Florida Historic Trails Association, c/o Milledge Murphey, Ph.D., 1815 N.W. 7th Pl., Gainesville, FL 32603, (352) 373-9234.
Length: 5.37 miles (loop). *Route:* The trail begins at the Visitors Center, heads to the fort, then to Spanish Pond, the Theodore Roosevelt Area, and Willie Browne Cemetery, then returns to the start. *Terrain:* Roads and

dirt paths. *Cycling:* Appropriate. *Awards:* Medal $6.50; Patch $4.00; Repeat Pin $2.50 (The miles for this trail and others sponsored by the same organization may be aggregated to qualify for the Florida Historic Trails Association 100 Mile Hiking Award—Medal $6.50; Patch $4.00; Repeat Pin $2.50.). *Submit:* Group leader's certification of completion, plus completed 22-item questionnaire. *Register:* In advance. *Sites:* Fort Caroline Replica, Spanish Pond, Willie Browne Cemetery, Alligator Pond, Willie Browne Home Ruins, Sgt. John Nathan Spearing Grave, St. Johns Bluff, Ribault Monument.

Ft. Clinch Environmental Trail

Location: Ft. Clinch State Park, Fernandina Beach, FL. *Theme:* Nature. *Sponsor:* Florida Historic Trails Association, c/o Milledge Murphey, Ph.D., 1815 N.W. 7th Pl., Gainesville, FL 32603, (352) 373-9234.
Length: 5 miles (loop). *Route:* The trail begins at the Youth Camp, includes the Willow Pond Nature Trail (Magnolia Loop), and goes to the fort, river and back to the start. *Terrain:* Roads and dirt trails. *Cycling:* Appropriate, except for dirt nature trails. *Awards:* Medal $6.50; Patch $4.00; Repeat Pin $2.50 (The miles for this trail and others sponsored by the same organization may be aggregated to qualify for the Florida Historic Trails Association 100 Mile Hiking Award—Medal $6.50; Patch $4.00; Repeat Pin $2.50). *Submit:* Group leader's certification of completion. *Register:* In advance. *Sites:* Fort Clinch, St. Mary's River.

Ft. Clinch Historic Trail

Location: Fernandina Beach, FL. *Theme:* Local history. *Sponsor:* Florida Historic Trails Association, c/o Milledge Murphey, Ph.D., 185 N.W. 7th Pl., Gainesville, FL 32603, (352) 373-9234.
Length: 16 miles (loop). *Route:* The trail begins at the Youth Camp, heads south through the city, north along the beach to the fort, then south to the start. *Terrain:* Woods, paved roads and beach. *Cycling:* Appropriate. *Awards:* Medal $6.50; Patch $4.00; Repeat Pin $2.50 (The miles for this trail and others sponsored by the same organization may be aggregated to qualify for the Florida Historic Trails Association 100 Mile Hiking Award—Medal $6.50; Patch $4.00; Repeat Pin $2.50).

Submit: Group leader's certification of completion and completed 16-item questionnaire. *Register:* In advance. *Sites:* Fort San Carlos Site, McClure's Hill, Atlantic Ocean, Fernandina Beach Chamber of Commerce Building, St. Mary's River, Fernandez Graves, Fort Clinch.

Fort George Historic Trail

Location: Jacksonville, FL. *Theme:* Local history. *Sponsor:* Florida Historic Trails Association, c/o Milledge Murphey, Ph.D., 1815 N.W. 7th Pl., Gainesville, FL 32063, (352) 373-9234.

Length: 6.4 miles (loop). *Route:* The trail begins at the Timucuan Preserve Kingsley Plantation, covers the Kingsley grounds, and includes the Saturiwa Trail through the Talbot Islands State Parks. *Terrain:* Paved roads, sidewalks, and walking paths. *Cycling:* Appropriate over the paved portions. *Awards:* Medal $6.50; Patch $4.00; Repeat Pin $2.50 (The miles for this trail and others sponsored by the same organization may be aggregated to qualify for the Historic Trails Association 100 Mile Hiking Award—Medal $6.50; Patch $4.00; Repeat Pin $2.50). *Submit:* Completed 33-item questionnaire. *Register:* In advance. *Sites:* Kingsley Plantation, Tabby Cabins, Planters Home, Visitor Center, Little Talbot Island, Saturiwa Trail.

Ft. Matanzas Historic Trail

Location: Ft. Matanzas National Monument, St. Augustine, FL. *Theme:* Historic fort. *Sponsor:* Florida Historic Trails Association, c/o Milledge Murphey, Ph.D., 1815 N.W. 7th Pl., Gainesville, FL 32063, (352) 373-9234.

Length: 1 mile (loop) plus boat ride to fort. *Route:* The trail begins in the parking area adjacent to the Visitors Center, follows a boardwalk nature trail, and loops back to the start. *Terrain:* Boardwalk and island fort. *Cycling:* Not recommended. *Awards:* Medal $6.50; Patch $4.00; Repeat Pin $2.50 (The miles for this trail and others sponsored by the same organization may be aggregated to qualify for the Florida Historic Trails Association 100 Mile Hiking Award—Medal $6.50; Patch $4.00; Repeat Pin $2.50.). *Submit:* Group leader's certification of completion, plus completed 39-item questionnaire. *Register:* In advance. *Sites:*

Visitors Center, Ft. Matanzas, Ribault Massacre Monument, Matanzas River.

Fort McCoy Historical Trail

Location: Fort McCoy, FL. *Theme:* Local history. *Sponsor:* Steve Rajtar, 1614 Bimini Dr., Orlando, FL 32806, (407) 894-7412, http://www.geocities.com/Yosemite/Rapids/8 428, e-mail rajtar@aol.com.

Length: 6.0 miles (loop). *Route:* The trail begins in Cougar Park and heads generally north, west and east to cover the roads in and near Fort McCoy before returning to the beginning. *Terrain:* Rural and city streets. *Cycling:* Appropriate. *Awards:* Patch $4.00. *Submit:* Patch order form. *Register:* Not required. *Sites:* Cook Company, Ft. McCoy School, Edmunds House, Masonic Lodge, Baptist Church, Fort McCoy Cemetery, Fort McCoy Library, Howell House Site, Cook Filling Station Site, Stephens House Site.

Fort Meade Historical Trail

Location: Fort Meade, FL. *Theme:* Local history. *Sponsor:* Steve Rajtar, 1614 Bimini Dr., Orlando, FL 32806, (407) 894-7412, http://www.geocities.com/Yosemite/Rapids/8 428, e-mail rajtar@aol.com.

Length: 6.8 miles (loop). *Route:* The trail begins at Peace River Park, heads west past the original fort site, winds through town, and returns to the beginning. *Terrain:* City streets. *Cycling:* Appropriate. *Awards:* Patch $4.00. *Submit:* Patch order form. *Register:* Not required. *Sites:* Edgewood Cemetery, Jackson Memorial, Christ Episcopal Church, First Baptist Church, Reif House, Bank Building, Galilee Baptist Church, St. Paul A.M.E. Church, Tillis Monument, Second Fort Site.

Fort Pickens Historical Trail

Location: Santa Rosa Island near Pensacola, FL. *Theme:* Historic fort. *Sponsor:* Michael M. Sams, Troop 3, Cokesbury United Methodist Church, 5725 N. 9th Ave., Pensacola, FL 32504, (850) 477-0852.

Length: 10 miles (loop). *Route:* The trail begins at the group camp west of Battery Langdon, heads westward to circle the fort, and returns through the campground to the start. *Terrain:* Roads and bike trails. *Cycling:* Appropriate. *Awards:* Medal $4.00; Patch $3.00. *Submit:* Completed 14-item questionnaire. *Register:* Not required. *Sites:*

Battery Langdon, WWII Tower, Battery Cooper, Langdon Beach, Battery Wirth, Fort Pickens, Battery Truman, Battery Payne.

Frostproof Historical Trail

Location: Frostproof, FL. *Theme:* Local history. *Sponsor:* Steve Rajtar, 1614 Bimini Dr., Orlando, FL 32806, (407) 894-7412, http://www.geocities.com/Yosemite/Rapids/8 428, e-mail rajtar@aol.com.

Length: 4.7 miles (loop). *Route:* The trail begins near the baseball diamond at the east end of Wall St., heads north on Lake Ave., west on CR 630, south on Palm Ave., and loops through downtown Frostproof. *Terrain:* City streets. *Cycling:* Appropriate. *Awards:* Patch $4.00. *Submit:* Patch order form. *Register:* Not required. *Sites:* First Presbyterian Church, First Baptist Church, Church of Christ, Gammon House, Brantley Building, Milton Store, Citizens Bank, Ramon Theater, Brown House, First Assembly of God.

Fruitland Park Historical Trail

Location: Fruitland Park, FL. *Theme:* Local history. *Sponsor:* Steve Rajtar, 1614 Bimini Dr., Orlando, FL 32806, (407) 894-7412, http://www.geocities.com/Yosemite/Rapids/8 428, e-mail rajtar@aol.com.

Length: 8.9 miles (loop). *Route:* The trail begins at the library, heads north to the English Colony area, heads through Fruitland Park south by Crystal and Mirror Lakes, and returns to the beginning. *Terrain:* City streets. *Cycling:* Appropriate. *Awards:* Patch $4.00. *Submit:* Patch order form. *Register:* Not required. *Sites:* Mainewood, Shiloh Cemetery, Fair Oaks, Holy Trinity Episcopal Church, Casino, Lee House, Hillcrest, Lake Griffin State Park, Bosworth House.

Gainesville Historical Trail

Location: Gainesville, FL. *Theme:* Local history and architecture. *Sponsor:* Steve Rajtar, 1614 Bimini Dr., Orlando, FL 32806, (407) 894-7412, http://www.geocities.com/ Yosemite/Rapids/8428, e-mail rajtar@aol. com.

Length: 9.0 miles (loop). *Route:* The trail begins and ends at Roper Park, looping through the historic northeast neighborhood, the area south of E. University Ave., the courthouse area, and the commercial area west of Main St. *Terrain:*

City streets. *Cycling:* Appropriate. *Awards:* Patch $4.00. *Submit:* Patch order form. *Register:* Not required. *Sites:* Epworth Hall, Tigert House, Thomas Center, Adkins House, Murphree House, Kirby Smith School, Matheson House, State Theatre, Commercial Hotel, Clock Tower.

Geneva-Chuluota Historical Trail

Location: Geneva and Chuluota, FL. *Theme:* Local history. *Sponsor:* Steve Rajtar, 1614 Bimini Dr., Orlando, FL 32806, (407) 894-7412, http://www.geocities.com/ Yosemite/Rapids/8428, e-mail rajtar@aol. com.

Length: Three loops totaling 9.9 miles, plus 21.7 miles driving between loops. *Route:* The trail begins at the Geneva Historical and Genealogical Museum, and loops through Geneva. Then after driving to the old settlement of Osceola, there is a walking loop and a drive to Fort Lane and two other sites on the way to Chuluota. In Chuluota, there is a walking loop beginning and ending at the VFW Post. *Terrain:* Paved streets and dirt roads. *Cycling:* Appropriate, but difficult in places. *Awards:* Patch $4.00. *Submit:* Patch order form. *Register:* Not required. *Sites:* Geneva Community Center, Geneva Cemetery, Geneva Methodist Church, Osceola Ruins, Flynt and Rehbinder Store, Cook's Ferry, Stationmaster's House, Lake Catherine Inn.

Goldenrod Historical Trail

Location: Winter Park, FL. *Theme:* Local history. *Sponsor:* Steve Rajtar, 1614 Bimini Dr., Orlando, FL 32806, (407) 894-7412, http://www.geocities.com/Yosemite/Rapids/8 428, e-mail rajtar@aol.com.

Length: 8.9 miles (loop). *Route:* The trail begins and ends at the shopping center near the intersection of Aloma Ave. and Howell Branch Rd., covering portions of Orange and Seminole counties. *Terrain:* City streets. *Cycling:* Appropriate. *Awards:* Patch $4.00. *Submit:* Patch order form. *Register:* Not required. *Sites:* Gospel Light Baptist Church, Community House, Aloma Baptist Church, Slovak Garden, Bower-Dike House, Johnston House, Spelzenhausen's Stores, Civic Center.

Groveland-Mascotte Historical Trail

Location: Groveland and Mascotte, FL. *Theme:* Local history. *Sponsor:* Steve Rajtar,

1614 Bimini Dr., Orlando, FL 32806, (407) 894-7412, http://www.geocities.com/ Yosemite/Rapids/8428, e-mail rajtar@aol. com.

Length: 9.5 miles (loop). *Route:* The trail starts in Groveland, follows SR 50 westward to and through Mascotte, and then heads eastward back to Groveland. *Terrain:* City streets. *Cycling:* Appropriate. *Awards:* Patch $4.00. *Submit:* Patch order form. *Register:* Not required. *Sites:* Groveland Elementary School, Edge Building, Greater Harmony Missionary Baptist Church, Lake Audrey, Zion Lutheran Church, Mascotte Cemetery, Mascotte United Methodist Church, First Baptist Church.

Gulfport Historical Trail

Location: Gulfport, FL. *Theme:* Local history. *Sponsor:* Steve Rajtar, 1614 Bimini Dr., Orlando, FL 32806, (407) 894-7412, http://www.geocities.com/Yosemite/Rapids/8 428, e-mail rajtar@aol.com.

Length: 9.9 miles (loop). *Route:* The trail begins on Beach Blvd. between 28th and 29th Sts., heads east and south to Tampa Bay, west to former Fiddler's Flats, north to Stetson University Law School, then heads through town back to the starting point. *Terrain:* City streets. *Cycling:* Appropriate. *Awards:* Patch $4.00. *Submit:* Patch order form. *Register:* Not required. *Sites:* Steinwinder House, City Hall, Barnett's Bluff, Casino, McLellan House, Fiddler's Flats, The Cedars, Prigun Apartments, Historical Museum, Scout Hall.

Haines City Historical Trail

Location: Haines City, FL. *Theme:* Local history and architecture. *Sponsor:* Steve Rajtar, 1614 Bimini Dr., Orlando, FL 32806, (407) 894-7412, http://www.geocities.com/ Yosemite/Rapids/8428, e-mail rajtar@aol. com.

Length: 7.2 miles (loop). *Route:* The trail begins and ends at the city park across from the railroad station, heads east through downtown, and then loops south and east of Lake Tracy. *Terrain:* City streets. *Cycling:* Appropriate. *Awards:* Patch $4.00. *Submit:* Patch order form. *Register:* Not required. *Sites:* Central Grammar School, Clay Cut, St. Mark's Episcopal Church, Van Buren Hotel, More Building, Polk Hotel, Garrett House, Van-Rook Inn, Polk Arcade, Randall House.

Hawthorne Historical Trail

Location: Hawthorne, FL. *Theme:* Local history and architecture. *Sponsor:* Steve Rajtar, 1614 Bimini Dr., Orlando, FL 32806, (407) 894-7412, http://www.geocities.com/ Yosemite/Rapids/8428, e-mail rajtar@aol. com.

Length: 3.7 miles (loop). *Route:* The trail begins near the center of Hawthorne, heads north on NW 6th St. to the residential area in the northwest section, then follows Johnson St. south through the commercial area, winds through the residential southeast section, heads north on Johnson St., and returns to the starting point. *Terrain:* City streets. *Cycling:* Appropriate. *Awards:* Patch $4.00. *Submit:* Patch order form. *Register:* Not required. *Sites:* Galilee Baptist Church, Shell House, Church of God By Faith, Center Hotel, Hawthorne House, Railroad Junction, Strange House, McGinness House, Old Hawthorne Drugstore, Whitcomb House.

High Springs Historical Trail

Location: High Springs, FL. *Theme:* Local history and architecture. *Sponsor:* Steve Rajtar, 1614 Bimini Dr., Orlando, FL 32806, (407) 894-7412, http://www.geocities.com/ Yosemite/Rapids/8428, e-mail rajtar@aol. com.

Length: 4.1 miles (loop). *Route:* The trail begins on SE Railroad Ave., then winds through the streets of downtown High Springs to the railroad depot on the west end of town, then meanders eastwardly through commercial and residential neighborhoods to the starting point. *Terrain:* City streets. *Cycling:* Appropriate. *Awards:* Patch $4.00. *Submit:* Patch order form. *Register:* Not required. *Sites:* Allen Chapel A.M.E. Church, Mt. Olive Missionary Baptist Church, Grimes Grocery Store, Thomas Apartments, First Baptist Church, Peanut Mill, Priest Theater, Thomas' Drug Store, Railroad Depot.

Historic Melbourne Trail

Location: Melbourne and Eau Gallie, FL. *Theme:* Local History. *Sponsor:* Troop 323, c/o Amy M. Pierce, 440 Finch Dr., Satellite Beach, FL 32937-3704.

Length: 10.5 and 11.3 miles (loops). *Route:* The trail begins at the boardwalk at the Crane Creek Promenade, passes through Melbourne on New Haven and Strawbridge Aves. and Harbor City Blvd., passes through

Eau Gallie on Highland and Magnolia Aves., and returns south to the point of beginning. While in Melbourne, the route splits and offers the hiker a choice between a slightly longer route to the west, with additional sites. *Terrain:* City streets. *Cycling:* Possible, but check with sponsor if it qualifies for the award. *Awards:* Patch. *Submit:* Completed 24-27 item questionnaire. *Register:* Not required. *Sites:* Florida Air Academy, Strawberry Mansion, United Church of Christ, Pioneer Cemetery, Rossetter Memorial Park, Rossetter House, Holy Trinity Church, Melbourne High School, Crane Creek Promenade, "Doc" Sloan House.

Homosassa Historical Trail

Location: Homosassa and Homosassa Springs, FL. *Theme:* Local history and architecture. *Sponsor:* Steve Rajtar, 1614 Bimini Dr., Orlando, FL 32806, (407) 894-7412, http://www.geocities.com/Yosemite/Rapids/8428, e-mail rajtar@aol.com.

Length: 5.6 miles (loop). *Route:* The trail begins at Homosassa Springs State Wildlife Park, heads west past the Sugar Mill ruins, winds through downtown, then heads back to the point of beginning. *Terrain:* City streets. *Cycling:* Appropriate. *Awards:* Patch $4.00. *Submit:* Patch order form. *Register:* Not required. *Sites:* Yulee Sugar Mill Ruins, Dunn House, Homosassa Springs Park, Atlanta Fishing Club, Stage Stand Cemetery, Schoolhouse, Campbell House, Homosassa Hotel, Florida Kenwick Manor, Lumber Mill Site.

Hudson-Bayonet Point Historical Trail

Location: Hudson and Bayonet Point, FL. *Theme:* Local history. *Sponsor:* Steve Rajtar, 1614 Bimini Dr., Orlando, FL 32806, (407) 894-7412, http://www.geocities.com/Yosemite/Rapids/8428, e-mail rajtar@aol.com.

Length: 9.0 miles (loop). *Route:* The trail begins at the intersection of US 19 and Hudson Ave., goes east and south to Fivay, north and west to Bayonet Point, north and west to the residential area of Hudson, and east to the point of beginning. *Terrain:* City streets. *Cycling:* Appropriate. *Awards:* Patch $4.00. *Submit:* Patch order form. *Register:* Not required. *Sites:* Bear Creek Sink, Fivay Site, Hudson Cemetery, Hudson Springs, Hudson House, Rawls House, Methodist Church, Vereen Cemetery.

Indian Rocks Beach Historical Trail

Location: Indian Rocks Beach and Largo, FL. *Theme:* Local history and architecture. *Sponsor:* Steve Rajtar, 1614 Bimini Dr., Orlando, FL 32806, (407) 894-7412, http://www.geocities.com/Yosemite/Rapids/8428, e-mail rajtar@aol.com.

Length: 7.8 miles (loop). *Route:* The trail begins in Largo Narrows Nature Park on the mainland, then cross to the barrier island, heads south to the end of the city, follows Gulf Blvd. north to about 27th Ave., and then heads south and back across the bridge to the point of beginning. *Terrain:* City streets. *Cycling:* Appropriate. *Awards:* Patch $4.00. *Submit:* Patch order form. *Register:* Not required. *Sites:* Hendrick House, Val's View, Breezes Grocery Store, Tompkins Building, Gardner House, Pueblo Village, Church of the Isles, Calvary Episcopal Church, Historical Museum, Kolb Park.

Interlachen Historical Trail

Location: Interlachen, FL. *Theme:* Local history. *Sponsor:* Steve Rajtar, 1614 Bimini Dr., Orlando, FL 32806, (407) 894-7412, http://www.geocities.com/Yosemite/Rapids/8428, e-mail rajtar@aol.com.

Length: 6.0 miles (loop). *Route:* The trail begins near the intersection of Commonwealth and Atlantic and heads west to Pineview Cemetery, east through Interlachen, north to Pinelawn Cemetery, west on SR 20, north on Grand Ave. to the library and Baptist Church, and then south to the starting point. *Terrain:* City streets. *Cycling:* Appropriate. *Awards:* Patch $4.00. *Submit:* Patch order form. *Register:* Not required. *Sites:* Brush General Store, Sister Spring Cemetery, Interlachen Community School, Keuka Site, Lakeview Hotel, St. John's Catholic Church, St. Andrew's Episcopal Church, Interlachen Methodist Church, Interlachen Baptist Church.

Inverness Historical Trail

Location: Inverness, FL. *Theme:* Local history. *Sponsor:* Steve Rajtar, 1614 Bimini Dr., Orlando, FL 32806, (407) 894-7412, http://www.geocities.com/Yosemite/Rapids/8428, e-mail rajtar@aol.com.

Length: 9.4 miles (loop). *Route:* The trail

begins at Wallace Brook City Park, heads
south on the Withlacoochee State Trail to
Fort Cooper, then goes north through town
and back to the beginning. *Terrain:* City
streets. *Cycling:* Appropriate. *Awards:* Patch
$4.00. *Submit:* Patch order form. *Register:*
Not required. *Sites:* Masonic Temple, Crown
Hotel, Inverness Woman's Club, Citrus
County Courthouse, Railroad Station, Hicks
House, Dampier House, Oak Ridge
Cemetery, Fort Cooper, Savary House.

Kenansville Historical Trail

Location: Kenansville, FL. *Theme:* Local
history. *Sponsor:* Steve Rajtar, 1614 Bimini
Dr., Orlando, FL 32806, (407) 894-7412,
http://www.geocities.com/Yosemite/Rapids/8
428, e-mail rajtar@aol.com.
Length: 8.8 miles (loop). *Route:* The trail
begins and ends at the schoolhouse, and
covers the former site of Whittier, plus
"downtown" Kenansville. *Terrain:* Mostly
city streets, with a short stretch on grassy
roads. *Cycling:* Appropriate. *Awards:* Patch
$4.00. *Submit:* Patch order form. *Register:*
Not required. *Sites:* Kenansville Cemetery,
Red Gator Lounge, First Missionary Baptist
Church of Kenansville, First State Bank,
Heartbreak Hotel, Webb's General Store, Post
Office, W.H. Phillips House, Kenansville
School.

Kissimmee Historical Trail

Location: Kissimmee, FL. *Theme:* Local
history and architecture. *Sponsor:* Steve
Rajtar, 1614 Bimini Dr., Orlando, FL 32806,
(407) 894-7412, http://www.geocities.com/
Yosemite/Rapids/8428, e-mail rajtar@aol.
com.
Length: 11.3 miles (loop). *Route:* The trail
begins and ends at Lakefront Park, and winds
through the older portions of Kissimmee and
North Kissimmee. *Terrain:* City streets.
Cycling: Appropriate. *Awards:* Patch $4.00.
Submit: Patch order form. *Register:* Not
required. *Sites:* American Legion Home,
KAST Club, Monument of States, Bethel
A.M.E. Church, Osceola County Courthouse,
Willson House, First Baptist Church, Winn-
Hunter House, Holy Redeemer Catholic
Church, Citizens' State Bank, High School.

Korona Historical Trail

Location: Flagler County, FL. *Theme:*
Local history. *Sponsor:* Steve Rajtar, 1614

Bimini Dr., Orlando, FL 32806, (407) 894-
7412, http://www.geocities.com/Yosemite/
Rapids/8428, e-mail rajtar@aol.com.
Length: 20.0 miles (loop). *Route:* The trail
begins at the Knox Bridge, heads west to
Korona, then east and north to the
Bulowville ruins, then south and east back to
the beginning. *Terrain:* Rural roads. *Cycling:*
Appropriate. *Awards:* Patch $4.00. *Submit:*
Patch order form. *Register:* Not required.
Sites: Bulowville, St. Mary's Church, Kings
Road, Dixie Highway, Knox House.

La Crosse-Santa Fe Historical Trail

Location: La Crosse and Santa Fe, FL.
Theme: Local history. *Sponsor:* Steve Rajtar,
1614 Bimini Dr., Orlando, FL 32806, (407)
894-7412, http://www.geocities.com/
Yosemite/Rapids/8428, e-mail rajtar@aol.
com.
Length: 7.8 miles (loop). *Route:* The trail
begins in La Crosse near the intersection of
SR 121 and CR 1493, loops through La
Crosse, heads north to and through Santa Fe,
then returns to the beginning. *Terrain:* City
streets and rural roads. *Cycling:* Appropriate.
Awards: Patch $4.00. *Submit:* Patch order
form. *Register:* Not required. *Sites:* Potato
Growers Association, Newbern House,
Methodist Episcopal Church, La Crosse
Baptist Church, Harris Commissary, Roberts
Store, Santa Fe Baptist Church, Futch House.

Lady Lake Historical Trail

Location: Lady Lake, FL. *Theme:* Local
history and architecture. *Sponsor:* Steve
Rajtar, 1614 Bimini Dr., Orlando, FL 32806,
(407) 894-7412, http://www.geocities.com/
Yosemite/Rapids/8428, e-mail rajtar@aol.
com.
Length: 5.1 miles (loop). *Route:* Starting at
Town Park, the trail heads west, north and
east to the residential area east of US 441,
then south along that road, and north to the
point of beginning. *Terrain:* City streets.
Cycling: Appropriate. *Awards:* Patch $4.00.
Submit: Patch order form. *Register:* Not
required. *Sites:* Railroad Station, Lady Lake
United First Methodist Church, Mt. Pleasant
Baptist Church, Dyches House, Iglesie de
Dios Pentecostal Church, Cottom's Garage,
Hanging Tree, General Feed Store.

Lake Apopka Historical Bike Trail

Location: Western Orange and Eastern

Lake Counties, FL. *Theme:* Local history, recreation. *Sponsor:* Steve Rajtar, 1614 Bimini Dr., Orlando, FL 32806, (407) 894-7412, http://www.geocities.com/Yosemite/Rapids/8428, e-mail rajtar@aol.com.

Length: 56.5 miles (loop). *Route:* The trail begins in Killarney, and proceeds counter-clockwise around Lake Apopka through Oakland, Tildenville, Winter Garden, Ocoee, Apopka, Plymouth, Zellwood, Tangerine, Astatula, Ferndale, and Montverde. *Terrain:* Paved and unpaved roads. *Cycling:* Appropriate. *Awards:* Patch $4.00. *Submit:* Patch order form. *Register:* Not required. *Sites:* Woodlawn Villa, Vick House, Michael Hardware Store, Lakeview High School, Edgewater Hotel, Withers-Maguire House, Astatula Cemetery, West Orange Trail, Montverde Academy, Mucklands.

Lake Helen-Cassadaga Historical Trail

Location: Lake Helen and Cassadaga, FL. *Theme:* Local history and architecture. *Sponsor:* Steve Rajtar, 1614 Bimini Dr., Orlando, FL 32806, (407) 894-7412, http://www.geocities.com/Yosemite/Rapids/8428, e-mail rajtar@aol.com.

Length: 9.5 miles (loop). *Route:* The trail begins at Lake Colby Park, heads north to wind through Lake Helen, then heads back south to visit both the Spiritualist and Non-Spiritualist portions of Cassadaga, before returning to Lake Colby. *Terrain:* City streets. *Cycling:* Appropriate. *Awards:* Patch $4.00. *Submit:* Patch order form. *Register:* Not required. *Sites:* Cassadaga Cemetery, Luffman House, Cassadaga Hotel, Andrews House, Harmony Hall, Mills House, Colby Memorial Temple, Florida National Bank, Bingham Hall, Mt. Zion Baptist Church.

Lake Hollingsworth Historical Trail

Location: Lakeland, FL. *Theme:* Local history and architecture. *Sponsor:* Steve Rajtar, 1614 Bimini Dr., Orlando, FL 32806, (407) 894-7412, http://www.geocities.com/Yosemite/Rapids/8428, e-mail rajtar@aol.com.

Length: 5.6 miles (loop). *Route:* The trail begins adjacent to Florida Southern College, winds north through the Dixieland neighborhood, tours the Frank Lloyd Wright architecture of the college, and then circles Lake Hollingsworth just to the south of the college. *Terrain:* City streets. *Cycling:* Appropriate. *Awards:* Patch $4.00. *Submit:* Patch order form. *Register:* Not required. *Sites:* Southside Baptist Church, Thad Buckner Building, Lake Morton Bed & Breakfast, Danforth Chapel, Annie Pfeiffer Chapel, Spivey Memorial, Joseph-Reynolds Hall, Edge Hall, Hindu Garden of Meditation, Cleveland Heights.

Lake Mary Historical Trail

Location: Lake Mary, FL. *Theme:* Local history and architecture. *Sponsor:* Steve Rajtar, 1614 Bimini Dr., Orlando, FL 32806, (407) 894-7412, http://www.geocities.com/Yosemite/Rapids/8428, e-mail rajtar@aol. com.

Length: 9.7 miles (loop). *Route:* The hike begins and ends at the Frank Evans Center, loops through downtown Lake Mary, and visits the site of the New Upsala settlement. *Terrain:* City streets, some dirt roads. *Cycling:* Appropriate, but some portions difficult. *Awards:* Patch $4.00. *Submit:* Patch order form. *Register:* Not required. *Sites:* Lake Mary First Presbyterian Church, Wyman's Garage, Lake View Lodge, Gleason's Store, Tableau Square, New Upsala Cemetery, Douglas Building.

Lake of the Hills Historical Trail

Location: Lake of the Hills, FL. *Theme:* Local history and architecture. *Sponsor:* Steve Rajtar, 1614 Bimini Dr., Orlando, FL 32806, (407) 894-7412, http://www.geocities.com/Yosemite/Rapids/8428, e-mail rajtar@aol.com.

Length: 9.4 miles (loop). *Route:* The trail begins at the Eagle Ridge Shopping Center, heads east to circle around Starr Lake with a good view of Bok Tower, and returns to the beginning. *Terrain:* City streets and paved country roads. *Cycling:* Appropriate. *Awards:* Patch $4.00. *Submit:* Patch order form. *Register:* Not required. *Sites:* Wolfe House, Lake View Apartments, Ekeland Store, Community Center, Chalet Suzanne, Moule House, Hutchens House, Casa Jannotta, Mountain Lake, Big Oak Motel.

Lake Pasadena Historical Trail

Location: Rural Pasco County, FL. *Theme:* Local history. *Sponsor:* Steve Rajtar, 1614 Bimini Dr., Orlando, FL 32806, (407) 894-7412, http://www.geocities.com/Yosemite/Rapids/8428, e-mail rajtar@aol.com.

Length: 7.7 miles (loop). *Route:* The trail begins at Williams Cemetery, heads northward and eastward, north of the lake. It then heads south on Fort King Rd. to the intersection with Bozeman Rd., and returns on roughly the same route. *Terrain:* City streets and country roads. *Cycling:* Appropriate. *Awards:* Patch $4.00. *Submit:* Patch order form. *Register:* Not required. *Sites:* Solberg House, Dew House, Himmelwright House, Linda Vista Store, Earnestville Site, Fordyce House, Freedtown Site, Pasadena Church, Lake Pasadena, Williams Cemetery.

Lake Wales Historical Trail

Location: Lake Wales, FL. *Theme:* Local history and architecture. *Sponsor:* Steve Rajtar, 1614 Bimini Dr., Orlando, FL 32806, (407) 894-7412, http://www.geocities.com/ Yosemite/Rapids/8428, e-mail rajtar@aol. com.

Length: 11.9 miles (loop). *Route:* The trail begins on the western shore of Lake Wailes, heads north and includes Spook Hill, winds through the downtown historic district, and covers the varied architectural styles in the neighborhood south of the lake before returning to the beginning. *Terrain:* City streets. *Cycling:* Appropriate. *Awards:* Patch $4.00. *Submit:* Patch order form. *Register:* Not required. *Sites:* Tillman House, Johnson Funeral Home, T.J. Parker Building, Citizens Bank, Rhodes Building, Ridge Drug Store, Rhodesbilt Arcade Building, Hotel Dixie Walesbilt, Caldwell-Temple Building, Scenic Theatre.

Lakeland Historical Trail

Location: Lakeland, FL. *Theme:* Local history. *Sponsor:* Steve Rajtar, 1614 Bimini Dr., Orlando, FL 32806, (407) 894-7412, http://www.geocities.com/Yosemite/Rapids/8 428, e-mail rajtar@aol.com.

Length: 9.8 miles (loop). *Route:* The trail begins just north of Lake Morton, winds through the old downtown along Main St. and Tennessee Ave., then covers some of the more recent portions of the city. *Terrain:* City streets. *Cycling:* Appropriate. *Awards:* Patch $4.00. *Submit:* Patch order form. *Register:* Not required. *Sites:* Polk Theater, Van Huss Building, All Saints Episcopal Church, Lakeland Terrace Hotel, Frances Langford Promenade, Florida Hotel, Deen-

Bryant Building, Munn Building, Bowyer Block, Kentucky Building.

Land O'Lakes Historical Trail

Location: Land O'Lakes, FL. *Theme:* Local history. *Support:* Steve Rajtar, 1614 Bimini Dr., Orlando, FL 32806, (407) 894-7412, http://www.geocities.com/Yosemite/Rapids/8 428, e-mail rajtar@aol.com.

Length: 7.5 miles (loop). *Route:* The trail begins near the Community Center, heads south past Lake Patience Rd., then north to Dupree Gardens, and southward along Land O'Lakes Blvd. to the point of beginning. *Terrain:* City streets. *Cycling:* Appropriate. *Awards:* Patch $4.00. *Submit:* Patch order form. *Register:* Not required. *Sites:* Clark House, Gower's Corners, Hale House, Community Center, Sanders Memorial School, Cypress Tree, Law House, Riegler House.

LaNoChe Trails

Location: Winn Dixie Scout Reservation, Paisley, FL. *Theme:* Nature. *Sponsor:* Central Florida Council, BSA, 1951 S. Orange Blossom Tr., Apopka, FL 32703, (407) 889-4403, fax (407) 889-4406.

Length: Bear Paw Trail, Big Stump Trail—2 hours (very muddy), Cateye Trail—after dark, Hydrowatch Trail, Lake Norris Aquatic Trail, Perimeter Trail—8.0 miles (loop), Sulphur Springs Trail, Trapper Creek Nature Trail. *Routes:* Most of the trails begin at the nature center. Check there for maps and more details. *Terrain:* Woods, sometimes wet. *Cycling:* Not recommended. *Awards:* Patch. *Submit:* Certification of completion of any three trails. *Register:* Upon arrival at the camp.

Largo Historical Trail

Location: Largo, FL. *Theme:* Local history and architecture. *Sponsor:* Steve Rajtar, 1614 Bimini Dr., Orlando, FL 32806, (407) 894-7412, http://www.geocities.com/Yosemite/ Rapids/8428, e-mail rajtar@aol.com.

Length: 6.4 miles (loop). *Route:* The trail starts on Bay Dr. near the intersection with Missouri Ave., heads east on Bay Dr. and loops through the northeast section, then heads west on Bay Dr. to 24th St., then loops through the southwest section and returns via 1st Ave. SW to the starting point. *Terrain:* City streets. *Cycling:* Appropriate. *Awards:*

Patch $4.00. *Submit:* Patch order form. *Register:* Not required. *Sites:* Largo Cemetery, Johnson House, Gainey Building, Smith House, Largo Church of Christ, Perkins House, Kilgore Manor, Ulmer House, Christ Presbyterian Church, American Legion Hall.

Leesburg Historical Trail

Location: Leesburg, FL. *Theme:* Local history. *Sponsor:* Steve Rajtar, 1614 Bimini Dr., Orlando, FL 32806, (407) 894-7412, http://www.geocities.com/Yosemite/Rapids/8428, e-mail rajtar@aol.com.

Length: 10.0 miles (loop). *Route:* The trail begins at Herlong Park and generally heads east on US 441, south on Mills St., west on Main St., south on Childs St., west on Dixie Ave., north on 14th St., west on Main St., through Lone Oak Cemetery, past Carver Heights High School, south on 13th St., east and west on Main St. and east and north past the railroad depot to the starting point. *Terrain:* City streets. *Cycling:* Appropriate. *Awards:* Patch $4.00. *Submit:* Patch order form. *Register:* Not required. *Sites:* St. Stephen A.M.E. Church, St. Paul A.M.E. Church, Skeen Elementary School, Lone Oak Cemetery, Hawkins House, First Baptist Church, Historical Museum, Morrison Memorial Methodist Church, Pythian Building.

Longwood Historical Trail

Location: Longwood, FL. *Theme:* Local history and architecture. *Sponsor:* Steve Rajtar, 1614 Bimini Dr., Orlando, FL 32806, (407) 894-7412, http://www.geocities.com/Yosemite/Rapids/8428, e-mail rajtar@aol.com.

Length: 7.8 miles (loop). *Route:* The trail begins in Big Tree Park, heads into and through the downtown historic area, then back to the point of beginning. *Terrain:* City streets. *Cycling:* Appropriate. *Awards:* Patch $4.00. *Submit:* Patch order form. *Register:* Not required. *Sites:* Old Longwood School, Longwood Cemetery, Beesley-Milwee House, Niemeyer House, Bradlee-MacIntyre House, Longwood Hotel, Christ Episcopal Church, Inside-Outside House, Henck-Tinker Building, Henck House.

Loxahatchee Run

Location: Tanah Keeta Scout Reservation, Tequesta, FL. *Theme:* Recreation and local history. *Sponsor:* Gulf Stream Council, BSA, 2935 Australian Ave. N, Palm Beach Gardens, FL 33410-6329, (56194-8585.

Length: 8 miles (straight). *Route:* The trail begins at the park on Indian Town Rd. where it is crossed by the Loxahatchee River and ends downstream where the river reaches Tanah Keeta Scout Reservation. *Terrain:* River, often blocked by logs or cypress knees along the first half. *Cycling:* Impossible; this is a canoe trail. *Awards:* Medal $12.50; Patch $2.50; Jacket Patch $7.50. *Submit:* Group leader's certification of completion of trail and service project, plus essay. *Register:* Not required. *Sites:* Loxahatchee River, Trapper Nelson Interpretive Site, Jonathan Dickinson State Park.

Maitland Historical Trail

Location: Maitland, FL. *Theme:* Local history and architecture. *Sponsor:* Steve Rajtar, 1614 Bimini Dr., Orlando, FL 32806, (407) 894-7412, http://www.geocities.com/Yosemite/Rapids/8428, e-mail rajtar@aol.com.

Length: 9.1 miles (loop). *Route:* The trail begins in Fort Maitland Park, heads south through a 1920s residential area, then north through the business district, then back to the beginning. *Terrain:* City streets. *Cycling:* Appropriate. *Awards:* Patch $4.00. *Submit:* Patch order form. *Register:* Not required. *Sites:* Lawrence-Chubb House, Thurston House, Church of the Good Shepherd, Chadburne Hall, Madlyn Baldwin Center for Birds of Prey, Maitland Art Center, Telephone Museum, Maitland Historical Museum, Barnett Bank.

McIntosh Historical Trail

Location: McIntosh, FL. *Theme:* Local history and architecture. *Sponsor:* Steve Rajtar, 1614 Bimini Dr., Orlando, FL 32806, (407) 894-7412, http://www.geocities.com/Yosemite/Rapids/8428, e-mail rajtar@aol.com.

Length: 5.7 miles (loop). *Route:* The trail begins at the park at the intersection of Ave. F and 6th St., winds through the entire historic district, and ends at its starting point. *Terrain:* City streets. *Cycling:* Appropriate. *Awards:* Patch $4.00. *Submit:* Patch order form. *Register:* Not required. *Sites:* Gist-Norsworthy House, Estridge

House, McIntosh Presbyterian Church, First Baptist Church, McIntosh Christian Church, Huff Packing House, Old Telephone Exchange, Tunipseed House, Allen House, Gist-Tully House.

Melbourne Beach Historical Trail

Location: Melbourne Beach and Indialantic, FL. *Theme:* Local history. *Sponsor:* Steve Rajtar, 1614 Bimini Dr., Orlando, FL 32806, (407) 894-7412, http://www.geocities.com/Yosemite/Rapids/8428, e-mail rajtar@aol.com.

Length: 9.0 miles (loop). *Route:* The trail starts at Spessard Holland Park, heads south to the House of Refuge site, then north to Ocean Ave., west to River Rd., and generally north, east and south to the point of beginning. *Terrain:* City streets. *Cycling:* Appropriate. *Awards:* Patch $4.00. *Submit:* Patch order form. *Register:* Not required. *Sites:* Myrtle Cottage, Ballard Pine Tree, Ryckman House, Melbourne Beach Community Chapel, Villa Marine Hotel, Beaujean House, Woman's House.

Melbourne Village Historical Trail

Location: Melbourne Village and Melbourne, FL. *Theme:* Local history. *Sponsor:* Steve Rajtar, 1614 Bimini Dr., Orlando, FL 32806, (407) 894-7412, http://www.geocities.com/Yosemite/Rapids/8428, e-mail rajtar@aol.com.

Length: 10.9 miles (loop). *Route:* The trail begins and ends on New Haven Ave., west of Melbourne. It proceeds west on New Haven to loop through Melbourne Village, then goes east on New Haven and south through the campus of Florida Institute of Technology, then returns on New Haven west past the Florida Air Academy to the starting point. *Terrain:* City streets. *Cycling:* Appropriate. *Awards:* Patch $4.00. *Submit:* Patch order form. *Register:* Not required. *Sites:* Deer Head Hammock, Florida Institute of Technology, Little Red Schoolhouse, Florida Air Academy, Village Hall, Erna Nixon Hammock, Wood House.

Melrose Historical Trail

Location: Melrose, FL. *Theme:* Local history and architecture. *Sponsor:* Steve Rajtar, 1614 Bimini Dr., Orlando, FL 32806, (407) 894-7412, http://www.geocities.com/Yosemite/Rapids/8428, e-mail rajtar@aol.com.

Length: 4.5 miles (loop). *Route:* The trail begins near the intersection of Bellamy Ave. and Hampton St., winds throughout the town, and returns to the point of beginning. *Terrain:* City streets. *Cycling:* Appropriate. *Awards:* Patch $4.00. *Submit:* Patch order form. *Register:* Not required. *Sites:* Nondenominational Church, Mossman House, Tillman House, Rosewood Cottage, Chiappini Service Station, Eliam-Melrose Cemetery, Davis Railroad Depot, Mosley House, Vogelbach Drugstore, Melrose Woman's Club.

Micanopy Historical Trail

Location: Micanopy and Evinston, FL. *Theme:* Local history. *Sponsor:* Steve Rajtar, 1614 Bimini Dr., Orlando, FL 32806, (407) 894-7412, http://www.geocities.com/Yosemite/Rapids/8428, e-mail rajtar@aol.com.

Length: 10.3 miles (loop). *Route:* The trail begins along Cholokka Blvd., heads east on Tuscawilla Rd., south on US 441 and east on county roads to Evinston, then returns to wind through Micanopy. *Terrain:* City streets and dirt roads. *Cycling:* Appropriate. *Awards:* Patch $4.00. *Submit:* Patch order form. *Register:* Not required. *Sites:* Mountain Garage, Little Story House, Micanopy Banking Company, Shettleworth House, Barron House, Evins House, Stewart-Merry House, Barr-Smyth House, Micanopy Cemetery, Little Red Schoolhouse.

Mike Machek Trail

Location: Tanah Keeta Scout Reservation, Tequesta, FL. *Theme:* Nature. *Sponsor:* Tanah Keeta Scout Reservation, Boy Scout Rd., Tequesta, FL 33469, (561) 746-8749 or (561) 844-0279.

Length: 5.2 miles (loop). *Route:* The trail begins and ends at the main parking lot, and loops through most of the reservation. *Terrain:* Sand, swamp and woods. *Cycling:* Not allowed. *Awards:* Patch $2.00. *Submit:* No requirement. *Register:* Upon arrival at reservation.

Minneola Historical Trail

Location: Minneola and Mohawk, FL. *Theme:* Local history. *Sponsor:* Steve Rajtar, 1614 Bimini Dr., Orlando, FL 32806, (407) 894-7412, http://www.geocities.com/Yosemite/Rapids/8428, e-mail rajtar@aol.com.

Length: 7.0 miles (loop). *Route:* The trail begins at Clermont Waterfront Park, heads south and east to Mohawk, then returns to the main portion of Minneola to return to the beginning. *Terrain:* City streets. *Cycling:* Appropriate. *Awards:* Patch $4.00. *Submit:* Patch order form. *Register:* Note required. *Sites:* Skyline Motel, Citrus Tower, Minneola Cemetery, First Baptist Church of Minneola, Minneola Elementary School, Lakes & Hills, Christian and Missionary Alliance Church, Heddon House.

Montverde Historical Trail

Location: Montverde and Ferndale, FL. *Theme:* Local history. *Sponsor:* Steve Rajtar, 1614 Bimini Dr., Orlando, FL 32806, (407) 894-7412, http://www.geocities.com/Yosemite/Rapids/8428, e-mail rajtar@aol.com.

Length: 7.1 miles (loop). *Route:* The trail begins in Kirk Park, heads south on 6th St., west on Porter Ave., loops through the campus of Montverde Academy, heads northwest through Ferndale, then returns southeast on CR 455 back to Kirk Park. *Terrain:* City streets and paved country roads. *Cycling:* Appropriate. *Awards:* Patch $4.00. *Submit:* Patch order form. *Register:* Not required. *Sites:* Conrad Lehmann Building, Rast Library, D.A.R. Hall, McCammack Hall, Kreke Science Building, Donnelly Building, Schoolhouse, Montverde United Methodist Church, Montverde Cemetery.

Mount Dora Historical Trail

Location: Mount Dora, FL. *Theme:* Local history. *Sponsor:* Steve Rajtar, 1614 Bimini Dr., Orlando, FL 32806, (407) 894-7412, http://www.geocities.com/Yosemite/Rapids/8428, e-mail rajtar@aol.com.

Length: 9.7 miles (loop). *Route:* The trail begins near the Lakeside Inn and heads south to Lake Dora, then goes north and west toward Tavares before heading east, south, and winding through downtown Mount Dora. *Terrain:* City streets. *Cycling:* Appropriate. *Awards:* Patch $4.00. *Submit:* Patch order form. *Register:* Not required. *Sites:* First Presbyterian Church, McDonald Stone House, Pine Forest Cemetery, Unity House, Mount Olive A.M.E. Church, Ice House Theater, Educational Hall, First Methodist Church, St. Edwards Episcopal Church, Royellou Museum.

New Port Richey Historical Trail

Location: New Port Richey, Port Richey and Elfers, FL. *Theme:* Local history. *Sponsor:* Steve Rajtar, 1614 Bimini Dr., Orlando, FL 32806, (407) 894-7412, http://www.geocities.com/Yosemite/Rapids/8428, e-mail rajtar@aol.com.

Length: 8.7 miles (loop). *Route:* The trail begins at Sims Park, heads west and then north parallel to the Pithlachascotee River, crosses it, and heads downtown to finish back at Sims Park. *Terrain:* City streets. *Cycling:* Appropriate. *Awards:* Patch $4.00. *Submit:* Patch order form. *Register:* Not required. *Sites:* Baker House, Edenfield Store, Elfers State Bank Building, West Elfers Cemetery, Oelsner Mound, VFW Hall, Pasco Hardware Building, Butler House, Kentucky Inn, Pasco Building.

New Smyrna Beach Historical Trail

Location: New Smyrna Beach, FL. *Theme:* Local history. *Sponsor:* Steve Rajtar, 1614 Bimini Dr., Orlando, FL 32806, (407) 894-7412, http://www.geocities.com/Yosemite/Rapids/8428, e-mail rajtar@aol.com.

Length: 9.6 miles (loop). *Route:* The trail includes downtown New Smyrna Beach, plus a portion of the Flagler Ave. historic area. *Terrain:* City streets. *Cycling:* Appropriate. *Awards:* Patch $4.00. *Submit:* Patch order form. *Register:* Not required. *Sites:* Christ Episcopal Church, Stone Wharf, Turnbull House Ruins, Garbordy's Canal, Riverview Hotel, Sugar Mill Ruins, St. Rita's Mission, Sacred Heart Church, Chisholm School, Swoope Building.

Newberry Historical Trail

Location: Newberry, FL. *Theme:* Local history. *Sponsor:* Steve Rajtar, 1614 Bimini Dr., Orlando, FL 32806, (407) 894-7412, http://www.geocities.com/Yosemite/Rapids/8428, e-mail rajtar@aol.com.

Length: 3.1 miles (loop). *Route:* The trail begins and ends in the parking lot just north of the intersection of SW 1st Ave. and 4th St., and winds through the entire downtown area. *Terrain:* City streets. *Cycling:* Appropriate. *Awards:* Patch $4.00. *Submit:* Patch order form. *Register:* Not required. *Sites:* Commercial Hotel, Bank of Newberry, Kincaid Building, Barry Building, White Building, Pickett Building, Holt House, Knight House, Cheves Bros., Norfleet House.

Northern Levy County Historical Trail

Location: Chiefland, Williston and Bronson, FL. *Theme:* Local history. *Sponsor:* Steve Rajtar, 1614 Bimini Dr., Orlando, FL 32806, (407) 894-7412, http://www.geocities. com/Yosemite/Rapids/8428, e-mail rajtar@ aol.com.

Length: 10.0 miles (three loops). *Route:* The trail begins with a loop walking route winding through downtown Chiefland, then after driving to Williston continues with a loop walking route there, and after driving to Bronson concludes with a loop walking route there. *Terrain:* City streets. *Cycling:* Appropriate. *Awards:* Patch $4.00. *Submit:* Patch order form. *Register:* Not required. *Sites:* Hardeetown Hotel, Rodgers Park, Masonic Lodge, Bronson Baptist Church, Levy County Courthouse, United Methodist Church, Hester House, Rock Hill Baptist Church, Chiefland Public Library, Chiefland Baptist Church.

Oak Hill Historical Trail

Location: Oak Hill, FL. *Theme:* Local history. *Sponsor:* Steve Rajtar, 1614 Bimini Dr., Orlando, FL 32806, (407) 894-7412, http://www.geocities.com/Yosemite/Rapids/8 428, e-mail rajtar@aol.com.

Length: 6.4 miles (loop). *Route:* The trail begins behind the library, heading east and north to the river, then south past City Hall, north to the cemetery, and back to the library in the middle of the town. *Terrain:* City streets. *Cycling:* Appropriate. *Awards:* Patch $4.00. *Submit:* Patch order form. *Register:* Not required. *Sites:* St. Martha's Baptist Church, Oak Hill Cemetery, Packing House, VIA Headquarters, McCullough Boarding House, Howse House, Threlkeld House, Bennett House.

Oakland Historical Trail

Location: Oakland, FL. *Theme:* Local history and architecture. *Sponsor:* Steve Rajtar, 1614 Bimini Dr., Orlando, FL 32806, (407) 894-7412, http://www.geocities.com/ Yosemite/Rapids/8428, e-mail rajtar@aol. com.

Length: 11.1 miles (loop). *Route:* The trail begins at the County Line Station of the West Orange Trail, passes through Killarney and Tildenville, and passes through downtown Oakland. *Terrain:* City streets. *Cycling:* Appropriate. *Awards:* Patch $4.00. *Submit:* Patch order form. *Register:* Not required. *Sites:* First Presbyterian Church, Tildenville, West Orange Baptist Church, Mount Zion A.M.E. Church, Charles Tilden House, Sadler House, Michael Hardware Store, Speer Park, Oakland Cemetery, Brock House.

Ocala Historical Trail

Location: Ocala, FL. *Theme:* Local history and architecture. *Sponsor:* Steve Rajtar, 1614 Bimini Dr., Orlando, FL 32806, (407) 894-7412, http://www.geocities.com/Yosemite/ Rapids/8428, e-mail rajtar@aol.com.

Length: 9.0 miles (loop). *Route:* The trail begins with a loop through a portion of the historic area in the southeast section, then south and west to former Marti City, then heads north and loops through the northwest and northeast sections before returning to the southeast historic district and the starting point. *Terrain:* City streets. *Cycling:* Appropriate. *Awards:* Patch $4.00. *Submit:* Patch order form. *Register:* Not required. *Sites:* Mount Zion A.M.E. Church, Union Train Station, Coca-Cola Bottling Plant, United Hebrew Synogogue, Ritz Apartments, Grace Episcopal Church, Marion Block Building, Francis Marion Hotel, Dunn House, Miller House.

Ocoee Historical Trail

Location: Ocoee, FL. *Theme:* Local history. *Sponsor:* Steve Rajtar, 1614 Bimini Dr., Orlando, FL 32806, (407) 894-7412, http://www.geocities.com/Yosemite/Rapids/8 428, e-mail rajtar@aol.com.

Length: 7.4 miles (loop). *Route:* The trail begins and ends at Tiger Minor Park, and covers downtown Ocoee. *Terrain:* City streets. *Cycling:* Appropriate. *Awards:* Patch $4.00. *Submit:* Patch order form. *Register:* Not required. *Sites:* Ocoee Christian Church, Scott Medical Office, Withers-Maguire House, West House, Railroad Depot, Blakely House, Bank of Ocoee, Ocoee Cemetery.

Old Cutler Trail

Location: Miami, FL. *Theme:* Route of pioneer trail created in 1882. *Sponsor:* South Florida Council, BSA, 15255 NW 82nd Ave., Miami Lakes, FL 33016, (305) 364-0020.

Length: 13 miles (straight). *Route:* The trail begins at the Torch of Friendship on Biscayne Blvd., heads south, and ends at

Chapman Field Park. *Terrain:* Sidewalks and bicycle paths. *Cycling:* Possible, but does not qualify for awards. *Awards:* Medal $3.00; Patch $3.00 (design changes annually). *Submit:* No requirement. *Register:* Pre-register for a price discount; this is an annual hike, held in late November or early December. *Sites:* Torch of Friendship, DuPont Plaza Hotel, Brickell Park, Vizcaya, Fitzpatrick Plantation, Villa Serena, Wainwright Park, Coral Rock Bluffs, Museum of Science and Space Transit Planetarium, Dinner Key, Peacock Inn Site, Fairchild Tropical Garden, The Barnacle, Plymouth Church, Larkin Home.

Oldsmar Historical Trail

Location: Oldsmar, FL. *Theme:* Local history. *Sponsor:* Steve Rajtar, 1614 Bimini Dr., Orlando, FL 32806, (407) 894-7412, http://www.geocities.com/Yosemite/Rapids/8 428, e-mail rajtar@aol.com.

Length: 7.3 miles (loop). *Route:* The trail begins at R.E. Olds Park, follows the shore of Tampa Bay eastward, heads north to Tampa Bay Downs racetrack, then returns to wind through downtown Oldsmar and return to the finish. *Terrain:* City streets. *Cycling:* Appropriate. *Awards:* Patch $4.00. *Submit:* Patch order form. *Register:* Not required. *Sites:* Wayside Inn Site, Library, Firehouse, Oldsmar Woman's Club, London House, Thompson House, Methodist Parsonage, Mitchell House, Oldsmar Elementary School, United Methodist Church.

Orange City Historical Trail

Location: Orange City, FL. *Theme:* Local history. *Sponsor:* Steve Rajtar, 1614 Bimini Dr., Orlando, FL 32806, (407) 894-7412, http://www.geocities.com/Yosemite/Rapids/8 428, e-mail rajtar@aol.com.

Length: 15.6 miles (loop). *Route:* The trail begins in Blue Spring State Park, heads east to wind through Orange City, then returns to the park for a visit to the spring and the Thursby mansion. *Terrain:* City streets, plus a boardwalk in the park. *Cycling:* Appropriate. *Awards:* Patch $4.00. *Submit:* Patch order form. *Register:* Not required. *Sites:* Blue Spring, French House, Albertus Cottage, Thursby House, First Congregational Church, A.M.E. Church, Dickinson Memorial Library, Orange City United Methodist Church, DeYarman Hotel.

Orlando Historic Trail

Location: Orlando, FL. *Theme:* Local history. *Sponsor:* Corb Sarchet, 132 Waverly Pl., Orlando, FL 32806, (407) 648-9636.

Length: 5.5 miles (loop). *Route:* The trail begins at the Orlando Centroplex, winds through the city, and returns to the start. *Terrain:* City streets. *Cycling:* Appropriate. *Awards:* Patch $2.75; Certificate n/c. *Submit:* Completed 46-item questionnaire. *Register:* Not required. *Sites:* Davis Armory, Orlando Arena, Leedy Park, Central Florida Sports Hall of Fame, Cracker Mural, Empire Hotel, Church Street Historic District, Dr. Phillips Home, Knox-Bacon Building, Angebilt Hotel, Guernsey Building, Orange County Courthouse, Lake Eola Park, Oriental Garden

Orlando Lake Cherokee Historical Trail

Location: Orlando, FL. *Theme:* Local history and architecture. *Sponsor:* Steve Rajtar, 1614 Bimini Dr., Orlando, FL 32806, (407) 894-7412, http://www.geocities.com/ Yosemite/Rapids/8428, e-mail rajtar@aol. com.

Length: 6.0 miles (loop). *Route:* The trail begins at the southeast corner of Lake Cherokee, heads west and north along Honeymoon Row, north to Anderson St., loops on Lake Ave., continues west and heads north into downtown Orlando as far north as Central Blvd., then heads south to loop through Greenwood Cemetery and return to the starting point. *Terrain:* City streets. *Cycling:* Appropriate. *Awards:* Patch $4.00. *Submit:* Patch order form. *Register:* Not required. *Sites:* Downtown Baptist Church, O'Neal House, Cherokee Junior High School, Gunby House, Engleman House, Beardall House, St. Regis Apartments, Cohoon Houses, Ohev Shalom Synagogue, Greenwood Cemetery.

Orlando Lake Eola Historic Trail

Location: Orlando, FL. *Theme:* Local history. *Sponsor:* Steve Rajtar, 1614 Bimini Dr., Orlando, FL 32806, (407) 894-7412, http://www.geocities.com/Yosemite/Rapids/8 428, e-mail rajtar@aol.com.

Length: 6.7 miles (loop). *Route:* The trail begins just north of Colonial Dr. on Garland Ave., then heads east and south and winds through downtown Orlando as far south as Church St., circling Lake Eola, before returning to the starting point. *Terrain:* City streets. *Cycling:* Appropriate. *Awards:* Patch $4.00. *Submit:* Patch order form. *Register:* Not required. *Sites:* St. James Catholic Church, Dolive Building, St. George Orthodox Church, Beacham Theatre, Church Street Station, Angebilt Hotel, The Fidelity Building, Rosalind Club, Murphy & Autrey Arcade, Empire Hotel.

Orlando Lake Lucerne Historic Trail

Location: Orlando, FL. *Theme:* Local history and architecture. *Sponsor:* Steve Rajtar, 1614 Bimini Dr., Orlando, FL 32806, (407) 894-7412, http://www.geocities.com/Yosemite/Rapids/8428, e-mail rajtar@aol.com. *Length:* 4.6 miles (loop). *Route:* The trail begins and ends on Gore St. west of Orange Ave., and includes a loop to the Amtrak station and Orlando Regional Medical Center, a loop around Lake Lucerne, and a portion of downtown Orlando from Pine St. southward. *Terrain:* City streets. *Cycling:* Appropriate. *Awards:* Patch $4.00. *Submit:* Patch order form. *Register:* Not required. *Sites:* Kuhl-Delaney Building, Bridges House, Norment House, Rogers Building, Hughey Peninsula, Wellborn Apartments, First Presbyterian Church, Fire Station No. 1.

Orlando West Side Historic Trail

Location: Orlando, FL. *Theme:* Local history. *Sponsor:* Steve Rajtar, 1614 Bimini Dr., Orlando, FL 32806, (407) 894-7412, http://www.geocities.com/Yosemite/Rapids/8428, e-mail rajtar@aol.com. *Length:* 4.4 miles (loop). *Route:* The trail begins on Colonial Dr. just north of the Orlando Arena, heads south and west through the Orlando Centroplex, south on Parramore Ave., east on South St., north on Hughey Ave., and west on Colonial Dr. to the start, and includes many of the smaller streets within that area. *Terrain:* City streets. *Cycling:* Appropriate. *Awards:* Patch $4.00. *Submit:* Patch order form. *Register:* Not required. *Sites:* Shiloh Baptist Church, Mt. Zion Missionary Baptist Church, Jones House, Callahan Neighborhood Center, Federal Courthouse, Hill-Tillinghast House, Davis Armory, Ebenezer United Methodist Church, Crooms House.

Ormond Beach Historical Trail

Location: Ormond Beach, FL. *Theme:* Local history. *Sponsor:* Steve Rajtar, 1614 Bimini Dr., Orlando, FL 32806, (407) 894-7412, http://www.geocities.com/Yosemite/Rapids/8428, e-mail rajtar@aol.com. *Length:* 7.4 miles (loop). *Route:* The trail begins at Granada Riverfront Park, heads south on Beach St., loops west and north on the mainland, then crosses the Halifax River for a loop on the barrier island, and then returns west across the bridge to the starting point. *Terrain:* City streets. *Cycling:* Appropriate. *Awards:* Patch $4.00. *Submit:* Patch order form. *Register:* Not required. *Sites:* Ormond Hotel Site, The Casements, Cobb Cottage, Marsh House, Dix House, McNary House, Ormond Beach Woman's Club, Lippincott Mansion, Ames House, Riverway.

Osceola-Olustee Historic Trail

Location: Olustee, FL. *Theme:* Civil War battle—February 20, 1864. *Sponsor:* Florida Historic Trails Association, c/o Milledge Murphey, Ph.D., 1815 N.W. 7th Pl., Gainesville, FL 32603, (352) 373-9234. *Length:* 22.4 miles (straight). *Route:* The trail begins 6.9 miles north of the I-10 overpass on US 441, and ends at the battlefield near Olustee. *Terrain:* Woods and roads. *Cycling:* Not permitted. *Awards:* Medal $6.50; Patch $4.00; Repeat Pin $2.50 (The miles for this trail and others sponsored by the same organization may be aggregated to qualify for the Florida Historic Trails Association 100 Mile Hiking Award—Medal $6.50; Patch $4.00; Repeat Pin $2.50.). *Submit:* Group leader's certification of completion and completed 19-item questionnaire. *Register:* In advance. *Sites:* Battlefield Monuments, UDC Monument, Interpretive Center, Fire Tower.

Oviedo Historical Trail

Location: Oviedo, FL. *Theme:* Local history and architecture. *Sponsor:* Steve Rajtar, 1614 Bimini Dr., Orlando, FL 32806, (407) 894-7412, http://www.geocities.com/Yosemite/Rapids/8428, e-mail rajtar@aol.com. *Length:* 12.1 miles (loop). *Route:* The trail begins at the Lawton Grove Park, passes through the Lake Charm community, downtown Oviedo, and Slavia, before returning to the start. *Terrain:* City streets and dirt roads. *Cycling:* Appropriate. *Awards:*

Patch $4.00. *Submit:* Patch order form. *Register:* Not required. *Sites:* First United Methodist Church of Oviedo, Sweetwater Park, Chamber of Commerce, Lake Charm Memorial Chapel, Grant Chapel A.M.E. Church, Fountainhead Missionary Baptist Church, Memorial Building.

Paisley Historical Trail

Location: Paisley, FL. *Theme:* Local history. *Sponsor:* Steve Rajtar, 1614 Bimini Dr., Orlando, FL 32806, (407) 894-7412, http://www.geocities.com/Yosemite/Rapids/8 428, e-mail rajtar@aol.com.

Length: 13.5 miles (loop). *Route:* The trail begins at the Clearwater Lake Recreation Area in the Ocala National Forest, heads southwest on CR 42, and then north on a forest road. The trail then heads east on a soft sand forest road, or the hiker can retrace steps on paved roads to the northeast, then heads through the middle of Paisley on CR 42 back to the beginning. *Terrain:* Paved country roads and a hard dirt forest road, plus either a soft sand forest road or a retracing on the hard dirt and paved road. *Cycling:* Appropriate, but difficult on the soft sand portion. *Awards:* Patch $4.00. *Submit:* Patch order form. *Register:* Not required. *Sites:* Ponceannah Cemetery, Ponceannah Site, Bayview Site, Lightwood Camp Site, Lookout Fire Tower, Disney Homestead Site, Paisley Methodist Church, Paisley Baptist Church, Hethcox House, Johnson's Corner.

Palatka Historical Trail

Location: Palatka and Peniel, FL. *Theme:* Local history. *Sponsor:* Steve Rajtar, 1614 Bimini Dr., Orlando, FL 32806, (407) 894-7412, http://www.geocities.com/Yosemite/Rapids/8428, e-mail rajtar@aol.com.

Length: 10.5 miles (loop). *Route:* The trail begins on Madison St. near the river, heads west to 19th St., south to Twigg St., then winds through the historic and downtown areas to return to the start. *Terrain:* City streets. *Cycling:* Appropriate. *Awards:* Patch $4.00. *Submit:* Patch order form. *Register:* Not required. *Sites:* St. Monica's Catholic Church, St. Joseph's Academy, St. Mark's Episcopal Church, Graham Hotel Site, Bronson-Mulholland House, Peniel Baptist Church, Ravine Gardens, Finley House, Central Academy High School, Woman's Club.

Palm Bay Historical Trail

Location: Palm Bay and Malabar, FL. *Theme:* Local history. *Sponsor:* Steve Rajtar, 1614 Bimini Dr., Orlando, FL 32806, (407) 894-7412, http://www.geocities.com/ Yosemite/Rapids/8428, e-mail rajtar@aol. com.

Length: 9.4 miles (loop). *Route:* The trail begins at Huggins Park in Malabar, heads east and north on Dixie Highway across Turkey Creek to loop through Palm Bay and head south to the starting point. *Terrain:* City streets. *Cycling:* Appropriate. *Awards:* Patch $4.00. *Submit:* Patch order form. *Register:* Not required. *Sites:* St. Joseph's Catholic Church, Carter House, Goode House, Pospisil House, Conkling House, Weber House, Knecht House Site, Henley House, Malabar Millworks, Lockmar Site.

Pasadena Historical Trail

Location: St. Petersburg, FL. *Theme:* Local history. *Sponsor:* Steve Rajtar, 1614 Bimini Dr., Orlando, FL 32806, (407) 894-7412, http://www.geocities.com/Yosemite/Rapids/8 428, e-mail rajtar@aol.com.

Length: 10.4 miles (loop). *Route:* The trail starts at Abercrombie Park, heads north and west through the Bayshore Homes subdivision, then south on Park St. and east on Central Ave. to a loop through Pasadena, and then returns to the starting point via Central Ave. and Park St. *Terrain:* City streets. *Cycling:* Appropriate. *Awards:* Patch $4.00. *Submit:* Patch order form. *Register:* Not required. *Sites:* Bayshore Homes Midden Mound, Narvaez Mounds, Bayshore Homes Temple Mound, Pasadena Community Church, White Cross Hospital, Taylor Office, Admiral Farragut Academy, Pasadena Estates, Casa Coe da Sol, Casa de Muchas Flores.

Pass-A-Grille Historical Trail

Location: St. Petersburg Beach, FL. *Theme:* Local history. *Sponsor:* Steve Rajtar, 1614 Bimini Dr., Orlando, FL 32806, (407) 894-7412, http://www.geocities.com/Yosemite/Rapids/8428, e-mail rajtar@aol.com.

Length: 6.5 miles (loop). *Route:* The trail begins on 87th Ave. and heads south on Gulf Blvd., which becomes Pass-a-Grille Way. It continues south to 1st Ave., and then turns north on Gulf Ave. to the point of beginning, with small jogs onto side streets. *Terrain:* City streets. *Cycling:* Appropriate. *Awards:*

Patch $4.00. *Submit:* Patch order form.
Register: Not required. *Sites:* St. John's
Catholic Church, Don Ce-Sar Hotel,
McPherson House, Thayer House, Marine
Apartments, Phillips Cabin, Watson House,
Sea Call, Castle Hotel, Duffy Building.

Pensacola Historical Trail

Location: Pensacola, FL. *Theme:* Local
history. *Sponsor:* John Steiger, 8100
Monticello Dr., Pensacola, FL 32514, (850)
477-0122; jsteiger@pcola.gulf.net.
Length: 4 miles (loop). *Route:* The trail
begins at the intersection of Gregory and
Alcaniz, heads north to Wright, west to
Palafox, north to Brainerd, west to Spring,
and back to the start via Spring, Desoto,
Baylen, Wright, Palafox, Zarragossa, Adams,
Government and Alcaniz. *Terrain:* City
streets. *Cycling:* Appropriate. *Awards:* Medal
$4.00; Patch $2.00. *Submit:* Completed 10-
item questionnaire. *Register:* Not required.
Sites: Fort George, North Hill Preservation
District, Perry House, Lee Square, Miranda
Square, Christ Church, St. Michael's Church,
Plaza Ferdinand VII, Hispanic Building,
Transportation Building, Lavalle House, Julee
Cottage, Tivoli Complex, Old Christ Church,
Dorothy Walton House, St. Michael's
Cemetery, Dorr House.

Pensacola Naval Air Station Historical Trail

Location: Pensacola Naval Air Station,
Pensacola, FL. *Theme:* Local and military
history. *Sponsor:* John Steiger, 8100
Monticello Dr., Pensacola, FL 32514, (850)
477-0122; jsteiger@pcola.gulf.net.
Length: 10 miles (near loop). *Route:* The
trail begins at Sherman Field near the
airstrip, heads east to the shore, then west to
the Naval Aviation Museum (less than a mile
from the start). *Terrain:* Roads. *Cycling:*
Appropriate. *Awards:* Medal $4.00; Patch
$2.00. *Submit:* Completed 15-item
questionnaire. *Register:* Not required. *Sites:*
Sherman Field Control Tower, U.S. Coast
Guard Pensacola Light Station, Fort
Barrancas, Barrancas National Cemetery,
Seaplane Ramps, U.S.S. Lexington, Chevalier
Field, U.S. Naval Hospital, Naval Aviation
Memorial Chapel, Naval Aviation Museum,
Advanced Redoubt.

Pierson Historical Trail

Location: Pierson and Bishopville, FL.
Theme: Local history. *Sponsor:* Steve Rajtar,
1614 Bimini Dr., Orlando, FL 32806, (407)
894-7412, http://www.geocities.com/
Yosemite/Rapids/8428, e-mail rajtar@aol.
com.
Length: 9.1 miles (loop). *Route:* The trail
begins at the intersection of US 17 and
Second Ave., heads south to Bishopville, then
north to Washington Ave., and south to the
point of beginning. *Terrain:* Paved country
roads. *Cycling:* Appropriate. *Awards:* Patch
$4.00. *Submit:* Patch order form. *Register:*
Not required. *Sites:* J. Peterson House, Mount
Zion Primitive Baptist Church, Ellis National
Bank, Methodist Church, Alhambra Grove,
Moulton-Woods Ditch, Gunter Store,
Ebenezer Lutheran Church, Killarney Farms.

Pine Castle Historical Trail

Location: Pine Castle, FL. *Theme:* Local
history. *Sponsor:* Steve Rajtar, 1614 Bimini
Dr., Orlando, FL 32806, (407) 894-7412,
http://www.geocities.com/Yosemite/Rapids/8
428, e-mail rajtar@aol.com.
Length: 13.3 miles (loop). *Route:* The trail
begins in Pine Castle, heads north to the Fort
Gatlin site, then south through Pine Castle,
Edgewood, Belle Isle, and Taft, and back to
the beginning. *Terrain:* City streets. *Cycling:*
Appropriate. *Awards:* Patch $4.00. *Submit:*
Patch order form. *Register:* Not required.
Sites: Pine Castle Elementary School, Lake
Jennie Jewel, Lake Gem Mary, First Baptist
Church, Crittenden Boat Ramp, Pine Castle
United Methodist Church, McCall's Drug
Store, Woman's Club, Girl Scout Little
House, Folk Art Center.

Pinellas Point Historical Trail

Location: St. Petersburg, FL. *Theme:* Local
history. *Sponsor:* Steve Rajtar, 1614 Bimini
Dr., Orlando, FL 32806, (407) 894-7412,
http://www.geocities.com/Yosemite/Rapids/8
428, e-mail rajtar@aol.com.
Length: 9.5 miles (loop). *Route:* The trail
begins at Pinellas Point Park, heads north
and west to Maximo Point, loops through
Maximo Park, heads north and west to loop
through Eckerd College, then heads east and
south to the starting point. *Terrain:* City
streets. *Cycling:* Appropriate. *Awards:* Patch
$4.00. *Submit:* Patch order form. *Register:*
Not required. *Sites:* Pinellas Point Temple

Mound, Maximo Point, Canton Street Midden Mound, Maximo Park, White Monument, Eckerd College, Gibbs High School, St. Bartholomew's Episcopal Church, Glen Oak Cemetery.

Plant City Historical Trail

Location: Plant City, FL. *Theme:* Local history. *Sponsor:* Steve Rajtar, 1614 Bimini Dr., Orlando, FL 32806, (407) 894-7412, http://www.geocities.com/Yosemite/Rapids/8 428, e-mail rajtar@aol.com.

Length: 7.8 miles (loop). *Route:* The trail begins on US 92 west of town, heads east and north to the former settlement of Shiloh, then south to wind through Plant City and west to return to the starting point. *Terrain:* City streets. *Cycling:* Appropriate. *Awards:* Patch $4.00. *Submit:* Patch order form. *Register:* Not required. *Sites:* Shiloh Cemetery, Allen House, Holy Name Catholic Church, First Baptist Church, Plant City High School, Lee Building, Bank of Plant City, Hillsboro State Bank, Herring Store, Union Depot.

Plymouth Historical Trail

Location: Plymouth, FL. *Theme:* Local history and architecture. *Sponsor:* Steve Rajtar, 1614 Bimini Dr., Orlando, FL 32806, (407) 894-7412, http://www.geocities.com/ Yosemite/Rapids/8428, e-mail rajtar@aol. com.

Length: 9.6 miles (loop). *Route:* The trail begins and ends at Errol Plaza on US 441, and passes through Errol Estate, McDonald and downtown Plymouth. *Terrain:* Paved and unpaved roads. *Cycling:* Appropriate. *Awards:* Patch $4.00. *Submit:* Patch order form. *Register:* Not required. *Sites:* Shiloh Missionary Baptist Church, McDonald, Merrimack, Plymouth Citrus Fruit Growers Association, Plymouth Baptist Church, Errol Estate.

Port Orange–Ponce Inlet Historical Trail

Location: Port Orange, FL. *Theme:* Local history. *Sponsor:* Steve Rajtar, 1614 Bimini Dr., Orlando, FL 32806, (407) 894-7412, http://www.geocities.com/Yosemite/Rapids/8 428, e-mail rajtar@aol.com.

Length: 11.0 miles (double loop). *Route:* The trail begins in downtown Port Orange and heads north and west to the Sugar Mill Gardens, and back to the start. After driving across the river, it loops through the city of Ponce Inlet. *Terrain:* City streets. *Cycling:* Appropriate. *Awards:* Patch $4.00. *Submit:* Patch order form. *Register:* Not required. *Sites:* Ponce Park Site, Ponce de Leon Inlet Lighthouse, Pacetti Homestead Site, Dunlawton Plantation Ruins, Grace Episcopal Church, Ponce Hotel Site, Bob's Bluff, Gamble House, Green Mound.

Port Tampa Historical Trail

Location: Tampa, FL. *Theme:* Local history. *Sponsor:* Steve Rajtar, 1614 Bimini Dr., Orlando, FL 32806, (407) 894-7412, http://www.geocities.com/Yosemite/Rapids/8 428, e-mail rajtar@aol.com.

Length: 10.0 miles (loop). *Route:* The trail begins at Picnic Island Park, heads northeast into Port Tampa, winds through town, and returns southwest to Picnic Island. *Terrain:* City streets. *Cycling:* Appropriate. *Awards:* Patch $4.00. *Submit:* Patch order form. *Register:* Not required. *Sites:* Railroad Spur Line, First Baptist Church, Mt. Zion A.M.E. Church, Silveus House, Port Tampa Park, Masonic Temple, Johnson-Wolff House, Hanks' Corner, West Shore High School, Fitzgerald Building.

Reddick Historical Trail

Location: Reddick, FL. *Theme:* Local history and architecture. *Sponsor:* Steve Rajtar, 1614 Bimini Dr., Orlando, FL 32806, (407) 894-7412, http://www.geocities.com/Yosemite /Rapids/8428, e-mail rajtar@aol. com.

Length: 4.2 miles (loop). *Route:* The trail begins at the Community House, heads south and then north on Gainesville Rd., winds through the former downtown area, and returns to the point of beginning. *Terrain:* City streets. *Cycling:* Appropriate. *Awards:* Patch $4.00. *Submit:* Patch order form. *Register:* Not required. *Sites:* Reddick State Bank, Jones House, Anderson House, Reddick House, Monticello Cemetery, Fridy House, Light House, Reddick School, Reddick Presbyterian Church, Drug Store.

Rochelle Historical Trail

Location: Reddick, FL. *Theme:* Local history. *Sponsor:* Steve Rajtar, 1614 Bimini Dr., Orlando, FL 32806, (407) 894-7412, http://www.geocities.com/Yosemite/Rapids/8 428, e-mail rajtar@aol.com.

Length: 9.6 miles (loop). *Route:* The trail begins along CR 234 where it crosses the creek within the Lochloosa Wildlife Management Area, heads south to Oak Ridge Cemetery, then north past the point of beginning to loop through Rochelle, and then south back to the beginning. *Terrain:* Paved and dirt country roads. *Cycling:* Appropriate. *Awards:* Patch $4.00. *Submit:* Patch order form. *Register:* Not required. *Sites:* Paynes Prairie, D. Zetrouer House, Methodist Church Site, Hall Chapel United Methodist Church, Rochelle School, Jolly House, J. Zetrouer House, Collins House, Oak Ridge Cemetery.

Ruskin Historical Trail

Location: Ruskin, FL. *Theme:* Local history. *Sponsor:* Steve Rajtar, 1614 Bimini Dr., Orlando, FL 32806, (407) 894-7412, http://www.geocities.com/Yosemite/Rapids/8 428, e-mail rajtar@aol.com.

Length: 8.0 miles (loop). *Route:* The trail begins at Commongood Park, then heads south to the intersection with College Ave., west and north through town, and west to Shell Point before returning. *Terrain:* City streets. *Cycling:* Appropriate. *Awards:* Patch $4.00. *Submit:* Patch order form. *Register:* Not required. *Sites:* Thomas Mound Site, Miller House, Dickman House, Shell Point, Coffee Cup Restaurant, Ruskin United Methodist Church, Ruskin Inlet .

Safety Harbor Historical Trail

Location: Safety Harbor, FL. *Theme:* Local history. *Sponsor:* Steve Rajtar, 1614 Bimini Dr., Orlando, FL 32806, (407) 894-7412, http://www.geocities.com/Yosemite/Rapids/8 428, e-mail rajtar@aol.com.

Length: 9.5 miles (loop). *Route:* The trail begins in Phillippe County Park, heads south to The Springs, south to loop past the Safety Harbor Museum and Lover's Oak, west and north to Sylvan Abbey Cemetery, east on Main St., and north on Phillippe Parkway to the point of beginning. *Terrain:* City streets. *Cycling:* Appropriate. *Awards:* Patch $4.00. *Submit:* Patch order form. *Register:* Not required. *Sites:* Phillippe Park Temple Mound, Hotel St. James, Phillippe Park Burial Mound, Tucker House, Safety Harbor Midden Mound, DeSoto Landing Site, Sylvan Abbey Cemetery, The Springs.

St. Augustine Historic Trail

Location: St. Augustine, FL. *Theme:* Local history. *Sponsor:* Florida Historic Trails Association, c/o Milledge Murphey, Ph.D., 1815 N.W. 7th Pl., Gainesville, FL 32603, (352) 373-9234.

Length: 8 miles (loop). *Route:* The trail begins at the parking lot of the Mission of Nombre de Dios, winds through the city, and returns to the start. *Terrain:* City streets. *Cycling:* Appropriate. *Awards:* Medal $6.50; Patch $4.00; Repeat Pin $2.50 (The miles for this trail and others sponsored by the same organization may be aggregated to qualify for the Florida Historic Trails Association 100 Mile Hiking Award—Medal $6.50; Patch $4.00; Repeat Pin $2.50.). *Submit:* Group leader's certification of completion and completed 57-item questionnaire. *Register:* In advance. *Sites:* Mission of Nombre de Dios and La Lache Shrine, Great Cross, Oldest Wooden Schoolhouse, Chapel of Nombre de Dios, Public Burying Grounds, Flagler College, Spanish National Tourist Office, Ancient City Baptist Church, Markland Place, Public Market Building, Plaza de la Constitution, Ponce de Leon Statue, Oldest Store Museum, Oldest House, Ximenes-Fatio House, Bridge of Lions, Oglethorpe Monument, St. Francis Barracks State Arsenal, Castillo de San Marcos.

St. Cloud Historical Trail

Location: St. Cloud, FL. *Theme:* Local history and architecture. *Sponsor:* Steve Rajtar, 1614 Bimini Dr., Orlando, FL 32806, (407) 894-7412, http://www.geocities.com/ Yosemite/Rapids/8428, e-mail rajtar@aol.com.

Length: 11.8 miles (loop). *Route:* The trail begins near the Hamilton Disston Sugar Plantation Marker on 9th St., passes through residential areas, and ends back in the central business section. *Terrain:* City streets. *Cycling:* Appropriate. *Awards:* Patch $4.00. *Submit:* Patch order form. *Register:* Not required. *Sites:* Railroad Passenger Station, Mount Peace Cemetery, Episcopal Church of St. Luke and St. Peter, St. Cloud Cannery, Citizens State Bank, St. Cloud Presbyterian Church, Tourist Club House, Dodds House, First United Methodist Church, Veterans Memorial Park, G.A.R. Memorial Hall.

St. Petersburg Historical Trail

Location: St. Petersburg, FL. *Theme:* Local

history. *Sponsor:* Steve Rajtar, 1614 Bimini Dr., Orlando, FL 32806, (407) 894-7412, http://www.geocities.com/Yosemite/Rapids/8428, e-mail rajtar@aol.com.

Length: 9.5 miles (loop). *Route:* The trail begins and ends at the parking area on 2nd Ave. N, east of 1st St. It winds through downtown St. Petersburg as far south as 11th Ave. S, west to 10th St., and north to 7th Ave. N. *Terrain:* City streets. *Cycling:* Appropriate. *Awards:* Patch $4.00. *Submit:* Patch order form. *Register:* Not required. *Sites:* Florida National Bank, Al Lang Field, St. Mary's Roman Catholic Church, Kress Building, Manual Training School, Alexander Hotel, Equitable Building, Pheil Building, Detroit Hotel, Snell Arcade.

San Antonio-St. Joseph Historical Trail

Location: San Antonio, St. Joseph and St. Leo, FL. *Theme:* Local history. *Sponsor:* Steve Rajtar, 1614 Bimini Dr., Orlando, FL 32806, (407) 894-7412, http://www.geocities.com/Yosemite/Rapids/8428, e-mail rajtar@aol.com.

Length: 11.3 miles (loop). *Route:* The trail begins in San Antonio, heads north to St. Joseph, then southeast to Lake Jovita, south through San Antonio, east to St. Leo College, west to wind through San Antonio, and north to the starting point. *Terrain:* City and paved country roads. *Cycling:* Appropriate. *Awards:* Patch $4.00. *Submit:* Patch order form. *Register:* Not required. *Sites:* Sacred Heart Church, Dooner House, Saint Leo Abbey Church, Saint Edward Hall, Our Lady of Lourdes Grotto, Hack House, Garden of Gethsemane Grotto, Saint Anthony School, Saint Anthony Church, San Antonio Plaza.

Sanford Historical Trail

Location: Sanford, FL. *Theme:* Local history and architecture. *Sponsor:* Steve Rajtar, 1614 Bimini Dr., Orlando, FL 32806, (407) 894-7412, http://www.geocities.com/Yosemite/Rapids/8428, e-mail rajtar@aol.com.

Length: 10.1 miles (loop). *Route:* The trail begins in the municipal lot near the courthouse, passes through the Georgetown community to the Fort Reid site, then north to and through the downtown historical area. *Terrain:* City streets. *Cycling:* Appropriate. *Awards:* Patch $4.00. *Submit:* Patch order form. *Register:* Not required. *Sites:* Log cabin Legion Home, Fort Mellon Park, Henry Shelton Sanford Library and Museum, Mayfair Hotel, St. James A.M.E. Church, Sanford Ball Park, Hopper Academy, Sanford Middle School, Florida Student Museum, All Souls Catholic Church, First Baptist Church.

Sebastian Historical Trail

Location: Sebastian and Roseland, FL. *Theme:* Local history. *Sponsor:* Steve Rajtar, 1614 Bimini Dr., Orlando, FL 32806, (407) 894-7412, http://www.geocities.com/Yosemite/Rapids/8428, e-mail rajtar@aol.com.

Length: 6.2 miles (two loops). *Route:* The trail begins at Moore's Point on the St. Sebastian River, and loops through Roseland back to the point of beginning. The second loop begins at the park in Sebastian, heads north on Indian River Dr., west on Main St., south on Louisiana Ave., and east on Fellsmere Rd. to the point of beginning. *Terrain:* City streets. *Cycling:* Appropriate. *Awards:* Patch $4.00. *Submit:* Patch order form. *Register:* Not required. *Sites:* Sebastian Methodist Church, Bartram Trail Site, Spanish Fleet Survivors and Salvors Camp Site, Hardee Monument, Wauregan, Pelican Island National Wildlife Refuge, Sebastian Inlet, City Hall.

Seville Historical Trail

Location: Seville and Bakersburg, FL. *Theme:* Local history. *Sponsor:* Steve Rajtar, 1614 Bimini Dr., Orlando, FL 32806, (407) 894-7412, http://www.geocities.com/Yosemite/Rapids/8428, e-mail rajtar@aol.com.

Length: 10.8 miles (loop). *Route:* The trail circles through Seville, then heads south on US 17 to Bakersburg, and returns north to the point of beginning. *Terrain:* City and paved country roads. *Cycling:* Appropriate. *Awards:* Patch $4.00. *Submit:* Patch order form. *Register:* Not required. *Sites:* Trinity United Methodist Church, Baptist Church, Methodist Cemetery, CY Ranch, Bakersburg Hotel Site, Hotel Seville, Village Improvement Association, Raulerson House, Seville Grammar School, City Hall.

Tampa Historic Trail

Location: Tampa, FL. *Theme:* Local history. *Sponsor:* Florida Historic Trails

Association, c/o Milledge Murphey, Ph.D., 1815 N.W. 7th Pl., Gainesville, FL 32603, (352) 373-9234.

Length: 11 miles (loop). *Route:* The trail follows sidewalks through Ybor City, downtown Tampa, the University of Tampa, and Bayshore Blvd. *Terrain:* City sidewalks. *Cycling:* Appropriate. *Awards:* Medal $6.50; Patch $4.00; Repeat Pin $2.50 (The miles for this trail and others sponsored by the same organization may be aggregated to qualify for the Florida Historic Trails Association 100 Mile Hiking Award—Medal $6.50; Patch $4.00; Repeat Pin $2.50.). *Submit:* Group leader's certification of completion and completed questionnaire. *Register:* In advance. *Sites:* Ice Palace, Tampa Bay Hotel, Harbour Island, Florida Aquarium, El Pasaje Hotel, Cigar Makers' Homes, Ybor City Museum, Tampa Theatre, Pirate Ship, Marti Park.

Tampa Heights Historical Trail

Location: Tampa, FL. *Theme:* Local history and architecture. *Sponsor:* Steve Rajtar, 1614 Bimini Dr., Orlando, FL 32806, (407) 894-7412, http://www.geocities.com/Yosemite/Rapids/8428, e-mail rajtar@aol.com.

Length: 7.0 miles (loop). *Route:* The trail begins and ends at Robles Park and winds through the area of Tampa bounded roughly by Buffalo Ave. on the north, Nebraska Ave. on the east, Scott St. on the south, and Tampa St. on the west. *Terrain:* City streets. *Cycling:* Appropriate. *Awards:* Patch $4.00. *Submit:* Patch order form. *Register:* Not required. *Sites:* Palm Avenue Baptist Church, Stovall House, Schaarai Zedek Temple, Larson House, Rodolph Sholom Synagogue, Arguelles House, First Congregational Church, Clayton House, Tampa Heights Presbyterian Church, Robles Park.

Tangerine Historical Trail

Location: Tangerine, FL. *Theme:* Local history and architecture. *Sponsor:* Steve Rajtar, 1614 Bimini Dr., Orlando, FL 32806, (407) 894-7412, http://www.geocities.com/Yosemite/Rapids/8428, e-mail rajtar@aol.com.

Length: 9.0 miles (loop). *Route:* The trail begins and ends at Johnston Hall, and loops around Lake Ola, including both nearby cemeteries. *Terrain:* City streets and unpaved roads. *Cycling:* Appropriate. *Awards:* Patch

$4.00. *Submit:* Patch order form. *Register:* Not required. *Sites:* Dixie Highway, Lake Ola, Congregational Church, Evergreen Cemetery, Tangerine Improvement Society, Trimble Park, Sloewood, Johnston Hall, Marot Store.

Tarpon Springs Historical Trail

Location: Tarpon Springs, FL. *Theme:* Local history. *Sponsor:* Steve Rajtar, 1614 Bimini Dr., Orlando, FL 32806, (407) 894-7412, http://www.geocities.com/Yosemite/Rapids/8428, e-mail rajtar@aol.com.

Length: 12.9 miles (loop). *Route:* The trail begins at Fred Howard Beach, heads east and north to Anclote, then heads southeast and winds through downtown Tarpon Springs, including the sponge docks and Spring Bayou, before returning west to the starting point. *Terrain:* City streets. *Cycling:* Appropriate. *Awards:* Patch $4.00. *Submit:* Patch order form. *Register:* Not required. *Sites:* Anclote Manor, Deserters Hill, Bigelow House, DeGolier House, Clemson House, St. Nicholas Greek Orthodox Cathedral, Safford House, Sponge Docks, Sponge Exchange.

Tavares Historical Trail

Location: Tavares, FL. *Theme:* Local history. *Sponsor:* Steve Rajtar, 1614 Bimini Dr., Orlando, FL 32806, (407) 894-7412, http://www.geocities.com/Yosemite/Rapids/8428, e-mail rajtar@aol.com.

Length: 4.4 miles (loop). *Route:* The trail begins on US 441 between Texas and Joanna Aves., heads south to Wooten Park, then winds throughout downtown Tavares to end at the starting point. *Terrain:* City streets. *Cycling:* Appropriate. *Awards:* Patch $4.00. *Submit:* Patch order form. *Register:* Not required. *Sites:* Lake County Courthouse, Railroad Station, Union Congregational Church, Nutt House, Bank of Tavares, Carriage House, Smythe House, Hux House, Abrams House, Ridge Park.

Temple Terrace Historical Trail

Location: Temple Terrace, FL. *Theme:* Local history and architecture. *Sponsor:* Steve Rajtar, 1614 Bimini Dr., Orlando, FL 32806, (407) 894-7412, http://www.geocities.com/Yosemite/Rapids/8428, e-mail rajtar@aol.com.

Length: 5.1 miles (loop) with an optional extension to 12.5. *Route:* The trail begins near the intersection of 56th St. and Bullard

Pkwy. and heads east to Glen Arven Ave. for a loop through the original country club and residential development. It then proceeds north, east and south to pass by Florida College and returns north to the point of beginning. *Terrain:* City streets. *Cycling:* Appropriate. *Awards:* Patch $4.00. *Submit:* Patch order form. *Register:* Not required. *Sites:* Morocco Club, Terrace Apartments, Old Hunting Lodge, Gillett House, Temple Terrace Hotel, Pilcher House, Krumick House, Hamner House, Campbell House, Fowler House.

10 Commandments Hike

Location: Coral Gables, FL. *Theme:* The 10 Commandments, as interpreted by 10 different churches. *Sponsor:* South Florida Council, BSA, 15255 NW 82nd Ave., Miami Lakes, FL 33016, (305) 364-0020.

Length: 6.2 miles (loop) (can vary from year to year). *Route:* The trail begins at a designated church, at which the hikers will hear a talk on the First Commandment. They then walk to the second, where they hear a talk on the Second Commandment, and so on. The route may vary from year to year depending on which churches have been selected. *Terrain:* City streets. *Cycling:* Not permitted. *Awards:* Patch $4.00 (design changes annually). *Submit:* No requirement. *Register:* Pre-register for a price discount; this is an annual hike, held on the day before Palm Sunday.

Titusville Historical Trail

Location: Titusville and La Grange, FL. *Theme:* Local history. *Sponsor:* Steve Rajtar, 1614 Bimini Dr., Orlando, FL 32806, (407) 894-7412, http://www.geocities.com/ Yosemite/Rapids/8428, e-mail rajtar@aol. com.

Length: 6.7 miles (loop). *Route:* The trail begins at Veterans Memorial Park, heads northwest to the southern edge of La Grange, then south on Dixie Hwy. to reach Titusville, where it winds westward through the streets and then heads north through downtown on Washington Ave. (US 1) and east to the starting point. *Terrain:* City streets. *Cycling:* Appropriate. *Awards:* Patch $4.00. *Submit:* Patch order form. *Register:* Not required. *Sites:* La Grange Community Church, Florida Theater, First Methodist Church, Pritchard House, Titusville Hardware Store, Titus

House, Denham Department Store, Duren Building, North Brevard Historical Museum, Spell Building.

Tomoka Historical Trail

Location: Volusia County, FL. *Theme:* Local history. *Sponsor:* Steve Rajtar, 1614 Bimini Dr., Orlando, FL 32806, (407) 894-7412, http://www.geocities.com/Yosemite/ Rapids/8428, e-mail rajtar@aol.com.

Length: 13.1 miles (loop). *Route:* The trail begins and ends at James Ormond Tomb Park, heads south on the Old Dixie Highway to Mount Oswald, north to Tomoka State Park, and then back to the start. *Terrain:* Country roads. *Cycling:* Appropriate. *Awards:* Patch $4.00. *Submit:* Patch order form. *Register:* Not required. *Sites:* Tomokie Fountain, Tomoka State Park, Carrickfergus, Damietta, Mount Oswald, Knox House, Number Nine Plantation, James Ormond Park, Ormond-Fairchild Oak, Harwood House.

Trenton Historical Trail

Location: Trenton, FL. *Theme:* Local history. *Sponsor:* Steve Rajtar, 1614 Bimini Dr., Orlando, FL 32806, (407) 894-7412, http://www.geocities.com/Yosemite/Rapids/8 428, e-mail rajtar@aol.com.

Length: 2.8 miles (loop). *Route:* The trail begins near the railroad depot and heads south on Main St. to wind through downtown before returning to the starting point. *Terrain:* City streets. *Cycling:* Appropriate. *Awards:* Patch $4.00. *Submit:* Patch order form. *Register:* Not required. *Sites:* Gilchrist County Courthouse, Coca Cola Building, Trenton Church of Christ, Trenton Hotel, Gilchrist County Jail, Warehouse, Railroad Depot, First Baptist Church, Bank Building, City Hall.

Trilacoochee Historical Trail

Location: Trilby and Lacoochee, FL. *Theme:* Local history. *Sponsor:* Steve Rajtar, 1614 Bimini Dr., Orlando, FL 32806, (407) 894-7412, http://www.geocities.com/ Yosemite/Rapids/8428, e-mail rajtar@aol. com.

Length: 6.9 miles (loop). *Route:* The trail begins on US 301 and heads north to the site of Fort Dade, where Fort King Rd. crosses the Withlacoochee River, then heads south and west to loop through Trilby, east through

Lacoochee, and then west to the point of beginning. *Terrain:* Country roads. *Cycling:* Appropriate. *Awards:* Patch $4.00. *Submit:* Patch order form. *Register:* Not required. *Sites:* Masonic Lodge, Stephens Grocery, Trilby Cemetery, Cummer House, Cummer Sons Commissary, Smith Store, Trilby United Methodist Church, Abbott House, Hartley Pressing Club, Couey House.

University of Florida Historical Trail

Location: Gainesville, FL. *Theme:* History of the university. *Sponsor:* Steve Rajtar, 1614 Bimini Dr., Orlando, FL 32806, (407) 894-7412, http://www.geocities.com/Yosemite/Rapids/8428, e-mail rajtar@aol.com.

Length: 6.0 miles (loop). *Route:* The trail begins at the Student Union and generally heads south to Archer Rd., east to SW 13th St., north to University Ave., west to Woodlawn Dr., west and south on Fraternity Dr., and east on Museum Rd. to the starting point. *Terrain:* City streets. *Cycling:* Appropriate. *Awards:* Patch $4.00. *Submit:* Patch order form. *Register:* Not required. *Sites:* J. Wayne Reitz Union, Jennings Hall, University Auditorium, Tigert Hall, Shands Hospital, Flint Hall, College of Law, Florida Field, Century Tower, Bryan Hall.

Vero Beach Historical Trail

Location: Vero Beach, FL. *Theme:* Local history. *Sponsor:* Steve Rajtar, 1614 Bimini Dr., Orlando, FL 32806, (407) 894-7412, http://www.geocities.com/Yosemite/Rapids/8428, e-mail rajtar@aol.com.

Length: 5.9 miles (loop). *Route:* The trail begins and ends downtown near the old Power Plant, heads south on Old Dixie Highway past the cemetery, then east, north and west to wind through the town. *Terrain:* City streets. *Cycling:* Appropriate. *Awards:* Patch $4.00. *Submit:* Patch order form. *Register:* Not required. *Sites:* Driftwood Resort, Heritage Center, Crestlawn Cemetery, Florida Theater, Pocahontas Park, Railroad Station, Pocahontas Building, Graves House, DuBose Jewelry Co., Pueblo Arcade.

Waldo Historical Trail

Location: Waldo, FL. *Theme:* Local history and architecture. *Sponsor:* Steve Rajtar, 1614 Bimini Dr., Orlando, FL 32806, (407) 894-7412, http://www.geocities.com/Yosemite/Rapids/8428, e-mail rajtar@aol.com.

Length: 3.1 miles (loop). *Route:* The trail begins near the intersection of SW 2nd Pl. and SW 5th Blvd., winds through the streets of downtown Waldo, and returns to the starting point. *Terrain:* City streets. *Cycling:* Appropriate. *Awards:* Patch $4.00. *Submit:* Patch order form. *Register:* Not required. *Sites:* Alexander Store, Sparkman Store, Schenk Hardware, Granger House, Seigler House, Episcopal Church, Strickland House, Waldo School, Pettit House, Cigar Factory.

Welaka Historical Trail

Location: Welaka, FL. *Theme:* Local history. *Sponsor:* Steve Rajtar, 1614 Bimini Dr., Orlando, FL 32806, (407) 894-7412, http://www.geocities.com/Yosemite/Rapids/8428, e-mail rajtar@aol.com.

Length: 5.1 miles (loop). *Route:* The trail begins in the Mud Springs Trail parking lot of the Welaka State Forest, heads north on SR 309 and winds through town, then returns south to its point of beginning. *Terrain:* City streets and some dirt roads. *Cycling:* Appropriate. *Awards:* Patch $4.00. *Submit:* Patch order form. *Register:* Not required. *Sites:* Florida State Fish Hatchery, Welaka Aquarium, Sunnyside Hotel, Bryant's Wharf, Sportsman's Lodge, Town Hall, Morris House, Fox Pond, Sulphur Springs, McLeod House.

West Tampa Historical Trail

Location: Tampa, FL. *Theme:* Local history and architecture. *Sponsor:* Steve Rajtar, 1614 Bimini Dr., Orlando, FL 32806, (407) 894-7412, http://www.geocities.com/Yosemite/Rapids/8428, e-mail rajtar@aol.com.

Length: 11.0 miles (loop). *Route:* The trail begins and ends in McFarlane Park, and covers the portion of Tampa roughly bounded by Dale Mabry Hwy., Interstate 275, North Blvd. and Columbus Dr. *Terrain:* City streets. *Cycling:* Appropriate. *Awards:* Patch $4.00. *Submit:* Patch order form. *Register:* Not required. *Sites:* Garcia and Vega Company, Cigar Factory Sites, Mount Olive A.M.E. Church, Arenas Building, West Tampa Junior High School, Orient Building, First Baptist Church of West Tampa, O'Halloran House, Bethel A.M.E. Church.

Windermere Historical Trail

Location: Windermere and Gotha, FL. *Theme:* Local history and architecture.

Sponsor: Steve Rajtar, 1614 Bimini Dr., Orlando, FL 32806, (407) 894-7412, http://www.geocities.com/Yosemite/Rapids/8 428, e-mail rajtar@aol. com.

Length: 10.0 miles (loop). *Route:* The trail begins at Windermere Elementary School, passes through Gotha, and winds through Windermere. *Terrain:* Paved and unpaved roads. *Cycling:* Appropriate. *Awards:* Patch $4.00. *Submit:* Patch order form. *Register:* Not required. *Sites:* Windermere Union Church, Town Hall, First Baptist Church, Town Office, Finders Keepers, Isleworth, Palmer Park, Palm Cottage Gardens, Park Among the Lakes, Gotha Memorial Park.

Winter Garden Historical Trail

Location: Winter Garden, FL. *Theme:* Local history and architecture. *Sponsor:* Steve Rajtar, 1614 Bimini Dr., Orlando, FL 32806, (407) 894-7412, http://www.geocities. com/Yosemite/Rapids/8428, e-mail rajtar@ aol.com.

Length: 10.1 miles (loop). *Route:* The trail begins and ends at the parking lot of the shopping center at the intersection of Dillard St. and Cypress St. The route includes Beulah. *Terrain:* City streets. *Cycling:* Appropriate. *Awards:* Patch $4.00. *Submit:* Patch order form. *Register:* Not required. *Sites:* First Baptist Church, Lakeview High School, State Bank of Winter Garden, Dave Starr Park, First United Methodist Church, City Hall, Maxey Recreation Center.

Winter Haven Historical Trail

Location: Winter Haven, FL. *Theme:* Local history. *Sponsor:* Steve Rajtar, 1614 Bimini Dr., Orlando, FL 32806, (407) 894-7412, http://www.geocities.com/Yosemite/Rapids/8 428, e-mail rajtar@aol.com.

Length: 9.0 miles (loop). *Route:* The trail begins and ends on Ave. C SW, loops west, then heads east and north to Ave. T, then south along 6th St. W to meander through downtown toward the beginning. *Terrain:* City streets. *Cycling:* Appropriate. *Awards:* Patch $4.00. *Submit:* Patch order form. *Register:* Not required. *Sites:* Grace Lutheran Church, Ritz Theatre, St. Joseph's Catholic Church, Inman Park, Beymer Memorial Methodist Church, Schneider House, Central Baptist Church, Boyd House, Lake Region Hotel, Postal Building.

Winter Park Historical Canoe Trail

Location: Winter Park, FL. *Theme:* Local history, recreation. *Sponsor:* Steve Rajtar, 1614 Bimini Dr., Orlando, FL 32806, (407) 894-7412, http://www.geocities.com/ Yosemite/Rapids/8428, e-mail rajtar@aol. com.

Length: 12.0 miles (loop). *Route:* The trail begins at Fort Maitland Park, and follows the shores of Lakes Maitland, Osceola, and Virginia. *Terrain:* Lakes and connecting canals. *Cycling:* Impossible—must be paddled. *Awards:* Patch $4.00. *Submit:* Patch order form. *Register:* Not required. *Sites:* Sandscove, MacCaughey-Taylor House, Alabama Hotel, Kraft Azalea Gardens, The Palms, Carlova, Martin Hall, Knowles Memorial Chapel, Rollins College, Dinky Dock.

Winter Park Historical Trail

Location: Winter Park, FL. *Theme:* Local history and architecture. *Sponsor:* Steve Rajtar, 1614 Bimini Dr., Orlando, FL 32806, (407) 894-7412, http://www.geocities.com/ Yosemite/Rapids/8428, e-mail rajtar@aol. com.

Length: 12.0 miles (loop). *Route:* The trail begins in the parking lot near the railroad station, heads through Hannibal Square, Rollins College, Kraft Azalea Gardens, and through the Park Avenue shopping area to the point of beginning. *Terrain:* City streets, with a short area on dirt roads. *Cycling:* Appropriate. *Awards:* Patch $4.00. *Submit:* Patch order form. *Register:* Not required. *Sites:* Winter Park Historical Association Museum, Ideal Woman's Club, Knowles Memorial Chapel, Peckham House, The Palms, Albin Polasek Galleries, Ward Cottage.

Winter Springs Historical Trail

Location: Winter Springs, FL. *Theme:* Local history. *Sponsor:* Steve Rajtar, 1614 Bimini Dr., Orlando, FL 32806, (407) 894-7412, http://www.geocities.com/Yosemite/ Rapids/8428, e-mail rajtar@aol.com.

Length: 19.4 miles (loop). *Route:* The trail begins and ends at Central Winds Park, and follows SR 434 and side roads throughout the community. *Terrain:* Paved and unpaved roads. *Cycling:* Appropriate, but difficult in some areas. *Awards:* Patch $4.00. *Submit:* Patch order form. *Register:* Not required. *Sites:* Tuskawilla Landing, Gee Hammock,

White's Wharf Site, Whitney Grove Site, Solary's Wharf Site, City Hall.

Yankeetown Historical Trail

Location: Yankeetown and Inglis, FL. *Theme:* Local history. *Sponsor:* Steve Rajtar, 1614 Bimini Dr., Orlando, FL 32806, (407) 894-7412, http://www.geocities.com/ Yosemite/Rapids/8428, e-mail rajtar@aol. com.

Length: 9.1 miles (loop). *Route:* The trail starts in Inglis, on US 19 just south of SR 40, and heads west on SR 40, south on SR 40A, and east on Riverside Dr. through Yankeetown to return to the point of beginning. *Terrain:* City streets. *Cycling:* Appropriate. *Awards:* Patch $4.00. *Submit:* Patch order form. *Register:* Not required. *Sites:* Parsons Memorial Presbyterian Church, Church of God, Log Landing, Izaak Walton Lodge, Palm Cottage, Yankeetown School, Cedar Landing.

Ybor City Historical Trail

Location: Tampa, FL. *Theme:* Local history. *Sponsor:* Steve Rajtar, 1614 Bimini Dr., Orlando, FL 32806, (407) 894-7412, http://www.geocities.com/Yosemite/Rapids/8 428, e-mail rajtar@aol.com.

Length: 6.7 miles (loop). *Route:* The trail begins and ends in the city parking lot adjacent to Ybor Square, at the intersection of 9th Ave. and 13th St. It meanders throughout the former cigar-manufacturing neighborhood, including an older residential area several blocks to the east. *Terrain:* City streets. *Cycling:* Appropriate. *Awards:* Patch $4.00. *Submit:* Patch order form. *Register:* Not required. *Sites:* La Union Marti-Maceo, Cherokee Club, United Secret Orders Hall, El Liceo Cubano, Circulo Cubano de Tampa, Centro Asturiano, La Joven Francesa Bakery, Columbia Restaurant.

Zellwood Historical Trail

Location: Zellwood, FL. *Theme:* Local history. *Sponsor:* Steve Rajtar, 1614 Bimini Dr., Orlando, FL 32806, (407) 894-7412, http://www.geocities.com/Yosemite/Rapids/8 428, e-mail rajtar@aol.com.

Length: 9.8 miles (loop). *Route:* The trail begins and ends near the intersection of Orange Blossom Tr. and Jones Ave., reaching to the edge of Tangerine. *Terrain:* Paved and unpaved roads. *Cycling:* Appropriate. *Awards:* Patch $4.00. *Submit:* Patch order form. *Register:* Not required. *Sites:* Hampden-DuBose Academy, Gainesboro, Zellwood Mucklands, Dixie Highway, Methodist Church, Grasmere.

Zephyrhills Historical Trail

Location: Zephyrhills, FL. *Theme:* Local history. *Sponsor:* Steve Rajtar, 1614 Bimini Dr., Orlando, FL 32806, (407) 894-7412, http://www.geocities.com/Yosemite/Rapids/8 428, e-mail rajtar@aol.com.

Length: 7.8 miles (loop). *Route:* The trail begins and ends in front of the library on 5th Ave., and winds through the streets of downtown Zephyrhills. *Terrain:* City streets. *Cycling:* Appropriate. *Awards:* Patch $4.00. *Submit:* Patch order form. *Register:* Not required. *Sites:* Geiger House, Parsons House, First Baptist Church, Zephyr Park, Trottman House, Geiger Cemetery, Oakside Cemetery, Mueller Studios.

Other Florida Awards

Trailwalker Program—Free Patches for completion of 10, 20 or 30 trails in state forests. Director, Division of Forestry, 3125 Conner Blvd., Tallahassee, FL 23299-9904.

Formerly Sponsored Trails

Downtown Tallhassee Historic Trail
Peace River Historic Wilderness Canoe Trail
Orlando Ten Commandments Hike

GEORGIA

Andersonville Prison Historical Trail

Location: Andersonville, GA. *Theme:*

Military prisoners of war. *Sponsor:* BSA Troop 231, 125 S. Jackson St., Americus, GA 31709.

Length: 3 miles (straight). *Route:* The trail begins at the Visitor Center, proceeds through the national cemetery to the prison site, then ends in the town of Andersonville. *Terrain:* Paved roads for most, open grassy areas for a portion. *Cycling:* Appropriate only on the roads. *Awards:* Patch $3.50. *Submit:* Completed 60-item questionnaire. *Register:* Not required. *Sites:* Minnesota Monument, Andersonville National Cemetery, POW Museum, Pennsylvania Monument, Visitor Center, Connecticut Monument, Indiana Monument, Providence Spring Pavilion, Castle Reed, Town of Andersonville Museum, Wirz Plaque, Andersonville Restaurant, Blacksmith Shop, Woman's Relief Corps Monument.

Big Rock Trail

Location: Camp Rainey Mountain, Clayton, GA. *Theme:* Recreation. *Sponsor:* Camp Rainey Mountain, Northeast Georgia Council, BSA, P.O. Box 6049, Athens, GA 30604, (706) 548-5293.

Length: 1 mile (loop). *Route:* The trail leaves the campground from Alto Campsite, and steeply climbs up to a large rock outcropping overlooking the camp and the valley, then returns by the same route. *Terrain:* Steep mountainside. *Cycling:* Impossible. *Awards:* Patch $1.50. *Submit:* No requirement. *Register:* Not required.

Chickamauga Military Trails

Location: Chickamauga Battlefield, Ft. Oglethorpe, GA. *Theme:* Civil War battle— September 19-20, 1863. *Sponsor:* Rossville Kiwanis Club, P.O. Box 488, Rossville, GA 30741, (706) 255-9025 or (706) 756-0333.

Length: Bragg Hike, 7 miles (loop). Cannon Hike, 14 miles (loop). Chickamauga Nature Trail, 5 miles (loop). Confederate Line Trail, 6 miles (loop). Historical Battlefield Trail, 14 miles (loop). Memorial Trail, 12 miles (loop). Perimeter Trail, 20 miles (loop). *Routes:* All are loop trails, generally beginning and ending just south of the park headquarters. *Terrain:* Paved and dirt roads, woods. *Cycling:* Not recommended. *Awards:* Medal $5.00; 7 Patches $2.50 each (A $2.50 100-Mile Hiking Award patch is available to anyone who completes all 7 Chickamauga Trails and the Blue Beaver Trail on Lookout Mountain, TN.). *Submit:* Completed questionnaires for each trail. *Register:* Not required. *Sites:* Visitors Center, Florida Monument, Snodgrass House, Jay's Mill Site, Kelly House, Smith's Monument, Wilder Tower, Heg's Monument, Brotherton Cabin, Texas Monument, General Lytle's Monument, Cross Monument, 125th Ohio Monument, 29th Georgia Monument, Hall House Plaque, 2nd Ohio Monument, Alexander House Plaque, Baldwin's Monument, King's Monument, Deshler's Monument.

Cumberland Island Historic Trail

Location: Cumberland Island, east of St. Mary's, GA. *Theme:* Nature, history of the island. *Sponsor:* Al Pearson, Troop 222, P.O. Box 222, St. Mary's, GA 31558, (912) 882-3551.

Length: 6 miles (loop). *Route:* The trail begins at Seacamp Dock, loops south to the Dungeness ruins, and northeast to the Atlantic Ocean, and returns to the dock. *Terrain:* Dirt roads. *Cycling:* Possible, but call ahead of time to see if you can bring a bicycle on the ferry. *Awards:* Patch $3.25. *Submit:* Completed 14-item questionnaire. *Register:* Pre-registration for the trail is not required, but a reservation for the ferry must be made with the National Park Service up to 11 months in advance. *Sites:* Seacamp Dock, Dungeness Dock, Old Ice House Museum, Visitor Center, Dungeness Ruins, Wild Horses, Green-Miller Cemetery.

Fort Benning Historic Trail

Location: Fort Benning, GA. *Theme:* History of the army base. *Sponsor:* Chattahoochee Council, BSA, 1710 Buena Vista Rd., P.O. Box 5425, Columbus, GA 31906-0425, (706) 327-2634.

Length: Route A—1 mile (straight). Route B—5 miles (straight). Route C—13 miles (straight). *Route:* The trail begins at the National Infantry Museum and winds through the base to end at the Assistant Commandant's Quarters (Route A), the Infantryman Statue (Route B), or the Federal Road Crossing (Route C). *Terrain:* Paved roads. *Cycling:* Possible, but contact the base first for permission (does not qualify for awards). *Awards:* Patch $3.00. *Submit:* Completed 25-item questionnaire. *Register:* Advisable with base. *Sites:* National Infantry Museum, Patch School, Kashita Town Monument, POW Monument, D.A.R.

Monument, Chinese Arch, School of the Americas, Officer's Club, The Infantry Chapel, Assistant Commandant's Quarters, Riverside, Doughboy Stadium, Railroad Station, Old Cooks and Bakers School, Cuartels, Infantryman Statue, Playhouse, Airborne Training Area, Office of the Staff Judge Advocate, Fire Station, Campbell King Horse Bowl, First Gymnasium, Infantry Hall, OCS Hall of Fame, Lavoie Community Life Center, Cussetah Town.

Historic Augusta Trail

Location: Downtown Augusta, GA. *Theme:* Local history. *Sponsor:* Georgia-Carolina Council, BSA, 1252 Gordon Park Rd., Augusta, GA 30901-4471, (706) 826-4471.
Length: 6 miles (straight). *Route:* The trail begins at the Harris House near the Augusta Canal and winds through the city to end at the Old Government House. *Terrain:* City streets. *Cycling:* Appropriate. *Awards:* Patch $1.25. *Submit:* Completed 12-item questionnaire. *Register:* Not required. *Sites:* Confederate Monument, Harris House, Confederate Powder Works, Savannah River, Augusta Canal, Celtic Cross, Meadow Garden, St. Paul's Church, Old Medical College, Signers' Monument, Old Government House, Augusta Museum, Boyhood Home of Woodrow Wilson.

Jimmy Carter Historical Hike

Location: Plains, GA. *Theme:* Life of Pres. Jimmy Carter. *Sponsor:* Jimmy Carter Historical Hike, Boy Scouts of America-Troop 231, 125 S. Jackson St., Americus, GA 31709.
Length: 5.0 miles (loop). *Route:* The trail begins at the former Plains High School and proceeds along Paschall St., Thomas St., Church St., Old Plains Hwy., Archery Rd., Bob Hale Rd., Main St. and ends on Bond St. *Terrain:* Sidewalks. *Cycling:* Possible, but discouraged. *Awards:* Patch $3.75. *Submit:* Completed 52-item questionnaire. *Register:* Not required. *Sites:* Plains United Methodist Church, Carter Boyhood Home, Railroad

Depot, 1950s Carter Residence, Golden Peanut Company, Lebanon Cemetery, Billy Carter's Service Station, Carter Compound.

Kennesaw Mountain Historical Trails

Location: Kennesaw Mountain National Battlefield Park, GA. *Theme:* Civil War battles—June, 1864. *Sponsor:* Kemo Trails, c/o BSA Troop 116, P.O. Box 512, Acworth, GA 30101.
Length: 5, 10 and 16 miles (loops). *Route:* The trail begins at the Visitor Center, climbs Kennesaw Mountain, and heads south to loop back to the start at any of three points. *Terrain:* Steep mountain, woods paths. *Cycling:* Not recommended. *Awards:* Patch $3.50; 3 Segment Strips $0.50 each. *Submit:* Completed questionnaire. *Register:* Not required. *Sites:* Kennesaw Mountain, Visitor Center, Little Kennesaw Mountain, Pigeon Hill, Cheatham Hill, Kolb's Farm.

Stone Mountain Historical Trail

Location: Stone Mountain Park, GA. *Theme:* Geology and Civil War history. *Sponsor:* Cherokee Trail and Campsites, P.O. Box 708, Tucker, GA 30084.
Length: 8 miles (loop). *Route:* The trail begins at Confederate Hall and climbs to the peak of the mountain, then back down along the same route, and around the base of the mountain back to the start. *Terrain:* Moderately steep rocky trail on mountain, paved sidewalk and easy dirt path around base. *Cycling:* Impossible on mountain, appropriate for base. *Awards:* Medal $3.00; Patch $2.50; Repeat Patch $3.00. *Submit:* Group leader's certificate of completion. *Register:* Not required. *Sites:* Confederate Hall, Memorial Hall, Railroad Station, Grist Mill, Mountainside Sculpture, Covered Bridge.

Formerly Sponsored Trails

Atlanta I.O.U. Trail
Brasstown Bald Mt. Trail
Columbus Historical Trail
North Cohutta Sapp Mt. Trail

HAWAII

Hawaii Heritage Trail

Location: Honolulu, HI or Hilo, HI (1 award for either). *Theme:* History of Hawaii. *Sponsor:* Na Mokupuni 'O Lawelawe Lodge, 567, c/o Aloha Council, BSA, 42 Puiwa Rd., P.O. Box 1100, Honolulu, HI 96808-1100, (808) 595-6366.

Length: 5 miles (loop) in Honolulu or 4 miles (loop) in Hilo. *Route:* In Honolulu, the trail begins and ends at the Aloha Tower, after winding through downtown. *Terrain:* City streets. *Cycling:* Appropriate. *Awards:* Patch $2.50. *Submit:* No requirement. *Register:* Not required. *Sites:* Aloha Tower, Falls of Clyde, Mission Houses, Kawaiahao Church, King Kamehameha Statue, Judiciary Building, Band Stand, Iolani Palace, Hawaii Archives, Iolani Barracks, First Mausoleum & Crypt, Library of Hawaii, Old Municipal Building, State Capitol, Eternal Flame, New Municipal Building, Washington Place, Royal Mausoleum, Foster Botanic Gardens, WWII Memorial, U.S. Immigration Office, YMCA Building, Adobe School House, Banyan Tree, Our Lady of Peace Cathedral, St. Andrew's Cathedral, Captain Cook Memorial Tablet.

Formerly Sponsored Trails

Haleakala Trail
The Hawaiiana Trail

IDAHO

Table Rock Trail

Location: Driggs, ID. *Theme:* Scenic mountain climbing. *Sponsor:* Teton Peaks Council, BSA, 574 4th St., Idaho Falls, ID 83401, (208) 522-5155; Dave Kirk, Scout Camp Director, P.O. Box 2854, Pocatello, ID 83201, (208) 233-4600.

Length: 16.0 miles (loop). *Route:* The trail begins at the base of Teton Mountain in Driggs, heads up the mountainside until it reaches a plateau, and then returns. Or, hikers may continue from the plateau down the other side of the mountain to the Alaskan Basin near Alta, WY. *Terrain:* Steep mountainside. *Cycling:* Not possible. *Awards:* Medallion $3.75. *Submit:* Group leader's certificate of completion. *Register:* Call in advance, register upon arrival. *Sites:* Snake River, Jackson Hole Site, Tetons Peak Mountains, Mirror Lake.

ILLINOIS

Abraham Lincoln Trail

Location: New Salem to Springfield, IL. *Theme:* Abraham Lincoln's walking route. *Sponsor:* Abraham Lincoln Council, BSA, 1911 W. Fairhills Mall, W. Monroe at Chatham Rd., Springfield, IL 62704-1596, (217) 546-5570.

Length: 20 miles (straight). *Route:* The trail begins at New Salem State Park and heads southeasterly near SRs 97 and 125. *Terrain:* Secondary roads, byways and trails. *Cycling:* Appropriate. *Awards:* Medal $4.00; Patch $2.00; 3 Repeat Patches $5.00 each. *Submit:* No requirement. *Register:* Not required.

Adventurer Award

Location: DuPage County, IL. *Theme:* Nature. *Sponsor:* Forest Preserve District of DuPage County, Oak Brook, IL 60301, (708) 790-4900 ext. 243, or Three Fires Council, BSA, 415 N. 2nd St., St. Charles, IL 60174-1254, (630) 584-9250.

Length: Varies. *Routes:* Each forest preserve or other natural area has its own trail or activity related to outdoor education and recreation. The areas are:. Blackwell Forest Preserve (Warrensville)—Compass Course. Danada Equestrian Center (Wheaton)—Guided Tour. Fullersburg Woods Environmental Center (Oak Brook)—Which-a-Way Trail. Greene Valley Forest Preserve (Woodridge)—Tricky Tree—Key Trail. Kline Creek Farm (West Chicago)—Visit to restored, working farm. Lyman Woods (Downers Grove)—Outings. Maple Grove Forest Preserve (Downers Grove)—Nature Treasure Hunt Trail. Outdoor Education Camp (Darien)—The Mystery of Nature program. Waterfall Glen Forest Preserve (Darien)—Orienteering Trail. Willowbrook Wildlife Haven (Glen Ellyn)—Nature Trail. *Terrain:* Varies. *Cycling:* Not recommended. *Awards:* Patch; Segments. *Submit:* Contact sponsor for specific requirements. *Register:* At each park upon arrival.

Algonquin Woods Nature Trail

Location: Des Plaines, IL. *Theme:* Nature. *Sponsor:* Karl Lindahl, 8705 W. Sunset Rd., Niles, IL 60714-1822, (847) 692-2065.

Length: 5.5 miles (loop). *Route:* The trail begins and ends at the Izaak Walton League, Des Plaines Chapter #206, 1841 S. River Rd., Des Plaines. *Terrain:* Woods. *Cycling:* Not recommended. *Awards:* Patch $3.50. *Submit:* No requirement. *Register:* At least 2 weeks in advance.

Beating the Bounds Trail

Location: Evanston, IL. *Theme:* Local History. *Sponsor:* Barbara Roberts, 1139 Chicago Ave., Evanston, IL 60202, (847) 864-2132.

Length: 15.0 miles (loop). *Route:* The trail begins at the Field House on the shore of Lake Michigan, heads north along the lake, then west, south, east, south, and east along the city limits, and north along the lake to the point of beginning. *Terrain:* City streets.

Cycling: Appropriate. *Awards:* Patch $2.00. *Submit:* Map signed by group hikemaster confirming completion of trail. *Register:* Not required. *Sites:* Northwestern University, Grosse Point Lighthouse, Evanston Art Center, Clark Square Park, Skokie Swift Tracks, Calvary Cemetery, Water Reclamation Plant, Landing Strip, Eadie Field, Dyche Stadium.

Big Foot Trail

Location: Cook County Forest Preserve, IL. *Theme:* Recreation. *Sponsor:* Indian Portage Trails, 11140 S. Trumbull, Chicago, IL 60655-3530.

Length: 13 miles (loop). *Route:* The trail starts at Camp Sullivan, heads east roughly following 143rd St., follows power lines westward, heads south roughly following Harlem Ave., and returns to the start. *Terrain:* Woods and fields. *Cycling:* Possible over most of the trail. *Awards:* Patch $2.00; Repeat, Snow, Rain and Camping Segments $0.80 each. *Submit:* No requirement. *Register:* Not required. *Sites:* Bachelors Grove Cemetery, Old Stone Quarry, Rubio Woods Forest Preserve.

Big Quarry Trail

Location: Cook County, IL. *Theme:* Recreation. *Sponsor:* Sauk Thorn Creek Trails, Inc., c/o Eleanor Blouin, HC 81, Box 9407, Cassville, MO 65625, (417) 271-4020.

Length: 10.0 miles (straight). *Route:* The trail begins at 154th St. and Paxton and ends at Lake Wampum. *Terrain:* City streets. *Cycling:* Possible. *Awards:* Patch $3.25. *Submit:* Patch order form. *Register:* Not required.

Blackhawk Trail

Location: Camp Lowden, Oregon, IL. *Theme:* Chief Blackhawk. *Sponsor:* Blackhawk Area Council, BSA, P.O. Box 4085, 1800 Seventh Ave., Rockford, IL 61110-0585, (815) 397-0210.

Length: 20 miles (loop). *Route:* The trail begins at Camp Lowden and follows the Rock River to Lorado Taft's statue of Blackhawk in Lowden Memorial Park. *Terrain:* Woods. *Cycling:* Not recommended. *Awards:* Medal; Patch. *Submit:* List of 16 identified trees and a 250-word report on Blackhawk. *Register:* Advance registration required. *Sites:* Blackhawk Statue, Lowden State Park, Rock River, Kyte River.

Cahokian Trail

Location: Maryville, IL. *Theme:* Indian Mounds. *Sponsor:* Troop 81, 5806 SR 162, Maryville, IL 62034, (618) 288-6049.

Length: 18 miles (straight). *Route:* The trail begins on the island in Horseshoe Lake, follows the shore around the island, and heads south past I 55/70 to Cahokia Mounds State Historic Site where it loops through the park to end at the interpretive center. *Terrain:* Woods and roads. *Cycling:* Not appropriate. *Awards:* Patch $2.00. *Submit:* Patch request. *Register:* Not required. *Sites:* Cahokia Mounds, Horseshoe Lake, Woodhenge, Interpretive Center.

Cedar Creek Trail

Location: London Mills, IL. *Theme:* Nature. *Sponsor:* W.D. Boyce Council, BSA, 614 N. Madison, Peoria, IL 61603, (309) 673-6136.

Length: 2, 5 or 12 miles (loops). *Route:* The trail follows the perimeter of the Ingersoll Scout Reservation along Cedar Creek. *Terrain:* Woods. *Cycling:* Not appropriate. *Awards:* Patch $2.00; Mile Segments $1.00. *Submit:* Request for patches. *Register:* At least 2 weeks in advance.

Chicago Lincoln Avenue Trail

Location: Chicago, IL. *Theme:* Local history. *Sponsor:* Troop 881 Trail Committee, c/o Bryan Albro, 1146 W. Mallard Dr., Palatine, IL 60067-6641, (847) 991-6793.

Length: 7.0 miles (straight). *Route:* The trail begins in Lincoln Park and heads southeast on Lincoln Ave. to end at River Park. *Terrain:* City streets (completely wheelchair accessible). *Cycling:* Appropriate. *Awards:* Patch $1.50; C.L.A. Border Strip (for repeat hikers) $0.50; Zoo Border Strip (for visit to Lincoln Park Zoo) $0.50; History Border Strip (for tour of Chicago Historical Society) $0.50; Nature Border Strip (for visit to Academy of Sciences, Nature Museum) $0.50; C.L.A. Braille Patch Border Strip (for non-sighted hikers or their guides) $0.50. *Submit:* Patch order form. *Register:* Not required. *Sites:* Lincoln Monument, Augustana Hospital, Grant Hospital, Biograph Theater, St. Alphonsus Church, Hild Library, Swedish Covenant Hospital, Lincoln Square.

Chicago Portage National Historic Site Trail

Location: Along the Des Plaines River south of US 66 near Chicago, IL. *Theme:* History of Chicago Portage. *Sponsor:* Sauk Thorn Creek Trails, Inc., c/o Eleanor Blouin, HC 81, Box 9407, Cassville, MO 65625, (417) 271-4020.

Length: 4.0 miles (loop). *Route:* The trail begins at the parking lot on the south side of US 66 just east of the Des Plaines River, heads generally south through the Ottawa Woods Forest Preserves past the Catherine Mitchell Lagoon, then east along the railroad tracks, south and west through the Chicago Portage Preserve, and north along the river to the point of beginning. *Terrain:* Woods. *Cycling:* Not appropriate. *Awards:* Patch $3.75; Repeat Feather $1.75. *Submit:* Patch order form. *Register:* Not required. *Sites:* Chicago Lake Plain, Portage Road, Laughton's Trading Post Site, Prescott's Island, Portage Creek, Walls' Meander, Diversion Channel, Laughton's Ford, Stony Ford.

Chief Che-Che-Pin-Qua Trail

Location: Thatcher Woods near Chicago, IL. *Theme:* Local History. *Sponsor:* Sauk Thorn Creek Trails, Inc., c/o Eleanor Blouin, HC 81, Box 9407, Cassville, MO 65625, (417) 271-4020.

Length: 10.0 miles (straight). *Route:* The trail begins at the Thatcher Woods parking lot, heads north along the edge of a field, then goes through the forest preserve to Devon Ave. *Terrain:* Field and woods. *Cycling:* Not appropriate. *Awards:* Patch $3.75; Repeat Feather $1.75. *Submit:* Patch order form. *Register:* Not required. *Sites:* Dam No. 4 South.

Chief Chicagou Trail

Location: Chicago, IL. *Theme:* Local history. *Sponsor:* Sauk Thorn Creek Trails, c/o Eleanor Blouin, HC 81, Box 9407, Cassville, MO 65625, (417) 271-4020.

Length: 14.0 miles (straight). *Route:* The trail begins at the statue in Jackson Park on Hayes Dr., then goes east to south Lake Shore Dr., north along the lakefront, west on North Ave., and north on Clark St. to end at the Chicago Academy of Science. *Terrain:* City streets. *Cycling:* Appropriate. *Awards:* Patch $3.75; Repeat Feather $1.75. *Submit:* Patch order form. *Register:* Not required. *Sites:* Chicago Academy of Science, Lake Michigan, 1893 Columbian Exposition Site, Jackson Park.

Chief Illini Trail

Location: Shelbyville, IL. *Sponsor:* Lincoln Trails Council, Order of the Arrow, 262 W. Prairie Ave., Decatur, IL 62522-1221, (217) 429-2326. *Theme:* Recreation.

Length: Chief Illini Trail 11 miles; Little Chief Illini Trail is the first 2 miles of the trail. *Route:* The trail goes in either direction from Lone Point Campground to Eagle Creek State Park. *Terrain:* Rolling hills and open prairies. *Cycling:* Not appropriate. *Awards:* Chief Illini Patch $3.00; Little Chief Illini Patch $1.75. *Submit:* Patch order form. *Register:* Not required.

Chief Saugnash Trail

Location: Cook County, IL. *Sponsor:* Sauk Thorn Creek Trails, Inc., c/o Eleanor Blouin, HC 81, Box 9407, Cassville, MO 65625, (417) 271-9407.

Length: 11.0 miles (loop). *Route:* The trail begins at Harms Woods, heads to Miami Wood, and returns. *Terrain:* City streets. *Cycling:* Possible. *Awards:* Patch $3.25. *Submit:* Patch order form. *Register:* Not required.

Chief Shabbona Trail

Location: Channahon, IL. *Theme:* Chief Shabbona. *Sponsor:* Snyder Watson, 1515 Burry Ave., Joliet, IL 60435, (815) 727-7054.

Length: 16.5 miles (straight). *Route:* The trail begins at Lock No. 6 and heads westward along the I & M Canal to end at Gebhard Woods State Park. *Terrain:* Canal towpath. *Cycling:* Not recommended. *Awards:* Patch $2.50; Repeat Patch $2.50; Miniature Canoe Paddle $2.50. *Submit:* No requirement. *Register:* Not required. *Sites:* Gebhard Woods State Park, I & M Canal, Illinois-Michigan State Park, Lock No. 6, Shabbona's Grave, Dresden Atomic Energy Generating Station, Evergreen Cemetery.

Des Plaines River Tecumseh Trail

Location: Northeastern corner of IL. *Theme:* Recreation. *Sponsor:* Makajawan Lodge 40, Northeast Illinois Council, BSA, 2745 Skokie Valley Rd., Highland Park, IL 60035, (847) 433-1813.

Length: 6.5 miles (straight). *Route:* The trail begins at the north end of Sterling Lake off Russell Rd. and proceeds south along the Des Plaines River to end at Wadsworth Rd. *Terrain:* Woods. *Cycling:* Not appropriate. *Awards:* Patch $4.00. *Submit:* Request for patches. *Register:* Not required. *Sites:* Sterling Lake, Van Patten Woods Forest Preserve, Des Plaines River Brige #1, Wadsworth Prairie, McCarty Road Bridge.

Discovery '76 Trail

Location: Chicago, IL. *Theme:* History, patriotism and nature. *Sponsor:* Troop 881 Trail Committee, c/o Bryan Albro, 1146 W. Mallard Dr., Palatine, IL 60067-6641, (847) 991-6793.

Length: Varies (you design your own route). *Route:* The trail is designed by the hikers—must contain at least three points of historic, patriotic or natural interest. *Terrain:* Depends on individual trail route. *Cycling:* Depends on individual trail route. *Awards:* Patch $1.00. *Submit:* No requirement. *Register:* Not required. *Sites:* Depends on trail route.

Eagle Trail

Location: Belleville, IL (formerly known as the Belleville Historical Trail). *Theme:* Recreation. *Sponsor:* Okaw Valley Council, BSA, 1801 N. 17th St., Belleville, IL 62223, (618) 236-3320.

Length: 8 miles (loop). *Route:* The trail begins at the main Camp Vandeventer parking lot, winds through the camp along a horse trail, the camp boundary, and the edge of Fountain Creek, and returns to the start. *Terrain:* Woods. *Cycling:* Not recommended. *Awards:* Patch $4.00; 2 Feather Repeat Pins $2.00 each. *Submit:* Group leader's certification of completion. *Register:* At least 3 days in advance.

Fort Dearborn Hiking Trails

Location: Chicago, IL. *Theme:* Recreation. *Sponsor:* Chicago Area Council, BSA, 730 W. Lake St., Chicago, IL 60661, (312) 559-0990.

Length: Border Trail, 20.0 miles (straight). Duneland Trail, 10.8 miles (loop). Indian Reserve Trail, 15.8 miles (straight). Trail Awinding, 16.8 miles (loop). Upward Trail, 13.5 miles (loop). *Routes:* The Upward Trail and Trail Awinding begin and end at Camp Kiwanis in the Palos Hills Forest Reserve. The

Indian Reserve Trail begins at the Trailside Museum in Thatcher Woods, passes through Camp Fort Dearborn, and ends at Northwestern Woods near Des Plaines. The Duneland Trail begins and ends at the campground at Indiana Dunes State Park. The Border Trail begins at Belleau Woods Memorial at Des Plaines, passes through Camp Dan Beard and Camp Baden-Powell, and ends at Lions Woods near Des Plaines. *Terrain:* Roads, woods, beach. *Cycling:* Not recommended. *Awards:* Medal. *Submit:* Group leader's certification of completion of all 5 hikes, plus visits to the Chicago Academy of Sciences Museum and Fort Dearborn. *Register:* For Upward Trail and Trail Awinding, upon arrival at Camp Kiwanis; not required for the rest. *Sites:* Little Red Schoolhouse, Chicago Academy of Sciences Museum, Indiana Dunes State Park, Fort Dearborn, St. James Cemetery, Trailside Museum, Armitage Avenue Dam, Old Indian Cemetery, Dempster Dam, Belleau Woods Memorial, Devon Dam.

Fort Dearborn Massacre Trail

Location: Chicago, IL. *Theme:* Massacre near the fort. *Sponsor:* Troop 881 Trail Committee, c/o Bryan Albro, 1146 W. Mallard Dr., Palatine, IL 60067-6641, (847) 991-6793.
Length: 2 miles (straight). *Route:* The trail begins at Pioneer Court and follows Michigan Avenue to the former site of the Illinois Central Station. *Terrain:* City street. *Cycling:* Appropriate. *Awards:* Patch $2.00. *Submit:* No requirement. *Register:* Not required. *Sites:* Fort Dearborn Site, Massacre Site, Tribune Tower, Equitable Building, Wrigley Building, Michigan Avenue Bridge, Standard Oil Building, Chicago Public Library Cultural Center, Prudential Building.

Frank Lloyd Wright Heritage Trail

Location: Oak Park to River Forest, IL. *Theme:* Architecture. *Sponsor:* Thatcher Woods Area Council, BSA, 407 Thomas St., Forest Park, IL 60130, (312) 386-8108.
Length: 6.2 miles (straight). *Route:* The trail begins at the Oak Park Visitors Center, winds through that town, then heads west to end near the Des Plaines River in the Forest Preserve in River Forest. *Terrain:* City streets. *Cycling:* Appropriate. *Awards:* Patch $1.50. *Submit:* No requirement. *Register:* Not required. *Sites:* Oak Park Visitors Center,

Lake Street, Grace Episcopal Church, First United Church, Second Scoville Building, Unity Temple, Horse Show Fountain, Scoville Park, Edward W. McCready House, C.A. Sharpe House, Herman W. Mallen House, Hemingway House, James Hall Taylor House, Edwin H. Cheney House, Harry C. Goodrich House, First United Methodist Church, William G. Fricke House, Edgar Rice Burroughs House, Vernon S. Watson House, Frank Lloyd Wright Studio, Robert N. Erskine House, Harry S. Adams House, Frank Lloyd Wright House, Ginkgo Tree Book Shop, Austin Gardens, Trailside Museum, River Forest Methodist Church, Pilgrim Congregational Church, Thatcher Woods, Harlem School.

Indian Portage Trails

Location: Near Chicago, IL. *Theme:* Indian trails. *Sponsor:* Indian Portage Trails, 11140 S. Trumbull, Chicago, IL 60655-3530.
Length: Ausaganashkee Trail, 15.0 miles (loop). Gau-Nash-Ke Trail, 17.3, 20.3, or 16.0 miles (loop). Sheshikmaos Trail—17.3 miles (loop). *Routes:* Ausaganashkee begins at Rocky Glen Forest Preserve and follows the Des Plaines River and Chicago Sanitary and Shipping Canal. Gau-Nash-Ke begins at Camp Kiwanis and circles Saganashkee Slough. Sheshikamaos begins at the Little Red School House parking lot and follows the Illinois and Michigan Canal before circling back through the woods to the start. *Terrain:* Woods. *Cycling:* Not recommended. *Awards:* 3 Patches $2.00 each which form 1 large patch; Repeat Feather $0.50; Snow, Rain and Camping Segments $0.80 each. *Submit:* No requirement. *Register:* Not required. *Sites:* Argonne National Laboratory, White Oak Woods, Crooked Creek Woods, Swallow Cliff, Ruins of Athens, Limestone Quarry, Beeline Bog, Waterfall Glen, Tomahawk Slough, St. James Church, Cal-Sag Bridge, Atomic Waste Burial Site, Little Red School House, Long John Slough, Old Sacred Heart Church, Indian Signal Station.

Indian Trail Tree Trail

Location: Near Chicago, IL. *Theme:* Local history. *Sponsor:* Sauk Thorn Creek Trails, Inc., c/o Eleanor Blouin, HC 81, Box 9407, Cassville, MO 65625, (417) 271-4020.
Length: 12.0 miles (straight). *Route:* The trail begins at the north side of Devon Ave. in

Dam No. 4 East Preserve and heads north to end at the picnic area of Dam No. 1 Woods. *Terrain:* Woods. *Cycling:* Not appropriate. *Awards:* Patch $3.75; Repeat Feather $1.75. *Submit:* Patch order form. *Register:* Not required. *Sites:* Dam No. 4 South, Dam No. 1.

Lewis & Clark Trail

Location: Wood River, IL. *Theme:* Route of Lewis & Clark. *Sponsor:* Lewis & Clark Trail Association, P.O. Box 385, Wood River, IL 62095.

Length: 13.5 miles (straight). *Route:* The trail begins at the Lewis & Clark Monument near Hartford, and follows the Mississippi River northward. *Terrain:* Levee along river. *Cycling:* Appropriate. *Awards:* Medal $3.50; Patch $2.50; Repeat Patch $1.00; Neckerchief $1.00; Anniversary Patch $1.25. *Submit:* No requirement. *Register:* Advance registration required. *Sites:* Lincoln-Douglas Square, Illinois Power Company Power Plant, Lock & Dam No. 26, Lovejoy Monument, Alton City Cemetery, Piasa Bird Painting, Lover's Leap, Oakwood Cemetery.

Lincoln Bicycle Trail

Location: Springfield, IL. *Theme:* Abraham Lincoln. *Sponsor:* Abraham Lincoln Council, BSA, P.O. Box 7125, Springfield, IL 62791-7125, (217) 546-5570, fax (217) 546-0598, alcbsa@juno.com.

Length: 25.0 miles (straight). *Route:* The trail begins at New Salem and ends a Stuart Park near Veterans Pkwy. *Terrain:* Roads. *Cycling:* Required. *Awards:* 25-Mile Patch $3.00; 50-Mile Patch $3.00. *Submit:* Patch order form. *Register:* Not required.

Lincoln Circuit Trail

Location: Champaign and Vermillion Counties, IL. *Theme:* Portion of the route traveled by Abraham Lincoln when he rode to the circuit courts in 1847-59 between Urbana and Danville. *Sponsor:* Ralph Kuchenbrod, 202 Western Dr., St. Joseph, IL 61873, (217) 469-7088.

Length: 18.5 miles (straight). *Route:* The trail begins in the Salt Fork Forest Preserve and heads east to finish in Kickapoo State Park. *Terrain:* Gravel and paved country roads, secondary road, and a wooded cross-country trail. *Cycling:* Not recommended. *Awards:* Patch $2.00. *Submit:* Patch request. *Register:* Not required. *Sites:* DAR 1922

Monument, Pollywog Strip Mines, Friend of Lincoln Monument, Middle Fork River.

Lincoln Heritage Trail

Location: Springfield, IL. *Theme:* Abraham Lincoln. *Sponsor:* John Washburn, 2051 S. Gate Dr., Decatur, IL 62521.

Length: 10-20 miles (loop or straight). *Route:* The actual trail route is to be determined by the group, but the suggested start is the Lincoln Home Visitors' Center. For the award, hikers must visit 3 specified sites and 2 additional sites from a list of 6. *Terrain:* City streets. *Cycling:* Appropriate. *Awards:* Patch $2.00. *Submit:* No requirement. *Register:* Not required. *Sites:* Old State House, Lincoln Tomb, Lincoln Home, Lincoln Family Church, New Salem Park, Lincoln R.R. Depot, Lincoln Law Office, Marine Bank, Visitors' Center.

Lincoln Heritage Trail

Location: Springfield, IL. *Theme:* Abraham Lincoln. *Sponsor:* Abraham Lincoln Council, BSA, P.O. Box 7125, Springfield, IL 67291-7125, (217) 546-5570, fax (217) 546-0598, alcbsa@juno.com.

Length: Less than 2 miles (straight). *Route:* This is a set of four tours, to be done during the weekend of the Lincoln Pilgrimage (see the information under the Lincoln Trail). The visits are to New Salem Village, Lincoln's Home, the Old Capitol and Lincoln's Tomb. *Terrain:* City streets. *Cycling:* Not appropriate. *Awards:* 4 Patches $3.00 each. *Submit:* Patch order form. *Register:* In advance, along with registration for the Pilgrimage.

Lincoln Land Cub Trail

Location: Springfield, IL. *Theme:* Abraham Lincoln. *Sponsor:* Abraham Lincoln Council, BSA, P.O. Box 7125, Springfield, IL 62791-7125, (217) 546-5570, fax (217) 546-0598, alcbsa@juno.com.

Length: Less than 2 miles (straight). *Route:* The route includes the Old State Capitol, the Lincoln Home, and at least two of the following: New Salem State Park, the Long Nine Building, the Lincoln Law Office, the Great Western Railroad Depot, the Lincoln Family Church, the Springfield Marine Bank and the St. Nicholas Hotel. *Terrain:* City streets. *Cycling:* Not permitted. *Awards:* Patch. *Register:* In advance, to receive certification form. *Submit:* Completed to certification.

Lincoln Trail

Location: New Salem State Park to Stuart Park, Springfield, IL. *Theme:* Abraham Lincoln. *Sponsor:* Abraham Lincoln Council, BSA, P.O. Box 7125, Springfield, IL 62791-7125, (217) 546-5570, fax (217) 546-0598, alcbsa@juno.com.

Length: 20.0 miles (straight). *Route:* The trail goes from New Salem State Park to Lincoln's tomb. Annually, this may be done as a group pilgrimage, and the EPA will also offer a patch that day for hikers who gather litter along the trail. *Terrain:* Roads. *Cycling:* Not appropriate. *Awards:* Medal $5.00; First-Time Patch (Illinois Lincolnland Trail) $2.00; First Repeat Patch (New Salem Railsplitter) $5.00; Second Repeat Patch (Debates With Stephen Douglas) $5.00; Third Repeat Patch (Farewell to Springfield) $5.00; Pilgrimage Patch $3.00. *Submit:* For the first hike, the unit leader must confirm that the hiker has read a book on Abraham Lincoln and has written a 300-word report. No requirement other than hiking is required for repeat hikes. Register:. *Register:* For the Pilgrimage, preregistration with the sponsor at least 4 days before the event is encouraged, so Pilgrimage awards may be waiting at the beginning of the trail. *Sites:* Oak Ridge Cemetery, Lincoln Tomb, Restored New Salem Village, State Capitol.

Little Woodsman Nature Trails

Location: Cook County, IL. *Theme:* Nature. *Sponsor:* Sauk Thorn Creek Trails, Inc., c/o Eleanor Blouin, HC 81, Box 9407, Cassville, MO 65625, (417) 271-4020.

Trails: Trailside Museum (no nature trails). Sandridge Nature Center (has trails). Little Red Schoolhouse, (15-, 30- and 60-minute walks). Pilcher Park Nature Museum, (several trails). River Trail Nature Center, (has trails). Crabtree Nature Center, (20 to 90 minutes each trail). *Route:* Each of the six forest preserves has a nature center which must be visited, and all of the nature trails at each center must be walked to qualify for awards. *Terrain:* Woods. *Cycling:* Not appropriate. *Awards:* Medal $3.50; Center (Smokey the Bear) Patch $3.00; 6 Section Patches $3.00 each; Repeat Feather $1.75. *Submit:* Request for patches. *Register:* Not

required. *Sites:* Little Red Schoolhouse, Flowing Well, French Fort, Conservatory, Miniature Train.

Martyrdom Trail

Location: Nauvoo to Carthage, IL. *Theme:* Joseph Smith's character and accomplishments. *Sponsor:* Orville Hale, Martyrdom Trail Committee, P.O. Box 223, Rt. 1, Box 57, Nauvoo, IL 62345, (217) 453-6543.

Length: 23 miles (straight). *Route:* The trail generally follows the 1843 Nauvoo-Carthage Road. *Terrain:* Lightly traveled rural roads. *Cycling:* Appropriate. *Awards:* Patch $2.50. *Submit:* No requirement. *Register:* At least 14 days in advance. *Sites:* Joseph Smith Farmstead, LDS Visitors Center, Pioneer Cemetery, Carthage Jail and Visitors Center, Times & Seasons Building, Browning Home and Gunshop, Cultural Hall, Joseph Smith Historic Center, Old Saints Cemetery, Webb Blacksmith Shop, Nauvoo State Park, E.P. Colton House.

Mi-Tig-Wa-Ti Trail

Location: Cook County, IL. *Theme:* Recreation. *Sponsor:* Sauk Thorn Creek Trails, Inc., c/o Eleanor Blouin, HC 81, Box 9407, Cassville, MO 65625, (417) 271-4020.

Length: 13.0 miles (straight). *Route:* The trail begins at Bemis Woods and ends at Brezina Woods. *Terrain:* City streets. *Cycling:* Possible. *Awards:* Patch $3.25. *Submit:* Patch order form. *Register:* Not required.

Oak Ridge Cemetery Trails

Location: Oak Ridge Cemetery, Springfield, IL. *Theme:* Abraham Lincoln. *Sponsor:* Abraham Lincoln Council, BSA, P.O. Box 7125, Springfield, IL 62791-7125, (217) 546-5570, fax (217) 546-0598, alcbsa@juno.com. *Lengths:* Introductory Trail, 0.5 hours. Intermediate Trail, 1.5 hours. Advanced Trail, 1.5 hours. *Route:* The Introductory Trail focuses on the Lincoln Tomb. The Intermediate Trail includes the Lincoln Tomb and the Korean and Vietnam Memorials. The Advanced Trail involves compass headings in the old section of the cemetery. *Terrain:* Sidewalks. *Cycling:* Not appropriate. *Awards:* 3 Patches $3.50 each. *Submit:* Patch order form. *Register:* Not required.

Old Nauvoo Trail

Location: Nauvoo, IL. *Theme:* History of town. *Sponsor:* Old Nauvoo Trail, c/o Cynthia B. House, 716 E. Oakton St., Arlington Heights, IL 60004.

Length: Estimated 7 hours to walk. *Route:* The trail begins at the Visitors Center, loops through downtown, and returns to the start. *Terrain:* City streets. *Cycling:* Possible, but does not qualify for awards. *Awards:* Patch $2.50. *Submit:* No requirement. *Register:* Required for trail guide. *Sites:* Visitors Center, Statue Gardens, Scovil Bakery, Jonathan Browning House and Gunshop, Brigham Young House, Print Shop, Times and Seasons Printing Office, Mansion House, Brick Kiln, Webb Wagon and Blacksmith Shop, Temple Sunstone, Wilford Woodruff House, Graves of Joseph, Emma and Hyrum Smith, Joseph W. Cooledge House, Historical Society Museum, Heber C. Kimball House, Nauvoo Temple Site.

Oxpojke Trail

Location: Bishop Hill, IL. *Theme:* Local history. *Sponsor:* Bishop Hill Heritage Association, P.O. Box 1853, Bishop Hill, IL 61419, (309) 927-3504.

Length: 11 miles (loop). *Route:* The trail begins and ends at the north end of the main road through Bishop Hill, just before the bridge over the Edwards River, and circles Red Oak Grove. *Terrain:* City streets and woods that have not been well maintained. *Cycling:* Not recommended. *Awards:* Patch $1.25. *Submit:* No requirement. *Register:* Upon arrival at Steeple Building. *Sites:* Grist Mill Sites, Dairy Caves, Brick Kiln, Burial Ground, Saw Mill, Dugouts.

Palos Pioneer Trail

Location: Country Lane Woods near Chicago, IL. *Theme:* Nature and local history. *Sponsor:* Sauk Thorn Creek Trails, Inc., c/o Eleanor Blouin, HC 81, Box 9407, Cassville, MO 65625, (417) 271-4020.

Length: 15.0 miles (loop). *Route:* The trail begins and ends at the parking lot off Mannheim Rd. *Terrain:* Woods. *Cycling:* Not appropriate. *Awards:* Patch $3.75; Repeat Feather $1.75. *Submit:* Patch order form. *Register:* Not required. *Sites:* Hogwash Slough, Tuma Lake, Tomahawk Slough, Bull Frog Lake, Maple Lake, Willow Springs.

Pecatonica Prairie Path

Location: Pecatonica, IL. *Theme:* Nature and recreation. *Sponsor:* Dave Derwent, President, Pecatonica Prairie Path, Inc., 248 W. Horner St., P.O. Box 534, Pecatonica, IL 61063 (815) 239-2180.

Length: 21 miles (straight). *Route:* The trail goes from Meridian Rd. to Hillcrest Rd., through Winnebago, Pecatonica, Ridott and Freeport. *Terrain:* Original railroad grade ballast. *Cycling:* Appropriate. *Awards:* Patch $1.00. *Submit:* No requirement. *Register:* Not required.

Pierce Lake Trail

Location: Rockford, IL. *Theme:* Recreation. *Sponsor:* Bryce J. Russell, 5904 Princess Dr., Rockford, IL 61109-1840, (815) 398-7455.

Length: 6.0 miles (loop). *Route:* The trail begins at the Boy Scout camping area at Pierce Lake and circles the shore with a trail marked with blue dots and blue triangles. *Terrain:* Woods. *Cycling:* Not appropriate. *Awards:* Patch $3.50; Anniversary Patch (changes each year) $4.00; Duck Design Back Patch $6.00. *Submit:* Patch order form. *Register:* Not required. *Sites:* Pierce Lake, Lone Rock.

Potawatomi Trail

Location: Pekin, IL. *Theme:* Recreation and nature. *Sponsor:* Pekin Recreation Dept., 1701 Court St., Pekin, IL 61554, (309) 347-7275.

Length: 7.0 miles (loop). *Route:* The trail begins and ends at the totem pole located behind the stables in McNauthton Park and follows the route designated by the red markers. *Terrain:* Woodland path. *Cycling:* Not appropriate. *Awards:* Patch $2.00. *Submit:* Request for patches (can purchase in the Park District Recreation Office). *Register:* Not required. *Sites:* Lick Creek, Totem Pole, Delwood Camp, Lick Creek Golf Course, Augsburg Church, Bailly Cemetery.

Rapatuck Trail

Location: Fellheimer Scout Reservation, east of Knoxville, IL. *Theme:* Recreation. *Sponsor:* Illowa Council, BSA, 311 E. Main St., Room 607, Galesburg, IL 61401-4895, (309) 343-1145.

Length: 5-16 miles (loop). *Route:* The trail begins at the camp visitor center, and makes loops of 5, 10 and 16 miles which return to the start. *Terrain:* Woods. *Cycling:* Not recommended. *Awards:* 3 Patches $2.50 each; Pin $3.50; Back Patch $15.00; Rain Spirit, Sun Spirit and Arctic Patches $3.50 each. *Submit:* No requirement. *Register:* Advance registration required. *Sites:* Covered Bridge, Grist Mill Remains, Coal Veins, Spoon River, Ancient Quarry, Stage Coach Station.

Red Caboose Trail

Location: Wheaton and West Chicago, IL. *Theme:* Chicago, Aurora and Elgin Railway. *Sponsor:* Three Fires Council, BSA, 415 N. Second St., St. Charles, IL 60174, (630) 584-9250.

Length: 11.36 miles (straight). *Route:* The trail begins at the Diecke Scout Center in Wheaton and heads northwest along the C.A.&E. railroad grade to end at Pratt's Wayne Woods Forest Preserve. *Terrain:* Asphalt, crushed stone, and dirt path. *Cycling:* Appropriate (part of Illinois Prairie Path bicycle route). *Awards:* Patch $4.00. *Submit:* No requirement. *Register:* Not required. *Sites:* Jewell Road Station, Pleasant Hill Station, Geneva Road Station, Klain Farm, Timber Ridge Forest Preserve, DuPage River, Prince Crossing Station, Wayne Substation, Lakewood Station, St. Andrews Station, Smith Road Station, Pratt's Wayne Woods Forest Preserve, West Wayne Siding, Hemp Mill.

River Ridge Back Pack Trail

Location: Forest Glen Preserve, Westville, IL. *Theme:* Nature. *Sponsor:* Piankeshaw Council, BSA, 704 N. Hazel, Danville, IL 61832.

Length: 11 miles (loop). *Route:* The trail begins and ends at the entrance to the "Old Barn Trail" and includes a portion of the Vermillion River bank. *Terrain:* Varied. *Cycling:* Not recommended. *Awards:* Patch $3.00. *Submit:* No requirement. *Register:* Advance registration required. *Sites:* Nature Center, Ranger Station, Visitor Center, Observation Tower, Arboretum, Tree Research Area.

Rock Cut Trail

Location: Rockford, IL. *Theme:* Recreation. *Sponsor:* Bryce J. Russell, 5904 Princess Dr., Rockford, IL 61109-1840, (815) 398-7455.

Length: 6.0 miles (loop). *Route:* The trail begins at the Boy Scout camping area, heads west to the edge of Rock Cut State Park, then southeast and east to circle Pierce Lake, then west to the point of beginning. *Terrain:* Woods. *Cycling:* Not appropriate. *Awards:* Patch $3.50. *Submit:* Patch order form. *Register:* Not required. *Sites:* Willow Creek, Pierce Lake.

Rock Island Arsenal Historical Trail

Location: Rock Island, IL. *Theme:* History of the Rock Island Arsenal. *Sponsor:* Rock Island Arsenal Historical Trail Committee, c/o Troop 664, P.O. Box 2744, Davenport, IA 52809; or Douglas C. Scovil, 2009 Ninth Ave., Rock Island, IL 61201, (309) 788-8811.

Length: 10.0 miles (loop). *Route:* After getting onto the island and going through the security gatehouse, the trail begins at Memorial Park and heads west on Rodman Ave., then crosses the Mississippi River at Fort Armstrong Ave. and crosses back to the island, heads east along the north bank, does a double loop to cover the eastern end of the island, and heads west to the point of beginning. *Terrain:* Roads. *Cycling:* Not appropriate. *Awards:* Patch $2.50. *Submit:* Order form on the bottom of the permission slip. *Register:* Two weeks in advance (only open on weekends and national holidays). *Sites:* Arsenal Sandstone Buildings, Clock Tower Building, Colonel Davenport's House, John M. Browning Memorial Museum, Lock and Dam No. 15, Rodman Monument, Rock Island Arsenal National Cemetery, Rock Island Prison Barracks.

Running Deer Trail

Location: Dirksen Park, Pekin, Il. *Theme:* Recreation and nature. *Sponsor:* Pekin Recreation Dept., 1701 Court St., Pekin, IL 61554, (309) 347-7275.

Length: Just over 3 miles (loop). *Route:* The trail begins and ends at the parking area on Rte. 98, just north of McNaughton Park and loops to the west and then to the east. *Terrain:* Woodland paths. *Cycling:* Not appropriate. *Awards:* Patch $2.00. *Submit:* Request for patches (they may be purchased in the Park District Recreation Office). *Register:* Not required. *Sites:* RC Flying Field, Archery Range.

Sac-Fox Trail

Location: Andalusia, IL. *Theme:* Memorial

to Chief Black Hawk and his Indian tribes. *Sponsor:* Troop 109, P.O. Box 232, Moline, IL 61265.

Length: 15 miles (loop). *Route:* The trail begins at Loud Thunder Boy Scout Camp, and circles Lake George to return to the start. *Terrain:* Wilderness. *Cycling:* Not recommended. *Awards:* Medal $5.00; Patch $2.50. *Submit:* Signed credentials (received upon advance registration). *Register:* Advance registration required.

Sauk-Thorn Creek Trail

Location: Cook County, IL. *Theme:* Recreation. *Sponsor:* Sauk Thorn Creek Trails, Inc., c/o Eleanor Blouin, HC 81, Box 9407, Cassville, MO 65625, (417) 271-4020.

Length: 18.5 miles (straight). *Route:* The trail begins at Torrence and Glenwood-Lansing Rd. and heads to Sauk Lake. *Terrain:* Roads. *Cycling:* Possible. *Awards:* Patch $3.25. *Submit:* Patch order form. *Register:* Not required.

Sauk Thorn Creek Training Trails

Location: Cook County Forest Preserves District, IL. *Theme:* Recreation. *Sponsor:* Sauk Thorn Creek Trails, Inc., c/o Eleanor Blouin, HC 81, Box 9407, Cassville, MO 65625, (417) 271-4020.

Lengths and Forest Division: Big Bend Lake, 5.0 miles (straight) Des Plaines. Bull Frog Lake, 6.0 miles (straight) Palos. Golf Course, 5.0 miles (loop), North Branch. Indian Boundary, 7.0 miles (straight) Indian Bound. Laughing Squaw, 8.0 miles (loop) Palos. Little Red Schoolhouse, 6.5 miles (straight) Palos. Miami Indians, 5.0 miles (loop) North Branch. North Creek, 5.5 miles (straight) Thorn Creek. Salt Creek, 6.0 miles (loop) Salt Creek. Sauk Trail Road,5.0 miles (straight) Thorn Creek. Skokie Lagoons, 6.5 miles (straight) Skokie. *Terrain:* Hiking, cycling and bridle paths. *Cycling:* Appropriate over a portion of the trails. *Awards:* Patch for each trail $2.75. *Submit:* Patch order form. *Register:* Not required. *Sites:* Tomahawk Slough, Bullfrog Lake, Papoose Lake, Horse Collar Slough, St. James Church Site, Wampum Lake, John McCoy Homesite, St. Joseph Cemetery, Pioneer Cabin Site, Forty Acre Woods.

Scouting Prayer Trail

Location: National Shrine of Our Lady of the Snows, Belleville, IL. *Theme:* Duty to God. *Sponsor:* Catholic Committee on Scouting, P.O. Box 372, Belleville, IL 62222.

Length: 5.0 miles (loop). *Route:* The trail begins and ends at the Visitors Center, and includes walking twice around the perimeter of the Shrine, plus the loop through the Way of the Cross area. *Terrain:* Roads. *Cycling:* Not appropriate. *Awards:* Patch $4.50. *Submit:* Patch application form (patches are available at the Visitors Center at the end of the hike). *Register:* Not required. *Sites:* Church of Our Lady of the Snows, Agony Garden, Fathers' Memorial Wall, Annunciation Garden, Mothers' Prayer Walk, Resurrection Garden, Rosary Court, Christ the King Chapel, Mary Chapel.

She-Ka-Gong Trail

Location: Chicago, IL. *Theme:* Local history. *Sponsor:* Sauk Thorn Creek Trails, c/o Eleanor Blouin, HC 81, Box 9407, Cassville, MO 65625, (417) 271-4020.

Length: 12.0 miles (straight). *Route:* The trail begins at the Museum of Science and Industry and heads east on 57th St., north along the lakefront, west on Balbo Dr., north on Columbus Dr., west on Congress Pkwy., and north on Michigan Ave. to the Water Tower. *Terrain:* City streets. *Cycling:* Appropriate. *Awards:* Patch $3.75; Repeat Feather $1.75. *Submit:* Patch order form. *Register:* Not required. *Sites:* Water Tower, Museum of Science and Industry, Shedd Aquarium, Museum of Natural History, McCormick Place, Adler Planetarium, Art Institute, Buckingham Fountain, Lincoln Monument.

Spokes on the Wheel Auto Tour

Location: Hancock County, IL. *Theme:* Early Mormon history. *Sponsor:* Old Nauvoo Trail, c/o Cynthia B. House, 716 E. Oakton St., Arlington Heights, IL 60004.

Length: Mileage will vary. *Route:* The trail begins at the Nauvoo Restoration Inc. Visitor Center and proceeds through many cities in the county to return to the start. *Terrain:* Roads. *Cycling:* Possible, but cars are recommended. *Awards:* Patch $2.50. *Submit:* No requirement. *Register:* Required for route map. *Sites:* Joseph Smith Homestead, Carthage Jail, Webster Community Church, Fort Edward Memorial, Yelrome Site, Geode Glen Park, Nauvoo State Park, Keokuck Dam.

Spoon River Valley Trail

Location: Fulton County, IL. *Theme:* Nature and history. *Sponsor:* Spoon River Scenic Committee, P.O. Box 59, Ellisville, IL 61431.

Length: 55 miles (straight). *Route:* The trail begins at London Mills and generally follows the Spoon River to Dickson Mounds. *Terrain:* Varies. *Cycling:* Appropriate over many sections. *Awards:* Medal $2.75; Section Patches $1.00 each. *Submit:* No requirement. *Register:* Not required. *Sites:* Dickson Mounds State Museum, Mt. Pisgah, Rice Lake Wildlife Refuge, Gobbler's Knob, Riverside Park, Lakeland Park.

Stephenson-Black Hawk Trail

Location: Lena, IL. *Theme:* Black Hawk War and local history. *Sponsor:* Stephenson County Convention & Visitors Bureau, 2047 AYP Rd., Freeport, IL 61032.

Length: 13 miles (loop). *Route:* The trail passes through the town of Lena and rural areas to the north and west. It can be begun at any of the 10 points of interest. *Terrain:* County and township roads. *Cycling:* Appropriate. *Awards:* Medal, Patch. *Submit:* Completed application. *Register:* Not required. *Sites:* Dodd's Stage Coach Inn, High Point Hill, Lena Water Tower, Lake Le-Aqua-Na, Pioneer Cemetery, Lena Maid Meat Processing Plant, Grist Mill, William Waddams Monument, Stephenson-Black Hawk Pursuit Trail, Crossroads Cemetery, Montague Homestead.

Sun Singer Trail

Location: Monticello, IL. *Theme:* Recreation. *Sponsor:* Sun Singer Trail Committee, P.O. Box 50, Monticello, IL 61856.

Length: 28.25 miles (straight). *Route:* The trail endpoints are at Bryant College and McClure Realty. *Terrain:* Dense woods. *Cycling:* Not recommended. *Awards:* Medal; Patch. *Submit:* Group leader's certification of completion. *Register:* Advance registration required. *Sites:* Bryant College, Allerton Park, Pioneer Cemetery, Lost Garden, Sun Singer Statue.

Trail of the Fu Dogs

Location: Monticello, IL. *Theme:* Recreation. *Sponsor:* Sun Singer Trail Committee, P.O. Box 50, Monticello, IL 61856.

Length: 19.25 miles (straight). *Route:* The trail begins at Bryant College and proceeds by car to Lost Garden, where walking starts, then ends at McClure Realty. *Terrain:* Dense woods. *Cycling:* Not appropriate. *Awards:* Medal; Patch. *Submit:* Group leader's certification of completion. *Register:* Advance registration required. *Sites:* Sunken Garden, Allerton House, Garden of the Fu Dogs, Formal Gardens, House of the Gold Buddhas.

Trail of the Lagoons

Location: Cook County, IL. *Theme:* Recreation. *Sponsor:* Sauk Thorn Creek Trails, Inc., c/o Eleanor Blouin, HC 81, Box 9407, Cassville, MO 65625, (417) 271-4020.

Length: 14.0 miles (loop). *Route:* The trail begins at Harms Woods, heads to Skokie Lagoons, and returns. *Terrain:* City streets. *Cycling:* Possible. *Awards:* Patch $3.25. *Submit:* Patch order form. *Register:* Not required.

U.S. Grant Pilgrimage

Location: Galena, IL. *Theme:* The 18th President of the U.S. *Sponsor:* Blackhawk Area Council, BSA, c/o Galena Chamber of Commerce, 101 Bouthillier, Galena, IL 61036, (815) 777-0203.

Length: Approx. 5 miles (straight). *Route:* The hike begins at the Honeywell Micro Switch Plant west of Galena High School, and ends across the Galena River at Grant's home. *Terrain:* City streets. *Cycling:* Not permitted. *Awards:* 3" Patch $1.50; 6" Patch $5.00; Commemorative Patch $5.00; Back Patch $10.00; Belt Buckle $10.00; Neckerchief $4.00; Hat $5.00; Hat Pin $2.00; Mug $5.00. *Submit:* No requirement. *Register:* Required in advance. This is an annual event, generally held at the end of April. *Sites:* Chamber of Commerce, New Foot Bridge, Grant Park, Grant's Home.

Wacca Lake Trail

Location: Nashville, IL. *Theme:* Recreation. *Sponsor:* Wacca Lake Trail, c/o Nashville Pharmacy, 117 W. St. Louis St., Nashville, IL 62263, (618) 327-8522.

Length: 9.0 miles (loop). *Route:* The trail begins on the shore of Wacca Lake, south of Little Bear Camping Area. It circles the lake counter-clockwise and returns to the start. *Terrain:* Gravel road and woods. *Cycling:*

Not recommended. *Awards:* Medal $4.00; Patch $2.50; Repeat Patch $1.00. *Submit:* No requirement. *Register:* Advance registration required.

William D. Boyce Trail

Location: Ottawa, IL. *Theme:* William D. Boyce, organizer of the BSA. *Sponsor:* W.D. Boyce Council, BSA, 614 NE Madison Ave., Peoria, IL 61603, (309) 673-6136, (800) 369-5069.

Length: 16.0 miles (straight). *Route:* The trail begins in Starved Rock State Park and heads through Utica and to Ottawa along the towpath of the I & M Canal. *Terrain:* Roads and canal towpath. *Cycling:* Not appropriate. *Awards:* Medal $3.00; Patch $2.00. *Submit:* Patch request. *Register:* In advance. *Sites:* W.D. Boyce Statue, Ottawa Ave. Cemetery, Buffalo Rock State Park, Lasalle County Historical Museum, Father Marquette Memorial, Illinois-Michigan Canal, Halfway House.

Wolf Lake Trail

Location: William W. Powers Conservation Area near Chicago, IL. *Theme:* Nature and conservation. *Sponsor:* Sauk Thorn Creek Trails, c/o Eleanor Blouin, HC 81, Box 9407, Cassville, MO 65625, (417) 271-4020.

Length: 8.5 miles (loop). *Route:* The trail begins and ends at the parking lot near the superintendent's office at the northwest end of the park. *Terrain:* Woods. *Cycling:* Not appropriate. *Awards:* Patch $3.75; Repeat Feather $1.75; Back Patch $5.25. *Submit:* Awards order form. *Register:* Only for groups of more than 25 people. *Sites:* Wolf Lake.

Other Illinois Awards

Century Club Awards—4 main patches for hiking (100 miles), canoeing (100 miles), cycling (250 miles) and camping (25 nights) $1.50 each; markers for additional miles $0.25 each. Sponsored by Century Club Awards, Inc., 1715 Hollow St., McHenry IL 60050.

Hikers Club Award (Sauk Thorn Creek Trails)—Main patch $3.75, Mile strips for 50, 100, 300 and 500 miles $3.75 each. Sponsored by Sauk Thorn Creek Trails, Inc., c/o Eleanor

Blouin, HC 81, Box 9407, Cassville, MO 65625, (417) 271-4020.

Formerly Sponsored Trails

Amaquonsippi Trail
Arboretum Trail
Campground Road Training Trail
Cantigny-McCormick Trail
Cantigny Woods Training Trail
Carl Sandburg Trail
Chicago Fire Dept. Ranger Trails
Chicago Portage Trail
Chief Senachwine Trail
Decatur Historic Trail
Eagle Cliff Wilderness Trail
Embarrass River Trail
Fort Beggs Trek
Fort Russell Wilderness Trail
Four Seasons Nature Trail
Freedom of the Press Trail
George McClung-A. Lincoln Trail
George W. Dolton Trail
Grafton-Marquette Trail
Graw-Mill Trail
Illini Trail
Indian Butterfield Trail
John Mason Peck Pilgrimage Trail Hike
Keepataw Trail
Kewanee Stagecoach Trail
Leekwinai Trail
Lewis & Clark Pilgrimage Trail
Lincoln Douglas Trail
Marquette's Landing Trail
Massacre Trace
Metamore Courthouse Trail
Moccasin Gap Trail
Notched Hoe Trail
Ozark Shawnee Trail
Peoria-Galena Coach Road Trail
Piasa Red Bird Trail
Portage Trail
Red Covered Bridge Trail
Sandridge Nature Training Trail
Shawneetown St. Louis Trail
Somme Woods Training Trail
Springtime Nature Trail
Thomas Lincoln Hist. Scout Pilgrimage
Three Rivers Trail
Tomahawk Trail
Turtle Head Lake Training Trail
Wood River Massacre Historic Trail

INDIANA

Al White Trail

Location: Camp Bradford, Indianapolis, IN. *Theme:* Recreation. *Sponsor:* Crossroads of America Council, BSA, 1900 N. Meridian St., Indianapolis, IN 46202, (317) 925-1900.

Length: 8 miles (loop). *Route:* The trail starts at the dedication marker in the camporee field, proceeds along Sycamore Creek, and returns to the start. *Terrain:* Hilly woods. *Cycling:* Not recommended. *Awards:* Patch $2.50. *Submit:* No requirement. *Register:* Not required.

American Heritage Trail

Location: Bear Wallow Hill, Nashville, IN. *Theme:* Revolutionary War history. *Sponsor:* Trail Headquarters, 3980 N. Bear Wallow Rd., Nashville, IN 47448-9451, (812) 988-2636.

Length: 12.1 miles (loop). *Route:* The trail begins and ends at the Trail Headquarters at Bear Wallow Hill. *Terrain:* Cross-country. *Cycling:* Not permitted. *Awards:* Ft. McHenry Medal $5.00; Spirit of '76 Patch $4.00; Historic Flags Patch $4.00; Presidential Seal Patch $4.00; 4 Repeat pins $2.00 each; Neckerchief $6.50; Certificate $0.15 (Miles for this and other trails sponsored by the same organization may be aggregated toward patches for 50, 100, 200, 300 & 500 total miles.). *Submit:* No requirement. *Register:* Advance registration required. *Sites:* Circle of Historic American Flags.

Bears of Blue River Trail

Location: Shelbyville, IN. *Theme:* Indian and pioneer routes. *Sponsor:* Shelby County Historical Society, 52 W. Broadway, Shelbyville, IN 46176, (317) 392-4634; or Jack Warble, (317) 398-6931.

Length: 14.8 miles (straight). *Route:* The trail begins at the Big Blue River Bridge on US 52, follows the river bank, passes through Freeport, and follows the old Morristown-Shelbyville toll road, and ends at the WSVL Radio Station. *Terrain:* Roads and river bank. *Cycling:* Not recommended. *Awards:* Medal; Patch; Repeat patch. *Submit:* Awards order form. *Register:* In advance. *Sites:* Hog Back Ridge, Fox Bridge, Freeport, Marion.

Brown County Bike Trail

Location: Brown County, IN. *Theme:* Recreation and scenery. *Sponsor:* Trail Headquarters, 3980 N. Bear Wallow Rd., Nashville, IN 47448-9451, (812) 988-2636.

Length: 25.8 miles (loop). *Route:* The trail begins and ends at the Bear Wallow Trail Headquarters. *Terrain:* Hilly dirt roads. *Cycling:* Permitted. *Awards:* Medal $6.00; Patch $5.00. *Submit:* Group leader's certificate of completion. *Register:* 1 week in advance.

Chain O' Lakes Canoe Trail

Location: Chain-O-Lakes Park, Noble County, IN. *Theme:* Recreation. *Sponsor:* Pokagon-Kekiona Trails, Inc., P.O. Box 192, Angola, IN 46703, (219) 833-1550.

Length: 6.0 miles (loop). *Route:* The trail begins at the eastern end of Sand Lake, then heads westward along the northern shores of Sand Lake, Weber Lake, Mud Lake, River Lake and Miller Lake, then heads back along their southern shores to the point of beginning. *Terrain:* Lakes and connecting rivers. *Cycling:* Impossible. *Awards:* Patch $3.00. *Submit:* Group leader's certification of completion. *Register:* Not required.

Chain O' Lakes Trail

Location: Chain-O-Lakes Park, Noble County, IN. *Theme:* Recreation. *Sponsor:* Pokagon-Kekionga Trails, Inc., P.O. Box 192, Angola, IN 46703, (219) 833-1550.

Length: 10 miles (loop). *Route:* The trail may be started at either the group campsite or the parking lot near Sand Lake. *Terrain:* Woods. *Cycling:* Not recommended; canoeing a 6-mile trail in the park also qualifies for the awards. *Awards:* Medal $3.00; Patch $3.00; Repeat Pins $1.00 each. *Submit:* Group leader's certification of completion of hike and anti-litter project. *Register:* Not required. *Sites:* Old School House, Sand Lake, Miller River, Lake Bowen.

Chank-Ten-Un-Gi Trail

Location: Indianapolis, IN. *Theme:* Indian Trail Route. *Sponsor:* Crossroads of America

Council, BSA, 1900 N. Meridian St., Indianapolis, IN 46202, (317) 925-1900.
Length: 16 miles. *Route:* The trail begins at Camp Belzer and ends at the County Dock. *Terrain:* Dirt path, roads, woods. *Cycling:* Not permitted. *Awards:* Medal; Patch; 4 Repeat Arrow Points. *Submit:* Group leader's certificate of completion. *Register:* At least two weeks in advance. *Sites:* County Line Boat Dock, Geist Reservoir, Explorer Canoe Base, Fall Creek Road, Indianapolis Water Company, Belzer Reservation.

Chief Little Turtle Trail

Location: Anthony Wayne Reservation, Ft. Wayne, IN. *Theme:* History of reservation, Miami Indians, and Chief Little Turtle. *Sponsor:* Pokagon-Kekionga Trails, Inc., P.O. Box 192, Angola, IN 46703, (219) 833-1550.
Length: 10 miles (loop). *Route:* The trail begins and ends at the Camp Little Turtle Office, looping through most of the reservation. *Terrain:* Woods. *Cycling:* Not recommended. *Awards:* Medal $3.00; Patch $3.00. *Submit:* Group leader's certification of completion of hike and anti-litter project. *Register:* At least 1 week before hiking.

Clark's Advance Trail

Location: Vincennes, IN. *Theme:* Route taken by George Rogers Clark to capture Fort Sackville. *Sponsor:* Larry Benson, 148 Pine View Dr., Vincennes, IN 47591.
Length: 10.2 miles (straight). *Route:* The trail begins on the Indiana side of the Wabash River on Vigo St., and heads southward to the Clark Memorial in Vincennes. *Terrain:* Roads. *Cycling:* Appropriate. *Awards:* Patch $2.50. *Submit:* No requirements. *Register:* Not required. *Sites:* Clark Memorial, Vincennes Visitors Center.

Covered Bridge Trail

Location: Montezuma, IN. *Theme:* Covered bridges. *Sponsor:* Paul K. Bartlow, 420 Madison, Box 538, Montezuma, IN 47862, (765) 245-2728.
Length: 22.0 miles (loop). *Route:* The trail begins on a road north of the Ferndale Bait Shop, heads south and west to cross Rocky Fork Creek and Raccoon Creek, then northeast along Raccoon Creek and over the Mansfield Dam to the point of beginning. *Terrain:* Blacktop, gravel and unimproved

roads. *Cycling:* Permitted. *Awards:* Patch $2.50. *Submit:* Request for patches. *Register:* At least one week in advance. *Sites:* Mansfield Reservoir, Mansfield Dam, Fallen Rocks, Three Covered Bridges.

Deer Hollow Trek

Location: Anthony Wayne Reservation, Ft. Wayne, IN. *Theme:* Recreation. *Sponsor:* Pokagon-Kekionga Trails, Inc., P.O. Box 192, Angola, IN 46703, (219) 833-1550.
Length: 5 miles (loop). *Route:* The trail begins and ends at the Camp Little Turtle Office, circling around Auburn Lodge. *Terrain:* Woods. *Cycling:* Not recommended. *Awards:* Patch $3.00. *Submit:* Group leader's certification of completion of hike and anti-litter project. *Register:* At least 1 week before hiking. *Sites:* Jack Noll Chapel, Totem Pole, Long Lake, Rock Lake.

Flags of Our Nation Trail

Location: Bear Wallow Hill, Nashville, IN. *Theme:* Historical American Flags. *Sponsor:* Trail Headquarters, 3980 N. Bear Wallow Rd., Nashville, IN 47448-9451, (812) 988-2636.
Length: 12.1 miles (loop). *Route:* The trail begins and ends at the Trail Headquarters at Bear Wallow Hill. *Terrain:* Cross-country. *Cycling:* Not permitted. *Awards:* Medal; Patch (Miles for this and other trails sponsored by the same organization may be aggregated toward patches for 50, 100, 200, 300 & 500 total miles.). *Submit:* Patch order form. *Register:* Advance registration required. *Sites:* Display of American flags.

Flags of the Nations Trail

Location: Bear Wallow Hill, Nashville, IN. *Theme:* Outdoor Flag Exposition. *Sponsor:* Trail Headquarters, 3980 N. Bear Wallow Rd., Nashville, IN 47448-9451, (812) 988-2636.
Length: 13.0 miles (loop). *Route:* The trail begins and ends at the Trail Headquarters at Bear Wallow Hill. *Terrain:* Cross-country. *Cycling:* Not permitted. *Awards:* Medal; Patch (Miles for this and other trails sponsored by the same organization may be aggregated toward patches for 50, 100, 200, 300 & 500 total miles); Northwest Mountie Patch; Bavarian Dancers Patch; South American Flags Patch; Neckerchief . *Submit:* Patch order form. *Register:* Advance registration required. *Sites:* Display of foreign flags.

Foster Park Trail

Location: Foster Park, Ft. Wayne, IN. *Theme:* Physical fitness and history of David and Samuel Foster. *Sponsor:* Pokagon-Kekionga Trails, Inc., P.O. Box 192, Angola, IN 46703, (219) 833-1550.

Length: 6.5 miles (loop). *Route:* The trail begins at the park entrance, north of the golf course. It heads north along St. Mary's River to the Oakdale St. Bridge, turns and follows the river south to the Stellhorn Bridge (Lower Huntington Rd.), turns and returns to the start. *Terrain:* Riverbank. *Cycling:* Not recommended. *Awards:* Patch $3.00. *Submit:* Group leader's certification of completion of hike and anti-litter project. *Register:* Not required. *Sites:* Swinging Bridge, St. Mary's River.

Franke Park Trek

Location: Franke Park, Ft. Wayne, IN. *Theme:* Nature (formerly called Cub-Brownie Nature Trail). *Sponsor:* Pokagon-Kekionga Trails, Inc., P.O. Box 192, Angola, IN 46703, (219) 833-1550.

Length: 1.5 miles (loop). *Route:* The trail begins at the pond pavilion at the west end of Shoaff Lake, circles through the park and back to the start. *Terrain:* Woods and fields. *Cycling:* Not recommended. *Awards:* Patch $3.00. *Submit:* Group leader's certification of completion of hike and anti-litter project. *Register:* Not required. *Sites:* Australian Adventure, Soap Box Derby Track, African Veldt Animal Building.

Hindostan Falls Trail

Location: Loogootee, IN. *Theme:* Local history. *Sponsor:* Jack Stuckey, 307 Riley St., Loogootee, IN 47553, (812) 295-2321.

Length: 16.0 miles (straight). *Route:* The trail begins in downtown Lagootee and ends at the Schoak, IN Overlook Park near the White River. *Terrain:* Backroads. *Cycling:* Appropriate. *Awards:* Medal; Patch; Pin; Repeat Pin. *Submit:* Group leader's certificate of completion. *Register:* One week in advance. *Sites:* Courthouse, Overlook Park, Hindostan Falls, Judd Rock, White River, Old Mill, Old Stage Coach Road, Houton House, Houghton Bridge.

Indiana Lincoln Trail

Location: Maxville to Lincoln City, IN. *Theme:* Route taken by Lincoln when Abraham was 22 years old (also called Lincoln Boyhood Trail). *Sponsor:* Buffalo Trace Council, BSA, P.O. Box 3245, 1050 Bayard Park Dr., Evansville, IN 47731-3245, (812) 423-5246.

Length: 17 miles (straight). *Route:* The trail begins at the Ferry Landing Park and heads northeast to the Lincoln Memorial Shrine. *Terrain:* Rural roads. *Cycling:* Appropriate. *Awards:* Patch $4.00. *Submit:* Group leader's certification of completion. *Register:* Not required. *Sites:* Lincoln Living Farm, Sarah Lincoln Grigsby's Homesite and Grave, Lincoln Memorial Shrine, Lincoln Cabin Site, Pigeon Church, Nancy Hanks Lincoln's Grave, Old Mill Site, Fire Tower.

Johnny Appleseed Trek

Location: Ft. Wayne, IN. *Theme:* History and times of Johnny Appleseed. *Sponsor:* Pokagon-Kekionga Trails, Inc., P.O. Box 192, Angola, IN 46703, (219) 833-1550.

Length: 8 miles (loop). *Route:* The trail can start at either Johnny Appleseed Park or Bloomingdale Park, and hikers proceed to the other and return to their chosen start point. *Terrain:* City greenways. *Cycling:* Appropriate. *Awards:* Medal $3.00; Patch $3.00; Repeat Pin $1.00. *Submit:* Group leader's certification of completion of hike and anti-litter project. *Register:* Not required. *Sites:* Bloomingdale Park, Johnny Appleseed Park, Johnny Appleseed Grave Site, County Memorial Coliseum.

Kekionga Trail

Location: Ft. Wayne, IN. *Theme:* Historic Old Fort and City. *Sponsor:* Pokagon-Kekionga Trails, Inc., P.O. Box 192, Angola, IN 46703, (219) 833-1550.

Length: 10 miles (loop). *Route:* The trail begins at Historic Fort Wayne (Old Fort) heads south to cut through the city along Jefferson and returns to the Fort. *Terrain:* Paved streets. *Cycling:* Appropriate. *Awards:* Medal $3.00; Patch $3.00. *Submit:* Group leader's certification of completion of hike and anti-litter project. *Register:* Not required. *Sites:* Fort Wayne Children's Zoo, GTE Telephone Museum, Deihm Museum, Foellinger-Freiman Botanical Conservatory, Allen County-Ft. Wayne Historical Society Museum, Swinney Homestead.

Kil-So-Quah Trail

Location: Huntington Reservoir,

Huntington, IN. *Theme:* Wabash River area. *Sponsor:* Pokagon-Kekionga Trails, Inc., P.O. Box 192, Angola, IN 46703, (219) 833-1550.

Length: 10 miles (loop). *Route:* The trail begins at the north end of the Huntington Dam, circles the reservoir, and returns to the start. *Terrain:* Woods. *Cycling:* Not recommended. *Awards:* Patch $3.00; Repeat Pin $1.00. *Submit:* Group leader's certification of completion of hike and anti-litter project. *Register:* Not required. *Sites:* Huntington Reservoir, Huntington Dam, Huntington Municipal Airport.

Larry L. Ayers Memorial Trail

Location: Shelburn, IN. *Theme:* Memorial to Larry L. Ayers. *Sponsor:* Jack P. Taylor, 28 Washington St., Shelburn, IN 47879, (812) 397-2219.

Length: 11 or 15 miles (loops). *Route:* The trail begins and ends near the intersection of Griffith and Washington Sts., heads north on Thomas St., then heads east to circle the cemetery and Larry's house. *Terrain:* Foothills. *Cycling:* Not appropriate. *Awards:* Medal $2.75; Patch $1.25; Neckerchief $2.00; Slide $0.80. *Submit:* Request for patches. *Register:* At least 2 days in advance. *Sites:* Larry's House, Larry's Grave.

Laughery Creek Trail

Location: Aurora to Versailles State Park, IN. *Theme:* Laughery Creek Massacre—August 24, 1781. *Sponsor:* Lloyd Martin, 6442 Lousse Ln., Cincinnati, OH 45248, (513) 574-3864.

Length: Aurora to Friendship Section—24 miles (straight). Friendship to Versailles Section—12 miles (straight)

Routes: The first section begins at the entrance to the Riverview Cemetery, and ends at the Walter Cline Muzzle Loading Rifle Range, where the second section begins and proceeds to the covered bridge in Versailles State Park. *Terrain:* Little used rural roads. *Cycling:* Appropriate. *Awards:* 2 Patches. *Submit:* No requirement. *Register:* Not required. *Sites:* Riverview Cemetery, McGuire's Fort, Indian Mounds, Grist Mill Site, Busching Covered Bridge, Versailles State Park.

Lincoln Homesite Trail

Location: Troy, IN. *Theme:* Historic route taken by Abraham Lincoln as a boy. *Sponsor:*

Ron Alstadt, 20 Ornament Ln., Santa Claus, IN 47549, (812) 544-2200.

Length: 1.5 miles. *Route:* The trail begins at the Lincoln Memorial State Park across the Ohio River from the ferry dock, and ends at the foundation remnants of Lincoln's boyhood home. *Terrain:* Dirt backroads. *Cycling:* Appropriate. *Awards:* Patch $1.75. *Submit:* Request for patches. *Register:* Not required. *Sites:* Lincoln Memorial State Park, Ohio River, Lincoln's Boyhood Home, Log Cabin Foundation.

Mastodon Trek

Location: Anthony Wayne Reservation, Ft. Wayne, IN. *Theme:* Recreation. *Sponsor:* Pokagon-Kekionga Trails, Inc., P.O. Box 192, Angola, IN 46703, (219) 833-1550.

Length: 5 miles (loop). *Route:* The trail begins and ends at the Camp Little Turtle Office, passing near site of discovery of mammoth fossil. *Terrain:* Woods. *Cycling:* Not recommended. *Awards:* Patch $3.00. *Submit:* Group leader's certification of completion of hike and anti-litter project. *Register:* At least 1 week before hiking.

Me-Te-A Trail

Location: Metea County Park, Allen County, IN. *Theme:* History and nature. *Sponsor:* Pokagon-Kekionga Trails, Inc., P.O. Box 192, Angola, IN 46703, (219) 833-1550.

Length: 2.0 miles (loop). *Route:* The trail begins at the marked trailhead along the ridge line, follows the Raccoon Trail west along the ridge, then east along Cedar Creek where it turns into the Softshell Turtle Trail, then loops through the Muskrat Trail, and heads south and (after a couple more loops), heads back to the start. *Terrain:* Woods. *Cycling:* Not appropriate. *Awards:* Medal $3.00; Patch $3.00. *Submit:* Request for awards. *Register:* Not required. *Sites:* Sassafras Pass Overlook, Cedar Creek.

Mississinewa Trail

Location: Peru, IN. *Theme:* Mississinewa River area, park and dam. *Sponsor:* Pokagon-Kekionga Trails, Inc., P.O. Box 192, Angola, IN 46703, (219) 833-1550.

Length: 10 miles (loop). *Route:* The trail begins and ends at the south parking lot of the Frances Slocum Picnic Area at the east end of the Mississinewa Dam. *Terrain:* Steep wooded hills. *Cycling:* Not recommended.

Awards: Medal $3.00; Patch $3.00; Repeat Pin $1.00. *Submit:* Group leader's certification of completion of hike and anti-litter project. *Register:* Not required. *Sites:* Frances Slocum State Forest, Mississinewa Reservoir and Dam, Frances Slocum Grave.

Muskhogen Trail

Location: Angel Mounds State Historic Site, Evansville, IN. *Theme:* Indian Lore. *Sponsor:* Troop 301, BSA, 2109 Lincoln Ave., Evansville, IN 47714.

Length: 6.75 miles (loop). *Route:* The trail begins at the Interpretive Center, takes a 2.85-mile loop through the Indian village area, then a 3.9-mile loop through the adjoining woods. *Terrain:* Woods. *Cycling:* Not recommended. *Awards:* Medal $4.50; Patch $2.50; Tomahawk Repeat Pin $2.50. *Submit:* No requirement. *Register:* Advance registration with site personnel requested. *Sites:* Angel Mounds Memorial, Interpretive Center.

Ouabache Trail and Trek

Location: Ouabache State Park, Bluffton, IN. *Theme:* Former "Greatest Wildlife Laboratory in U.S.". *Sponsor:* Pokagon-Kekionga Trails, Inc., P.O. Box 192, Angola, IN 46703, (219) 833-1550.

Length: Trail, 10 miles (loop). Trek, 2.8 miles (loop). *Route:* The trail begins at the fire tower, meanders through the park, and returns to the start (shortcut for the trek). *Terrain:* Woods. *Cycling:* Not recommended. *Awards:* Trail Medal $3.00; Trail Patch $3.00; Trail Repeat Patch $0.50; Trek Patch $3.00. *Submit:* Group leader's certification of completion of hike and anti-litter project. *Register:* Not required. *Sites:* Fire Tower, Wildlife Exhibits, Kunkel Lake.

Pit Lake Trek

Location: Anthony Wayne Reservation, Ft. Wayne, IN. *Theme:* Recreation. *Sponsor:* Pokagon-Kekionga Trails, Inc., P.O. Box 192, Angola, IN 46703, (219) 833-1550.

Length: 5 miles (loop). *Route:* The trail begins and ends at the Camp Little Turtle Office, looping around Pit Lake. *Terrain:* Woods. *Cycling:* Not recommended. *Awards:* Patch $3.00. *Submit:* Group leader's certification of completion of hike and anti-litter project. *Register:* At least 1 week before hiking. *Sites:* Water Tower, Totem Pole, Pit Lake, Halls Point.

Pokagon Trail and Trek

Location: Pokagon State Park, Angola, IN. *Theme:* History of territory that was once the home of Potawatomi chiefs. *Sponsor:* Pokagon-Kekionga Trails, Inc., P.O. Box 192, Angola, IN 46703, (219) 833-1550.

Length: Trail, 8.0 miles (loop). Trek, 3.5 miles (loop). *Route:* The trail starts at the Youth Campground or Wildlife Exhibit Pens, meanders through the park, and returns to the start (shortcut for the trek). *Terrain:* Woods. *Cycling:* Not recommended. *Awards:* Trail Medal $3.00; Trail Patch $3.00; Trail Repeat Patch $0.50; Trek Patch $3.00. *Submit:* Group leader's certification of completion of hike and anti-litter project. *Register:* Not required. *Sites:* Saddle Barn, Wildlife Exhibit Pens, Toboggan Slide, Lake James, Nature Center, Potawatomi Inn.

Potawatomi Trail Hike

Location: Chesterton, IN. *Theme:* Annual event. *Sponsor:* Calumet Council, BSA, 8751 Calument Ave., Munster, IN 46321-2593, (219) 836-1720.

Length: 10 miles. *Route:* The hike begins at the City West Shelter of the Indiana Dunes State Park. *Terrain:* Contact sponsor. *Cycling:* Not permitted. *Awards:* Patch $4.50. *Submit:* Purchase patches at the event. *Register:* At the beginning of the hike.

Riley Trail

Location: Maxwell, IN. *Theme:* James Whitcomb Riley. *Sponsor:* Randall Shepherd, c/o Hancock County Historical Society, 7859 E. 200 S., P.O. Box 375, Greenfield, IN 46140.

Length: 12 miles (straight). *Route:* The trail begins at Hancock County Road 500 N in Maxwell and generally follows Brandywine Creek to end at Riley's boyhood home. *Terrain:* Mostly off-road. *Cycling:* Not recommended. *Awards:* Medal $3.25; Patch $1.00. *Submit:* No requirement. *Register:* Advance registration required. *Sites:* C.C. Irving Animal Farm, Old Log Jail, Chapel in the Park, Mitchell House, Riley Boyhood Home.

Salamonie Trail

Location: Salamonie River State Forest near LaGro, IN. *Theme:* Salamonie River area. *Sponsor:* Pokagon-Kekionga Trails, Inc., P.O. Box 192, Angola, IN 46703, (219) 833-1550.

Length: 8 miles (loop). *Route:* The trail begins at the parking lot on top of the Salamonie Dam, meanders westward nearly to the park boundary, and returns to the start. *Terrain:* Rural roads. *Cycling:* Appropriate. *Awards:* Medal $3.00; Patch $3.00; Repeat Pins $1.00 each. *Submit:* Group leader's certification of completion of hike and anti-litter project. *Register:* Not required. *Sites:* Salamonie Dam, Cable Car, Hominy Ridge Falls, Hominy Lake, Stone Bridge.

Ten O'Clock Line Trail

Location: Nashville, IN. *Theme:* Indian settlers movement. *Sponsor:* Trail Headquarters, 3980 N. Bear Wallow Rd., Nashville, IN 47448-9451, (812) 988-2636.

Length: 16.0 miles (straight). *Route:* The trail begins in Brown County State Park and ends in Yellowwood Forest. *Terrain:* Hills. *Cycling:* Not permitted. *Awards:* Medal $6.00; Trail Patch $5.00 (Miles for this and other trails sponsored by the same organization may be aggregated toward patches for 50, 100, 200, 300 & 500 total miles); Camper Patch; 4 Repeat Pins; 4 Seasonal Overnight Patches; Neckerchief. *Submit:* Contact Sponsor for information. *Register:* 1 week in advance. *Sites:* Bowie Knife Knob, Lake Strahl, Fire Tower, Schooner Creek.

Tulip Tree Trace

Location: Nashville, IN. *Theme:* Recreation. *Sponsor:* Trail Headquarters, 3980 N. Bear Wallow Rd., Nashville, IN 74748-9451, (812) 988-2636.

Length: 18.0 miles (straight). *Route:* The trail begins in Morgan-Monroe Forest and ends in Yellowwood Forest. *Terrain:* Cross-country hills. *Cycling:* Not permitted. *Awards:* Medal $6.00; Patch $5.00 (Miles for this and other trails sponsored by the same organization may be aggregated toward patches for 50, 100, 200, 300 & 500 total miles); 4 Repeat Pins; State Seal Patch; Camper Patch; Neckerchief. *Submit:* Patch order form. *Register:* 1 week in advance.

Wabash Heritage Trail

Location: Battle Ground, IN. *Theme:* Local history. *Sponsor:* Wabash Heritage Trail, P.O. Box 366, Battle Ground, IN 47920, (765) 567-2147.

Length: 6.5 miles (straight). *Route:* The trail begins at a sign next to the Wabash River 0.7 miles south of the SR 52 overpass, and heads north along the river to the Tippecanoe Battlefield Park. *Terrain:* Woods and riverbank. *Cycling:* Not recommended. *Awards:* Patch $3.50. *Submit:* No requirement. *Register:* Not required. *Sites:* Old Davis Ferry Bridge, Heron Island Wildlife Preserve, Tippecanoe Battlefield Park, Battlefield Memorial, Prophets Rock, Tecumseh Trails Park, Davis Ferry Park, McAllister Park, Mascouten Park.

Whitewater Canal Trail

Location: Laurel, IN. *Theme:* History of the Waterway Canal system. *Sponsor:* Trail Headquarters, 3980 N. Bear Wallow Rd., Nashville, IN 47448-9451, (812) 988-2636.

Length: 11.7 miles (straight). *Route:* The trail begins at the feeder dam near Laurel, IN, and heads east to end just east of Brookville. *Terrain:* Cross-country. *Cycling:* Not permitted. *Awards:* Medal $6.00; Patch $5.00 (Miles for this and other trails sponsored by the same organization may be aggregated toward patches for 50, 100, 200, 300 & 500 total miles); 4 Repeat Pins; Duck Creek Aqueduct Patch; Overnighter Patch; Neckerchief. *Submit:* Request for patches. *Register:* 1 week in advance. *Sites:* Grist Mill Museum, Millville Lock, Boundary Hill Railroad Cut, Aqueduct.

Yellowwood Trail

Location: Bear Wallow Hill, Nashville, IN. *Theme:* Native wildlife. *Sponsor:* Trail Headquarters, 3980 N. Bear Wallow Rd., Nashville, IN 47448-9451, (812) 988-2636.

Length: 11.5 miles (straight). *Route:* The trail begins in the Morgan-Monroe Forest and ends at the Trail Headquarters at Bear Wallow Hill. *Terrain:* Hills and woodlands. *Cycling:* Not permitted. *Awards:* Medal $6.00; Patch $5.00 (Miles for this and other trails sponsored by the same organization may be aggregated toward patches for 50, 100, 200, 300 & 500 total miles.). *Submit:* Request for patches. *Register:* Advance registration required.

Formerly Sponsored Trails

Adena Trek
Anthony Wayne Trail
Bartholomew Trail

Central Canal Towpath Trek
Chief Kikthawenund Trail
Clark State Forest Trail
Cumberland Trail
Ell River Kenapocomoco Trail
Fall Creek Massacre Trail
Fort Harrison Trail
Fort Wayne Segment
Francis Slocum Trail
Freedom Trail
Guthrie Trail
Harrison Trail
Harrison-Riley Trek

Hoosier Lincoln Trail
Kekionga Segment
Ledgerwood Canoe Trail
Lincoln Prairie Pilgrimage
Lincoln Wilderness Pilgrimage
Ma-Ko-Ko-Mo Trail
Simon Kenton Bike Trail
T.C. Steele Trail
Tippecanoe River Trail
Wapihani Trails
Wayne Trace Segment
Woapikamikunk Trail
Wyandotte Trail

IOWA

American Gothic Trail

Location: Eldon, IA. *Theme:* Physical fitness and American heritage. *Sponsor:* Mark A. Ballard, 703 W. Walnut, Eldon, IA 52554, (641) 652-3130.

Length: 10 miles. *Route:* Not fixed—any 10 miles in or near Eldon will qualify for the award. Suggested routes are Eldon to Selma and return on either side of the Des Moines River, or Eldon to or from the Cliffland Access Area north of Eldon along the Des Moines River. *Terrain:* Roads. *Cycling:* Appropriate. *Awards:* Patch $4.00; Coffee Mug $6.00 (An additional Three Trails Patch is available for $1.50 for hiking this, the Diamond Trail and the Chief Wapello Trail.). *Submit:* No requirement. *Register:* Not required. *Sites:* American Gothic Gift Shop, Lions Club Park, American Gothic House, Sioc Cemetery, Old Bearing Tree Marker, Indian Mounds, Eldon Public Library, Old Log Cabin, Vesser Creek, Sac-Fox and Ioway Indian Battleground, Wapello County Fairgrounds, Jordan House Site, Stone House, Iowaville Cemetery.

Buffalo Bill Trail

Location: LeClaire, IA. *Theme:* "Buffalo Bill" Cody. *Sponsor:* Troop 95-BSA, 4908 Lorton Ave., Davenport, IA 52807,   (319) 359-0814.

Length: 10 miles (nearly a loop). *Route:* The trail begins at the Green Tree Memorial along the Mississippi River, loops through town, and ends at City Park 1 block from Green Tree. *Terrain:* City streets. *Cycling:* Appropriate; driving by car also qualifies for the awards. *Awards:* Medal $2.75; Patch $1.50. *Submit:* No requirement. *Register:* Not required. *Sites:* Green Tree Memorial, Old Limestone Quarry, Smith House, Dawley House, Old Market Square, Gamble House, Joe Barnes' Grave, Glendale Cemetery, Silver Creek, Kattenbracker House, Buffalo Bill's Boyhood Home, Tromley House, Clark House, Van Sant House, Buffalo Bill Museum, Lone Star Steamboat.

Charles Larpenteur Trail

Location: Little Sioux, IA. *Theme:* History of area and an early pioneer. *Sponsor:* Mid-America Council, BSA, 12401 W. Maple Rd., Omaha, NE 68164-1853, (402) 431-9272.

Length: 20 miles (loop). *Route:* The trail begins and ends at Little Sioux Scout Ranch. *Terrain:* Bluffs and plains. *Cycling:* Not recommended. *Awards:* Trail Patch $3.00; Scout Ranch Patch $1.50; Footprint $0.50; Scout Ranch Mug $2.50. *Submit:* No requirement. *Register:* At least 2 weeks in advance. *Sites:* Settler's Corral, Pete's Lookout, Charles Larpenteur Grave, Preparation Canyon, Sioux Burial Grounds, Preparation Cemetery.

Chief Wapello Trail

Location: Ottumwa to Agency City, IA.

Theme: Local history. *Sponsor:* Chief Wapello Trail Committee, Inc., 111 N. Webster, Ottumwa, IA 52501, (641) 684-6255.

Length: 11 miles (straight). *Route:* The trail begins at Ottumwa Park, follows the Des Moines River, and ends at Chief Wapello's Grave in Agency City. *Terrain:* Gravel roads, timber, underbrush, rocky areas and swamp. *Cycling:* Not recommended. *Awards:* Medal $4.50; Patch $2.00; Repeat Patch $2.00; Hat Pin $1.50; Mug $2.50 (An additional Three Trails Patch is available for $1.50 for hiking this, the Diamond Trail and the American Gothic Trail.). *Submit:* No requirement. *Register:* Not required. *Sites:* Sugar Creek, Garrison Rock, Horsethief Cave, Cliffland, Garrison Cemetery, Chief Wapello's Grave, Indian Springs, Agency Cemetery.

Diamond Canoe Trail

Location: Newton, IA. *Theme:* Physical fitness. *Sponsor:* Diamond Trail, Inc., P.O. Box 555, Newton, IA 50208.

Length: 22 to 50 miles (straight). *Route:* The trail begins in Cambridge and goes along the South Skunk River to Trails End at Galesburg Rd. To qualify for the patch, one must canoe at least from Colfax to Trails End. *Cycling:* Impossible, must be canoed. *Awards:* Patch $1.25; Canoe mugs $1.50. *Submit:* Request for patches. *Register:* 10 days in advance.

Diamond Trail

Location: Reasoner and Reynolds, IA. *Theme:* Iowa railroad movement; wagon trains. *Sponsor:* Dean Revell, 310 E. 16th St. N, Newton, IA 50208, (641) 792-7610; Troop 354, c/o Mary Crum, 201 Blair St., Kellogg, IA 50135-1165, (641) 526-3424.

Length: 17 miles (loop). *Route:* The trail begins and ends at Reasnor Ball Park, and for a large portion of the route follows the bank of the South Skunk River. *Terrain:* Timber, underbrush, rocky areas and swamp. *Cycling:* Not permitted. *Awards:* Patch $3.25; Cup $1.50; Three Trail Patch $1.50 (for hiking this, American Gothic and Wapello Trails). *Submit:* Request for patches. *Register:* 10 days in advance. *Sites:* Sandstone Bluff, Indian Lookout, Fairview Cemetery, Red Iron Bridge, Sand Mountains, Franklin Crossing, Draper Marsh, Petrified Tree Branch.

Hoover Trail

Location: Rochester to Cedar Valley, IA.

Theme: Herbert Hoover. *Sponsor:* Hoover Trail Committee, P.O. Box 444, West Branch, IA 52358, (319) 643-5567.

Length: 17 miles (loop). *Route:* The trail begins at Cedar Valley Park, follows the Cedar River north to Cedar Valley, then crosses the river and follows it south to Rochester Park, then back north to the start. *Terrain:* Woods and fields. *Cycling:* Not recommended; a 41-mile canoe trail also qualifies for the awards. *Awards:* Medal $3.50; Patch $2.00; Repeat Patch $2.00; Canoe Patch $2.00; Camp Patch $2.00; Rain Patch $2.00; Jacket Patch $3.00; Hat Pin $1.25. *Submit:* Group leader's certification of completion. *Register:* Advance registration required. *Sites:* West Branch Heritage Museum, Lime Kiln, Friends' Church Cabin, Maxson Farm, Cedar Valley Quarries.

Kate Shelley Trail

Location: Boone, IA. *Theme:* Local history. *Sponsor:* Kate Shelley Trail, Inc., P.O. Box 134, Boone, IA 50036.

Length: 25 miles (loop). *Route:* The trail begins at the Boy Scout cabin in McHose Park, runs through Boone, follows the Des Moines River and returns to the start. *Terrain:* Roads and woods. *Cycling:* Not recommended. *Awards:* Medal $6.00; Patch $4.00. *Submit:* No requirement. *Register:* Advance registration required. *Sites:* Mamie Eisenhower Birthplace, First School House, Kate Shelley High Bridge, Milton Lott's Grave.

Little Sioux Trails

Location: Little Sioux Scout Ranch, Little Sioux, IA. *Theme:* Recreation and local history. *Sponsor:* Mid-America Council, BSA, 12401 W. Maple Rd., Omaha, NE 68164-1853, (402) 431-1853. *Lengths:* Blue & Gold Trail, 5 miles (loop). Blue Trail, 5 miles (loop). Brown Trail, 2 miles (loop). Gold Trail, 2.5 miles (loop). Red Trail, 5 miles (loop). White Trail, 5.5 miles (loop). *Routes:* All trails are loops beginning and ending at the same location at the camp. *Terrain:* Steep wooded hills and valleys. *Cycling:* Not recommended. *Awards:* Patch. *Submit:* No requirement. *Register:* At least 2 weeks in advance.

Meskwakie Hiking And Canoe Trail

Location: Maquoketa, IA. *Theme:* Recreation. *Sponsor:* Meskwakie Trail

Committee, c/o Dr. M.A. Dalchow, 314 W. Platte St., Maquoketa, IA 52060, (563) 652-3811.

Length: 25 miles (loop) hiking or 50 miles (straight) canoeing. **Route:** The canoe route begins at Dunlap Park and heads downstream on the Maquoketa River to Camp Iten Boy Scout Camp, then back upstream 1 mile to Joinerville. The hiking trail begins at the home of Dr. M.A. Dalchow, 314 W. Platte St., Maquoketa, heads upriver to the Chenelworth Bridge, then north to the caves, and back to the start via CR Y-31 and the riverbank. **Terrain:** Roads, river bluffs, farms. **Cycling:** Not recommended. **Awards:** Medal $2.00 (with imprint $3.00); Brassard $1.00. **Submit:** No requirement. **Register:** Not required. **Sites:** Monticello Dam, Picture Rock Park, Supple Bridges, Joinerville Park, Maquoketa Caves.

Old Capitol Trail

Location: Iowa City, IA. **Theme:** Local history. **Sponsor:** Old Capitol Trail, P.O. Box 2060, Iowa City, IA 52244, (319) 337-9623.

Length: 17 miles (loop). **Route:** The trail begins at Turkey Creek Camp Site, follows Prairie des Chien Rd. to Iowa City and returns to start on Old US 218 and Prairie

des Chien Rd. **Terrain:** Roads. **Cycling:** Appropriate. **Awards:** Medal $3.50; Patch $2.00. **Submit:** Group leader's certification of completion. **Register:** At least 3 days in advance. **Sites:** Coralville Dam, Robert Lucas Grave, Old Survey Marker, Plum Grove, College Park, Iowa City Stage Stop, Pentacrest of SUI, Old Capitol, MacLean Hall, MacBride Hall, SUI President's Home.

Sac and Fox Trail

Location: Cedar Rapids, IA. **Theme:** Recreation. **Sponsor:** City of Cedar Rapids Park Department, Indian Creek Nature Center, 6665 Otis Rd. SE, Cedar Rapids, IA 52403, (319) 362-0664.

Length: 7.5 miles (straight). **Route:** The trail endpoints are East Post Rd. and the Cole St. parking lot, and follows the banks of Indian Creek and the Cedar River. **Terrain:** Packed dirt and mowed grass. **Cycling:** Appropriate. **Awards:** Patch. **Submit:** No requirement. **Register:** Not required.

Formerly Sponsored Trails

Bo Qui Trail
Delaware County Monument Trail
Sho-Quo-Quon Geode Trail

KANSAS

Council Grove Historic Trail

Location: Council Grove, KS. **Theme:** Santa Fe Trail. **Sponsor:** Troop 59 BSA, Faith Lutheran Church, 1716 Gage St., Topeka, KS 66604, (785) 273-2251, (785) 272-4214.

Length: 10.0 miles (straight). **Route:** The trail begins at the Kaw Indian Agency Headquarters building, heads northwest into Council Grove, west through town, and south to the Council Grove Cemetery. **Terrain:** Roads. **Cycling:** Possible. **Awards:** Patch. **Submit:** Group leader's certificate of completion. **Register:** In advance. **Sites:** Madonna of the Trail, Hays House, Father Padilla's Monument, Pioneer Jail, Old Kaw Mission, Hermits Cave, Last Chance Store,

Custer Elm, Old Bell Monument, Post Office Oak.

Curtis Trail And Trek

Location: Topeka, KS. **Theme:** Life of Charles Curtis, Vice President of the U.S. **Sponsor:** The Curtis Trail, BSA Troop 59, Faith Lutheran Church, 1716 Gage St., Topeka, KS 66604, (785) 273-2251, (785) 272-4214.

Length: Trail, 10 miles (straight). Trek, 4 miles (loop). **Route:** The trail begins at 37th St. and Topeka Ave., and ends at the State Capitol. The Trek begins at the Capitol, loops through the city, and returns to the start. **Terrain:** City streets. **Cycling:** Appropriate.

Awards: Trail Patch $2.00; Trek Patch $1.25. *Submit:* Group leader's certification of completion. *Register:* Advance registration required. *Sites:* State Capitol, Curtis Home, Railroad Station, Copeland House, Old Stockade Site, State Historical Society Building, G.A.R. Memorial Building, Topeka Cemetery, Columbian Building.

Elk River Hiking Trail

Location: Elk City Lake, Independence, KS. *Theme:* Recreation. *Sponsor:* Project Manager, Corps of Engineers, Elk City Lake, P.O. Box 567, Independence, KS 67301, (620) 331-0315; order patches from Wilderness Specialties, P.O. Box 841, Newton, KS 67114-0841, (316) 283-6583.

Length: 15 miles (straight). *Route:* The trail endpoints are located just north of the river on US 160 and the Corps of Engineers Project Office just west of the dam, and follows the shore of the lake and river in between. *Terrain:* Woods. *Cycling:* Not recommended. *Awards:* Patch. *Submit:* No requirement. *Register:* Not required.

Fort Leavenworth Heritage Trail

Location: Fort Leavenworth, KS. *Theme:* History of the army base. *Sponsor:* Harold Youth Center, Bldg. 1056, Heritage Trail Coordinator/Youth Services, Fort Leavenworth, IS 66027-5093.

Length: 6.0 and 13.0 miles (loops). *Route:* Both hike routes begin and end at Camp Miles. *Terrain:* Dirt and paved roads. *Cycling:* Does not qualify for award. *Awards:* Patch $2.25. *Submit:* Patch order form and confirmation of spending two days and one night along the trail and participation in one retreat ceremony. *Register:* At least 2 weeks in advance. *Sites:* Frontier Army Museum, St. Ignatius Chapel, James Franklin Bell Hall, Dickinson Hall, National Cemetery, Munson Army Hospital, U.S. Disciplinary Barrack, Sutler's Home.

Fort Riley Trail

Location: Fort Riley, KS. *Theme:* History of the army base. *Sponsor:* Scouting Coordinator, DPCA Attn: AFZN-PA-CFF, Bldg. #5800, Fort Riley, KS 66442, (785) 239-9200.

Length: 10 miles (straight). *Route:* The trail begins at the Great War Memorial, winds through the base and ends at the campground at Moon Lake. *Terrain:* Road. *Cycling:* Possible, but inquire ahead for permission. *Awards:* Patch $4.00. *Submit:* Group leader's certification of completion of hike and overnight camping. *Register:* At least 45 days in advance of hike. *Sites:* First Territorial Capitol, U.S. Cavalry Museum, Custer House, Buffalo Corral, Camp Funston, Locomotive 6072, Old Trooper Monument, Artillery Parade Field, Colonel's Row, Commanding General's Quarters, St. Mary's Chapel, Old Parsonage, Post Sutler's Store, Wounded Knee Monument, Ogden Monument, Post Cemetery.

General Walt Trail

Location: Waubaunsee County, KS. *Theme:* General Lewis W. Walt. *Sponsor:* General Walt Trail, 1020 SE Monroe, Topeka, KS 66612.

Length: 32.4 miles (straight). *Route:* The trail begins at General Walt's birthplace, a mile south of Harveyville, and goes to the Zwanziger Museum in Alma. *Terrain:* Easy path. *Cycling:* Not recommended. *Awards:* Patch $1.50. *Submit:* No requirement. *Register:* Advance registration required. *Sites:* Birthplace of General Walt, Zwanziger Museum, Lake Waubaunsee, Flint Hills.

Historic Trails of Rice County

Location: Rice County, KS. *Theme:* Historic routes passing through Rice County. *Sponsor:* Ron Harkrader, Troop 101 BSA, c/o Coronado Quivira Museum, 105 W. Lyon, Lyons, KS 67554 (620) 257-2186.

Length: 38 miles (straight). *Route:* There are three segments, the 11-mile Coronado-Padilla Route west of Lyons, the 6-mile Quivira Route east of Lyons, and the 21-mile Kaw Segment further to the east. The trail runs roughly east to west. *Terrain:* Foothills and woodlands. *Cycling:* Not appropriate. *Awards:* Patch $1.00. *Submit:* Request for patches and description of project which improved and preserved the trail. *Register:* At least 10 days in advance. *Sites:* Stone Corral, Kaw Indian Camp Site, Cow Creek Crossing Station, Buffalo Bill Well, Wagon Train Massacre Site, Plum Buttes, Jarvis Creek Massacre Site, Father Padilla Cross, Plum Buttes Massacre Site, Wagon Train Raid Site.

Kansas Capitols Trail

Location: Lecompton to Tecumseh, KS.

Theme: Early state capitols. *Sponsor:* Troop 18 BSA, P.O. Box 1, Tecumseh, KS 66542; Dave Gary, 7331 SE SR 40, Tecumseh, KS 66542-9785, (785) 379-9525; Dennis Eisenbarth, 2623 SE Granger Ct., Topeka, KS 66605, (785) 267-2028.

Length: 22.5 miles (straight). *Route:* The trail begins at the campground at Coon Point near SR 40, heads north to Lecompton, and west through Grover to Tecumseh. *Terrain:* Roads. *Cycling:* Not appropriate. *Awards:* Patch $5.00 ($1.00 fee is required upon registration, whether one wants a patch or not). *Submit:* To qualify for awards, one must spend at least two days and one night on the trail. *Register:* At least two weeks in advance. *Sites:* Historical Society Museum, Constitution Hall, Fort Titus Site, Kriepe House, Strickler House, Leupold House, Hoagland Castle Site, Garvey's Retreat.

Neodesha Historical Trail

Location: Wilson County and Neodesha, KS. *Theme:* History of Neodesha. *Sponsor:* Troop 28 BSA, United Methodist Church, Neodesha, KS 66757.

Length: 10-15 miles (loop). *Route:* The trail begins and ends at the museum located near the reconstructed first successful commercial producing oil well in Kansas-Norman No. 1. *Terrain:* Roads. *Cycling:* Appropriate. *Awards:* Patch. *Submit:* No requirement. *Register:* Not required. *Sites:* Grist Mill, Fall River, Lovers' Cave, Water Works, Little Bear Mound, Legion Bridge, Norman No. 1 Museum, Mill Street Bridge, Verdigris River, Hell's Cave, GAR Monument.

Old Santa Fe Trail

Location: Burlingame to Council Grove Lake, KS. *Theme:* Route of historic Santa Fe Trail. *Sponsor:* Jayhawk Area Council, BSA, Rm. 222, 215 E. Eighth St., Topeka, KS 66603, (785) 354-2541.

Length: 55 miles (straight). *Route:* The trail begins in Burlingame just west of the Scout Hall Shelter and heads west to Council Grove, but may also be hiked in the opposite direction. *Terrain:* Rural roads. *Cycling:* Appropriate. *Awards:* Patch. *Submit:* No requirement. *Register:* Not required. *Sites:* Agnes Cemetery, Rock House, Old Stone Building, Elm Creek Mail Station, 1879 Building, Stone Cave, Stone House, Dragoon Grave, Stone Inn, ICBM Site, Unknown Indian Monument, Oldest Cowboy Jail, Madonna of the Trail, Council Oak, Last Chance Store, Post Office Oak, Old Kaw Mission, Hays Tavern.

Old Santa Fe Trail of McPherson County

Location: McPherson, KS. *Theme:* Historic pioneer route. *Sponsor:* Troop 133, c/o Gene Ewing, 1562 16th Ave., McPherson, KS 67460, (620) 241-4387.

Length: Bison Route: 16.0 miles (straight). Empire Route: 20.0 miles (straight). *Route:* The Bison Route begins at the Dry Turkey Creek Crossing and Boy Scout Campground and heads west to the McPherson County line. The Empire Route begins at the east McPherson County line and heads west to the Dry Turkey Creek Crossing and campground. *Terrain:* Sandy, gravel road. *Cycling:* Recommended. *Awards:* 2 patches $2.00 each. *Register:* A few days in advance. *Submit:* Patch request. *Sites:* Ed Miller's Grave, Fuller's Ranch, Empire Cemetery, Old Mill Museum, Cottonwood Grove Cemetery, Stone Corral, Gunsight Notch, Walnut Creek Crossing, Fort Zarah, Pawnee Rock.

Pike-Long Trail

Location: Alden, KS. *Theme:* Exploration route of Zebulon Pike and Maj. Stephen H. Long. *Sponsor:* Troop 164 BSA, c/o Lyons Kiwanis Club, P.O. Box 267, Lyons, KS 67554; Ron Harkrader, (620) 257-2186.

Length: 3.0 miles (straight). *Route:* The trailheads are the bridges crossing the Arkansas River, due south on Alden and the next one to the east. *Terrain:* Riverbank. *Cycling:* Not appropriate. *Awards:* Patch. *Submit:* Request for patches. *Register:* In advance. *Sites:* Arkansas River.

Rimrock Trail

Location: Theodore Naish Scout Reservation, Bonner Springs, KS. *Theme:* Recreation and nature. *Sponsor:* Camping Service, Heart of America Council, BSA, 10210 Holmes Rd., Kansas City, MO 64131, (816) 942-9333 or (800) 776-1110.

Length: 12.5 miles (loop). *Route:* The trail begins and ends at the Campmaster Cabin at Central Camp, Camp Naish, and loops along the nearby bluffs. *Terrain:* Hilly and rocky. *Cycling:* Not allowed. *Awards:* Medal $5.00; Patch $4.00. *Submit:* Completed patch order form. *Register:* At least 2 weeks in advance. *Sites:* Lake of the Forest, Kaw River Valley, Lookout Point, Boone Overlook, Ghost Circle, Copperhead Point, Table Rocks, Needle Point.

Formerly Sponsored Trails

Perry Lake Trail
Santa Fe Trail

KENTUCKY

Api-Su-Ahts Trail

Location: Grayson Lake, Grayson, KY. *Theme:* Scenic trail. *Sponsor:* Tim Wilson, U.S. Army Corps of Engineers, Grayson Lake Station, 50 Launch Ramp Rd., Grayson, KY 41143, (606) 474-5815. *Lengths:* 1st loop, 2.9 miles. 2nd loop, 7.8 miles. 3rd loop, 5.9 miles. 4th loop, 6.7 miles. *Route:* The 1st loop begins and ends at Camp Webb. The 2nd loop begins and ends at Frazier Falls. The 3rd loop begins at the Lookout Tower. The 4th loop branches off from the 3rd loop. *Terrain:* Woodland hills. *Cycling:* Not permitted. *Awards:* Patch. *Register:* Not required. *Submit:* Request for patches. *Sites:* Deer Creek, Frazier Falls, Grayson Lake, Lookout Tower, Camp Webb.

Buena Vista Trail

Location: Audubon Scout Reservation, Owensboro, KY. *Theme:* Recreation. *Sponsor:* Audubon Council, BSA, P.O. Box 280, 330 Allen St., Owensboro, KY 42302.
Length: 9 miles (loop). *Route:* This is a circular route surrounding Lake Herndon, which could be started at any point on the trail. *Terrain:* Woods. *Cycling:* Not recommended. *Awards:* Patch. *Submit:* Completed 10-item questionnaire. *Register:* Not required. *Sites:* Jesse James Cave, Lake Herndon.

Buffalo Trace Trail

Location: Maysville, KY. *Theme:* Recreation. *Sponsor:* Scioto Area Council, BSA, P.O. Box 1305, 612 Masonic Bldg., Portsmouth, OH 45662.
Length: 28 miles (straight). *Route:* The trail begins in Maysville and goes south through Washington, Murphysville, and Sardis, to end at Blue Licks Battlefield State Park. *Terrain:* Rural roads. *Cycling:* Not recommended. *Awards:* Medal $5.50. *Submit:* Group leader's certification of completion. *Register:* At least 10 days before hiking, contact 1 of 2 listed individuals, as they take down some signs between hikes to prevent vandalism.

Buffalo Trail

Location: Frankfort, KY. *Theme:* Historic buffalo route. *Sponsor:* Wah-La-Ha—Buffalo Trail, Inc., 420 Ewing St., Frankfort, KY 40601.
Length: 5.5 miles (straight). *Route:* The trail begins at the rear of the Old State Capitol Building and ends at the E-W Connector, where the Wah-La-Ha Trail begins. *Terrain:* Streets and woods. *Cycling:* Not recommended. *Awards:* Medal $3.00; Patch $2.00; 1st and 2nd Repeat Pins $1.50 each. *Submit:* Completed 5-item questionnaire. *Register:* Request hike date in advance. *Sites:* Fort Hill, Old State Capitol, Fort Boone.

Capitol View Trail

Location: Frankfort, KY. *Theme:* Early Kentucky history. *Sponsor:* Troop 281, c/o Rick Haydon, 525 Grama Dr., Frankfort, KY 40601, (502) 227-2162.
Length: 15 miles (straight). *Route:* The trail begins and Silver Lake, south of Stedmantown, and ends at Fort Hill near the Kentucky River. *Terrain:* Cross-country. *Cycling:* Not recommended. *Awards:* Patch $3.00. *Submit:* Request for patches. *Register:* At least 2 weeks in advance. *Sites:* Leestown Settlement, Cook Cabin, Fort Hill, Lakeview Park.

Caveland Trail

Location: Mammoth Cave, KY. *Theme:* Nature. *Sponsor:* So-Ky Trails, Inc., P.O. Box 404, Bowling Green, KY 42101-0404.

Length: 10 miles (straight). *Route:* The trail begins at the Capitol Hill Community Center on SR 259 and ends at the Mammoth Cave Visitor Center. *Terrain:* Back roads and woods trails. *Cycling:* Not recommended. *Awards:* Medal. *Submit:* List of 15 identified trees. *Register:* Not required. *Sites:* Mammoth Cave Visitor Center, Joppa Church, Historic Entrance, Dixon Cave.

Collie Ridge Composite Hike

Location: Mammoth Cave, KY. *Theme:* Recreation. *Sponsor:* So-Ky Trails, Inc., P.O. Box 404, Bowling Green, KY 42101-0404.

Length: 11.9 miles (straight). *Route:* The trail begins at the group campsite near the Maple Springs Ranger Station and ends at Jaggers Cemetery. *Terrain:* Back roads. *Cycling:* Possible over most, unlikely on spur trails. *Awards:* Patch $2.12. *Submit:* No requirement. *Register:* Not required. *Sites:* Jaggers Cemetery, Good Spring Church.

Cumberland State Resort Park Trails

Location: Daniel Boone National Forest, Corbin, KY. *Theme:* Scenic. *Sponsor:* Gift Shop, Cumberland Falls State Park, 7351 SR 90, Corbin, KY 40701, (606) 528-4121. *Lengths:* Moonbow Trail, 10.8 miles. Cumberland River Trail, 5.0 miles. Laurel Trail, 0.25 mile. Civilian Conservation Corps Memorial Trail, 1.0 mile. Campers Path, 0.5 mile. Cumberland Falls Trail, 0.5 mile. Rock House Trail, 0.125-0.5 mile. Connector Trail, 0.25 mile. Eagle Falls Trail, 1.5 miles. Blue Bend Trail, 4.5 miles. Anvil Branch Trail, 2.5 miles. Wildflower Loop Trail, 1.25 miles. *Routes:* See trail brochure from sponsor. *Terrain:* Varies. *Cycling:* Possible on some trails. *Awards:* 2 Patches $3.50 (oval) and $2.50 (round). *Submit:* Request for patches. *Register:* Not required.

Freedom Trail

Location: Camp Nelson, Nicholasville, KY. *Theme:* History of Camp Nelson. *Sponsor:* Troop 115, P.O. Box 1214, Nicholasville, KY 40356.

Length: Available from sponsor. *Route:* The trail covers 8 acres within Camp Nelson Heritage Park. *Terrain:* Available from sponsor. *Cycling:* Available from sponsor. *Awards:* Patch $5.00. *Submit:* Completed 4-item questionnaire. *Register:* Not required.

Iron Furnace Trail

Location: Jackson, KY. *Theme:* Local history. *Sponsor:* Anthony Scott, 963 Highland Ave., Jackson, KY 41339, (606) 666-2884.

Length: 10.5 miles. *Route:* Available from sponsor. *Terrain:* Available from sponsor. *Cycling:* Available from sponsor. *Awards:* Patch. *Submit:* Available from sponsor. *Register:* Available from sponsor.

Kentucky Lincoln Trail

Location: Elizabethtown to Hodgenville, KY. *Theme:* Abraham Lincoln's Boyhood. *Sponsor:* Talligewi Lodge #62 Order of the Arrow, Lincoln Heritage Council, BSA, P.O. Box 32113, Louisville, KY 40233-2113.

Length: 33 miles (straight). *Route:* The trail begins at the high school in Elizabethtown and ends at the Abraham Lincoln National Historical Park near Hodgenville. *Terrain:* Country roads. *Cycling:* Does not qualify for awards. *Awards:* Patch $5.00 (the Kentucky Trails Back Patch is available for $8.00 when this and the Lincoln Memorial Trail are completed). *Submit:* Request for patches; the trip must include a backpacking campout at Knobs Creek. *Register:* At least two weeks prior to the hike, and the registration request must be accompanied by a 200-word book report on a book about the life of Abraham Lincoln. *Sites:* Knob Creek, Lincoln Memorial.

Land Between the Lakes Trails

Location: Golden Pond, KY. *Theme:* Recreation. *Sponsor:* Jerry Conley, Tennessee Valley Authority, 100 Van Morgan Dr., Golden Pond, KY 42211, (270) 924-2032. *Lengths:* Canal Loops Trail, 14.0 miles. Fort Henry Trail, 26.0 miles. North-South Trail, 55.0 miles. *Routes:* Available from sponsor. *Terrain:* Woods. *Cycling:* Not appropriate. *Awards:* Patch $4.00; Canal Loops Patch $3.00; Fort Henry Patch $3.00; North-South Patch $3.00. *Submit:* Request for patches. *Register:* Not Required.

Lincoln Memorial Trail

Location: Knob Creek to Hodgenville, KY.

Theme: Abraham Lincoln. *Sponsor:* Talligewi Lodge #62 Order of the Arrow, Lincoln Heritage Council, BSA, P.O. Box 32113, Louisville, KY 40233-2113.

Length: 14 miles (straight). *Route:* This is intended as the second day for the Kentucky Lincoln Trail, from Lincoln's boyhood home at Knob Creek to Hodgenville. *Terrain:* Country roads. *Cycling:* Not recommended. *Awards:* Patch $5.00 (the Kentucky Trails Back Patch is available for $8.00 upon completion of this and the Kentucky Lincoln Trail). *Register:* At least two weeks in advance. *Submit:* Request for patch. *Sites:* Knob Creek, Lincoln Memorial.

Long Hunter's Trek

Location: Daniel Boone National Forest, Louisville, KY. *Theme:* Scenic views of Red River Gorge. *Sponsor:* Troop 321, c/o Larry Tour, 210 Doorshire Ct., Louisville, KY 40245, (502) 245-6254; or Lincoln Heritage Council, BSA, 824 Phillips Ln., Louisville, KY 40245, (502) 361-1513.

Length: 13.1 miles (loop). *Route:* The trail loops through Red River Gorge Park. *Terrain:* Woodlands. *Cycling:* Not appropriate. *Awards:* Medal, Patch. *Register:* Not required. *Submit:* Group leader's certificate of completion.

Mammoth Cave Trail

Location: Mammoth Cave, KY. *Theme:* Nature. *Sponsor:* So-Ky Trails, Inc., P.O. Box 404, Bowling Green, KY 42101-0404.

Length: 13 miles (straight). *Route:* The trail begins at the junction of the boundary of Mammoth Cave National Park and Dennison Ferry Rd., and follows Little Jordan Cemetery Rd. and Maple Springs Ranger Station Rd. to the park Visitor Center. *Terrain:* County and backwoods roads and trails. *Cycling:* Not recommended. *Awards:* Patch. *Submit:* Completed 15-item questionnaire. *Register:* Not required. *Sites:* White Cave, Mammoth Dome Sink, Sunset Point, Visitor Center, Old Guides Cemetery.

The Massacre Trail

Location: Middletown, KY. *Theme:* Memorial to Indian massacres of 1781, 1786, and 1789. *Sponsor:* Historic Middletown, Inc., P.O. Box 43013, Middletown, KY 40253-0013.

Length: 12 miles (straight). *Route:* The trail begins at Middletown Christian Church and ends at Long Run Church on Long Run Rd. *Terrain:* Secondary roads. *Cycling:* Possible, but will not qualify for awards. *Awards:* Medal $3.00; Patch $2.00; Repeater Segments. *Submit:* No requirement. *Register:* Pre-registration not required, but check-in at starting point can only qualify for awards if done on first Saturday in either April or November. *Sites:* Middletown Christian Church, William Miller House, Capt. Benjamin Head House, John C. Marshall House, Chenoweth Fort-Springhouse, Middletown Inn, Joseph Abell House, John Bull House, Long Run Church, Davis Tavern.

Mischa Mokwa Adventure Trail

Location: Cumberland Gap National Historical Park, Middlesboro, KY and VA. *Theme:* Local history. *Sponsor:* Kirby Smith III, 424 Englewood Rd., Middlesboro, KY 40965, (606) 248-6014.

Length: 21 miles (straight). *Route:* The trail begins in the Wilderness Road Campground, heads east through the park, and ends in Ewing, VA. *Terrain:* Woods. *Cycling:* Not appropriate. *Awards:* Patch. *Submit:* Patch request. *Register:* Not required. *Sites:* Indian Rocks, Hensley Settlement, Martins Fork, Sand Cave, White Rocks.

Ohio River Trail

Location: Meade County, KY. *Theme:* Recreation. *Sponsor:* Ohio River Trail Corporation, P.O. Box 567, Brandenburg, KY 40108.

Length: 20.4 miles (loop). *Route:* The trail begins at the Nature Center in Otter Creek Park, follows the Ohio River westward to short stop checkpoint, then returns past Doe Valley on SRs 448 and 1638. A shortcut by the Olin Chemical Plant reduces the hike to 14 miles. *Terrain:* Gently rolling roads. *Cycling:* Appropriate. *Awards:* Medal $5.00; Patch. *Submit:* No requirement. *Register:* Advance registration required. *Sites:* Buttermilk Falls, Ohio River, Morgan's Cave, Rock Haven.

Ox Cart Trail

Location: Fairdale, KY. *Theme:* Ox cart trail route to Bullet County. *Sponsor:* G.E. GAns, 7711 Chet Ln., Louisville, KY 40214, (502) 367-7222; or Richard Shacklett, 10101 Jefferson Hill Rd., Fairdale, KY 40118, (502) 368-0949.

Length: 18.6 miles (loop). *Route:* The trail begins in the Jefferson County Forest at the foot of Holsclaw Hill Rd., leads to a huge hill, then continues to Brooks Hill Rd., Mt. Elmira Rd., Knoeb Creek Rd., and Mitchell Rd. to pass Tom Wallace Lake on the way back to the starting point. *Terrain:* Winding paved road. *Cycling:* Recommended. *Awards:* Medal; Patch. *Submit:* Group leader's certificate of completion. *Register:* One week in advance. *Sites:* Holsclaw Hill, Knoeb Creek, Elmira Church Ground, Horine Scout Reservation Plaque, Pioneer Cabins.

Pioneer Mountain Trail

Location: McKee Scout Reservation, 8 miles south of Mt. Sterling, KY. *Theme:* Old logging route. *Sponsor:* Blue Grass Council, BSA, 415 N. Broadway, Lexington, KY 40506.

Length: 8.0 miles. *Route:* Contact sponsor for map. *Terrain:* Rugged wilderness roads, streambeds and footpaths. *Cycling:* Not appropriate. *Awards:* Patch. *Submit:* Request for patches. *Register:* In advance for use of scout reservation.

Red River Gorge Trails

Location: Daniel Boone National Forest, Stanton, KY. *Theme:* Geological sites. *Sponsor:* Stanton Ranger District, Supervisor's Office, 1700 Bypass Rd., Winchester, KY 40391, (859) 745-3100. *Lengths:* Double Arch Trail (#201), 1.0 mile. Courthouse Rock Trail (#202), 2.2 miles. Auxier Branch Trail (#203), 0.8 mile. Auxier Ridge Trail (#204), 1.1 miles. Grays Arch Trail (#205), 0.9 mile. Cliff Trail (#206), 0.8 mile. Rock Bridge Trail (#207), 1.3 miles. Hidden Arch Trail (#208), 1.0 mile. Daniel Boone Hut Trail (#209), 0.7 mile. Bison Way Trail (#210), 0.8 mile. Sky Bridge Trail (#214), 0.9 mile. Whittleton Branch Trail (#216), 2.0 miles. Whittleton Arch Trail (#217), 0.2 mile. Angel Windows Trail (#218), 0.3 mile. Swift Camp Creek Trail (#219), 6.7 miles. Koomer Ridge Trail (#220), 2.3 miles. Rough Trail (#221), 7.2 miles. Pinch-Em-Tight Trail (#223), 1.8 miles. Silvermine Arch Trail (#225), 0.9 mile. Buck Trail (#226), 1.5 miles. Rush Ridge Trail (#227), 1.0 mile. Wildcat Trail (#228), 1.3 miles. Tower Rock Trail (#229), 1.0 mile. Princess Arch Trail (#233), 0.2 mile. Whistling Arch Trail (#234), 0.2 mile. Chimney Top Rock Trail (#235), 0.3 mile. *Routes:* Vary—check map and brochure from sponsor. *Terrain:* Varies, some steep. *Cycling:* Possible on some trails. *Awards:* Patch $3.00. *Submit:* Request for patches. *Register:* Not required.

Road Runner Trail

Location: Tom Wallace Lake Park, Jefferson County, KY. *Theme:* Scenic views of Tom Wallace Lake. *Sponsor:* Ms. Sandy Tucker, 11202 Holsclaw Hill Rd., Fairdale, KY 40118, (502) 368-8832.

Length: 10.0 miles. *Route:* The trail begins at Mitchell Hill Rd. and continues along Top Hill Rd., Jefferson Hill Rd., Keysferry Rd., Manslick Rd., and Mitchell Hill Rd. back to the starting point. *Terrain:* Paved roads. *Cycling:* Recommended. *Awards:* Patch. *Submit:* Group leader's certificate of completion. *Register:* In advance.

Shawnee Hunting Trails

Location: Lake Malone State Park, Greenville, KY. *Theme:* Woodland scenic cliffs. *Sponsor:* Tom Lewis, 202 Highland Dr., Greenville, KY 42345, (270) 338-3577. *Lengths:* Beaver Trail, 10 miles. Canyon Rim Trail, 14 miles. Lake Malone Trail, 10 miles. *Routes:* Beaver Trail begins at the bridge across the lake at the Shady Cliff boat dock, and ends at Robert Whittaker Rd. Lake Malone Trail begins and ends on the Thomas Younts farm on Dunmore Rd. leading through the park. Canyon Rim Trail begins at Jason Ridge Rd. passing through the gorge and ends at the Shady Cliff boat dock. *Terrain:* Canyon rims along the lake. *Cycling:* Impossible. *Awards:* Medal (Beaver-Shawnee Trail); 3 Patches. *Submit:* Group leader's certificate of completion. *Register:* At least one week in advance. *Sites:* Bear Bluff, Balance Rock, Beaver Dam, Beaver Dam, Canyon Rims, Cliff Canyon, Cliff Rocks, Lake Malone.

Sheltoweee Trace

Location: Daniel Boone National Forest, Southern Kentucky. *Theme:* Scenic sites of Morehead Ranger District. *Sponsor:* U.S. Forest Service, Morehead Ranger District, 2375 SR 801 South, Morehead, KY 40351, (606) 784-6478.

Length: 300+ miles. *Route:* The trail brochure includes all trails (start to finish) from the ranger station. *Terrain:* Hills and woodlands. *Cycling:* Not recommended.

Awards: Patch $4.00. *Submit:* Request for patches. *Register:* Not required.

Triple Arch Trail

Location: Daniel Boone National Forest, Louisville, KY. *Theme:* Climbing of three major peaks. *Sponsor:* Troop 321, c/o Larry Tour, 210 Doorshire Ct., Louisville, KY 40245, (502) 245-6254; or Lincoln Heritage Council, BSA, 824 Phillips Ln., Louisville, KY 40245, (502) 361-1513.
Length: 14.4 miles (loop). *Route:* The trail loops through Red River Gorge Park. *Terrain:* Woodlands with steep climbing. *Cycling:* Not appropriate. *Awards:* Medal; Patch. *Submit:* Group leader's certificate of completion. *Register:* Not required.

Wah-La-Ha Trail

Location: Frankfort, KY. *Theme:* Kentucky history. *Sponsor:* Wah-La-Ha—Buffalo Trail, Inc., 420 Ewing St., Frankfort, KY 40601.
Length: 7 miles (straight). *Route:* The trail begins across the E-W Connector at the end of the Buffalo Trail, heads north to cross the Kentucky River at Capital Ave., then around the Capitol and across the river on the Singing Bridge, to end at the Old State Capitol (where the Buffalo Trail starts). *Terrain:* City streets. *Cycling:* Appropriate. *Awards:* Medal $3.00; Patch $2.00; 1st and 2nd Repeat Pins $1.50 each. *Submit:* Completed 10-item questionnaire. *Register:* Request hike date in advance. *Sites:* Regional Jail, Kentucky Military History Museum, Vietnam Memorial, Rebecca and Daniel Boone's Grave, Old State Capitol, Floral Clock, New State Capitol.

Zollicoffer Trail

Location: Somerset, KY. *Theme:* Battle of Mill Springs—January 19, 1862. *Sponsor:* Troop 79, c/o Pat Green, Starview Dr., Somerset, KY 42501; or c/o Dr. Harry Kennedy, 340 Bogle St., Somerset, KY 42501, (606) 678-4155; or c/o Dr. Robert Drake, Jr., 121 Rebel Dr., Somerset, KY 42501, (606) 679-1449.
Length: 11.5 miles (straight). *Route:* The trail begins at the Pulaki County Park road sign on SR 80, heads west on SR 80 and south on SR 235 to the shore of Lake Cumberland. *Terrain:* Roads. *Cycling:* Possible, but check with sponsor to see if that qualifies for awards. *Awards:* Patch $3.00. *Submit:* Completed 10-item questionnaire. *Register:* Not required. *Sites:* National Cemetery, Oakalona Church, Zollicoffer Park Monument, Rifle Breastworks, Confederate Grave Marker, Delmer Nazarene Church.

Formerly Sponsored Trails

Arboretum Trail
Blue Grass Trail
Christopher Gist Trail
Dan Beard Memorial Trail
Dry Canteen Trail
Dug Road March
George Rogers Clark Trace
Hames Ridge Wilderness Trail
Horine Memorial Trail
Jefferson Forest Loop Trail
Kentucky Boone Trail
Kentucky Heritage Trail
Kentucky Zollicoffer Trail
Louisville Heritage Trail
Mammoth Cave Explorers Trail
Munfordville Battlefield Trek
Old Bison Trail
Perryville Pilgrimage Trek
River Overlook Trail
Roy G. Manchester Trail
Salt Rim Trail
Shaker Trail
Siltstone Trail
Silver Eagle Trail
Tom Wallace Forest Trail
Wagon Wheel Trace
Wilderness Road Trail
Windy Hollow Trail

LOUISIANA

Bienville Trail

Location: New Orleans, LA. *Theme:* Local history. *Sponsor:* R.J. Daret, 1312 Broadway, New Orleans, LA 70118, (504) 861-8611.

Length: 4.8 miles (straight). *Route:* The trail begins at Scout Island, follows Esplanade Dr., and ends in the French Quarter. *Terrain:* City streets. *Cycling:* Appropriate. *Awards:* Patch $2.00. *Submit:* No requirement. *Register:* Not required. *Sites:* New Orleans Museum of Art, Duelling Oaks, Spanish Custom House, Old Spanish Stables, Haunted House, Ursulines Convent, Beauregard House, Jackson Square, Saint Louis Cathedral, St. Anthony's Garden, Musee Conti Wax Museum, State Museum, International Trade Mart.

Capitol Historical Trail

Location: Baton Rouge, LA. *Theme:* Local history. *Sponsor:* Louisiana Hiking Trails, Inc., 1833 Cloverdale Ave., Baton Rouge, LA 70808, (225) 344-4287.

Length: 7 miles (straight). *Route:* The trail begins at the Parker Agricultural Center at the Louisiana State University campus and ends at the Capitol. *Terrain:* City streets. *Cycling:* Appropriate. *Awards:* Medal $3.75; Patch $2.00; Pin $1.50. *Submit:* Completed 13-item questionnaire. *Register:* Not required. *Sites:* Anglo-American Museum, Memorial Tower, Museum of Natural History, LSU Stadium, Magnolia Mound Plantation, Mississippi River, U.S.S. Kidd, Red Stick, Old State Capitol, Louisiana Arts and Science Center, New State Capitol, Governor's Mansion.

Carrollton Historical Trail

Location: New Orleans, LA. *Theme:* Route of New Orleans and Carrollton Railroad. *Sponsor:* R.J. Daret, 1312 Broadway, New Orleans, LA 70118, (504) 861-8611.

Length: 5.2 miles (straight). *Route:* The trail begins at Ben Franklin High School at 719 Carrollton and follows the train tracks to Lafayette Square. *Terrain:* City streets. *Cycling:* Appropriate. *Awards:* Patch $2.00. *Submit:* No requirement. *Register:* Not required. *Sites:* Camelback Houses, Dominican College, Doll House, Audubon Place, Tulane University, Loyola University, Audubon Park, Wedding Cake House, Sacred Heart Academy, Tara, Christ Church Cathedral, Unity Temple, Garden District, Julia Row, Lafayette Square, Gallier Hall.

Carruth Historic Trails

Location: Port Allen, LA. *Theme:* Local history. *Sponsor:* West Baton Rouge Historical Association—Trails, 845 N. Jefferson, Port Allen, LA 70767.

Length: 2 or 10 miles (loops). *Routes:* The trails start at the West Baton Rouge Museum and loop through city (10 miles) or rural (2 miles) areas to return to the museum. *Terrain:* City streets and river levee. *Cycling:* Appropriate. *Awards:* 2 Patches $2.00 each; Pin $1.00. *Submit:* Completed 9-item questionnaire. *Register:* Upon arrival at the museum. *Sites:* West Baton Rouge Museum, Historic Slave Cabin, Old Courthouse, Mississippi River, New Courthouse, Masonic Building.

Chalmette Historical Trail

Location: Chalmette, LA. *Theme:* Battle of New Orleans. *Sponsor:* David N. Liggio, Troop 79, BSA, P.O. Box 70, Arabi, LA 70032-0070, (504) 271-6400 or (504) 278-7458.

Length: 7 or 16 miles (straight). *Route:* The trail begins at the ferry landing in Scarsdale and follows the levee up the Mississippi River to Chalmette National Historical Park. *Terrain:* River levee. *Cycling:* Appropriate. *Awards:* Patch. *Submit:* No requirement. *Register:* At least 1 week in advance. *Sites:* Braithwaite Park, Chalmette National Historical Park, Caernarvon Canal, Cuban American Nickel Plant, de la Ronde Plantation House Ruins, St. Bernard State Park, Tenneco Oil Co. Refinery, Murphy Oil Co. Refinery, American Sugar Refinery, Kaiser Aluminum Plant.

Istrouma Trail

Location: Avondale Scout Reservation, Clinton, LA. *Theme:* Commemoration of founding of Baton Rouge. *Sponsor:* Istrouma Area Council, BSA, P.O. Box 66676, Baton Rouge, LA 70896, (225) 926-2697.

Length: 11 miles (loop). *Route:* The trail begins and ends at Hickory Hill and covers 33 numbered points on the reservation. *Terrain:* Woods. *Cycling:* Not recommended. *Awards:* Patch. *Submit:* Group leader's certification of completion. *Register:* At least 1 week in advance. *Sites:* Indian Mound, Grist Mill Remains, Lake Istrouma, Tigator Lake Dam, Caddo House, McGee Lake.

Little Red Church Historic Trail

Location: Destrehan, LA. *Theme:* History of the church. *Sponsor:* Craig N. Melancon, 10 Horse Shoe Ln., St. Rose, LA 70087-9656.

Length: 10 miles (straight). *Route:* The trail begins at the site of the Destrehan-Luling ferry landing, takes River Rd. north and west to the spillway levee in Norco, which takes the hikers northeast to the spillway campgrounds at the end. *Terrain:* Road and levee. *Cycling:* Appropriate. *Awards:* Patch. *Submit:* No requirement. *Register:* Not required. *Sites:* St. Charles Grain Elevator, Destrehan Manor House, Little Red Church, Shell Norco Manufacturing Complex, Ormond Plantation, Myrtleland Plantation, Bonnet Carre Spillway.

Spanish Fort Trail

Location: Metarie, LA. *Theme:* Historic Spanish fort. *Sponsor:* BSA Troop 269, P.O. Box 6245, Metarie, LA 70009.

Length: 9.5 miles (straight). *Route:* The trail begins at the intersection of Jefferson Davis Parkway and Tulane Ave., heads north along the parkway and Wisner Blvd. to Lake Ponchartrain, then west to the public boat launch area. *Terrain:* City streets. *Cycling:* Appropriate. *Awards:* Patch $5.00. *Submit:* Completed 16-item questionnaire. *Register:* Not required. *Sites:* St. Louis III Cemetery, Ft. St. John, Lighthouse, Plantation House, Beauregard Statue, Pan American Stadium, Bayou St. John, New Orleans Civil Defense Shelter, Mardi Gras Fountain.

Other Louisiana Awards

River Heritage Award—Mississippi River cruise and guided tour. Patch included in $4.50 price. New Orleans Steamboat Company, 2340 World Trade Center, New Orleans, LA 70130, (504) 586-8777.

U.S.S. Kidd Overnight Award—Overnight on a destroyer. Patch included in overnight price. U.S.S. Kidd, 305 S. River Rd., Baton Rouge, LA 70802, (225) 342-1942.

Formerly Sponsored Trails

Chitimacha Trail
Dogwood Trail
Fort Jackson Trail
Harahan Historic Trail
Harahan Levee Hike
Mansfield Battlepark Trail
Rocky Mt. Trail

MAINE

Colonial Ramblings

Location: York, ME. *Theme:* Local history. *Sponsor:* Virginia S. Spiller, Colonial Ramblings, 71 York St., York, ME 03909-1324.

Length: 1.6-5 miles (3 loops). *Route:* The trail begins at the Revolutionary Marker between the Town Hall and the First Parish Church, on the Village Green. *Terrain:* City sidewalks, woods trail, grass path, street shoulders. *Cycling:* Appropriate. *Awards:* Patch $4.00. *Submit:* Completed 10-item questionnaire. *Register:* Not required (but send $4.00 in advance for the trail guide). *Sites:* Emerson-Wilcox House, Old Gaol, Joseph Horn House, Old Schoolhouse, Green Dragon Inn, Jefferds Tavern, Barrell Mill Pond, John Hancock's Wharf, Soldiers Monument, Sewall's Bridge, Old Burying Ground, Ebenezer Coburn House, The Moulton Properties, Lt. Joseph Banks House, General John Harmon House, Nicholas Sewall House, Dr. Joseph Gilman House, Lt. Daniel Simpson House.

MARYLAND

Antietam Battlefield Historic Trail

Location: Sharpsburg, MD. *Theme:* Bloodiest day in the Civil War—September 17, 1862. *Sponsor:* Mason-Dixon Council, BSA, 18600 Crestwood, P.O. Box 2133, Hagerstown, MD 21742-2133, (301) 739-1211.

Length: 10.5 miles (loop). *Route:* The trail begins and ends at either the Visitors Center or the Rohrbach Camping Area. *Terrain:* Most of the trail is paved roads, with some dirt paths. *Cycling:* Appropriate on the road portions only. *Awards:* Patch $2.00; Medal $2.25 for completing this trail and the Appalachian Trail (Maryland segment), a portion of the C & O Historical Trail, and the Forbes Road Trail. *Submit:* Group leader's certification of completion. *Register:* Check in at visitor center. *Sites:* Visitors Center, Slave Auction Block, New York Monument, Dunkard Church, Mansfield Monument, Mumma Farm, Old Vermont Brigade Monument, Sunken Road, Burnside Bridge, McKinley Monument, Otto House, Lower Bridge, Hawkins Zouaves Monument, Jacob Grove House, National Cemetery, U.S. Soldiers Monument, Sherrick House, Bloody Lane.

Appalachian Trail

Location: Franklin County, PA and Washington County, MD. *Theme:* Recreation. *Sponsor:* Mason-Dixon Council, BSA, 18600 Crestwood, P.O. Box 2133, Hagerstown, MD 21742-2899, (301) 739-1211.

Length: 44 miles (straight). *Route:* The trail begins at the Potomac River in Maryland and runs northward to Camp Penn, just northeast of Waynesboro, PA. *Terrain:* Mountain ridges. *Cycling:* Not recommended. *Awards:* Patch $2.00; Medal $2.25 for completing this trail, the Antietam Battlefield Historic Trail, a portion of the C & 0 Canal Historical Trail, and the Forbes Road Trail. *Submit:* Group leader's certification of completion. *Register:* In advance.

Baltimore Historical Trails

Location: Baltimore, MD. *Theme:* Local History. *Sponsor:* Baltimore Area Council, BSA, 701 Wyman Park Dr., Baltimore, MD 21211-2899, (410) 338-1700.

Length: Cannon Segment, 7.5 miles (straight). Railroad Segment, 6.0 miles (straight). Shot Tower Segment, 5.0 miles (straight). Thinker Segment, 8.5 miles (straight). *Routes:* Cannon Segment—Eastern Ave. and Linwood to Fort McHenry. Railroad Segment—Carroll Park to Old Otterbein United Methodist Church. Shot Tower Segment—Maryland Historical Society at 201 W. Monument St. to Carroll Mansion. Thinker Segment—Lillie Carroll Jackson Museum, 1320 Eutaw Pl. to Baltimore Zoo. *Terrain:* City streets. *Cycling:* Appropriate. *Awards:* Medal $7.00; Patch $1.25; 4 Segments $0.70 each. *Submit:* No requirement. *Register:* Not required. *Sites:* Pulaski Monument, Observatory Tower, National Aquarium, U.S.S. Torsk, Shot Tower, Star-Spangled Banner House, Camden Railroad Station, U.S. Frigate Constellation, Baltimore Public Works Museum, Maryland Line Monument, Maryland Science Center and Planetarium, Charles P. McCormick Spice Co., Federal Hill Park, Poe Monument, Baltimore Museum of History, Fort McHenry, Baltimore Art Museum, Washington Monument, Carroll Mansion, Peabody Institute, Baltimore Zoo, Peale Museum, Mount Clare Mansion, Babe Ruth House, Railroad Museum, Baltimore Conservatory, Baltimore Arts Tower, Old Otterbein United Methodist Church, Francis Scott Key Monument, Lovely Lane Methodist Church, Lillie Carroll Jackson Museum, Basilica of the Assumption.

The Battle of Bladensburg and the Star Spangled Banner Trail

Location: Benedict to Bladensburg, MD. *Theme:* Battle of August 24, 1814. *Sponsor:* American Historical Trails, Inc., P.O. Box 769, Monroe, NC 28111-0769, (704) 289-1604, Carotrader@trellis.net.

Length: 53 miles (straight)—this was formerly a walking or biking trail, but the present sponsor recommends driving instead, stopping at the various sites. *Route:* The trail begins in Benedict, MD, and goes to

Nottingham and St. Thomas Church, Upper Marlboro, Melwood Park, and ends at Lincoln Cemetery in Bladensburg. *Terrain:* Paved roads. *Cycling:* Appropriate, can also be driven. *Awards:* Medal $6.50; Patch $2.25. *Submit:* Completion of 8-item questionnaire. *Register:* No requirement. *Sites:* John Halterman's Farm, St. Thomas Church, Benedict Marker, Beanes Grave, Battle of Bladensburg Historical Marker, Old Spring House, Nottingham Sign, Upper Marlboro, Floral Clock, Melwood Park House, Peace Cross, Ft. Lincoln Cemetery.

C & O Canal Historical Trail

Location: Hancock to Sandy Hook, MD. *Theme:* Route of Chesapeake and Ohio Canal. *Sponsor:* Mason-Dixon Council, BSA, 18600 Crestwood, P.O. Box 2133, Hagerstown, MD 21742-2133, (301) 739-1211.

Length: 184.5 miles (straight). *Route:* The segment of the trail qualifying one for an award is the 64.0 mile Crossed Flags Segment which runs from Hancock to Sandy Hook. *Terrain:* Canal towpath and roads. *Cycling:* Appropriate, and so is canoeing. *Awards:* Patch $2.00; 5 Segments $0.80 each; Medal for completion of 184.5 miles $4.50; Barge Pin for completing 184.5 miles twice $1.25; Medal $2.25 for completing Crossed Flags Segment, the Antietam Battlefield Historic Trail, the Maryland portion of the Appalachian Trail, and the Forbes Road Trail. *Submit:* Group leader's certification of completion. *Register:* In advance.

Colonial Annapolis Historical Trail

Location: Annapolis, MD. *Theme:* Local history. *Sponsor:* American Historical Trails, Inc., P.O. Box 769, Monroe, NC 28111-0769, (704) 289-1604, Carotrader@trellis.net.

Length: Route A, 7 miles (straight). Route B, 11 miles (straight). Route C, 14.5 miles (straight). *Route:* The trail begins at the parking lot behind the Maryland Department of Natural Resources at Taylor Ave., winds through Annapolis, and ends at the Hammond-Harwood House (Route A),

Stewart-Stone House (Route B), or the Quynn-Brewer House (Route C). *Terrain:* City streets. *Cycling:* Appropriate. *Awards:* Medal $6.00; Patch $2.25. *Submit:* Completed 50-item questionnaire. *Register:* Not required. *Sites:* State House, Taney Statue, Old Iron Cannon, Old Treasury Building, DeKalb Statue, Brooksby-Shaw House, Government House, Tomb of Sir Robert Eden, Sign O' the Whale, Summer Garden Theatre, Tobacco Prise House, Bordley-Randall House, Barrister's House, Monument to the French, Liberty Tree, Hammond-Harwood House, Ridout Homes, U.S. Naval Academy, U.S.S. Maine Memorial, Sign of the Bible, John Paul Jones' Sarcophagus, Stewart-Stone House, Quynn-Brewer House, Reynold's Tavern.

Defenders Trail

Location: Dundalk, MD. *Theme:* Battle of Northpoint—September, 1814. *Sponsor:* Dundalk-Patapsco Neck Historical Society, P.O. Box 21781, Dundalk, MD 21222.

Length: 10 miles (straight). *Route:* The trail begins at the Fort Howard Historic Marker and ends at North Point Shopping Center. *Terrain:* Paved road. *Cycling:* Appropriate. *Awards:* Patch $1.50. *Submit:* No requirement. *Register:* In advance. *Sites:* Aquila Randall Monument, Todds Inheritance, Ft. Howard Veterans Hospitalm Battle Acre, Ross' Death Site Marker, Cooks Tavern Site, Methodist Meeting House Marker.

Formerly Sponsored Trails

Annapolis Pathways
C & O Canal Towpath Trail
Chief Nemacolin's Trail
Eastern Short Trail
General A.P. Hill's Forced March
Governor Johnson Patriot Trail
Mansfield's Approach Trail
McLaw's Approach Trail
Monocacy Battle Trail
Sharpsburg Line Trail

MASSACHUSETTS

Appalachian Trail In Massachusetts

Location: Berkshire County, MA. *Theme:* Recreation. *Sponsor:* Great Trails Council, BSA, 88 Old Windsor Rd., Dalton, MA 01226, (413) 684-3542.

Length: 85 miles (straight). *Route:* The Massachusetts portion of the trail extends from the Connecticut border near Sage's Ravine and heads north to the Vermont border in Clarksburg State Forest. *Terrain:* Mountains. *Cycling:* Not recommended. *Awards:* Patch. *Submit:* Log of hikes. *Register:* Not required.

Blue Hills Trails

Location: Milton, MA. *Theme:* Nature. *Sponsor:* Witch Trail Committee, 157 Circuit Rd., Winthrop, MA 02152-2820, (617) 846-2626.

Length: 2 and 8 miles (loops). *Route:* The trails may be started either at the Trailside Museum on SR 138, or at Sayre Scout Reservation on Uniquity Rd. in Milton. *Terrain:* Woods. *Cycling:* Not recommended. *Awards:* Medal $2.50; 2 Patches $2.00 each. *Submit:* No requirement. *Register:* In advance. *Sites:* Trailside Museum, Stone Tower, Hancock Hill, Houghton Hill.

Boston Bicentennial Trail of Freedom

Location: Boston, MA. *Theme:* Revolutionary War history. *Sponsor:* American Historical Trails, Inc., P.O. Box 769, Monroe, NC 28111-0629, (704) 289-1604, Carotrader@trellis.net.

Length: 7.5 miles (straight). *Route:* The trail begins at Faneuil Hall, winds through Boston and ends at the Massachusetts State House (Route A), the Old North Church (Route B), the U.S. Frigate Constitution (Route C), or the Continental Bakery Site (Route D). *Terrain:* City streets. *Cycling:* Appropriate. *Awards:* Medal $6.50; 2 patches $2.25 each. *Submit:* Completed 70-item questionnaire. *Register:* Not required. *Sites:* Faneuil Hall, Boston Massacre Site, New England Courant Site, Old Corner Bookstore, Samuel Adams Statue, Old State House, Boston Tea Party Site, James Otis Home Site, Bunch of Grapes Tavern Site, Franklin's Birthplace, Old South Meeting House, Franklin Statue, Granary Burying Ground, Franklin Tomb, Boston Common, Revere Tomb, Kosciuszko Statue, Paul Revere House, Flagstaff Hill, Bunker Hill.

Bread and Roses Strike Trail

Location: Lawrence, MA. *Theme:* Mill workers' strike of 1912. *Sponsor:* Bread and Roses Strike Trail Associates, 37 Linehan St., Lawrence, MA 01841.

Length: 3.5 miles (loop). *Route:* The trail begins at 430 North Canal St., traces the steps of the strikers, and returns to the start. *Terrain:* City streets. *Cycling:* Appropriate. *Awards:* Patch $2.50. *Submit:* Completed 10-item questionnaire. Register In advance. *Sites:* Lawton's Hot Dog Stand, Dam Gatehouse, Great Stone Dam, Atlantic Mills, Lower Pacific Mill, Ayer Mills, Lawrence Duck Company Mills, Wood Worsted Mills, Everett Mill, Essex Company, American Woolen Company, Pemberton Park, Washington Mills.

Footsteps of Our Founders Trail

Location: Fall River, MA. *Theme:* Local history. *Sponsor:* Moby Dick Council, BSA, 39 Grove St., New Bedford, MA 02740-3498, (508) 993-9978 or (508) 678-2858.

Length: 6.5 miles (loop). *Route:* The trail may begin either at the Fall River Chamber of Commerce or at the Battleship Cove, and heads through the city's historic highlands. *Terrain:* City streets. *Cycling:* Appropriate. *Awards:* Patch. *Submit:* Group leader's certification of completion. *Register:* At least 3 weeks in advance. *Sites:* St. Anne's Church and Shrine, Columbia Street Historic District, St. Mary's Cathedral, B.M.C. Durfee High School.

Freedom Trail

Location: Boston, MA. *Theme:* Revolutionary War history. *Sponsor:* Boston Minuteman Council, BSA, 199 State St., 3rd Floor, Boston, MA 02109, (617) 723-0007, council@bsaboston.org.

Length: 5 miles (loop). *Route:* The trail begins and ends at the Boston Common

Visitor Information Booth, after visiting the U.S.S. Constitution at Charlestown, by following the red lines painted on the sidewalk. *Terrain:* City streets. *Cycling:* Appropriate. *Awards:* Medal $5.00; Patch $2.50; Hat Pin $2.25. *Submit:* Completed 11-item questionnaire, including signatures of persons present at 2 of the sites. *Register:* In advance. *Sites:* Boston Common, State House, Park Street Church, King's Chapel, Old Granary Burying Ground, Faneuil Hall, First Public School Site, Franklin Statue, Old Corner Book Store, Old South Meeting House, Franklin Birthplace, Old State House, Boston Massacre Site, Paul Revere House.

Hancock Shaker Trail

Location: Hancock Shaker Village, MA. *Theme:* Mid-19th century Shaker community. *Sponsor:* Great Trails Council, BSA, 88 Old Windsor Rd., Dalton, MA 01226, (413) 684-3542.

Length: 6 miles (nearly a loop). *Route:* The trail begins behind the Meeting House in the village, tours the village, then passes through Pittsfield State Forest and returns to near the start. *Terrain:* Roads, hills and valleys. *Cycling:* Not recommended. *Awards:* Patch. *Submit:* Completed 10-item questionnaire. *Register:* In advance. *Sites:* Hancock Shaker Village, Pittsfield State Forest, North Home Foundation, Meeting House, Holy Mount, Mt. Sinai.

Isaac Davis Trail

Location: Acton to Concord, MA. *Theme:* Route used by Captain Isaac Davis of Acton Minutemen in historic march to Concord on April 19, 1775. *Sponsor:* Scouters of the Isaac Davis Trail, P.O. Box 763, Acton, MA 01720.

Length: 7 miles (straight). *Route:* The trail begins at the home of Isaac Davis in Acton, and ends at the Old North Bridge in Concord. *Terrain:* Paved roads and dirt paths. *Cycling:* Not recommended. *Awards:* Medal $3.50; Patch $1.50; Hat Pins $1.50; Mug $3.50. *Submit:* Completed 10-item questionnaire. *Register:* In advance. *Sites:* Captain Davis Home, Old North Bridge, Acton Center Monument, Woodlawn Cemetery, Capt. Isaac Davis Monument, Old North Burying Ground.

Leslie's Retreat Trail

Location: Marblehead to Salem, MA.

Theme: Retraces British march of February 26, 1775. *Sponsor:* Witch Trail Committee, 157 Circuit Rd., Winthrop, MA 02152-2820, (617) 846-2626.

Length: 6 miles (straight) or 10 miles (loop). *Route:* The trail begins at Fort Sewall in Marblehead, takes SR 114 toward Salem, and ends at the Peabody Museum on Essex St. in Salem. *Terrain:* City streets. *Cycling:* Appropriate. *Awards:* Medal $2.50; Patch $2.00. *Submit:* Completed 13-item questionnaire. *Register:* In advance. *Sites:* Site of Old Meeting House, Old North Church, Home of Major John Pedrick, Abbot Hall, Home of Elbridge Gerry, Forest River, Home of John Glover, South River, Old Town House, St. Michael's Episcopal Church, North Bridge.

Pirate Legend Trail and Trek

Location: Lynn, MA. *Theme:* History of Lynn Woods. *Sponsor:* Witch Trail Committee, 157 Circuit Rd., Winthrop, MA 02152-2820, (617) 846-2626.

Length: Trail, 10 miles (loop). Trek, 4 miles (loop). *Route:* Both routes begin and end at the Western Gate of Lynn Woods, and cover the western side of the area. The 10-mile trail also includes a loop on the eastern side of Lynn Woods. *Terrain:* Well-defined woods paths. *Cycling:* Not recommended. *Awards:* Trail Medal $2.50; Trail Patch $2.00; Trek Medal $2.50; Trek Patch $2.00. *Submit:* No requirement. *Register:* In advance. *Sites:* Pirate Grave, Treasure Cave, Wolf Pits, Mt. Gilead, Walden Pond, Dungeon Rock, Burrill Hill, Tomlin's Swamp, Breed's Pond, Stone Tower, Ramsdell's Swamp.

Sky Line Trail

Location: Middlesex Fells Reservation, Stoneham, MA. *Theme:* Indian history. *Sponsor:* Witch Trail Committee, 157 Circuit Rd., Winthrop, MA 02152-2820, (617) 846-2626.

Length: 7 miles (loop). *Route:* The trail begins and ends at the parking lot of the MDC off SR 28, and circles the North, Middle, and South Reservoirs. *Terrain:* Woods. *Cycling:* Not recommended. *Awards:* Medal $2.50; Patch $2.00. *Submit:* No requirement. *Register:* In advance. *Sites:* Boston Skyline, Pine Hill, Bear Hill, Money Hill, Grinding Rock Hill, Winthrop Hill, Silver Mine, Panther Cave, Nanepashemet Hill, Gerry Hill.

Sons of Liberty Trail

Location: Lexington to Concord, MA. *Theme:* Route of British soldiers advancing to Concord on April 19, 1775. *Sponsor:* Witch Trail Committee, 157 Circuit Rd., Winthrop, MA 02152-2820, (617) 846-2626.

Length: 10 miles (straight). *Route:* The trail begins at the Lexington Green, heads west toward Concord, and ends at the information center at the North Bridge. *Terrain:* City streets and fields. *Cycling:* Not recommended. *Awards:* Medal $2.50; Patch $2.00. *Submit:* Completed 13-item questionnaire. *Register:* In advance. *Sites:* Buckman Tavern, Hancock-Clarke House, Jonathan Harrington House, Minute Man Boulder, Minute Man Statue, The Old Monument, Ye Old Burying Ground, Hayward's Well, Bloody Angle, Meriam's Corner, Old North Bridge, Wright's Tavern.

Spirit of '76 Trail

Location: Marblehead, MA. *Theme:* Revolutionary War history. *Sponsor:* Witch Trail Committee, 157 Circuit Rd., Winthrop, MA 02152-2820, (617) 846-2626.

Length: 2 miles (loop). *Route:* The trail begins and ends at the Marblehead Town Hall, and makes a loop through the center of Marblehead. *Terrain:* City streets. *Cycling:* Appropriate. *Awards:* Medal $2.50; Patch $2.00. *Submit:* Completed 15-item questionnaire. *Register:* In advance. *Sites:*

Spirit of '76 Painting, Abbot Hall, Col. Jeremiah Lee Mansion, 1680 Tavern, Home of Gen. John Glover, Crocker Park, King Hooper Mansion, Lafayette House, Lovis Cove, Fort Sewall, Elbridge Gerry Home, Old Burial Hill, Major John Pedrick's Home, Old Town House, Tory Headquarters.

Witch Trail

Location: Danvers to Salem, MA. *Theme:* 1692 witchcraft hysteria. *Sponsor:* Witch Trail Committee, 157 Circuit Rd., Winthrop, MA 02152-2820, (617) 846-2626.

Length: 10 miles (straight). *Route:* The trail begins at the old Village Training Field on Centre St. in Danvers, heads down Centre, Holton, Pine, Adams, Sylvan and High Sts. in Danvers, then south on SR 35 to Salem, where the trail loops through downtown to end at Gallows Hill Park. *Terrain:* City streets. *Cycling:* Appropriate. *Awards:* Medal $2.50; Patch $2.00. *Submit:* Completed 14-item questionnaire. *Register:* In advance. *Sites:* Charter St. Burial Ground, Witch House, Statue of Founder of Salem, Holten House, Essex Institute, Haines House, Wadsworth House, Watch House Hill, Ingersoll House, Foundation of Rev. Parris' House, Nurse Graveyard, Jail Site.

Former Sponsored Trail

Chelmsford-Concord Trail

MICHIGAN

Chief Pontiac Trail

Location: Pontiac, MI. *Theme:* Ottawa Indians and Chief Pontiac. *Sponsor:* Clinton Valley Council, BSA, P.O. Box 431173, 1100 County Center Dr., W., Pontiac, MI 48053-1173, (248) 338-0035.

Length: 16.7 miles (straight). *Route:* The trail begins in the Highland State Recreation Area near Teeple Hill, runs through the Barnfield Trial Area, Proud Lake State Recreation Area, and Wixom Road Picnic Area, and ends at the bridge over the Huron River in the Kensington Metropark. *Terrain:*

Hills, woods, dirt and blacktop roads. *Cycling:* Not recommended; a portion may be canoed. *Awards:* Medal and Patch $6.00; OA Medal and Patch $6.00; Honorary Medal n/c; Canoe Pin $1.50; Service Project Patch n/c; Winter Pin $1.50; Canoeist Patch $1.50; Winter Patch $1.50; Pioneer Patch $1.50. *Submit:* Group leader's certification of completion of hike, required essays, and hike reports. *Register:* At least 45 days in advance. *Sites:* Milford Dam, Mt. Omich, Haven Hill Lake, Beaumont Overlook, Proud Lake Nature Center.

Cuwe Wilderness Trail

Location: Northern Oakland County, MI.
Theme: Recreation. *Sponsor:* Tall Pine
Council, BSA, 202 E. Boulevard Dr., Flint, MI
48503-1894, (810) 235-2531.
Length: 22 miles (loop). *Route:* The trail
begins at the organizational campground on
McGinnes Rd., loops through the Holly
Recreation Area, and returns to the start.
Terrain: Woods, ridges, and marshes.
Cycling: Not recommended. *Awards:* Medal
$3.00; Patch $2.25. *Submit:* No requirement.
Register: Not required.

Potawatomi Trail

Location: Pinckney Recreation Area near
Ann Arbor, MI. *Theme:* Recreation. *Sponsor:*
Great Sauk Trail Council, BSA, 1979 Huron
Pkwy., Ann Arbor, MI 48104-4115, (734) 971-
7100.
Length: 17.0 miles (loop). *Route:* The trail
begins at Hadley Rd. south of Bruin Lake
Scout Camp, circles the recreation area and
returns to the start. *Terrain:* Woods. *Cycling:*
Not recommended. *Awards:* Medal $3.50;
Patch $2.75; Repeater Patch $2.75; Five-Mile
Patch $1.50. *Submit:* No requirement.
Register: Not required. *Sites:* Little Mackinac
Bridge, U of M Radiotelescope, George Game
Preserve, Silver Lake.

President Ford Trail

Location: Grand Rapids, MI. *Theme:*
President Gerald R. Ford. *Sponsor:* Gerald R.
Ford Council, BSA, 1935 Monroe Ave., NW,
Grand Rapids, MI 49505-6295, (616) 363-
3828.
Length: 2 miles (straight). *Route:* The trail
begins at the West Michigan Shores Service
Center at 1935 Monroe Ave., proceeds north
along Monroe, crosses the Grand River at
Michigan St., and ends at the Ford Museum.
Terrain: City streets. *Cycling:* Appropriate.
Awards: Medal $4.50; Patch $3.00; Mug
$3.00. *Submit:* 200 word essay plus group
leader's certification of hike (for patch) or
hike and 8-mile canoe float (for medal).
Register: In advance. *Sites:* Ford Museum,
Ford Federal Building, Ah-Nab-Awen Indian
Mounds, Fish Ladder, Hyser House, Grand
River, Calder Plaza.

Formerly Sponsored Trails

Au Sable Canoe Trek
Chief Noonday Trail
Freedom Trail
Golden Jubilee Trail
Grand Valley Trail
Greenstone Ridge Trail
Mackinac Bridge Trail
Murder Mountain Trail
Pere Marquette Pilgrimage
Saginaw Trail
Tecumseh Trail
Tonquish Trail
Wakazoo Trail
Wilderness Trail

MINNESOTA

Fort Snelling Historic Trail

Location: Minneapolis, MN. *Theme:* Local
history. *Sponsor:* Indianhead Council, BSA,
393 Marshall Ave. S., St. Paul, MN 55102-
1795, (651) 224-1891.
Length: 7.5 miles (straight). *Route:* The
trail begins near the pavilion in Minnehaha
Park, follows the Mississippi River south to
Pike Island, then circles the island shore.
Terrain: Dirt paths. *Cycling:* Not
recommended. *Awards:* Medal $7.00; Patch
$2.75. *Submit:* Completed 50-item

questionnaire and group leader's certification
of completion. *Register:* Not required. *Sites:*
Gunnar Wennerberg Statue, Minnehaha
Falls, Railroad Depot, Fort Snelling, Col.
John H. Stevens' House, Pike Island
Interpretive Center, Memorial Tree, Indian
Statue.

L'Etoile du Nor

Location: St. Paul, MN. *Theme:* Local
history—the name means "Trail of the North
Star". *Sponsor:* Indianhead Council, BSA, 393

Marshall Ave. So., St. Paul, MN 55102, (651) 224-4175.

Length: Approximately 4 miles (straight). *Route:* The trail begins at the James J. Hill house at 240 Summit Ave., heads northeast on John Ireland Blvd., south on Cedar St., west on Fourth St., through Town Square Park, north on St. Peter St., and ends on Seventh St. *Terrain:* City streets. *Cycling:* Possible. *Awards:* Medal $9.00; Patch $2.25. *Submit:* Completed order form. *Register:*

Not required. *Sites:* St. Paul Cathedral, State Capitol, Minnesota History Center, Civil War Monument, Central Presbyterian Church, Church of St. Louis, World Trade Center, Minnesota Public Radio Building, Cafesjian's Carousel, James J. Hill Public Library, Landmark Tower.

Formerly Sponsored Trail

Hiawatha Trail

MISSISSIPPI

Nathan Bedford Forrest Trail

Location: Baldwyn, MS. *Theme:* Route taken by attacking Confederate troops during key Civil War victory on June 10, 1864. *Sponsor:* Historical Hiking Trails, P.O. Box 17507, Memphis, TN 38187-0507, (901) 323-2739.

Length: 16 miles (loop). *Route:* The trail begins and ends at Brice's Crossroads Museum in Baldwyn, and passes through the town of Bethany. *Terrain:* Backroads. *Cycling:* Appropriate. *Awards:* Medal $3.25; Patch $1.25; Repeat Pin $0.75; Neckerchief $4.00; Neckerchief Slide $1.75. *Submit:* Group leader's certification of completion of hike and required reading, plus completed questionnaire. *Register:* At least 3 weeks in advance. *Sites:* Brice's Crossroads Museum.

Tuxachanie Trail

Location: McHenry, MS. *Theme:* Recreation. *Sponsor:* Tuxachanie Trail, Inc., P.O. Box 14, Gulfport, MS 39501.

Length: 11 miles (straight). *Route:* The trail begins at a well-marked trailhead parking lot on US 49 between McHenry and Saucier, and heads eastward to the P.O.W. Camp near Bethel Rd. 402. *Terrain:* Woods. *Cycling:* Appropriate. *Awards:* Patch $3.50. *Submit:* Completed 5-item questionnaire. *Register:* In advance. *Sites:* P.O.W. Camp Site, Airey Lake, Airey Lookout Tower, Copeland Spring.

Vicksburg National Military Park Trails

Location: Vicksburg, MS. *Theme:* Civil War Battles—1863. *Sponsor:* Eugene G. Buglewicz, 503 Lakeside Dr., Vicksburg, MS 39180 (as of 5/96 it was reported that Steven Elwart is now in charge—no new address available yet).

Lengths: National Military Park Trail, 14 miles (loop). National Military Park Trek, 7 miles (loop). National Military Park Scout Trail, 12 miles (loop). *Routes:* The 14-mile trail begins at the Visitor Center, heads north, then west, to the Yazoo River, east to Grant's Circle, then south to the start. The trek begins at the Visitor Center, loops northward to the Great Redoubt, then southward to Fort Garrott, then back to the start. The Scout Trail begins at the Visitor Center and generally follows the route of the 14-mile trail. *Terrain:* Woods. *Cycling:* Not recommended. *Awards:* NMPT Medal $3.00; NMPT Patch $2.50; NMPT Star $2.50; NMPT Hat Pin $1.00; Scout Trail Medal $3.50; Scout Trail Patch $2.50; Scout Trail Hat Pin $1.00; Trek Patch $2.50; Trek Hat Pin $1.00. *Submit:* Completed questionnaires and group leader's certification of completion. *Register:* Upon arrival at the park. *Sites:* Pemberton's Circle, Cairo Museum, Tilghman Memorial Circle, Great Redoubt, Vicksburg National Cemetery, Stockade Redan, Fort Hill, Union Navy Memorial, Minnesota Circle, Union Battery, Memorial

Arch, Railroad Redoubt, Fort Garrott, Surrender Site Monument, Hickenloop Statue, Minieball Monument.

Formerly Sponsored Trails

Beaver Dam Nature Trail
Chewalla Nature Trail

d'Iberville Trail
Grand Gulf Park Trail
Jefferson Davis Memorial Trail
Mississippi Chautaqua Trail
Peckerwood Nature Trail
Ship Island Trail
Tiak-Beauvoir Trail

MISSOURI

Babler Nature Trail

Location: Dr. Edmund A. Babler Memorial State Park, Chesterfield, MO 63005. *Theme:* Nature. *Sponsor:* Special Awards Co., 811 Lafayette, Webster Groves, MO 63119, (314) 961-2610.

Length: 10 miles (loop). *Route:* The trail meanders throughout the park and can be entered at numerous points. *Terrain:* Rugged. *Cycling:* Not recommended. *Awards:* Patch $2.15; First Repeat Patch $1.60; Second Repeat Patch $2.15. *Submit:* No requirement. *Register:* Not required. *Sites:* Wild Horse Creek, Jacob L. Babler Outdoor Education Center, Cochran Woods, Babler Southwoods Hollow.

Battle of Carthage Historical Trail

Location: Carthage, MO. Theme: 1864 Civil War Battle. *Sponsor:* Leonard Baker, 2224 W. Oak St., Carthage, MO 64836, (417) 358-7057.

Length: 10.0 miles. *Route:* Available from sponsor. *Terrain:* Available from sponsor. *Cycling:* Available from sponsor. *Awards:* Patch $3.00. *Register:* In advance. *Submit:* Request for patches.

Battle of Westport Historical Trail

Location: Kansas City, MO. *Theme:* Civil War battle—October 23, 1864. *Sponsor:* B.G. Sims, 8604 Arlington, Raytown, MO 64138.

Length: 20 miles (straight). *Route:* The trail begins at Loose Park, heads south on Wornall, east on Meyer Blvd. to Swope Park, south along the Big Blue River to end at the boy scout camp south of Minor Park. *Terrain:* City streets and woods. *Cycling:* Not recommended. *Awards:* Patch $3.50. *Submit:*

No requirement. *Register:* In advance. *Sites:* Loose Park, Byram's Ford Industrial Park, Wornall Home, Forest Hill Cemetery, Union Cemetery.

Beaumont Scout Reservation Hiking Trails

Location: Beaumont Scout Reservation, High Ridge, MO. *Theme:* Recreation. *Sponsor:* Camping Service, Greater St. Louis Area Council, BSA, 4568 W. Pine Blvd., St. Louis, MO 63108, (314) 361-0600. *Lengths:* Blue Trail, 4 miles (loop). Green Trail, 5 miles (loop). Red Trail, 5 miles (loop). Yellow Trail, 5 miles (loop). *Routes:* All trails begin and end at the Merle D. Shippey Memorial Trail Center, in the Harris Scoutcraft Field. *Terrain:* Woods. *Cycling:* Not recommended. *Awards:* Neckerchief Slide $1.25. *Submit:* No requirement. *Register:* At least 2 weeks in advance. *Sites:* Blackberry Hollow, Mud Cave, Toad Hollow, Cemetery Ridge, Indian Flint Pits, Lost Spring, Fabick Lake Dam.

Bee Tree Park Trails

Location: Bee Tree Park, South St. Louis County, MO. *Theme:* Recreation. *Sponsor:* Special Awards Co., 811 Lafayette, Webster Groves, MO 63119, (314) 961-2610.

Length: Bee Tree Trail, 0.3 mile (straight). Crows Roost Trail, 0.5 mile (straight). Mississippi Trail, 0.4 mile (straight). *Routes:* The Mississippi Trail begins at the Mansion and follows the course of the river and the Missouri Pacific Railroad track. It forks into the Crows Roost Trail, which heads into the woods at the southern tip of the park, and the Bee Tree Trail, which heads toward the gardens near the lake. *Terrain:* Woods.

Cycling: Not recommended. *Awards:* Patch $2.65; Repeat Patch $1.65. *Submit:* No requirement. *Register:* Not required. *Sites:* Golden Eagle Riverboat Museum.

Berryman Trail

Location: Mark Twain National Forest near Potosi, MO. *Theme:* Recreation. *Sponsor:* Special Awards Co., 811 Lafayette, Webster Groves, MO 63119, (314) 961-2610.

Length: 24 miles (loop). *Route:* The trail begins and ends at Berryman Camp on FR 2266 north of SR 8. *Terrain:* Woods and ridges. *Cycling:* Not recommended. *Awards:* Patch $3.00; First Repeat Patch $1.60; Second Repeat Patch $2.15. *Submit:* No requirement. *Register:* Not required. *Sites:* Berryman Camp, Harmon Spring Camp, Edward Beecher Camp, Brazil Creek Camp.

Black Buffalo Trail

Location: Sioux Passage Park, St. Louis County, MO. *Theme:* Recreation. *Sponsor:* Special Awards Co., 811 Lafayette, Webster Groves, MO 63119, (314) 961-2610.

Length: 4 miles (loop). *Route:* The trail begins on Old Jamestown Rd., just west of the park entrance, follows the perimeter of the park, and returns to the start. *Terrain:* Woods. *Cycling:* Not recommended. *Awards:* Patch $2.75. *Submit:* No requirement. *Register:* Not required.

Black Hawk Trail

Location: Troy and Moscow Mills, MO. *Theme:* Settlement of Lincoln County; Indian wars. *Sponsor:* Camping Service, Greater St. Louis Area Council, BSA, 4568 W. Pine Blvd., St. Louis, MO 63108, (314) 361-0600.

Length: 13.4 miles (loop). *Route:* The trail begins at Buchanan High School in Troy, tours the city, heads to Moscow Mills and returns to the start. *Terrain:* Roads. *Cycling:* Appropriate. *Awards:* Patch $2.50. *Submit:* Group leader's certification of completion. *Register:* At least 2 weeks in advance. *Sites:* Clark Home Site, Shapley Ross House, Mill Site Park, Wood's Fort, Sacred Heart Cemetery.

Carondelet-Jefferson Barracks Trail

Location: South St. Louis, MO. *Theme:* History of Carondelet and Jefferson Barracks.

Sponsor: Camping Service, Greater St. Louis Area Council, BSA, 4568 W. Pine Blvd., St. Louis, MO 63108, (314) 361-0600.

Length: 12 miles (loop). *Route:* The trail begins at Hilliker Picnic Shelter in Carondelet Park, heads south to Jefferson Barracks, and returns to the start. *Terrain:* City streets. *Cycling:* Appropriate. *Awards:* Patch $2.50. *Submit:* Group leader's certification of completion. *Register:* At least 2 weeks in advance. *Sites:* Quinn Chapel, Carondelet Markham Presbyterian Church, Carondelet Library, Steamboat Gothic Style House, Saints Mary & Joseph Catholic Church, Stone Row Houses, Hoffmeister Mortuary, Sisters of St. Joseph of Carondelet Convent, Hancock School, Odd Fellows Cemetery, Grant Shelter, Gethsemane Lutheran Church, Trinity Temple, Doerings Bakery, Jefferson Barracks County Park, Blow School.

Chubb Memorial Trail

Location: West Tyson County Park to Lone Elk County Park, St. Louis County, MO. *Theme:* Recreation. *Sponsor:* Special Awards Co., 811 Lafayette, Webster Groves, MO 63119, (314) 961-2610.

Length: 7 miles (straight). *Route:* The trail may be started at either endpoint, the Chubb Shelter in West Tyson, or at the trailhead in Lone Elk. The trail skirts the Meramec River and Castlewood State Park along the way. *Terrain:* Portions are rough. *Cycling:* Not recommended. *Awards:* Patch $2.50. *Submit:* No requirement. *Register:* Not required.

Covered Bridge Trail

Location: Antonia, MO. *Theme:* Local history. *Sponsor:* Antonia Memorial Sport Club, c/o A.M. McKenzie, Jr., 5218 SR 21, Imperial, MO 63052.

Length: 14 miles (straight). *Route:* The trail begins at Opal's Cafe on SR 21 north of Hillsboro and proceeds north through Antonia and Seckman to end at Lion's Den Camp. *Terrain:* Roads. *Cycling:* Appropriate. *Awards:* Patch $2.50. *Submit:* Group leader's certification of completion. *Register:* Not required. *Sites:* 1872 Covered Bridge, 1870 Blacksmith Shop, Frisco Hill.

Creve Coeur Park Trail

Location: Creve Coeur Lake Memorial Park, St. Louis County, MO. *Theme:* Recreation.

Sponsor: Special Awards Co., 811 Lafayette, Webster Groves, MO 63119, (314) 961-2610.

Length: 3 miles (loop). *Route:* The trail begins at the parking lot off the main entrance road, southeast of the first athletic field, circles the lake, and returns to the start. *Terrain:* Lakeshore and woods. *Cycling:* Not recommended. *Awards:* Patch $2.65. *Submit:* No requirement. *Register:* Not required.

Cuivre River Trail

Location: Cuivre River State Park, Troy, MO. *Theme:* Recreation. *Sponsor:* Special Awards Co., 811 Lafayette, Webster Groves, MO 63110, (314) 961-2610.

Length: 8 miles (straight). *Route:* The trail passes through the park and follows the Cuivre River along the western border of the park. *Terrain:* Woods. *Cycling:* Not recommended. *Awards:* Patch $2.65; First Repeat Patch $1.60; Second Repeat Patch $2.25. *Submit:* No requirement. *Register:* Not required.

Daniel Boone Trail

Location: Defiance, MO. *Theme:* Daniel Boone. *Sponsor:* Camping Service, Greater St. Louis Area Council, BSA, 4568 W. Pine Blvd., St. Louis, MO 63108, (314) 361-0600.

Length: 20 miles (straight). *Route:* The trail begins on Defiance Rd. on the west side of SR 94 in Defiance, MO. The trail passes through Matson, Augusta and Dutzow to end at the Boone Monument east of Marthasville. *Terrain:* Roads and woods. *Cycling:* Not recommended. *Awards:* Patch $2.50. *Submit:* Group leader's certification of completion. *Register:* At least 2 weeks in advance. *Sites:* Boone Monument, Femme Osage Creek, Daniel Boone Farm, David Bryan House, Daniel Boone Home.

Elephant Rocks Braille Trail

Location: Elephant Rocks State Park, Graniteville, MO. *Theme:* Origin of the elephant rocks. *Sponsor:* Special Awards Co., 811 Lafayette, Webster Groves, MO 63119, (314) 961-2610.

Length: 1 mile (loop). *Route:* The trail begins at the parking area, loops around the elephant rocks, and returns to the start. *Terrain:* Paved path. *Cycling:* Appropriate. *Awards:* Patch $1.90. *Submit:* No requirement. *Register:* Not required. *Sites:* Elephant Rocks, Taum Sauk Mountain.

Gateway West Historical Trail

Location: St. Louis, MO. *Theme:* Local history of westward expansion. *Sponsor:* Camping Service, Greater St. Louis Area Council, BSA, 4568 W. Pine Blvd., St. Louis, MO 63108, (314) 361-0600.

Length: 12 miles (loop). *Route:* The trail begins and ends at the Eads Bridge north of the Gateway Arch, and winds through downtown St. Louis. *Terrain:* City streets. *Cycling:* Appropriate. *Awards:* Patch $2.50. *Submit:* Group leader's certification of completion and completed 39-item questionnaire. *Register:* At least 2 weeks in advance. *Sites:* Old Court House, Jefferson National Expansion Memorial, Kiel Auditorium, Soldiers' Memorial, Christ Church Cathedral, Centenary Methodist Church, John Hall-Robert Campbell House, Millers Fountain, Union Station, Basilica of St. John the Baptist and Evangelist, Anheuser-Busch Brewery, Defense Mapping Agency, Chatillon-De Menil House, Busch Memorial Stadium, St. Mary of Victories Catholic Church, Soulard Market.

George Washington Carver Trail

Location: Neosho to Diamond, MO. *Theme:* George Washington Carver. *Sponsor:* Ozark Trails Council, BSA, 2806 E. Sunshine, Springfield, MO 64801, (417) 883-1636.

Length: 10 miles (straight). *Route:* The trail begins at Field School in Neosho and ends at the George Washington Carver National Monument near Diamond. *Terrain:* City streets, grass and gravel. *Cycling:* Possible, but does not qualify for awards. *Awards:* Medal $4.50; Patch $2.00. *Submit:* No requirement. *Register:* 2-week notice recommended. *Sites:* Birthplace Site, Rock Wall Overlook, Boy Carver Statue, Moses Carver Second Period Dwelling, Spring and Bridge, Persimmon Grove, Cemetery.

Green-Rock Trail

Location: Pacific, MO. *Theme:* Recreation. *Sponsor:* Camping Service, Greater St. Louis Area Council, BSA, 4568 W. Pine Blvd., St. Louis, MO 63108, (314) 361-0600.

Length: 10 miles (straight). *Route:* The trail begins at Rockwood Range Tract, travels through Greensfelder County Park, and ends at Rockwoods Reservations. *Terrain:* Woods. *Cycling:* Not recommended. *Awards:* Patch $2.50. *Submit:* Group leader's certification of completion. *Register:* At least 2 weeks in advance. *Sites:* Greensfelder Memorial, Radio Towers.

Greensfelder Park Nature Trail

Location: Greensfelder County Park, St. Louis County, MO. *Theme:* Nature. *Sponsor:* Special Awards Co., 811 Lafayette, Webster Groves, MO 63119, (314) 961-2610.

Length: 5 miles (loop). *Route:* The trail begins and ends immediately behind the visitor center. *Terrain:* Woods. *Cycling:* Not recommended. *Awards:* Patch $2.75. *Submit:* No requirement. *Register:* Not required.

Harry S Truman Trail

Location: Independence, MO. *Theme:* President Harry S Truman. *Sponsor:* Lloyd Hawkins, 20602 E. Blue Mills Rd., Independence, MO 64058.

Length: 5 to 13 miles. *Route:* Available from sponsor. *Terrain:* Available from sponsor. *Cycling:* Available from sponsor. *Awards:* Medal; Patch. *Register:* Available from sponsor. *Submit:* Available from sponsor. *Sites:* Harry Truman's boyhood home.

Henry Rowe Schoolcraft Trail

Location: Mark Twain National Forest near Potosi, MO. *Theme:* Henry Rowe Schoolcraft, Indian agent, explorer and geologist. *Sponsor:* Camping Service, Greater St. Louis Area Council, BSA, 4568 W. Pine Blvd., St. Louis, MO 63108, (314) 361-0600.

Length: 10 or 14 miles (loop). *Route:* The beginning and end of the 10- and 14-mile loops is on FR 2397 near Butcher Gulch. *Terrain:* Woods. *Cycling:* Not recommended. *Awards:* Patch $2.50. *Submit:* Group leader's certification of completion. *Register:* At least 2 weeks in advance. *Sites:* Miranda Meadow, Beaubien Camp, Schoolcraft Lake, North Pond, Clear Creek, Butcher Gulch, Frank Myers Ridge, Pettibone Pond.

Huzzah Wildlife Area Trail

Location: Huzzah State Wildlife Area near Leasburg, MO. *Theme:* Recreation. *Sponsor:* Special Awards Co., 811 Lafayette, Webster Groves, MO 63119, (314) 961-2610.

Length: 10 miles (straight). *Route:* The trail runs from the southern park boundary at Huzzah Creek to the Daniel Boone Park along the Meramec River. *Terrain:* Roads.

Cycling: Appropriate; or may be canoed on Meramec River. *Awards:* Patch $2.10. *Submit:* No requirement. *Register:* Not required.

Indian Mound Trail

Location: Kansas City, MO. *Theme:* Indian Mounds. *Sponsor:* Historic Trails Committee, P.O. Box 16532, Raytown, MO 64133-6532, (816) 537-5719; or Historic Trails Committee, 405 Allendale Ct., Greenwood, MO 64034.

Length: 8.0 miles (loop). *Route:* The trail may be begun at any point, and forms a loop in and to the south of North Terrace Park, including Cliff Dr. and Gladstone Blvd. *Terrain:* Woods trail, grassy areas, and boulevards. *Cycling:* Not appropriate. *Awards:* Medal $6.00; Patch $4.00. *Submit:* Hike report describing service project done on or for the trail. *Register:* In advance. *Sites:* Reservoir Hill, John Fitzgerald Kennedy Monument, Colonnade, Lexington Bridge, Kansas City Museum of History & Science, Thomas Hart Benton Monument, Scarritt's Point Monument, Indian Village Site.

Jefferson Barracks Historic Pilgrimage

Location: Jefferson Barracks, St. Louis, MO. *Theme:* History of Jefferson Barracks. *Sponsor:* Special Awards Co., 811 Lafayette, Webster Groves, MO 63119, (314) 961-2610.

Length: 8 miles (straight). *Route:* The trail begins at the Powder Magazine Museum and ends at the Parade Grounds. *Terrain:* Open fields. *Cycling:* Not recommended. *Awards:* Patch $2.25; Repeat Patch $2.25. *Submit:* No requirement. *Register:* Not required. *Sites:* Powder Magazine Museum, Scenic Circle, Laborer's House and Stable, Mississippi River, Parade Grounds and Buildings, Railroad Station, Old Ordnance Room.

Jefferson Barracks Historical Trail

Location: St. Louis, MO. *Theme:* Local history. *Sponsor:* Robert F. Shear, 5312 Michigan Ave., St. Louis, MO 63111, (314) 752-3916.

Length: 5 miles (loop). *Route:* The trail begins at the Stone Building, heads north to the National Cemetery, then returns to the start. *Terrain:* Roads. *Cycling:* Appropriate. *Awards:* Patch $1.75; Repeat Patch $0.75. *Submit:* No requirement. *Register:* Not required. *Sites:* Stone Building, Powder Magazine, National C.C.C. Museum, Labor

House Historical Marker, National Cemetery, Jefferson Barracks School, St. Bernadette. Catholic Church, Sylvan Springs

John J. Audubon Trail

Location: Mark Twain National Forest near Womack, MO. *Theme:* John J. Audubon, naturalist. *Sponsor:* Camping Service, Greater St. Louis Area Council, BSA, 4568 W. Pine Blvd., St. Louis, MO 63108, (314) 361-0600.

Length: 12 miles (loop). *Route:* The trail begins and ends at Bidwell Creek Ford on FR 2199, about 20 miles from Ste. Genevieve. *Terrain:* Rugged. *Cycling:* Not recommended. *Awards:* Patch $2.50. *Submit:* Group leader's certification of completion. *Register:* At least 2 weeks in advance.

Les Petites Cotes Trail

Location: St. Charles, MO. *Theme:* First capital of Missouri. *Sponsor:* Camping Service, Greater St. Louis Area Council, BSA, 4568 W. Pine Blvd., St. Louis, MO 63108, (314) 361-0600.

Length: 10 miles (loop). *Route:* The trail begins at the First Capitol building, located at the intersection of First Capitol Dr. and Main St. in St. Charles, covers major streets in the city and returns to the start. *Terrain:* City streets. *Cycling:* Appropriate. *Awards:* Patch $2.50. *Submit:* Group leader's certification of completion and completed 7-item questionnaire. *Register:* At least 2 weeks in advance. *Sites:* MKT Depot, St. Charles Market and Fish House, Lindenwood College, Atkinson House, American Legion Home, First Free Public School, St. Charles College, Borromeo Cemetery, Schemmer Bros. Wagon and Blacksmith Shop, Custom House, Seth Millington Home, Newbill-McElhiney Home, Academy of the Sacred Heart, Tiercerot-Krekel Home, Immanuel Lutheran Church, California House, Western House, Weeke Home.

Lewis and Clark Trail

Location: Jackson County, MO. *Theme:* Lewis and Clark Expedition. *Sponsor:* Historic Trails Committee, P.O. Box 16532, Raytown, MO 64133-6532, (816) 537-5719; or Historic Trails Committee, 405 Allendale Ct., Greenwood, MO 64034.

Length: 17.0 miles (straight). *Route:* The trail begins at La Benite Park in Courtney

and heads east (mostly along Atherton and Sibley Rds.) to end in Hayes Park in Sibley. *Terrain:* Roads. *Cycling:* Not appropriate. *Awards:* Medal $6.00; Patch $4.00. *Submit:* Hike report describing service project done on or for the trail. *Register:* In advance. *Sites:* ATSF Railroad, River Bluff Park, MoPac Railroad, Little Blue River, YMCA Camp Santosage, Coolane Farm, Pemberton House, Fort Osage Park, Sibley Cemetery.

Log Cabin Trail

Location: Pleasant Hill, MO. *Theme:* Local history. *Sponsor:* J.C. Hammontree, Rt. 2, 1216 College Hill, Pleasant Hill, MO 64080, (816) 981-2352.

Length: 13.2 miles (loop). *Route:* The trail begins at the overnight camping area at the east end of Loch Lenord, heads south through town, north to City Lake, east along County Line Rd., and south to the start. *Terrain:* Roads. *Cycling:* Appropriate. *Awards:* Patch $3.00. *Submit:* No requirement. *Register:* Not required. *Sites:* Old Church, Post Office, Memorial Hall, Scout Cabin, City Hall, Old Wooden Bridges, Rock Fence, World's Second-largest Greenhouse, Wooden Silo.

Lone Elk Trail

Location: Lone Elk County Park, St. Louis County, MO. *Theme:* Nature. *Sponsor:* Special Awards Co., 811 Lafayette, Webster Groves, MO 63119, (314) 961-2610.

Length: 3 miles (loop). *Route:* The trail begins northwest of the park's visitor center, circles the lake, and returns to the start. *Terrain:* Woods. *Cycling:* Not recommended. *Awards:* Patch $2.50; Repeat Patch $2.50. *Submit:* No requirement. *Register:* Not required.

Lone Jack Civil War Trail

Location: Jackson County, MO. *Theme:* 1862 Civil War Battle. *Sponsor:* Historic Trails Committee, P.O. Box 16532, Raytown, MO 64133-6532, (816) 537-5719; or Historic Trails Committee, 405 Allendale Ct., Greenwood, MO 64034.

Length: 17.0 miles (straight). *Route:* The trail begins at the parking lot of Missouri Town 1855, passes through Blue and Grey Park and the town of Lone Jack, and ends at the Lone Jack Battlefield Museum and Cemetery. *Terrain:* Country roads. *Cycling:*

Not appropriate. *Awards:* Medal $6.00; Patch
$4.00. *Submit:* Hike report with description
of service project done on or for trail.
Register: In advance. *Sites:* Native Hoofed
Animal Enclosure, Kemper Outdoor
Education Center, Lake Lotawana Overlook,
Adams Cemetery.

Lost Creek Trail

Location: Pendleton, MO. *Theme:* Oneota
Indians. *Sponsor:* Camping Service, Greater
St. Louis Area Council, BSA, 4568 W. Pine
Blvd., St. Louis, MO 63108, (314) 361-0600.
Length: 20 miles (loop). *Route:* The trail
begins and ends at the common ground area
of Pendleton, along the Norfolk and Western
railroad tracks just east of Hwy. B. *Terrain:*
Light duty and generally unimproved
roadways. *Cycling:* Appropriate. *Awards:*
Patch $2.50. *Submit:* Group leader's
certification of completion. *Register:* At least
2 weeks in advance.

Manuel Lisa Trail

Location: St. Louis, MO. *Theme:* Manuel
Lisa, an early fur trader. *Sponsor:* Camping
Service, Greater St. Louis Area Council, BSA,
4568 W. Pine Blvd., St. Louis, MO 63108,
(314) 361-0600.
Length: 20.4 miles (straight). *Route:* The
trail begins at the intersection of SR 94 and
Howell Rd., goes generally northward for 10
miles, then turns south and ends at the
visitors' center for the August A. Busch
Wildlife Area. *Terrain:* Roads. *Cycling:*
Appropriate. *Awards:* Patch $2.50. *Submit:*
Group leader's certification of completion.
Register: At least 2 weeks in advance. *Sites:*
Femme Osage Creek, Busch Wildlife Area.

Mark Twain Historical Trail

Location: Hannibal, MO. *Theme:* Mark
Twain. *Sponsor:* Mark Twain Historical Trail,
P.O. Box 101, Hannibal, MO 63401, (573) 221-
4157.
Length: 10 miles (loop). *Route:* The trail
begins at Mark Twain Cave, follows the
railroad tracks north to Riverview Park, then
returns to the start. *Terrain:* Roads and
woods. *Cycling:* Not recommended. *Awards:*
Patch; Repeat Patch. *Submit:* No
requirement. *Register:* Not required. *Sites:*
Mark Twain Cave, Tom & Huck Statue,
Lovers Leap, Riverview Park, Mark Twain
Statue.

Meramec Trail

Location: Meramec State Park, Sullivan,
MO. *Theme:* Recreation. *Sponsor:* Special
Awards Co., 811 Lafayette, Webster Groves,
MO 63119, (314) 961-2610.
Length: 6 miles (loop). *Route:* The trail
begins and ends near the cabin area and
includes the southwest corner of the
Meramec Upland Forest Natural Area.
Terrain: Woods. *Cycling:* Not recommended.
Awards: Patch $2.75; First Repeat Patch
$1.60; Second Repeat Patch $1.60. *Submit:* No
requirement. *Register:* Not required. *Sites:*
Meramec Caverns, La Jolla Springs, Cooper
Hollow, Fishers Cave, Breakdown Cave,
Campbell Hollow, Museum, Meramec River.

Moniteau Wilderness Trail

Location: Clark, MO. *Theme:* Nature and
local history. *Sponsor:* Moniteau Wilderness
Trail, Inc., P.O. Box 723, Moberly, MO 65270.
Length: 15 miles (loop). *Route:* Woods
route in the Rudolf Bennitt Wildlife Area.
Terrain: Backcountry trail. *Cycling:* Not
recommended. *Awards:* Patch $3.25; Medal;
Repeater Patch. *Submit:* Group leader's
request for awards. *Register:* In advance; trail
is closed during the firearms deer season.
Sites: Grave of Lt. Leonard Bradley, Boyhood
Home of Gen. Omar Bradley, Site of Sioux
Village.

Moses Austin Trail

Location: Clark National Forest northwest
of Potosi, MO. *Theme:* Moses Austin,
founder of Potosi. *Sponsor:* Camping Service,
Greater St. Louis Area Council, BSA, 4568 W.
Pine Blvd., St. Louis, MO 63108, (314) 361-
0600.
Length: 14.5 miles (loop). *Route:* The trail
begins and ends at the junction of a fire trail
and gravel road, 1.5 miles west of Washington
County Rd. 208. *Terrain:* Wilderness.
Cycling: Not recommended. *Awards:* Patch
$2.50. *Submit:* Group leader's certification of
completion. *Register:* At least 2 weeks in
advance.

1904 World's Fair Historical Trail

Location: St. Louis, MO. *Theme:* World's
Fair. *Sponsor:* Camping Service, Greater St.
Louis Area Council, BSA, 4568 W. Pine Blvd.,
St. Louis, MO 63108, (314) 631-0600.
Length: 10 miles (loop). *Route:* The trail
begins and ends at Balloon Field, just east of

the Jefferson Memorial, and winds through Forest Park and the campus of Washington University. *Terrain:* Roads and paths. *Cycling:* Appropriate. *Awards:* Patch $2.50. *Submit:* Group leader's certification of completion and completed 21-item questionnaire. *Register:* At least 2 weeks in advance. *Sites:* Confederate Memorial, St. Louis Science Center, World's Fair Pavilion, Jewel Box, St. Louis Municipal Opera, Ridgley Library, Jefferson Memorial, Brookings Hall, Art Museum, Francis Field.

Osage Wilderness Trail

Location: H. Roe Bartle Scout Reservation near Osceola, MO. *Theme:* Recreation. *Sponsor:* Heart of America Council, BSA, 10210 Holmes Rd., Kansas City, MO 64131-4200, (816) 942-9333.

Length: 14 miles (loop). *Route:* The trail begins and ends at the scout reservation office. *Terrain:* Rugged. *Cycling:* Not recommended, and does not qualify for awards. *Awards:* Patch $1.50. *Submit:* Group leader's certification of completion of hike and service project. *Register:* At least 2 weeks in advance. *Sites:* Harry S Truman Lake, "The Point", Ozark Mountains, Osage River.

Ozark Trail

Location: Southeastern Missouri. *Theme:* Recreation. *Sponsor:* Special Awards Co., 811 Lafayette, Webster Groves, MO 63119, (314) 961-2610.

Lengths: Between Rivers Section, 30 miles (straight). Blair Creek Section, 27 miles (straight). Current River Section, 35 miles (straight). Taum Sauk Section, 30 miles (straight). Trace Creek Section, 35 miles (straight). *Routes:* The Taum Sauk Section runs from SR 21 south of Ironton to the eastern border of the Mark Twain National Forest, passing through Johnson's Shut-Ins State Park. The Blair Creek Section runs from Indian Creek State Forest to SR 72 in the Mark Twain National Forest. The Trace Creek Section runs from the northwest end of the Taum Sauk Section to just south of where SR 8 crosses the Mark Twain National Forest. The Current River Section runs from US 60 in the Mark Twain National Forest to SR 104 in the Indian Creek State Forest. The Between Rivers Section runs from Eleven Point River to US 60, all in the Mark Twain National Forest. Other sections are proposed.

Terrain: Woods. *Cycling:* Not recommended. *Awards:* Patch $1.65; 5 Segments $1.25 each. *Submit:* No requirement. *Register:* Not required.

Pioneer Trace

Location: Beaumont Scout Reservation near High Ridge, MO. *Theme:* Recreation. *Sponsor:* Camping Service, Greater St. Louis Area Council, BSA, 4568 W. Pine Blvd., St. Louis, MO 63108, (314) 361-0600.

Length: 17 miles (loop). *Route:* The trail begins and ends near the pool and generally follows the borders of the reservation. *Terrain:* Rugged. *Cycling:* Not recommended. *Awards:* Patch $2.50. *Submit:* Group leader's certification of completion. *Register:* At least 2 weeks in advance. *Sites:* Periwinkle Glen, Lost Spring, Deer Point, Mystery Pond, Woodchuck Site, Dentree Ridge.

Plattin Hollows Trail

Location: Plattin, MO. *Theme:* Recreation. *Sponsor:* Camping Service, Greater St. Louis Area Council, BSA, 4568 W. Pine Blvd., St. Louis, MO 63108, (314) 361-0600.

Length: 14 miles (loop). *Route:* The trail begins and ends at the bridge over Dry Fork Creek on Doss Hollow Rd. *Terrain:* Hilly roads. *Cycling:* Appropriate. *Awards:* Patch $2.50. *Submit:* Group leader's certification of completion. *Register:* At least 2 weeks in advance.

Queeny Park Trails

Location: Queeny Park, St. Louis County, MO. *Theme:* Recreation. *Sponsor:* Special Awards Co., 811 Lafayette, Webster Groves, MO 63119, (314) 961-2610.

Length: Crow Hill Trail, 0.3 mile (straight). Dogwood Trail, 0.2 mile (straight). Fox Run Trail, 0.2 mile (straight). Hawk Ridge Trail, 3.3 miles (loop). Lake Spur Trail, 0.1 mile (straight). Owl Creek Trail, 0.8 mile (straight). White Oak Trail, 0.4 mile (straight). *Routes:* The Hawk Ridge Trail enters either off of Mason Rd. in the southeast or Wiedman Rd. in the northwest, and follows the perimeter of the park. The other trails cut through the central portion of the park. *Terrain:* Woods. *Cycling:* Not recommended. *Awards:* Patch $2.75. *Submit:* No requirement. *Register:* Not required.

Rockywood Trail

Location: Washington State Park, St. Louis County, MO. *Theme:* Recreation. *Sponsor:* Special Awards Co., 811 Lafayette, Webster Groves, MO 63119, (314) 961-2610.

Length: 10 miles (loop). *Route:* The trail begins and ends at the trail parking lot near the park's nature center. *Terrain:* Woods. *Cycling:* Not recommended. *Awards:* Patch $2.00. *Submit:* No requirement. *Register:* Not required.

St. Francois State Park Trails

Location: St. Francois State Park, Bonne Terre, MO. *Theme:* Recreation. *Sponsor:* Special Awards Co., 811 Lafayette, Webster Groves, MO 63119, (314) 961-2610.

Lengths: Missouri Trail, 0.5 mile (straight). Mooner's Hollow Trail, 2.7 miles (loop). Pike Run Trail, 11 miles (loop). Swimming Deer Trail, 2.7 miles (loop). *Routes:* Mooner's Hollow Trail begins and ends at the picnic area just east of the park entrance. The Swimming Deer Trail begins and ends at the camping area (parallel to which is the Missouri Trail) along the Big River. The Pike Run Trail begins and ends along the main park road south of the first picnic area and almost to the camping area. *Terrain:* Woods. *Cycling:* Not recommended. *Awards:* Patch $1.95. *Submit:* No requirement. *Register:* Not required.

St. Louis Pilgrimage

Location: St. Louis, MO. *Theme:* Local history. *Sponsor:* Special Awards Co., 811 Lafayette, Webster Groves, MO 63119, (314) 961-2610.

Length: 10 miles (approx.). *Route:* The route is to be determined by the group, and must include the sites listed below in no particular order. *Terrain:* City streets. *Cycling:* Appropriate. *Awards:* Patch $2.75. *Submit:* No requirement. *Register:* Not required. *Sites:* Basilica of St. Louis, Old Courthouse, Busch Memorial Stadium, Jefferson Memorial, Eads Bridge, Gateway Arch, Soldier's Memorial, Campbell House, Art Museum, Museum of Science and Natural History, Aloe Plaza, Millers Fountain, Chatillon-De Menil House, Jewel Box, Eugene Field House, Grant's Farm, Jefferson Barracks Historical Park, Municipal Opera, McDonnell Planetarium, St. Louis Zoo, Missouri Botanical Garden.

Santa Fe/Oregon/California Trail

Location: Jackson County, MO. *Theme:* Early pioneer trails. *Sponsor:* Historic Trails Committee, P.O. Box 16532, Raytown, MO 64133-6532, (816) 537-5719; or Historic Trails Committee, 405 Allendale Ct., Greenwood, MO 64034.

Lengths: Independence Section, 10.0 miles (straight). Raytown Section, 8.0 miles (straight). Kansas City Section, 9.0 miles (straight). *Routes:* The Independence Section begins at the Wayne City Landing overlook and ends at 47th St. The Raytown Section begins there and continues to Bannister Rd. The Kansas City Section begins there and ends at the Missouri/Kansas state line. *Terrain:* Roads. *Cycling:* Not appropriate. *Awards:* Medal $6.00; Patch $4.00. *Submit:* Hike report describing service project done on or for trail. *Register:* In advance. *Sites:* Mound Grove Cemetery, Truman Boyhood Home, 1827 Log Courthouse, 1859 Civil War Jail and Museum, Mormon Visitors Center, William M. Klien Park, Rice/Tremonti Home, R.L.D.S. Auditorium, R.L.D.S. Temple.

South St. Louis Trail

Location: South St. Louis, MO. *Theme:* Local history. *Sponsor:* Camping Service, Greater St. Louis Area Council, BSA, 4568 W. Pine Blvd., St. Louis, MO 63108, (314) 361-0600.

Length: 14 miles (loop). *Route:* The trail begins and ends in Tower Grove Park, and winds through most of South St. Louis. *Terrain:* City streets. *Cycling:* Appropriate. *Awards:* Patch $2.50. *Submit:* Group leader's certification of completion. *Register:* At least 2 weeks in advance. *Sites:* Friedrich von Steuben Statue, Bevo Mill, Lyle Mansion, Fountain Pond, Turkish Shelter, Music Stand, Coast Guard Base, Alexander von Humboldt Statue, William Shakespeare Statue, Bellerive Park, Carondelet Park, Alexian Brothers Hospital, Benton Park, Frank T. Hilliker Bridge, St. Francis de Sales Catholic Church, Tower Grove House, Shaw Mausoleum, Missouri Botanical Garden, Compton Hill Reservoir Park, World War I Cannon.

Taum Sauk Trail

Location: Pilot Knob, MO. *Theme:* Battle of Pilot Knob—1864. *Sponsor:* Camping Service, Greater St. Louis Area Council, BSA, 4568 W. Pine Blvd., St. Louis, MO 63108, (314) 361-0600.

Length: 20 miles (straight). *Route:* The trail begins at Ft. Davidson and ends at Johnson Shut-Ins State Park. *Terrain:* Woods. *Cycling:* Not recommended. *Awards:* Patch $2.50. *Submit:* Group leader's certification of completion. *Register:* At least 2 weeks in advance. *Sites:* Taum Sauk Mountain, Ft. Davidson, Shepherd Mountain, Russell Mountain, Mina Sauk Falls, Taum Creek, Devil's Toll Gate, Proffit Mountain.

Three Notch Trail

Location: S-F Scout Ranch near Ste. Genevieve, MO. *Theme:* Recreation. *Sponsor:* Camping Service, Greater St. Louis Area Council, BSA, 4568 W. Pine Blvd., St. Louis, MO 63108, (314) 361-0600.

Length: West Loop, 11 miles (loop). East Loop, 10 miles (loop). Combined, with Cutoff—17 miles (loop). *Route:* The West Loop begins at the Camporee Area and circles Eugene D. Nims Lake. The East Loop begins at the Castle Rock parking lot and generally follows Beard Ridge and Rutherford Ridge. *Terrain:* Rugged. *Cycling:* Not recommended. *Awards:* Patch $2.50; 3 Segments $0.35 each. *Submit:* Group leader's certification of completion. *Register:* At least 2 weeks in advance. *Sites:* Whiteoak Spring Branch, Ship Rock, Little St. Francis River, Anvil Rock, Wills Branch, Castle Rock, Little Rock Creek, Fern Grotto.

Tomahawk Trail

Location: Beaumont Scout Reservation, High Ridge, MO. *Theme:* Recreation. *Sponsor:* Camping Service, Greater St. Louis Area Council, BSA, 4568 W. Pine Blvd., St. Louis, MO 63108, (314) 361-0600.

Length: 10 miles (loop). *Route:* The trail begins and ends at the Shippey Trail Center, and approaches the perimeter of the reservation. *Terrain:* Woods. *Cycling:* Not recommended. *Awards:* Patch $2.50. *Submit:* Group leader's certification of completion. *Register:* At least 2 weeks in advance. *Sites:* Toad Hollow, Mud Cave, Blackberry Hollow, Little Antire Creek, Indian Flint Pits, Cub World.

Trace Creek Trail

Location: Mark Twain National Forest near Potosi, MO. *Theme:* Recreation. *Sponsor:* Special Awards Co., 811 Lafayette, Webster Groves, MO 63119, (314) 961-2610.

Length: 17 miles (straight). *Route:* The trail begins at the Hazel Creek Campground on FR 2408, and ends at SR 32. *Terrain:* Woods. *Cycling:* Not recommended. *Awards:* Patch $1.60; Repeat Patch $1.60. *Submit:* No requirement. *Register:* Not required.

West Tyson Park Trails

Location: West Tyson County Park, St. Louis County, MO. *Theme:* Recreation. *Sponsor:* Special Awards Co., 811 Lafayette, Webster Groves, MO 63119, (314) 961-2610. *Lengths:* Buck Run Trail, 0.3 mile (straight). Chinkapin Trail, 0.5 mile (straight). Chubb Trail, 7.5 miles (straight). Flint Quarry Trail, 0.8 mile (loop). Ridge Trail, 0.3 mile (straight). *Routes:* The Chubb Trail begins at its trail shelter (take left fork after entering park) and ends at Lone Elk. All other trails begin at the end of the road forming the right fork, ending at Chubb Trail (Ridge), trailhead (Flint Quarry), first parking area on right fork (Chinkapin) or camping area 3 (Buck Run). *Terrain:* Generally rugged. *Cycling:* Not recommended. *Awards:* Patch $2.75. *Submit:* No requirement. *Register:* Not required.

Whispering Pine Trail

Location: Hawn State Park, Farmington, MO. *Theme:* Recreation. *Sponsor:* Special Awards Co., 811 Lafayette, Webster Groves, MO 63119, (314) 961-2610.

Length: 10 miles (loop). *Route:* The trail begins and ends at the end of the road reached by turning right just after entering the park. *Terrain:* Woods. *Cycling:* Not recommended. *Awards:* Patch $2.25. *Submit:* No requirement. *Register:* Not required.

Formerly Sponsored Trails

Big Piney Trail
Big Spring Ozark Trail
Big Springs Trail
Black Madonna Trail
Butterfield Overland Trail
Chalk Bluff Trail
Clear Fork Trail
Doc Ferener Trail
Duchesne Trail
First Capitol Trail
Fort Osage Trail
Halls Ferry Historic Trail
Jesse James Pilgrimage Trail
Jim Bridger Pilgrimage Trail

Johnny Appleseed Pilgrimage Trail
Kit Carson Pilgrimage Trail
Lone Jack Battlefield Trail
Meramec Ridge Trail
Missouri Lead Belt Trail
Missouri Woodland Trail
Ouray Trace

Saxon Heritage Trail
Sioux Trail
Sunridge Tower Trails
Tower Rock Trail
Trail Awinding
Walter A. Favers Trail

MONTANA

None

NEBRASKA

Covered Wagon Trail

Location: Camp Eagle, Cedar Bluffs, NE.
Theme: Recreation. *Sponsor:* Mid-America
Council, BSA, 12401 W. Maple Rd., Omaha,
NE 68164-1853, (402) 431-9272.
Length: 10 miles (loop). *Route:* The trail
begins at Camp Eagle on the Covered Wagon
Scout Reservation, passes through Camp
Cedars, and returns to the start. *Terrain:*
Woods. *Cycling:* Not recommended. *Awards:*
Patch. *Submit:* No requirement. *Register:* At
least 2 weeks in advance. *Sites:* Platte River,
Beaver Lake.

Logan Fontenelle Trail

Location: Bellevue, NE. *Theme:* 19th
century local history. *Sponsor:* Mid-America
Council, BSA, 12401 W. Maple Rd., Omaha,
NE 68164-1853, (402) 431-9272.
Length: 12 miles (loop). *Route:* The trail
begins at Camp Wa-Kon-Da, winds through
Bellevue, and returns to the start. *Terrain:*
City streets. *Cycling:* Appropriate. *Awards:*
Medal $3.00; Patch $2.00; Trail Mug $3.00;
Camp Mug $2.50. *Submit:* Group leader's
certification of completion. *Register:* Two
weeks in advance. *Sites:* Logan Fontenelle
Grave, Mormon Hollow, John Dougherty
Indian Agency, Burlington Railroad Station,

Peter Sarpy Trading Post, Courthouse,
Strategic Aerospace Museum, Lucien
Fontenelle Blacksmith Shop, St. Columban
Fathers Mission, Reverend Hamilton's Home,
Presbyterian Church, Presbyterian Mission,
Log Cabin, Lucien Fontenelle Trading Post.

Mormon Historic P.L.S. Trail

Location: Columbus, NE. *Theme:* 1847
route of Mormons to Utah. *Sponsor:* Mid-
America Council, BSA, 12401 W. Maple Rd.,
Omaha, NE 68164-1853, (402) 431-9272.
Length: 10-59 miles (straight). *Route:* The
trail follows the historical route through the
Platte River Valley. The starting and ending
points can vary depending upon the desires
of the group. *Terrain:* Varies. *Cycling:* Not
recommended. *Awards:* Patch. *Submit:* No
requirement. *Register:* At least 2 weeks in
advance.

Formerly Sponsored Trails

Lone Tree Trail
Pioneer Mormon Trail
Prairie Schooner Trail

NEVADA

Basin & Range Trails

Location: Basin & Range area of NV.
Theme: Recreation. *Sponsor:* Boulder Dam Area Council, BSA, 1135 University Rd., Las Vegas, NV 89119-6605, (702) 736-4366 or fax (702) 736-0641.

Length: At least 6 miles. *Routes:* Individually-designed trails may qualify for awards. Suggested routes include:. Camp Bonanza to Lee Canyon Trail, (20 miles loop). Cranes Nest Rapids Hike, (10 miles loop). Eagle Eye-Bonanza Peak Trail, (12 miles loop). Mt. Charleston North Loop Trail, (18 miles loop). Mt. Charleston South Loop Trail, (18 miles loop). Mt. Charleston via Deer Creek Trail and North Loop Trail, (20 miles loop). Pinto Valley Hike, (15 miles loop). White Rock Canyon Hike, (6 miles loop). *Terrain:* Generally mountainous. *Cycling:* Not recommended. *Awards:* Patch. *Submit:* Group leader's certification of completion. *Register:* Not required.

Formerly Sponsred Trails

Historic Nevada Trail
Trail of the Foxtail Pine

NEW HAMPSHIRE

None

NEW JERSEY

Batona Trail

Location: Bass River State Forest, Gretna, NJ. *Theme:* Scenic forest area. *Sponsor:* Bass River State Park, P.O. Box 118, New Gretna, NJ 08224, (609) 327-1114. Order awards from Wharton State Forest, US 9, Batsto Historic Site Visitor Center, Batsto, NJ 08037, (609) 561-0024 or (609) 561-3262; or Lebanon State Forest, P.O. Box 215, New Lisbon, NJ 08064, (609) 726-1190.

Length: 52 miles. *Route:* See trail brochure. *Terrain:* Forest woodlands. *Cycling:* Not permitted. *Awards:* Medal; Patch; Pin. *Submit:* Request for awards. *Register:* Not required.

Battle of Monmouth Historic Trail

Location: Englishtown to Freehold, NJ. *Theme:* Battle of Monmouth—June 28, 1778. *Sponsor:* Monmouth Council, BSA, P.O. Box 188, Oakhurst, NJ 07755-0188, (732) 531-3636.

Length: 11 miles (straight). *Route:* The trail starts at Quail Hill Scout Reservation Lawrence Training Center and ends in Freehold. *Terrain:* Woods. *Cycling:* Not recommended. *Awards:* Medal $5.00; Patch $3.00. *Submit:* Completed 18-item questionnaire. *Register:* Two weeks in advance. *Sites:* Old Monmouth Court House, Hulse Memorial Home, Old Tennent Church, Cobb House, Battle of Monmouth Monument, Village Inn, St. Peter's Church, Monmouth Battlefield State Park, Molly Pitcher's Well, Molly Pitcher's Spring, Craig House.

Captain Joshua Huddy Revolutionary Trail

Location: Toms River, NJ. *Theme:* Captain Joshua Huddy, Revolutionary War hero. *Sponsor:* Jersey Shore Council, BSA, 1518 Ridgeway Rd., P.O. Box 1247, Toms River, NJ 08754-1247, (732) 349-1037.

Length: 7 miles (loop). *Route:* The trail begins at the BSA Service Center on Indian Hill Rd., heads south to Huddy Park, and returns to the start. *Terrain:* Roads. *Cycling:* Appropriate. *Awards:* Medal $9.00; Patch $2.00. *Submit:* Completed 23-item questionnaire. *Register:* Two weeks in advance. *Sites:* Cedar Grove Church, Ocean County Museum, Old Methodist Cemetery, Town Hall Square, Ocean County Court House, Huddy Park.

Cooper River Historical Trail

Location: Camden County, NJ. *Theme:* Cooper River, a tributary of the Delaware River. *Sponsor:* American Historical Trails, P.O. Box 769, 1902 Plyler Mill Rd., Monroe, NC 28111-0769, (704) 289-1604, Carotrader@trellis.net.

Length: 12.0 miles (straight). *Route:* The trail begins at Pomona Hall on Park Blvd. and Euclid Ave. in Camden. It ends at the Barclay Farmstead in Cherry Hill. *Terrain:* Sidewalks and roads. *Cycling:* Appropriate. *Awards:* Medal $6.50; Patch $2.25. *Submit:* 23-item questionnaire. *Register:* Not required. *Sites:* Harleigh Cemetery, Collins-Knight House, Hadrosaurus Dinosaur, Friends Meeting House, Indian King Tavern, Haddon Fortnightly, Greenfield Hall, Old Salem Road, Bonnie's Ridge, Croft Farm.

Covered Bridge Historical Trail

Location: Central NJ. *Theme:* Local history. *Sponsor:* George Washington Council, BSA, 62 S. Main St., Pennington, NJ 08534, (609) 737-9400.

Length: 18.0 miles. *Route:* Available from sponsor. *Terrain:* Available from sponsor. *Cycling:* Available from sponsor. *Awards:* Patch $2.00. *Submit:* Available from sponsor. *Register:* Available from sponsor.

History of the Glen Trail

Location: Camp Glen Gray, Mahwah, NJ. *Theme:* Recreation. *Sponsor:* Essex Council, BSA, 788 Bloomfield Ave., Verona, NJ 07044-

1302, (201) 857-0007; or Camp Glen Gray, 200 Midvale Mountain Rd., Mahwah, NJ 07430, (201) 327-7234.

Length: 9.8 miles (loop). *Route:* The trail begins near the Camp Office and Trading Post on the Red Card Trail, heads north and west along the Teepee Trail, crosses the Cannonball Road and Trail, heads south parallel to the Midvale-Suffern Trail, east along the Old Guard Trail, then south on the Cannonball Road and through the camp to end at the Trading Post. *Terrain:* Mountainous woods. *Cycling:* Not allowed. *Awards:* Medal; patch. *Submit:* 19-item questionnaire. *Register:* Send $1 per hiker for trail package. *Sites:* Sanders Farm, Post Foundation, View of New York City, Mothercroft, Wanaque Reservoir, Mother's Pavilion, Old Guard Cabin, The Library, Kidde-Miller Dam, 1917 Campsite.

Jockey Hollow Trail

Location: Gladston to Morristown, NJ. *Theme:* Recreation. *Sponsor:* Morris-Sussex Area Council, BSA, 12 Mt. Pleasant Tpk., Denville, NJ 07834, (973) 361-1800.

Length: 17.5 miles (straight). *Route:* The trail begins at the corner of SR 512 and Mendham Rd. in Gladstone and ends at the Ford Mansion and Historical Museum in Morristown. *Terrain:* Country roads. *Cycling:* Appropriate. *Awards:* Medal $4.00. *Submit:* Essay on Revolutionary War topic and stamped credential card. *Register:* At least 2 weeks in advance. *Sites:* Ford Mansion, Schiff Reservation, Jockey Hollow, Fort Nonsense, Tempe Wick House, Cross Estate, New Jersey Audubon Museum, Soldier Huts, Washington's Headquarters.

Millstone Valley Historic Trail

Location: Kingston to Manville, NJ. *Theme:* Route taken by Washington and his army after crossing the Delaware River on December 25, 1776. *Sponsor:* Thomas A. Edison Council, BSA, 2757 Woodbridge Ave., P.O. Box 855, Edison, NJ 08818-0855, (732) 494-0305.

Length: 10 miles (straight). *Route:* The trail starts at the intersection of SR 27 and the Delaware and Raritan Canal, and follows the Millstone River north to the Old Cemetery near the Weston Causeway. *Terrain:* Hilly roads. *Cycling:* Appropriate. *Awards:* Patch $2.00. *Submit:* Group leader's certification of completion. *Register:* In advance. *Sites:* Bernards Boat Rental, Old Forge, Lock Tenders Home, Old Mill Building, Rockingham House, Old Copper Mine, Griggstown Canal Lock, Griggstown Causeway, John Honeyman Home, Old Franklin Inn.

Palisades Historic Trails

Location: Alpine, NJ. *Theme:* Revolutionary War. *Sponsor:* Bergen Council, BSA, 22-08 SR 208 S, Fair Lawn, NJ 07410, (201) 791-8000.

Length: There are two trails, the Long Path (11.3 miles straight) and the Shore Trail (12.5 miles straight). Completion of either trail in either direction is required for the patch. Both trails must be hiked and a night must be camped at Camp Alpine for the medal. *Route:* The Long Path stretches from Fort Lee to Camp Alpine in Alpine, NJ, and is located on top of the area cliffs. The Shore Trail has the same beginning and end, but is located under the cliffs and is the more strenuous trail. *Terrain:* Roads and woods. *Cycling:* Not recommended. *Awards:* Medal $6.50; Patch $3.50. *Submit:* For the patch, credential card (sent upon registration) stamped at the visitor center in Fort Lee Historic Park, plus completed questionnaire. For the medal, also submit a 250-word essay. For each, submit completed order form. *Register:* Required. The trails are only open from March 15 to November 30, as the Palisades Interstate Park Commission officials consider them unsafe during the rest of the year. *Sites:* Women's Federation Monument, Cornwallis House, State Line Lookout, Fort Lee Visitor Center, Fort Lee Battle Monument, Alpine Lookout, George Washington Bridge, Rockefeller Lookout, Twombley Landing, Allison Overlook Park, Greenbrook Sanctuary, Ruckman Point.

Victorian Trail

Location: Cape May, NJ. *Theme:* Late 19th Century Victorian Architecture. *Sponsor:* Boy Scout Troop 84, P.O. Box 55, Cape May, NJ 08204, (609) 884-3947.

Length: 7.0 miles (loop). *Route:* The trail begins at the Cape May Welcome Center on Lafayette St., heads a little west, and then northeast on Lafayette St., south on Pittsburgh, west on Beach, and then winds through downtown to end at the start.

Terrain: City streets. *Cycling:* Appropriate. *Awards:* Patch $3.50. *Submit:* 38-item questionnaire. *Register:* Not required. *Sites:* Good House, Williams House, The Blue Pig, The Pink House, The Seven Sisters, The Merry Widow, Old Post Office, Cohen's Jewelry Store, Captain Mey's Inn, The Queen Victoria.

Victory Trail

Location: Elizabeth, NJ. *Theme:* Colonial era history of Elizabeth. *Sponsor:* Watchung Area Council, BSA, 1170 SR 22 W., Mountainside, NJ 07092, (908) 654-9191.

Length: Contact sponsor. *Route:* The trail begins at the foot of Elizabeth Ave. and Front St., and proceeds on First Ave., Fifth St., Pearl St., Broad St., Morris Ave., Westfield Ave., Galloping Hill Rd., Chestnut St., Stuyvesant Ave., W. Chestnut St., Caldwell Pl., Elmwood Ave., and Mountain Ave. *Terrain:* City streets. *Cycling:* Appropriate. *Awards:* Medal. *Submit:* 12-item questionnaire. *Register:* Not required. *Sites:* St. John's Parsonage House, Court House, First Presbyterian Church, Galloping Hill Inn, Connecticut Farms Church, Springfield Presbyterian Church, Springfield Town Boundary.

Yaw Paw Trails

Location: Ramapo Mountains, NJ. *Theme:* Recreation. *Sponsor:* Ridgewood-Glen Rock Council, BSA, 176 Rock Rd., Glen Rock, NJ 07452, (908) 444-4615.

Length: 18.5 miles total. *Routes:* There are 6 trails, all in the Oakland-Mahwah area. *Terrain:* Mountains. *Cycling:* Not appropriate. *Awards:* Patch. *Submit:* Group leader's certification of completion of all 6 trails. *Register:* Not required.

Other New Jersey Awards

Cub Paw Award—7 requirements, including 2 short hikes. Patch. Sponsored by Ridgewood-Glen Rock Council, BSA, 176 Rock Rd., Glen Rock, NJ 07452, (908) 444-4615.

Formerly Sponsored Trails

Cannonball Trail
Dale's Trail
Oyster Shell Road Historic Trail
Post Ford Historical Trail
Wayne Trail

New Mexico

Formerly Sponsored Trails
Old Ft. Wingate-Zuni Rd. Trail
Santa Fe Scout Trail

New York

Adam Helmer Historic Trail

Location: Herkimer, NY. *Theme:* Path of 24-year-old Revolutionary War scout who ran from Edmeston to Fort Herkimer to warn settlers of an impending Indian raid. *Sponsor:* General Herkimer Council, BSA, 427 N. Main St., P.O. Box 128, Herkimer, NY 13350, (315) 866-1540.
Length: 50 miles (straight). *Route:* The trail begins at the Carr Farm near Edmeston, and heads to the northeast through Richfield Springs to Fort Herkimer. *Terrain:* Woods and roads. *Cycling:* Not appropriate. *Awards:* Patch. *Submit:* Group leader's proof of completion of hike and two nights' camping. *Register:* Not necessary, but advisable. *Sites:* Fort Herkimer, Carr Farm, Jordanville, Columbia Center.

American 1779 March of Anthony Wayne Trail

Location: Stony Point, NY. *Theme:* Revolutionary War. *Sponsor:* Hudson Valley Council, BSA, Station Road Sq., SR 94, P.O. Box 374, Salisbury Mills, NY 12577-0374, (845) 497-7337.
Length: 12 miles (straight). *Route:* The trail runs from Bear Mountain to Stony Point, passing by Camp Bullowa. *Terrain:* Woods. *Cycling:* Not recommended. *Awards:* Medal $5.00; Patch $2.75. *Submit:* 200-word essay. *Register:* Not required. *Sites:* Stony Point Battlefield Museum, Harriman State Park.

Benjamin Tallmadge National Historic Trail

Location: Port Jefferson, Long Island, NY.

Theme: Revolutionary War battle and troop movement—November, 1780. *Sponsor:* John Aleksak, 56 Hewes St., Port Jefferson Station, NY 11776, (516) 928-2867; or Suffolk County Council, BSA, 7 Scouting Blvd., Medford, NU 11763, (516) 924-7010.
Length: 24 miles (straight). *Route:* The trail begins at Mount Sinai Harbor and ends at the Manor of St. George. *Terrain:* Roads. *Cycling:* Appropriate. *Awards:* Patch $5.00. *Submit:* No requirement (overnight camp required for awards). *Register:* At least 3 weeks in advance. *Sites:* Swezey House Site, Christopher Swezey's Mill Site, Ashton House, Cathedral Pines County Park, Lengyal House, Horman's Mill Site, Captain Williams Phillips House, Robert F. Hawkins House, First Presbyterian Church, Manor of St. George, Carman's Mill Site.

British 1777 General Clinton Trail

Location: Stony Point, NY. *Theme:* March of British army to attack forts at Bear Mountain. *Sponsor:* Hudson Valley Council, BSA, Station Road Sq., SR 94, P.O. Box 374, Salisbury Mills, NY 12577-0374, (845) 497-7337.
Length: 8 miles (straight). *Route:* The trail begins at Stony Point and heads north to end at Bear Mountain. *Terrain:* Roads and woods. *Cycling:* Not recommended. *Awards:* Medal $5.00; Patch $2.75. *Submit:* 200-word essay on a topic related to the area. *Register:* Not required. *Sites:* Fort Clinton, Bear Mountain State Trailside Museum and Zoo, Fort Montgomery, Stony Point Fort.

Brooklyn Historic Quest Trail

Location: Brooklyn, NY. *Theme:* History of

Brooklyn. *Sponsor:* Environmental Quest, Inc., 1715 Newkirk Ave., Brooklyn, NY 11226-6613, (718) 941-9835.

Length: 35 miles. *Route:* The trail begins in Brooklyn and ends at Floyd Bennett Field. *Terrain:* City streets. *Cycling:* Permitted. *Awards:* Patch $5.00. *Submit:* Completed questionnaire. *Register:* Upon arrival. *Sites:* Zoo.

Corning, Colonists, Cowboys and Crystal Historic Trail

Location: Corning, NY. *Theme:* Local history. *Sponsor:* Five Rivers Council, BSA, P.O. Box 5190, Horseheads, NY 14844-3861, (607) 776-3861.

Length: 3.5 miles (straight). *Route:* The trail begins at the Corning Museum of Glass and ends at the parking area at the intersection of Pultenay St. and SR 17E. *Terrain:* City streets. *Cycling:* Possible, but does not qualify for awards. *Awards:* Patch $3.00. *Submit:* Group leader's certification of completion and completed 132-item questionnaire. *Register:* Not required. *Sites:* Corning Museum of Glass, Corning Glass Center, Benjamin Patterson Inn, Chemung River, Rockwell Museum, DeMonstoy Cabin, Browntown School.

Elmira Historical Trail

Location: Elmira, NY. *Theme:* Local history. *Sponsor:* Five Rivers Council, BSA, P.O. Box 5190, Horseheads, NY 14844-5190, (607) 776-3861.

Length: 5 or 10 miles (straight). *Route:* The trail begins on West Water St. near SR 17, winds through Elmira, and ends at the Chemung County Historical Society Building. *Terrain:* City streets. *Cycling:* Appropriate. *Awards:* Medal $6.00; 10-mile Patch $4.00; 5-mile Patch $3.00. *Submit:* Completed 83-item questionnaire. *Register:* Not required. *Sites:* Civil War Monument, Woodlawn City Cemetery, 1862 Court House, Arnot Art Museum, Mark Twain's Grave, E.F.A. Building, Henry Brooks House, Harris Hall, Elmira College, Booth House, Old Second Street Cemetery, Riverfront Park, Elmira Savings and Loan, Soaring Sculpture, Elmira Correctional Facility, Woodlawn National Cemetery, First Baptist Church, Arnot House.

Lost City of Tryon Trail

Location: Ellison Park, Rochester, NY. *Theme:* Local history. *Sponsor:* Troop 55,

Covenant United Methodist Church, 1124 Culver Rd., Rochester, NY 14609.

Length: 1.5 miles (loop). *Route:* The trail begins and ends at the parking lot on N. Landing Rd., and does a figure eight south near the swamp. *Terrain:* Woods and roads. *Cycling:* Not recommended. *Awards:* Patch $2.75. *Submit:* Group leader's certification of completion. *Register:* Not required. *Sites:* Old Spring, Lookout Site of Butler's Rangers, Old Tryon House, Stone Steps in Old Garden, Indian Landing Rock, Fort Schuyler, Irondequoit Creek.

Millard Fillmore Historical Trail

Location: Millard Fillmore State Park, Moravia, NY. *Theme:* President Millard Fillmore. *Sponsor:* Cayuga County Historian, Historic Old Post Office, 157 Genesee St., Auburn, NY 13021-3423, (315) 253-1300.

Length: 12 miles (loop). *Route:* The trail begins and ends in the park, making a large loop through town. *Terrain:* City streets. *Cycling:* Appropriate. *Awards:* Medal $5.00. *Submit:* Completed 14-item questionnaire. *Register:* Not required. *Sites:* Fillmore's Birthplace, St. Matthew's Episcopal Church, Sally Robin's Grave, Deer Lodge, Fillmore Cabin Replica.

Nathan Hale Historic Trail

Location: Huntington, Long Island, NY. *Theme:* Nathan Hale and local history. *Sponsor:* Suffolk County Council, BSA, c/o Howard Gary, 31 Turtle Cove Ln., Huntington, NY 11743-3867; or Suffolk County Council, BSA, 7 Scouting Blvd., Medford, NY 11763, (516) 924-7010.

Length: 18.5 miles (straight). *Route:* The trail begins at the Silas Wood House on Park Ave. and ends at the Old Bethpage Village Restoration. *Terrain:* Roads. *Cycling:* Appropriate. *Awards:* Medal $3.00. *Submit:* Completed credential cards. *Register:* At least 3 weeks in advance. *Sites:* Old Burying Grounds, Powell House, The Old Presbyterian Church, Conklin House, The Town Historian Building, Walt Whitman House, New York State Fish Hatchery, Whaling Museum, Peace and Plenty Inn, Whitman-Place Home, Old Bethpage Village Restoration, Whitman-Rome Home, St. John's Episcopal Church, Jarvis House.

Niagara Frontier Trail

Location: Youngstown to Buffalo, NY.

Theme: Local history. *Sponsor:* Greater Niagara Frontier Council, BSA, 401-407 Maryvale Dr., Cheektowaga, NY 14225-2601, (716) 891-4073.

Length: 30 miles (straight). *Route:* The trail begins at Old Fort Niagara and ends at the Naval & Servicemen's Park. *Terrain:* Roads. *Cycling:* Appropriate, but this is intended to be done by car. *Awards:* Medal $4.50. *Submit:* Completed 35-item questionnaire. *Register:* Not required. *Sites:* Our Lady of Fatima Shrine, Old Fort Niagara, Whirlpool State Park, Devils Hole, Power Vista, Niagara Reservation State Park, Schoellkopf Geological Museum, Buffalo & Erie County Historical Museum, Buffalo Naval & Servicemen's Park.

The Old New York Historical Trail

Location: New York City, NY. *Theme:* Local history. *Sponsor:* Historical Trail Committee, Man-A-Hattin Lodge 82, W.W.W., c/o Pat Golland, 10 Park Ave. #4J, New York, NY 10016-4338, (212) 242-1100 ext. 240.

Length: 5.3 miles (straight). *Route:* The trail begins at the main gate of the Saint Mark's-in-the-Bowerie Church, winds through Manhattan, and ends at the Brooklyn Bridge, with one of the three listed side trips required for awards. *Terrain:* City streets. *Cycling:* Possible, but does not qualify for awards. *Awards:* Patch $2.50. *Submit:* Completed 11-item questionnaire. *Register:* Not required. *Sites:* Stuyvesant-Fish House, Alamo Sculpture, Cooper Union College, Chinatown, DeVinne Press Building, Shakespeare Festival Public Theater, Confucius Statue, Paolucci's Restaurant, Surrogate's Court, New York City Fire Museum, World Trade Center site, Battery Park, Castle Clinton, Statue of Liberty, Ellis Island, Fraunces Tavern, India House, New York Stock Exchange, Mariner's Church, Old Merchant's House, Puck Building.

Otetiana Council Trail

Location: Rochester, NY. *Theme:* New York State Barge Canal System. *Sponsor:* Otetiana Council, BSA, 474 East Ave., Rochester, NY 14607, (716) 244-4210.

Length: Approx. 15.0 miles (straight). *Route:* There are four approved routes:. Village of Brockport east to Long Pond Rd. in Greece; Long Pond Rd. in Greece west to

Brockport; Mitchell Rd. in Pittsford east to Macedon; or Macedon west to Mitchell Rd. in Pittsford. *Terrain:* Canal towpath. *Cycling:* Not appropriate. *Awards:* Medal; patch. *Submit:* For patch, group leader's certification of proof of completion of hike. For medal, also include 300-word essay. *Register:* In advance with sponsor. *Sites:* Canal Park, Lock 30.

Pelham Bay Park Historical Trail

Location: Long Island, NY. *Theme:* History of Pelham Bay Park. *Sponsor:* David Malitsky, Greater New York Council, BSA, Ranachua Lodge No. 4, 345 Hudson St., New York, NY 10014, (212) 242-1100.

Length: 8.9 miles (straight). *Route:* The trail begins at Turtle Cove, heads northeast to Hunter Island, southwest past the lagoon, and north to end at St. Paul's Cemetery. *Terrain:* Woods and roads. *Cycling:* Not appropriate. *Awards:* Patch $3.00. *Submit:* Request for patches. *Register:* Not required. *Sites:* Orchard Beach, Twin Islands, Mica Crystal Dike, Sphinx Rock, Pell Cemetery, St. Paul's Church, Split Rock, Glover's Rock, Carriage Shed, Mishow Rock.

Portage Trail

Location: Barcelona to Mayville, NY. *Theme:* Local history. *Sponsor:* Allegheny Highlands Council, BSA, 50 Hough Hill Rd., P.O. Box 0261, Falconer, NY 14733-0261, (716) 665-2697.

Length: 11.5 miles (straight) by car; 12.5 miles (straight) by foot; or 13.5 miles (straight) by canoe. *Route:* The trail begins at the Daniel Reed Memorial on the Lake Erie shore, and heads south through Westfield to Mayville. The canoe route goes upstream on Chautauqua Creek. *Terrain:* Roads. *Cycling:* Appropriate, or may be driven or canoed. *Awards:* Patch $2.50. *Submit:* No requirement. *Register:* Not required. *Sites:* Barcelona Lighthouse, Welch Plant, Grace Bedell Home, First County Office, First Church Building, McClurg Mansion, McMahan Homestead, Albion Tourge Home, Former Indian Village, Portage Trail Marker, Button's Inn Site, Daniel Reed Memorial, Water Divide, Mayville Cemetery, County Court House, Glen Mills and Falls.

Saratoga National Historic Trail

Location: Saratoga National Historical

Park, Stillwater, NY. *Theme:* Revolutionary War Battles of Saratoga. *Sponsor:* Twin Rivers Council, BSA, 253 Washington Ave. Ext., Albany, NY 12205, (518) 869-6436.

Length: 7.5 miles loop. *Route:* The trail begins behind the Visitor Center, heads south and east on the park tour road nearly to US 4, then north and east nearly back to US 4, and west back to the point of beginning. *Terrain:* Roads and dirt trails. *Cycling:* Appropriate. *Awards:* Patch $3.00; Medal $5.00. *Submit:* Completed questionnaire (picked up at Visitor Center). *Register:* Two weeks in advance. *Sites:* Freeman Farm Overlook, Benedict Arnold Boot Memorial, Chatfield Farm, Neilson Farm, Breymann Redoubt, Buygoyne's Headquarters, Balcarres Redoubt, Fraser Burial Site, Rockefeller Monument.

Ten Mile River Historic Trail

Location: Narrowsburg, NY. *Theme:* Recreation and history. *Sponsor:* Ten Mile River Scout Camps, 1481 CR 26, Narrowsburg, NY 12764, (845) 252-3911 ext. 160.

Length: 36 miles (straight). *Route:* The awards can be earned by hiking and/or canoeing at least 10 miles along the 36-mile route. *Terrain:* Woods. *Cycling:* Not recommended. *Awards:* Medal $10.00; "XIV", "XIX" and "50" Devices for ribbon of medal $1.50 each; 4" Patch $4.00; 6" Patch $6.00. *Submit:* Group leader's certification of completion of hike, conservation project, historic site visitation, and essay. *Register:* In advance. *Sites:* Stone Arch Bridge, Tusten Baptist Church, Zane Grey Museum, Roebling Bridge, Minisink Battlefield, Fort Delaware.

Vroman's Nose Historic Trail

Location: Vroman's Nose Mountain near West Middleburgh, NY. *Theme:* Recreation and local history. *Sponsor:* Otschodela Council, BSA, P.O. Box 1356, Oneonta, NY 13820-1356, (607) 432-6491.

Length: 1.8 miles (loop). *Route:* The trail begins and ends at the parking lot on West Middleburgh Rd. near Line Creek, and follows the cliff along the edge of the mountain. *Terrain:* Mountain. *Cycling:* Not recommended. *Awards:* Patch $3.00. *Submit:* Group leader's certification of completion and completed 13-item questionnaire. *Register:* Not required. *Sites:* Vroman's Nose Mountain, Schoharie Valley, 1853 Octagon House, Wilder Hook, Glacial Grooves, Stanton Hall, Vroman Massacre Site, Mattice Barn.

Westchester County Historic Trail

Location: Westchester County, NY. *Theme:* Local history. *Sponsor:* Westchester/Putnam Council, BSA, 41 Saw Mill River Rd., Hawthorne, NY 10532-1519, (914) 773-1135.

Length: Varies. *Route:* The route chosen will depend on which 7 of the 10 historic sites the hikers choose to visit. *Terrain:* Roads. *Cycling:* Appropriate, but it is intended to be a driving tour. *Awards:* Medal $2.75; Patch $2.00. *Submit:* Completed 39-item questionnaire. *Register:* Not required. *Sites:* Sunnyside, Thomas Paine Cottage, Cudner-Hyatt House and Museum, Lyndhurst, Philipsburg Manor Upper Mills, 1828 Quaker Meeting House, Bill of Rights Museum, John Jay Homestead State Historic Site, Van Cortlandt Manor, Glenview Mansion, St. Paul's Church National Historic Site, Washington's Headquarters Museum, The Hudson River Museum.

Formerly Sponsored Trails

Babylon Township Trail
Interloken System Trail
Patriots' Migration Trail
Revolutionary War Trail
Richard "Bull" Smith Historical Trail
Upper Mohawk Trail

NORTH CAROLINA

Appalachian Trail

Location: Western NC. *Theme:* Recreation. *Sponsor:* Rita Grindstaff, Appalachian Ranger District, Toecane Station, P.O. Box 128, Burnsville, NC 28714, (828) 682-6146. *Length:* 35.0 miles (straight). *Route:* This is a 35-mile stretch of the long Appalachian Trail. *Terrain:* Wooded hills and mountains. *Cycling:* Not appropriate. *Awards:* Patch $4.50. *Submit:* Request for patches. *Register:* Not required.

Asbury Trail

Location: Lake Junaluska, NC. *Theme:* Route taken by Rev. Mr. Francis Asbury, an early circuit rider. *Sponsor:* SEJ Commission on Archives & History, The United Methodist Church, Attention: Heritage Center, P.O. Box 67, Lake Junaluska, NC 28745, (828) 452-2881x781 or (828) 456-9226. *Length:* 22.6 miles (straight). *Route:* The trail begins at Mt. Sterling near the Tennessee/North Carolina border, and generally follows SR 284 and US 276 south to Cove Creek. *Terrain:* Some country roads, generally difficult mountains. *Cycling:* Not recommended. *Awards:* Medal $5.00; Patch $2.00. *Submit:* Group leader's certification of completion. *Register:* In advance. *Sites:* Mt. Sterling Gap, Indian Grave, Scottish Mountain, Louisa Chapel.

Bentonville Battlefield Trail

Location: Bentonville, NC. *Theme:* Civil War battle—March 19-21, 1865. *Sponsor:* T.L. Walden, P.O. Box 18832, Raleigh, NC 17619. *Length:* 14 miles (loop). *Route:* The trail begins at the Visitor Center, passes through Bentonville, and returns to the start. *Terrain:* Paved and dirt roads. *Cycling:* Appropriate. *Awards:* Patch $2.00. *Submit:* Completed 24-item questionnaire and group leader's certification of completion. *Register:* Not required. *Sites:* Visitor Center, Harper House, Federal Earth Works, Confederate Cemetery, Texas Monument, Cole Farmhouse Site, UDC Monument, Ebenezer Church.

Cape Fear Historical Trail

Location: Wilmington, NC. *Theme:* Local history. *Sponsor:* Cape Fear Council, BSA, 110 Longstreet Dr., P.O. Box 7156, Wilmington, NC 28406, (910) 395-1100. *Length:* 6 miles (loop). *Route:* The trail begins at the Price House at 514 N. Market St., heads north and west to Oakdale Cemetery, then south on Market St. to the Cape Fear River and other downtown sites, then returns to the start. *Terrain:* City streets. *Cycling:* Appropriate. *Awards:* Patch $1.40. *Submit:* No requirement. *Register:* Not required. *Sites:* Gilcrest House, Thalian Hall, St. Thomas Church, Bellamy Mansion, First Baptist Church, Bridges House, Harnett Memorial, St. James Cemetery, Temple of Israel, deRosset House, Chandler's Wharf, Burgwin-Wright House, Zebulon Latimer House, Masonic Temple, Cotton Exchange, U.S.S. North Carolina.

Great Smoky Mountains National Park Trails

Location: On south side of TN/NC border, north of Bryson City and Cherokee, NC. *Theme:* Recreation. *Sponsor:* Patches available at The Happy Hiker, 905 River Rd., Gatlinburg, TN 37738, (865) 436-6000. About one-third of the patches are also available at the national park headquarters on US 441 2 miles south of Gatlinburg. *Lengths:* Appalachian Trail, 49.0 miles (straight), Cataloochee Divide Trail, 11.5 miles (straight), Charlie's Bunyon Trail, 8.0 miles (loop), Clingman's Dome Trail, 1.0 miles (loop), Deep Creek Trail, 15.0 miles (straight), Derrick Knob Trail, Eagle Creek Trail, 9.0 miles (straight), Forney Ridge Trail, 16.0 miles (straight), Hazel Creek Trail, 6.6 miles (loop), Icewater Springs Trail, Mt. Guyot Trail, Peck's Corner Trail, Shuckstack Mountain Trail, 7.0 miles (loop), Silers Bald Trail, 10.0 miles (loop), Smokemont Trail, 6.0 miles (loop), Sterling Mountain Trail, 12.0 miles (loop), Tricorner Knob Trail. *Routes:* Vary—check park maps for details. *Terrain:* Mountains. *Cycling:* Not permitted. *Awards:* Patches for each trail named above $1.75 each at The Happy Hiker, $1.99 at park headquarters. *Submit:* No requirement. *Register:* Not required, but check park rules for overnight hikes.

Guilford Courthouse Historic Trail

Location: Guilford Courthouse National Military Park, Greensboro, NC. *Theme:* Revolutionary War battle—March 15, 1781. *Sponsor:* Old North State Council, BSA, 1405 Wester Terr., P.O. Box 29046, Greensboro, NC 27429-9046, (336) 378-9166.

Length: 6.5 miles (straight). *Route:* The trail begins at the Lake Brandt Marina, follows the railroad bed to the Visitors Center, and circles the park. *Terrain:* Roads and paved footpaths. *Cycling:* Appropriate. *Awards:* Medal $5.00; Patch $5.00. *Submit:* Completed 15-item questionnaire, stamped by park ranger. *Register:* Not required. *Sites:* Visitor Center, Guilford Courthouse, Caldwell Monument, Greene Monument, Delaware Monument, Maryland Monument, Francisco Monument, Schenck Monument.

Moore's Creek Battlefield Trail

Location: Currie, NC. *Theme:* Pre-Revolutionary War battle—February 27, 1776. *Sponsor:* Cape Fear Council, BSA, 110 Longstreet Dr., P.O. Box 7156, Wilmington, NC 28406, (910) 395-1100.

Length: 1.3 miles (loop). *Route:* The trail begins at the Visitor Center, and follows the History Trail, with a side loop around the Tarheel Trail, and back to the start. *Terrain:* Dirt paths. *Cycling:* Not recommended. *Awards:* Patch $2.00. *Submit:* Group leader's certification of completion. *Register:* Not required. *Sites:* Visitor Center, Stage Road Monument, Loyalist Monument, Reconstructed Bridge, Patriot Monument, Slocumb Monument, Moore Monument.

Raleigh Historical Trail

Location: Raleigh, NC. *Theme:* Local History. *Sponsor:* American Historical Trails, Inc., P.O. Box 769, Monroe, NC 28111, (704) 289-1604.

Length: 4.5 miles (loop). *Route:* The trail begins at the North Carolina Museum of History, 5 E. Edenton St., winds through downtown Raleigh, and returns to the point of beginning. *Terrain:* City streets. *Cycling:* Appropriate. *Awards:* Medal $6.00; Patch $2.25. *Submit:* Completed 23-item questionnaire. *Register:* Only necessary for arranging advance tours of Museum of History, Mordecai Historic Park, Legislative Building, State Capitol, or the Governor's Mansion. *Sites:* Badger-Iredell Law Office, North Carolina Archives and Library, Hawkins-Hartness House, Mordecai House, Andrew Johnson House, St. Mark's Chapel, Henry Clay Oak, Oakwood Historic District, Confederate Cemetery, Executive Mansion, Hebrew Cemetery, Sir Walter Raleigh Statue, Peace College.

Salisbury-Spencer Historical Trail

Location: Salisbury, NC. *Theme:* Local history. *Sponsor:* American Historical Trails, Inc., P.O. Box 769, Monroe, NC 28111, (704) 289-1604, Carotrader@trellis.net.

Length: Route A—4.2 miles (straight). Route B—8.5 miles (loop)

Route: The trail begins at the National Cemetery, winds through Salisbury, and ends at Grimes Mill (Route A) or the start (Route B). *Terrain:* City streets. *Cycling:* Appropriate. *Awards:* Medal $5.50; Patch $2.00. *Submit:* Completed 27-item questionnaire and group leader's certification of completion. *Register:* Not required. *Sites:* Andrew Jackson's Residence, Old Rowan Courthouse, Klutz Drug Store, Thomas Maxwell House, Governor Ellis House, Rowan Museum, Salisbury Female Academy, Grimes Mill, Leo Wallace, Sr. House, Confederate Monument, St. Luke's Episcopal Church, North Carolina Transportation Museum, Old English Cemetery, .

Formerly Sponsored Trails

Bob's Creek Pocket Wilderness Trail
Outer Banks Historical Trail

NORTH DAKOTA

None

OHIO

Anthony Wayne Trail (Fallen Timbers Segment)

Location: Grand Rapids to Maumee, OH. *Theme:* General "Mad" Anthony Wayne. *Sponsor:* Toledo Area Council, BSA, One Stranahan Sq., P.O. Box 337, Toledo, OH 43691-1492, (419) 241-7293.

Length: 15 miles (straight). *Route:* The trail begins at Providence Metropark Shelter House and ends at Sidecut Park. Until the Waterville Bridge, it follows the route of the Buckeye Trail. *Terrain:* Woods. *Cycling:* Not recommended. *Awards:* Medal $3.00; Patch $1.50; Segment Pin $0.95. *Submit:* No requirement. *Register:* At least 2 weeks in advance. *Sites:* Farnsworth Metro Park, Ludwig Mill, Fort Deposit Site, Bend View Park, Columbia House, Site of Battle of Fallen Timbers, Sidecut Metropark.

Anthony Wayne Trail (Fort Finney and Fort Hamilton Segments)

Location: Hamilton, Butler and Preble Counties, OH. *Theme:* General "Mad" Anthony Wayne. *Sponsor:* Dan Beard Council, BSA, 2331 Victory Pkwy., Cincinnati, OH 45206-2803, (513) 961-2336.

Length: Fort Finney Segment, 35.5 miles (straight). Fort Hamilton Segment, 32.8 miles (straight). *Route:* The Fort Finney Segment begins near Cincinnati, and follows the Great Miami River to the Anthony Wayne Hotel in Hamilton. The Fort Hamilton Segment begins at the hotel, takes SR 127 north across the river and westward into Indiana. *Terrain:* Roads. *Cycling:* Appropriate. *Awards:* Medal $3.00; 2 Patches $ 1.50 each; 2 Segment Pins $0.95 each. *Submit:* No requirement. *Register:* At least 2 weeks in advance. *Sites:* Ft. Dunlap, Anthony Wayne Hotel, Soldiers Monument.

Beaumont Trails

Location: Beaumont Scout Reservation, Rock Creek, OH. *Theme:* Recreation. *Sponsor:* Greater Cleveland Council, BSA, 2441 Woodland Ave., Cleveland, OH 44115-3295, (216) 861-6060 or fax (216) 861-3431. *Length:* Blue Trail, 4.0 miles (loop). Red Trail, 6.5 miles (loop). *Route:* The trails begin and end at the Trail Center on the west shore of the lake. The Red Trail stays north of the Grand River, while the Blue Trail follows the southern boundary of the reservation. *Terrain:* Woods and fields. *Cycling:* Not recommended. *Awards:* Patch $2.10. *Submit:* No requirement. *Register:* Not required.

Belden Camp Trail

Location: Belden Scout Camp, Grafton, OH. *Theme:* Recreation. *Sponsor:* Greater Cleveland Council, BSA, 2441 Woodland Ave., Cleveland, OH 44115-3295, (216) 861-6060 or fax (216) 861-3431.

Length: 5 miles (loop). *Route:* The trail begins at the Reception Center, follows the ridges along the ravine, and returns to the start. *Terrain:* Woods. *Cycling:* Not recommended. *Awards:* Patch $2.10. *Submit:* No requirement. *Register:* Not required.

Blue Heron Trail

Location: Dayton, OH. *Theme:* Recreation. *Sponsor:* BSA Troop 184, c/o Larry Young, 585 SR 571, Union City, OH 45390, (937) 968-5577.

Length: 15 miles (straight). *Route:* The trail begins at Huffman Dam northeast of Dayton, and follows the route of the Buckeye Trail west and north to Taylorsville Dam. *Terrain:* Woods. *Cycling:* Not recommended. *Awards:* Patch $5.00. *Register:* Not required. *Sites:* Great Miami River, Mad River, Taylorsville Dam, Huffman Dam.

Bluewater Training Trail

Location: Woodland Trails Boy Scout Reservation, Dayton, OH. *Theme:* Recreation. *Sponsor:* Miami Valley Council, BSA, 4999 Northcutt Pl., Dayton, OH 45414.

Length: 6.12 miles (loop). *Route:* The trail begins and ends at the main parking lot and circles Mystic Lake and a small portion of the reservation. *Terrain:* Woods. *Cycling:* Not recommended. *Awards:* Patch. *Submit:* No requirement. *Register:* Not required.

Buckeye Trail

Location: Throughout Ohio. *Theme:*

Recreation. *Sponsor:* Buckeye Trail Association, P.O. Box 254, Worthington, OH 43085.

Length: 1,158 miles (loop). *Route:* The trail makes a huge loop from Lake County in the northeast to Morgan County in the southeast, to Cincinnati in the southwest, to Defiance County in the northwest, and back to the start. *Terrain:* Varies. *Cycling:* Appropriate over many sections. *Awards:* Patch $2.30; 10k, 25k, 50k and 100k Patches $2.30 each. *Submit:* No requirement. *Register:* Not required.

Chief Blackhoof Trail

Location: St. Johns to Wapakoneta, OH. *Theme:* Catahecassa, also known as Shawnee Chief Blackhoof. *Sponsor:* Bill Collins, Fort Amanda Trading Post, Rt. 4, Fort Amanda Rd., Cridersville, OH 45806, (419) 657-6575.

Length: 8.5 miles (straight). *Route:* The trail begins at Chief Blackhoof Park in St. Johns, heads south along Blackhoof Creek, east along Blank Pike Rd., and north along Cemetery Rd. to end at the Neil Armstrong Museum in Wapakoneta. *Terrain:* Woods and roads. *Cycling:* Not recommended. *Awards:* Patch. *Submit:* Trail pamphlet stamped at Neil Armstrong Museum. *Register:* Not required. *Sites:* Neil Armstrong Museum, Blackhoof Park, Blackhoof Creek, St. Johns Cemetery.

Chief Wapa Tecumseh Trail

Location: Minster to Wapakoneta, OH. *Theme:* Indian lore. *Sponsor:* Paul Nuss, Rt. 1, New Knoxville, OH 45871.

Length: 24.5 miles (straight). *Route:* The trail begins at the State Office in Lake Loramie State Park, follows the Miami-Erie Canal northward, passes through New Knoxville and ends at Koneta Hotel in Wapakoneta. *Terrain:* Roads and canal edge. *Cycling:* Not recommended. *Awards:* Patch $1.00; Medal available for completion of this trail and Clear Water Trail, Fort Amanda-Fort Barbee Trail, and Miami-Erie Trail. *Submit:* Completed 8-item questionnaire. *Register:* Not required. *Sites:* Miami-Erie Canal, Neil Armstrong Airport, Neil Armstrong Space Museum, Koneta Hotel.

Clear Water Trail

Location: Wapakoneta, OH. *Theme:* Route of retreat of Shawnee Indians. *Sponsor:* Bill Collins, Fort Amanda Trading Post, Rt. 4, Fort Amanda Rd., Cridersville, OH 45806, (419) 657-6575.

Length: 18 miles (straight). *Route:* The trail begins at the Hamilton St. Bridge in Wapakoneta and generally follows the Auglaize River west and north to end at Fort Amanda State Park. *Terrain:* Roads. *Cycling:* Possible, but does not qualify for awards; may also be canoed on Auglaize River. *Awards:* Patch; Medal available for completion of this trail and Chief Wapa Tecumseh Trail, Fort Amanda-Fort Barbee Trail, and Miami-Erie Trail. *Submit:* No requirement. *Register:* Not required. *Sites:* Auglaize River, Thomas William Collins World Scout Museum, Fort Amanda State Park.

Cuyahoga Valley Trail

Location: Cuyahoga Valley National Recreation Area, Peninsula, OH. *Theme:* Recreation. *Sponsor:* Marnoc Lodge, O.A., Great Trail Council, BSA, P.O. Box 68, 1601 S. Main St., Akron, OH 44309-0068.

Length: 13 miles (loop). *Route:* The trail begins at Happy Days Lodge, heads west to the Cuyahoga River and follows it (and the Buckeye Trail) south, the north to Virginia Kendall Park, and back to the start. *Terrain:* Woods and roads. *Cycling:* Not recommended. *Awards:* Medal $3.00; Patch $3.00; Jacket Patch $3.00. *Submit:* No requirement. *Register:* Not required. *Sites:* Happy Days Lodge, Camp Butler, Kendall Lake, Camp Manatoc, Ice Box Cave, Ritchie Ledges.

Dan Beard Riverwalk Trail

Location: Cincinnati, OH. *Theme:* Local history. *Sponsor:* Dan Beard Council, BSA, 2331 Victory Pkwy., Cincinnati, OH 45206-2803, (513) 961-2336.

Length: 5 miles (loop). *Route:* The trail begins and ends at Fountain Square, and crosses the Ohio River into Covington, KY, and back. *Terrain:* City streets. *Cycling:* Appropriate. *Awards:* Medal. *Submit:* No requirement. *Register:* Not required. *Sites:* Daniel Carter Beard Park, Boy Scout Plaza, Riverfront Coliseum, L & N Bridge, Dan Beard House, Riverfront Stadium, General James Taylor Park, Covington Landing, Sawyer Point, Lytle Park, George Rogers Clark Park, Ohio River, Yeatman's Cove Park, Roebling Suspension Bridge.

Delphos Historical Trail

Location: Delphos, OH. *Theme:* Local history. *Sponsor:* Rock Rohrbacher, 420 S. Cass St., Delphos, OH 45833, (419) 695-7437.

Length: 7.5 miles (loop). *Route:* The trail begins and ends at the Delphos Public Library and winds through most of the downtown area. *Terrain:* City streets. *Cycling:* Not recommended. *Awards:* Patch $3.00. *Submit:* Group leader's certification of completion. *Register:* Not required. *Sites:* Delphos City Park, Civil War Statue, First Presbyterian Church, Westside Cemetery, Old Jefferson High School, American Legion Hall, Delphos Stone Quarry, Peltier Observatory, Canal Boat Display , Delphos Historical Museum, Delphos Manufacturing Co., St. John the Evangelist Catholic Church, First Hotel/Opera House, St. John's Cemetery, Lang Elevator, Stenles Delphos Brewery, Jennings Creek.

Emerald Necklace Trails

Location: Cuyahoga County, OH. *Theme:* Recreation. *Sponsor:* Greater Cleveland Council, BSA, 2441 Woodland Ave., Cleveland, OH 44115-3295, (216) 861-6060 or fax (216) 861-3431.

Lengths: Rocky River Segment (Leg 1), 9 miles (straight). Brecksville Segment (Leg 2), 12 miles (straight). Bedford Segment (Leg 3), 16 miles (straight). Chagrin Segment (Leg 4), 12 miles (straight). *Routes:* Leg 1 begins at the Mastic Picnic Area and goes south along the Rocky River to Albion Rd. just south of the Ohio Turnpike. Leg 2 begins at the south end of Leg 1 and heads east along US 176 to Meadows Area in Brecksville Reservation. Leg 3 then starts and heads north to Canal Rd., through Bedford Reservation, and east to the Shelter House in South Chagrin Reservation. Leg 4 then starts and follows the Chagrin River to North Chagrin Reservation and the endpoint at Squires Castle. *Terrain:* Paved bike paths and roads. *Cycling:* Appropriate. *Awards:* 4 Patches $2.50 each. *Submit:* No requirement. *Register:* Not required. *Sites:* Wallace Lake, Rocky River, Bonnie Park, Old Ohio Canal, Glacial Erratic Boulders, Tinkers Creek, Chagrin River, Squaw Rock, Squires Castle, Sunset Pond.

Four Rivers Trail

Location: Dayton, OH. *Theme:* Recreation. *Sponsor:* Four Rivers Trail Committee, c/o Troop 235 BSA, 825 Creighton Ave., Dayton, OH 45410.

Length: 11.5 miles (loop). *Route:* The trail begins and ends at the Riverbend Art Center, and follows the Stillwater River, Mad River, Great Miami River, and Wolf Creek. *Terrain:* Roads. *Cycling:* Appropriate. *Awards:* Patch $1.00. *Submit:* No requirement. *Register:* Not required. *Sites:* Dayton Art Institute, Carillon Park, Riverbend Art Center, Island Park, Dayton Water Treatment Plant, Dayton Power and Light Co. Power Station, Soldiers and Sailors Monument.

Glen Helen Scout Trail

Location: Yellow Springs, OH. *Theme:* Nature. *Sponsor:* Milton Lord, 1360 Rice Rd., Yellow Springs, OH 45387.

Length: 10 miles (loop). *Route:* The trail begins and ends at the Trailside Museum near Corry St., and generally follows Yellow Springs Creek and the Little Miami River. *Terrain:* Off-road. *Cycling:* Not recommended. *Awards:* Patch $2.00; 4 Seasonal Strips $0.50 each. *Submit:* No requirement. *Register:* In advance. *Sites:* Little Miami River, Trailside Museum, Outdoor Education Center, Indian Mound, Horace Mann Monument, Yellow Spring, Butterfly Preserve, Glen Barn, Swinging Bridge, Pompey's Pillar, Orator's Mound, Covered Bridge, Grinnell Mill, Glen Helen Building, Glen House.

Happy Hunting Ground Trail

Location: Woodland Trails Boy Scout Reservation, Dayton, OH. *Theme:* Recreation. *Sponsor:* Miami Valley Council, BSA, 4999 Northcutt Pl., Dayton, OH 45414.

Length: 12.78 miles (loop). *Route:* The trail begins and ends at the main parking lot and circles Mystic Lake and nearly all of the reservation. *Terrain:* Woods. *Cycling:* Not recommended. *Awards:* Patch. *Submit:* No requirement. *Register:* Not required.

Heritage Trail

Location: Findlay, OH. *Theme:* Recreation. *Sponsor:* Heritage Trail Coordinator, c/o Hancock Park District, 819 Park St., Findlay, OH 45840, (419) 423-6952.

Length: 20 miles (straight). *Route:* The trail begins along the Blanchard River just east of I-75, and follows the river eastward. *Terrain:* Sidewalks, roadways and paths.

Cycling: Appropriate; may also be canoed.
Awards: Medal $3.50; Patch $2.50. *Submit:*
Group leader's certification of completion,
plus completed 20-item questionnaire.
Register: Not required. *Sites:* Indian Green
Cemetery, Liberty Township Fire
Department, Liberty Landing, Blanchard
River, Great Karg Well Historic Site,
Waterfalls .

Hutch's Trail

Location: Seven Ranges Camp, Columbus.
Theme: An early surveyor (Hutch) who was
sent out by Pres. Jefferson to survey a portion
of Ohio, known as Seven Ranges. *Sponsor:*
Buckeye Council, 2301 13th St. NW, Canton,
OH 44708, (330) 580-4272, fax (330) 580-
4283.
Length: 5.0 miles (loop). *Route:* There is
no written hike plan—the route is marked
with blazes on the camp property. *Terrain:*
Woods. *Cycling:* Check with sponsor.
Awards: Patch $3.00 (includes tax and
shipping). *Submit:* Not required. *Register:*
Check in at camp office.

Johnny Appleseed Trail

Location: Mansfield, OH. *Theme:* Local
history. *Sponsor:* Heart of Ohio Council,
BSA, 445 W. Longview Ave. W., Mansfield,
OH 44901-1979, (419) 522-5091.
Length: 20.9 miles (straight). *Route:* The
trail begins at Charles Mill Dam and heads
south to end at Clear Fork State Park.
Terrain: Roads. *Cycling:* Appropriate.
Awards: Medal $2.75; Patch $1.50. *Submit:*
Group leader's certificate of completion.
Register: Not required. *Sites:* Corpus Massacre
Monument, Malabar Farm, Shambaugh
Pioneer Cemetery, Greentown, Pipe's Cliffs,
Malabar Inn, Abandoned Mine Shaft,
Helltown, Pleasant Hill Dam, Little Lyons
Falls, Big Lyons Falls, Mohican State Forest.

Kit Cricket Training Trail

Location: Cricket Holler Boy Scout
Reservation, Dayton, OH. *Theme:*
Recreation. *Sponsor:* Miami Valley Council,
BSA, 4999 Northcutt Pl., Dayton, OH 45414.
Length: 4.62 miles (loop). *Route:* The trail
begins and ends at Tait Lodge. *Terrain:*
Woods. *Cycling:* Not recommended. *Awards:*
Patch. *Submit:* No requirement. *Register:* Not
required.

Logan Trail

Location: Tar Hollow Forest near Adelphi,
OH. *Theme:* Recreation. *Sponsor:* The Logan
Trail, 643 Weyant Ave., Columbus, OH 42313,
(614) 235-7026.
Length: 10-21 miles (loop). *Route:* The trail
begins and ends at Pine Lake Dam, 1.2 miles
from the park entrance. The trail forms a
north loop of 10 miles (for patch) and a
south loop to bring the total to 21 miles (for
medal). *Terrain:* Woods. *Cycling:* Not
recommended. *Awards:* Medal $8.00; Patch
$2.00; Repeat Arrowhead $1.50. *Submit:* No
requirement. *Register:* Not required.

Miami-Erie Trail

Location: New Bremen to St. Mary's, OH.
Theme: Early canal transportation. *Sponsor:*
John Lunz, Jr., 302 Columbia St., St. Mary's,
OH 45885.
Length: 8 miles (straight). *Route:* The trail
begins at Lock #1 in New Bremen and follows
the canal northward to the U.R.W. Hall in St.
Mary's. *Terrain:* Canal towpath. *Cycling:* Not
recommended. *Awards:* Patch; Medal
available for completion of this trail and
Chief Wapa Tecumseh Trail, Clear Water
Trail, and Fort Amanda-Fort Barbee Trail.
Submit: No requirement. *Register:* Not
required. *Sites:* Canal Locks, St. Mary's River
Aqueduct.

Mill Creek Park Trail

Location: Mill Creek Park, Youngstown,
OH. *Theme:* Nature. *Sponsor:* Mahoning
Valley Council, BSA, 3712 Leffingwell Rd.,
Canfield, OH 44406, (330) 477-7248.
Length: 10 miles (loop). *Route:* The trail
begins and ends at the Park Office at
Glenwood and Falls Ave. *Terrain:* Woods.
Cycling: Not recommended. *Awards:* Patch
$3.50. *Submit:* Group leader's certification of
completion. *Register:* Not required. *Sites:*
Log Cabin, Lanternman's Mill, Ford Nature
Education Center.

Oak Openings Trail

Location: Oak Openings Metropolitan
Park, Toledo, OH. *Theme:* Recreation.
Sponsor: Toledo Area Council, BSA, One
Stranahan Sq., P.O. Box 337, Toledo, OH
43591-1492, (419) 241-7293.
Length: 17 miles (loop). *Route:* The trail
begins at the group camp off Oak Openings

Parkway, follows most of the park's perimeter, and returns to the start. *Terrain:* Woods. *Cycling:* Not recommended. *Awards:* Medal $3.00; Patch $1.50; 2nd Segment Pin $0.95; 3rd Segment Pin $0.95. *Submit:* Written hike report. *Register:* At least 2 weeks in advance.

Ohio City Trail

Location: Cleveland, OH. *Theme:* Local history. *Sponsor:* Greater Cleveland Council, BSA, 2441 Woodland Ave., Cleveland, OH 44115-3295, (216) 861-6060 or fax (216) 861-3431.

Length: 4.5 miles (loop). *Route:* The trail begins and ends at the Superior Viaduct Bridge, and winds through Ohio City, which merged with Cleveland in 1854. *Terrain:* City streets. *Cycling:* Appropriate. *Awards:* Patch $1.25. *Submit:* No requirement. *Register:* Not required. *Sites:* International Salt Co., St. Malachis Roman Catholic Church, Dr. George Crile Home, Five Mile Crib, Detroit Superior High Level Bridge, Franklin Castle, Archibald Willard Home, St. Herman's House of Hospitality, Ohio City Tavern, Marcus Hanna Home Site, St. Ignatius High School, John A. Heisman Home, Monroe Cemetery, St. Emeric Roman Catholic Magyar Church, Paul Laurence Dunbar Elementary School.

Red Stallion Training Trail

Location: Woodland Trails Boy Scout Reservation, Dayton, OH. *Theme:* Recreation. *Sponsor:* Miami Valley Council, BSA, 4999 Northcutt Pl., Dayton, OH 45414.

Length: 5.2 miles (loop). *Route:* The trail begins and ends at the nature area parking lot and circles the central portion of the reservation. *Terrain:* Woods. *Cycling:* Not recommended. *Awards:* Patch. *Submit:* No requirement. *Register:* Not required.

Shawnee Trail

Location: Portsmouth, OH. *Theme:* Recreation. *Sponsor:* Scioto Area Council, BSA, P.O. Box 1305, Portsmouth, OH 45662.

Length: 14 miles (loop). *Route:* The trail begins and ends at Camp Oyo, 6 miles west of Portsmouth. *Terrain:* Woods and ridges. *Cycling:* Not recommended. *Awards:* Patch $3.50. *Submit:* No requirement. *Register:* Upon arrival at Camp Oyo. *Sites:* Bear Creek Lake, Copperhead Fire Tower.

Thunderbird Trail

Location: Michaels Scout Camp, Franklin, OH. *Theme:* Recreation. *Sponsor:* Dan Beard Council, BSA, 2331 Victory Pkwy., Cincinnati, OH 45206, (513) 961-2336.

Length: 5 miles. *Route:* Route will be supplied by sponsor upon registration. *Terrain:* Woods. *Cycling:* Not recommended. *Awards:* Patch $2.25. *Submit:* No requirement. *Register:* In advance with camp ranger.

Towpath Trail

Location: Canal Fulton to Massillon, OH. *Theme:* Ohio Erie Canal. *Sponsor:* Buckeye Council, BSA, 2301 13th St. NW., Canton, OH 44708, (330) 580-4272, fax (330) 580-4283.

Length: 15 miles (loop). *Route:* The trail goes from Canal Fulton to Massillon and returns, following the canal. *Terrain:* Canal towpath. *Cycling:* Possible, but does not qualify for awards; route may also be canoed one direction, and walked back to the start. *Awards:* Patch. *Submit:* No requirement. *Register:* At least 2 weeks in advance. *Sites:* Ohio Erie Canal, Lock #4 Park, Butterbridge Road Bridge, McIntosh Indian Treaty Monument, Canal Days Museum, Crystal Springs.

Triangle Training Trail

Location: Triangle Park, Dayton, OH. *Theme:* Nature. *Sponsor:* Miami Valley Council, BSA, 4999 Northcutt Pl., Dayton, OH 45414.

Length: 6.21 miles (loop). *Route:* The trail begins and ends at the nature area parking lot on Ridge Ave. near Embury Park Rd., and follows the Stillwater and Great Miami Rivers. *Terrain:* Off-road. *Cycling:* Not recommended. *Awards:* Patch. *Submit:* No requirement. *Register:* Not required. *Sites:* Artillery Memorial Bridge, Dayton Museum of Natural History, Wegerzyn Garden Center.

Vesuvius Furnace Historical Trail

Location: Ironton, OH. *Theme:* One of the first iron blast furnaces in the Hanging Rock district. *Sponsor:* Scioto Area Council, BSA, P.O. Box 1305, Portsmouth, OH 45662.

Length: 16 miles (loop). *Route:* The trail begins and ends at Vesuvius Furnace Stack at Vesuvius Lake, 9 miles north of Ironton. *Terrain:* Woods. *Cycling:* Not recommended.

Awards: Medal $3.25; Patch $2.50. *Submit:* No requirement. *Register:* In advance. *Sites:* Lake Vesuvius, Storms Creek, Kimble Fire Tower, Vesuvius Furnace Stack.

Warren Western Reserve Historical Trail

Location: Warren, OH. *Theme:* Local history. *Sponsor:* Ron Kay, 8442 E. Market St., Warren, OH 44483, (330) 372-1049.

Length: 7 miles (loop). *Route:* The trail winds along the streets of downtown Warren. *Terrain:* City streets. *Cycling:* Appropriate. *Awards:* Patch $2.25. *Submit:* No requirement. *Register:* Not required. *Sites:* Courthouse, City Hall, Log Cabin, War Memorial.

Winter Bushwack

Location: Clifton Gorge State Nature Preserve, Clifton, OH. *Theme:* Recreation. *Sponsor:* BSA Troop 184, c/o Larry Young, 585 SR 571, Union City, OH 45390, (937) 968-5577.

Length: 10 miles (loop). *Route:* The trail begins and ends at the Jackson St. parking lot, 1 block from Clifton Mill, and follows the Little Miami River. *Terrain:* Woods. *Cycling:* Not recommended. *Awards:* Patch $7.50. *Submit:* No requirement. *Register:* By September 15, so patches can be ordered for those planning to hike during the winter season. *Sites:* John Bryan State Park, Clifton Gorge State Nature Preserve, Falls of the Little Miami, Devil's Gorge, The Bear's Den Interpretive Area, Jughandle Falls, Amphitheater Falls, Steamboat Rock, The Blue Hole.

Wright Memorial Trail

Location: Wright-Patterson Air Force Base, Dayton, OH. *Theme:* History of aviation. *Sponsor:* Wright Memorial Trail, P.O. Box 905, Fairborn, OH 45324.

Length: 12 miles (loop). *Route:* The trail begins at the Scout Camp north of Patterson Field, and circles it in a counter-clockwise loop, then returns to the start. *Terrain:* Roads. *Cycling:* Appropriate. *Awards:* Medal $2.50; Patch $1.50. *Submit:* Group leader's certification of completion of hike and conservation project. *Register:* At least 10 days in advance. *Sites:* Wright Brothers Hangar Site, Simms Station, Wright Brothers Memorial, Air Force Museum.

Zoar Valley Trail

Location: Bolivar to New Philadelphia, OH. *Theme:* Local history. *Sponsor:* Buckeye Council, BSA, 5136 Tuscarawas St. W., Canton, OH 44708.

Length: 12 miles (straight). *Route:* The trail begins at Ft. Laurens in Bolivar and ends at Schoenbrunn Village. *Terrain:* Woods, canal towpath, roads. *Cycling:* Not recommended. *Awards:* Medal $4.00. *Submit:* Group leader's certification of completion and overnight camping. *Register:* Not required except for campsite. *Sites:* Ft. Laurens, Schoenbrunn Village, Zoar Village, Ohio-Erie Canal, Camp Tuscazoar, Dover Dam.

Other Ohio Hiking Awards

Tecumseh 100-Mile Hiker Award—Sponsored by BSA Troop 184, c/o Larry Young, 585 SR 571, Union City, OH 45390, (937) 968-5577. Spear head patch for first 100 miles $4.00; additional 100 mile spear handle patches $2.00 each.

Formerly Sponsored Trails

Ah-Wen-Nah-Sa Trails
Anthony Wayne Trail (Fort Defiance Segment)
Anthony Wayne Trail (Fort Greenville Segment)
Anthony Wayne Trail (Fort Jennings Segment)
Anthony Wayne Trail (Fort Recovery Segment)
Anthony Wayne Trail (Fort St. Clair Segment)
Anthony Wayne Trail (Fort St. Mary's Segment)
Beaver Trail
Captain Martin Bates Trail
Chief Leatherlips Trace
Chief Tarhe Trail
Clear Fork Valley Trail
Clendening Trail
Columbus Historic Trail
Corpus Massacre Trail
Covered Bridge Trail
Faraway Trail
Flint Ridge Trail
Fort Amanda-Fort Barbee Trail
Freedom Trail
George Rogers Clark Trail
Golden Lamb Trail
Hawkeye Trail
Isaac Zane Trail

Kachina Trail
Kingfisher Trail
La Trainee de L'Explorateur Trail
Lima Historic Trail
Little Miami Trail
Lu-Del Village Trail
Miami Conservancy Trail
Miami Erie Canal Trail
Middletown Historic Trail
Moccasin Trail
Mohican Wilderness Trail
Ohio Hills Trail
Old Two-Path Trail

Paleo-Indian Trail
Put-In Bay Trail
Raccoon Trail
Sakemo Trail
Sandy Beaver Trail
Silver Moccasin Trail
Simon Kenton Trail
Spirit of '76 Trail
Tomahawk Trail
U.S. Grant Trail
Wilderness Trace
Wyandot Trail

OKLAHOMA

Chisholm Trail

Location: Grady County, OK. *Theme:* Nature and history. *Sponsor:* Carl Sikes, 322 Chickasha Ave., Chickasha, OK 73018, (405) 224-2716 or (405) 224-0888.

Length: 50 miles (straight). *Route:* The trail begins at the Old Withita Indian Village near Rush Springs and heads north to end at Silver City Cemetery north of Tuttle. *Terrain:* Backroads. *Cycling:* Appropriate. *Awards:* Patch $2.00. *Submit:* No requirement. *Register:* Not required. *Sites:* Old Brushycreek Cemetery, Rune Stones, Old Withita Indian Village, Moncrief Cemetery, Silver City Cemetery, Hybarger Hill.

Rock Mary Trail

Location: Hinton, OK. *Theme:* Sandstone

landmark. *Sponsor:* Last Frontier Council, BSA, 3031 NW 64, P.O. Box 75339, Oklahoma City, OK 73116.

Length: 8.5 miles (straight). *Route:* The trail begins at the recreation area in Red Rock Canyon State Park, heads north to Hinton, west to the windmill, south to the John Ballou Farm, and west to Rock Mary. *Terrain:* Roads and paths. *Cycling:* Not recommended. *Awards:* Patch. *Submit:* Group leader's certification of completion. *Register:* Not required. *Sites:* Rock Mary, Windmill.

Formerly Sponsred Trails

Fort Holmes Trail
Kamiachi Trail

OREGON

Rogue River Trail

Location: Siskiyou National Forest, OR. *Theme:* Recreation. *Sponsor:* Crater Lake Council, BSA, 3039 Hanley Rd., Central Point, OR 97502-1499, (541) 664-1444.

Length: 17 or 23 miles (straight) on foot or 40 miles (straight) floating. *Route:* The Upper Section (23 miles) begins at Graves Creek Boat Landing and follows the north bank of the river downstream to the Rogue

River Ranch at Marial. The Lower Section (17 miles) begins there and follows the north bank of the river to Foster Bar near Illahe. The float utilizes both sections of the river. *Terrain:* Woods or water. *Cycling:* Not recommended. *Awards:* Patch $2.50. *Submit:* Group leader's certification of hike or float, plus service project and 2 nights of camping. *Register:* Not required. *Sites:* Sanderson

Homesite, Sanderson Bridge, Rainie Falls, Tyree Rapids, Cedar Mountain Fault, Black Bear Lodge, Rogue River Ranch, Rodruguez Memorial, Marial Lodge, Sturgeon Hole, Rogue River, Inspiration Point.

Formerly Sponsored Trails
Scott Trail
Trail of Lewis & Clark

PENNSYLVANIA

Baker Trail

Location: Western PA. *Theme:* Recreation. *Sponsor:* American Youth Hostels, Inc., 6300 Fifth Ave., Pittsburgh, PA 15232, (412) 362-8181.

Length: 141 miles (straight). *Route:* The trail begins in Schenley along the Allegheny River and passes near Atwood, Plumville, McWilliams, North Freedom, Heathville, Summerville, Corsica and Fisher, and meets up with the North Country Trail in Allegheny National Forest. *Terrain:* Woods. *Cycling:* Not recommended. *Awards:* Patch. *Submit:* No requirement. *Register:* Not required. *Sites:* Crooked Creek State Park, Allegheny River, Mahoning Creek Lake, Cook Forest State Park.

The Benjamin Franklin Historical Trail

Location: Downtown Philadelphia, PA. *Theme:* Places and events important in the life of Benjamin Franklin. *Sponsor:* American Historical Trails, Inc., P.O. Box 769, Monroe, NC 28111-0769, (704) 289-1604, Carotrader@trellis.net.

Length: Route A, 4.5 miles. Route B, 7.5 miles. Route C, 8.3 miles. (each route ends 1.5 blocks from start). *Route:* The trail begins at reconstructed Franklin Court, Benjamin Franklin's home in Philadelphia. It winds through historic streets bounded by 2nd St., Pine St., 9th St. and New St. *Terrain:* City streets and sidewalks. *Cycling:* Appropriate. *Awards:* Medal $6.00; Patch $2.25. *Submit:* Completed form with answers to 37 (Route A), 47 (Route B), or 50 (Route C) questions

about sites visited along the trail. *Register:* Not required. *Sites:* Franklin Court, Atwater-Kent Museum, Public Ledger Building, Congress Hall, Independence Hall, Philosophical Hall, Bible Society Building, Mikveh Israel Cemetery, Pennsylvania Hospital, Mother Bethel Church, Thomas Neval Home, Hill-Physick-Weith House, Hopkinson House, Franklin Lamp, Wistar House, Mutual Assurance Company, Philadelphia Contributionship, First Pennsylvania Bank, Judge Lewis House Site, City Tavern, John Drinker House Site, Visitors Center, First U.S. Bank, Second U.S. Bank, Carpenters Hall, Library Hall, John Kinsey House Site, Charity School Site, Franklin Penny Bust, Christ Church, Elfreths Alley, Fireman's Hall Museum, Old First Reformed Church, Old St. Augustines Church, St. Georges Methodist Church, Franklin's Grave.

Braddock's Crossing Trail

Location: White Oak to Arona, PA. *Theme:* Recreation. *Sponsor:* John P. English, 1031 East End Ave., Pittsburgh, PA 15221, (412) 731-6651; or Greater Pittsburgh Council, BSA, Flag Plaza, 1275 Bedford Ave., Pittsburgh, PA 15219, (412) 471-2927 .

Length: 10 miles (straight). *Route:* The trail begins in White Oak and follows the Braddock Rd. to Arona. *Terrain:* Country roads. *Cycling:* Appropriate. *Awards:* Medal $4.50; Patch $3.00; Neckerchief $3.50. *Submit:* Group leader's certification of completion, plus 200-word essay. *Register:* Not required.

Carlisle Historical Trail

Location: Carlisle, PA. *Theme:* Local history. *Sponsor:* American Historical Trails, Inc., P.O. Box 769, Monroe, NC 28111-0769, (704) 289-1604, Carotrader@trellis.net.

Length: Route A, 4 miles (loop). Route B, 8 miles (loop). Route C, 6 miles (loop). *Route:* The trail begins and ends at Letort Park, and passes through downtown Carlisle. The longer two routes also go through Carlisle Army Barracks. *Terrain:* City streets. *Cycling:* Appropriate. *Awards:* Medal $6.00; Patch $2.25. *Submit:* Completed 60-item questionnaire. *Register:* Not required. *Sites:* Thomas Butler Home Site, Andre House, Carlisle Court House, George Washington Review Site, Green Tree Inn Site, Court House Monument, Trickett Hall Marker, Thomas Wilson House Site, Carlisle Fort Site, Soldiers Monument, Old Graveyard, Letort Park, Biddle Field Marker, Zion AME Church, Rush Campus Marker, Dickinson Campus Marker, John Gibson House, Carlisle Army Barracks, Carlisle Jail.

Delaware Canal Trail

Location: Eastern PA. *Theme:* Recreation and history. *Sponsor:* Bucks County Council, BSA, One Scout Way, P.O. Box 797, Doylestown, PA 18901-4915, (215) 348-9436.

Length: 10-48 miles (straight). *Route:* The trail follows the route of part of the 1831-1931 Delaware Canal. *Terrain:* Towpath. *Cycling:* Appropriate, as is canoeing. *Awards:* Patch; Canoe, Hiker, Biker and End-to-End Segments. *Submit:* Group leader's certification of completion. *Register:* In advance.

Delaware & Lehigh Canal Trail

Location: Hugh Moore Historical Park, Easton, PA. *Theme:* Canals. *Sponsor:* Hugh Moore Historical Park and Museums, 200 S. Delaware Dr., P.O. Box 877, Easton, PA 18044-0877, (610) 250-6700.

Length: 12.5 miles (loop). *Route:* The trail follows the banks of the Lehigh Canal and the Lehigh River from Durham Furnace at the junction of SRs 611 and 212, and ends at the Locktender's House at Chain Dam and Guardlock #8 in Hugh Moore State Park. *Terrain:* Paved and dirt paths. *Cycling:* Appropriate. *Awards:* Patch $2.50. *Submit:* No requirement. *Register:* Not required. *Sites:* Locktender's House Museum, Archives and Library, Canal Museum, Canal Boat Ride, Roosevelt State Park.

80 Miles of Wilderness Adventure

Location: Clearfield to North Bend, PA. *Theme:* Recreation. *Sponsor:* Bucktail Council, BSA, 209 First St., DuBois, PA 15801.

Length: 80 miles (straight), in 5 segments: 11.2 miles, Clearfield—Shawville; 20.5 miles, Shawville—Rolling Stone Bridge; 18.4 miles, Rolling Stone Bridge—Loop Run; 14.6 miles, Loop Run—Keating; 15.3 miles, Keating—North Bend. *Route:* The route is over the West Branch of the Susquehanna River from Witmer Park in Clearfield to North Bend. *Terrain:* River. *Cycling:* Not possible, as this is a canoe trail with several sections of whitewater or rapids. *Awards:* Patch $2.00; 5 Segments $.50 each. *Submit:* Completed award application. *Register:* Yes, by submitting BSA tour permit form to the sponsor. *Sites:* Fullerton Rocks, Uncle Petes Point, Old Grimes Rock, Button Riffle, Big Stepping Stones, Rams Horn, Moshannon Falls, Paddy Island.

Erie Historical Trail

Location: Erie, PA. *Theme:* Local history. *Sponsor:* Langundowi Lodge #46, French Creek Council, BSA, 1815 Robison Rd. W., Erie, PA 16509-4905, (814) 868-5571.

Length: 7 miles (straight). *Route:* The trail begins at the Old Land Lighthouse at the foot of Lighthouse St., winds 23 blocks to Cascade St., and ends at the foot of State St. *Terrain:* City streets. *Cycling:* Appropriate. *Awards:* Medal $5.00; Patch $2.50. *Submit:* Group leader's certification of completion. *Register:* In advance. *Sites:* Soldiers and Sailors Home, Old Land Lighthouse, Statue of Oliver Hazard Perry, Cascade Street Ship Yard, Flagship Niagara, Strong Mansion, General Anthony Wayne Blockhouse, Dickson's Tavern, Cashier's House, Boston Store Livery and Garage, Erie Club, Erie County Court House, Firefighters Historical Museum, Bowsprit of USS Wolverine, Horace Greely House, Old Custom House.

Forbes Road Trail

Location: Near McConnellsburg, PA. *Theme:* Route of overland trail first cleared by British general John Forbes during the French and Indian War. *Sponsor:* Mason-Dixon Council, BSA, 1200 Crestwood, P.O.

Box 2133, Hagerstown, MD 21742-2133, (301) 739-1211.

Length: 28 miles (straight). *Route:* The trail begins at Cowan's Gap State Park and ends at Hill Mountain, near the Bedford County line. *Terrain:* Woods. *Cycling:* Not recommended. *Awards:* Patch $1.50; Medal $2.25 for completing this trail and the Antietam Battlefield Historic Trail, the Maryland portion of the Appalachian Trail, and the C & O Canal Historical Trail. *Submit:* Group leader's certification of completion. *Register:* In advance. *Sites:* Cowan's Gap State Park, Ray's Hill Mountain, Raystown Path Marker, Burnt Cabins Site, Fort Littleton Site.

Forbes Trail

Location: Old Hannastown to Murryville, PA. *Theme:* Recreation. *Sponsor:* John P. English, 1031 East End Ave., Pittsburgh, PA 15221, (412) 731-6651; or Greater Pittsburgh Council, BSA, 1275 Bedford Ave., Pittsburgh, PA 15219, (412) 471-2927.

Length: 20 miles (straight). *Route:* The trail begins at Old Hannastown and heads to the end in Murrysville. *Terrain:* Mostly roads. *Cycling:* Not recommended. *Awards:* Medal $4.50; Patch $3.00; Neckerchief $3.50. *Submit:* Group leader's certification of completion, plus 200-word essay. *Register:* Not required. *Sites:* Hannastown Court House, Denmark Manor Church, Boyce Park, Turtle Creek.

Gettysburg Heritage Trails

Location: Gettysburg National Military Park, Gettysburg, PA. *Theme:* Civil War battle—July 1-3, 1863. *Sponsor:* York-Adams Area Council, BSA, 800 E. King St., York, PA 17403-1797, (717) 843-0901. *Lengths:* Billy Yank Trail—9 miles (loop). Johnny Reb Trail—3.5 miles (loop)

Routes: The trails begin and end at the Visitor Center and include the Gettysburg National Cemetery. A side trip to the Eisenhower National Historic Site is available. *Terrain:* Roads, paved and dirt paths. *Cycling:* Not recommended. *Awards:* Medal $3.75; Gettysburg Patch $1.75; Johnny Reb Segment $0.50; Billy Yank Segment $0.50; Eisenhower Segment $0.75. *Submit:* Group leader's certification of completion. *Register:* Upon arrival at Visitor Center. *Sites:* Electric Map, Bloody Run, Soldiers'

National Monument, Pennsylvania Memorial, First Minnesota Monument, Devil's Den, Granite Farm, Big Round Top, Wheatfield Road Batteries, Virginia Memorial, Leister House, Cemetery Hill, Spangler Meadow, Second Maryland Regiment Monument, Spangler's Spring, Cemetery Gate House, Pardee Field.

Harrisburg Historical Trail

Location: Downtown Harrisburg, PA. *Theme:* Historical places and events in the state capital. *Sponsor:* American Historical Trails, Inc., P.O. Box 769, Monroe, NC 28111-0769, (704) 289-1604, Carotrader@trellis.net.

Length: 6.0 miles (ends about 1 mile from start). *Route:* The trail begins at the parking lot on City Island, in the middle of the Susquehanna River. It parallels the river for a while, and winds through streets with attractive architecture. *Terrain:* City streets. *Cycling:* Appropriate. *Awards:* Patch $2.25. *Submit:* Completed 80-item questionnaire. *Register:* Not required . *Sites:* City Island, Walnut Street Bridge, Conrail Railroad Bridge, John Harris, Sr. Grave, Freedom Tree, Harris Ferry Marker, Harrisburg Tech H.S. Marker, Reading Railroad Bridge, John Harris Mansion, Harrisburg Rail Station, Zion Lutheran Church, Abraham Lincoln Marker, Market Square Pres. Church, Dauphin County Courthouse, Art Association of Harrisburg, Governor Schulze Mansion, Pennsylvania Banker's Assn., Faeger School, Harrisburg Public Library, Centennial Marker, Cathedral House, Bigler Mansion, Keystone Hall Plaque, Cameron House, Pennsylvania Bar Association, St. Patrick Church, Grace Methodist Church, The Capitol, Young Men's Christian Assn., Harrisburg Civic Club, Forster Street Bridge, Sunken Garden.

Horse-Shoe Trail

Location: Southeastern PA. *Theme:* Recreation. *Sponsor:* Horse-Shoe Trail Club, Attn: Treasurer, 509 Cheltena Ave., Jenkintown, PA 19046, (215) 887-1549.

Length: 130 miles (straight). *Route:* The trail begins at Valley Forge, heads westward roughly parallel to I-76, then meets the Appalachian Trail near Hershey. *Terrain:* Fields, forests and hills. *Cycling:* Appropriate. *Awards:* Patch. *Submit:* No requirement. *Register:* Not required. *Sites:* Warwick

County Park, Middle Mill Creek Wildlife Area, Cornwall Furnace, French Creek State Park, Valley Forge National Historical Park, Hopewell Village National Historic Site, Mt. Gretna.

Kinzua Bridge Historic Trail

Location: Kinzua Bridge State Park, Mt. Jewett, PA. *Theme:* Historic bridge. *Sponsor:* Allegheny Highlands Council, BSA, 50 Hough Hill Rd., P.O. Box 0261, Falconer, NY 14733-0261, (716) 665-2697.

Length: Varies. *Route:* The precise route will be worked out between the group and the local ranger. *Terrain:* Varies. *Cycling:* Not recommended. *Awards:* Medal; Neckerchief. *Submit:* Group leader's certification of completion of hike, overnight camping, and conservation project. *Register:* In advance. *Sites:* Kinzua Bridge.

Laurel Highlands Hiking Trail

Location: Rockwood, PA. *Theme:* Recreation. *Sponsor:* Laurel Ridge State Park, Rt. 3, Box 246, Rockwood, PA 15557.

Length: 70 miles (straight). *Route:* The trail is broken into 5 segments:. Yough Gorge, miles 0-19; Roaring Run, miles 19-32; First Turnpike, miles 32-46; Forbes Road, miles 46-57; Conemaugh Gorge, miles 57-70. *Terrain:* Woods. *Cycling:* Not recommended. *Awards:* Patch $1.50; 6 Segments $1.00 each. *Submit:* No requirement. *Register:* Not required.

Loyalsock Trail

Location: Williamsport, PA. *Theme:* Recreation. *Sponsor:* Alpine Club of Williamsport, P.O. Box 501, Williamsport, PA 17703-0501, (570) 322-7757.

Length: 59.28 miles (straight). *Route:* The trail begins on SR 87 9 miles north of the SR 87/Montoursville exit from I-180, and ends on US 220 about 3 miles north of Laporte. *Terrain:* Mountain ridges and streams. *Cycling:* Not recommended. *Awards:* Patch $1.50; Blaze $0.25; 35th Anniversary Pin $3.00. *Submit:* No requirement. *Register:* Not required. *Sites:* Worlds End State Park, High Knob, Kettle Creek Vista, Angel Falls, Allegheny Ridge, Mary's View, Eagles Mere Railroad, Wallis Road, Canyon Vista Trail, Rogers Road, Towanda Indian Trail.

Mid State Trail

Location: Central PA. *Theme:* Recreation.

Sponsor: PSOC Hiking Division, 4 Intramural Bldg., University Park, PA 16802; or Mid State Trail Association, 227 Kimport Ave., Boalsburg, PA 16827.

Length: 206 miles (straight). *Route:* The endpoints are US 22 east of Water St., to Blackwell on SR 414, passing through Thickhead Wild Area, Wolf Run Wild Area, White Mountain Wild Area, Stone Valley Recreation Area, Stone Valley Recreation Area, and 6 state parks. *Terrain:* Generally rocky. *Cycling:* Not recommended. *Awards:* Patch $1.00. *Submit:* No requirement. *Register:* Not required. *Sites:* Fire Towers, Still Ruins.

Minsi Trails Council Historic Trails

Location: Lehigh Valley, PA. *Theme:* Colonial era history. *Sponsor:* Minsi Trails Council, BSA, P.O. Box 20624, Lehigh Valley, PA 18002-0624, (610) 264-8551. *Lengths:* Colonial Trail, 12 miles (straight). Durham Trail, 12 miles (straight). Industrial Heritage Trail, 13 miles (loop). Moravian Trail, 14 miles (straight). Nazareth Trail, 13 miles (loop). Sullivan-Wilderness Trail, 12 miles (straight). Uncas Trail, 13.5 miles (straight). *Routes:* The Colonial Trail runs from the Zufluchtshaus (Shelter House) in Emmaus to Allentown. The Durham Trail runs from the Saugon Creek in Hellertown to the Durham Locks. The Industrial Heritage Trail is a loop in Northampton. The Moravian Trail runs from Bethlehem to Hellertown. The Nazareth Trail is a loop in Nazareth. The Uncas Trail runs from the Uncas grave site in Bethlehem to Easton. The Sullivan-Wilderness Trail runs from the Learns Tavern in Tannersville to Camp Minsi. *Terrain:* Woods and roads. *Cycling:* Not recommended. *Awards:* Medal $9.00 (for hiking any 5); Sullivan-Wilderness Segment $1.00; 6 Other Segments $0.60 each. *Submit:* Group leader's certification of completion. *Register:* In advance. *Sites:* Northampton County Historical Society Building, Hungry Hill Monument, Largest Linden Tree in the U.S., Edwin Drake Home, Iron Gate House, Union Cemetery, Durham Mill and Furnace, Boehm House, Edgar Fink Homestead, Canal Locks, George Taylor Home, Keek House, Hellertown Jail.

Philadelphia Bicentennial Trail of Freedom

Location: Philadelphia, PA. *Theme:*

Colonial era history. *Sponsor:* American Historical Trails, Inc., P.O. Box 769, Monroe, NC 28111-0769, (704) 289-1604, Carotrader@trellis.net.

Length: Route A, 5.25 miles (straight). Route B, 7 miles (loop). Route C—7.75 miles (straight). *Route:* The trail begins at the Visitor Center on Third and Chestnut Sts., does a double loop through the city, and ends at Old St. Mary's Church (Route A), the Philadelphia Exchange (Route B) or the Norris Row Site (Route C). *Terrain:* City streets. *Cycling:* Appropriate. *Awards:* Medal $6.00; U.S. Capitol Patch $2.25; Statue of Freedom Patch $2.25. *Submit:* Completed 75-item questionnaire. *Register:* Not required. *Sites:* Carpenters Hall, Pemberton House, Liberty Bell Pavilion, Old City Hall, George Washington Statue, Independence Hall, Free Quaker Meeting House, Betsy Ross House, Kosciuszko House, Reynolds-Morris House, Man Full of Trouble Tavern, John Penn House Site, 1st United States Bank, Robert Morris Statue, Todd-Moylan House, Old St. Joseph's Church, Bishop White House, St. Peter's Church, Judge Peters House Site, Head House.

Pittsburgh Hiking Trail

Location: Downtown Pittsburgh, PA. *Theme:* Local History. *Sponsor:* The Pittsburgh Hiking Trail, P.O. Box 97881, Pittsburgh, PA 15227.

Length: 11.0 miles (loop). *Route:* The trail runs in a circle around and through downtown Pittsburgh, starting and ending at Flag Plaza, but can be started and ended at any point along the way. *Terrain:* Sidewalks. *Cycling:* Appropriate. *Awards:* 3" patch $3.00; 4" patch $4.00. *Submit:* Completed 62-item questionnaire. *Register:* Not required. *Sites:* Flag Plaza, Scout Statue, Civic Arena, U.S.X. Tower, Post Office, First Lutheran Church, Gulf Tower, Law Enforcement Officers Memorial, Senator John Heinz Pittsburgh Regional History Center, Pittsburgh Public Theater, Allegheny Center Mall, Children's Museum, Buhl Planetarium, Roberto Clemente Bridge, H.J. Heinz Plant, Wholey's, Liberty Point State Park, Block House, Old County Jail, PPG Plaza.

Rachel Carson Trail

Location: Freeport, PA. *Theme:*

Recreation. *Sponsor:* American Youth Hostels, Inc., 6300 Fifth Ave., Pittsburgh, PA 15232, (412) 362-8181.

Length: 32.3 miles (straight). *Route:* The trail begins near Freeport on the Allegheny River in Allegheny County and runs through Harrison Hills Regional Park, near Springdale, Dorseyville, and ends in North Park. *Terrain:* Woods. *Cycling:* Not recommended. *Awards:* Patch. *Submit:* No requirement. *Register:* Not required. *Sites:* Birthplace of Rachel Carson, Allegheny River, Harrison Hills Regional Park, North Park.

Shenango Trail

Location: Northwest PA. *Theme:* Recreation. *Sponsor:* Langundowi Lodge #46, French Creek Council, BSA, 1815 Robison Rd. W., Erie, PA 16509-4905, (814) 868-5571.

Length: 18 miles. *Route:* Will be furnished by sponsor upon application for specific hiking date. *Terrain:* Woods. *Cycling:* Not recommended. *Awards:* Medal $6.00; Patch $2.50. *Submit:* Group leader's certification of completion. *Register:* In advance.

Susquehannock Trail

Location: Coudersport, PA. *Theme:* Recreation. *Sponsor:* Susquehannock Trail Club, P.O. Box 643, Coudersport, PA 16915.

Length: 85 miles (loop). *Route:* The trail forms a loop which may be hiked in sections, in either direction. *Terrain:* Old railroad grades, logging trails, roads and fire trails. *Cycling:* Not recommended. *Awards:* Brassard; Patch $2.50. *Submit:* Hike log showing completion of entire circuit. *Register:* Not required.

Valley Forge Historical Trail

Location: Valley Forge National Historical Park, PA. *Theme:* Revolutionary War history. *Sponsor:* Valley Forge Council, BSA, P.O. Box 806, Valley Forge, PA 19482, (610) 688-6900.

Length: 9 miles (loop). *Route:* The trail begins and ends at the Visitor Center, following the tour road. *Terrain:* Bike trail. *Cycling:* Appropriate. *Awards:* Medal; Patch. *Submit:* Completed questionnaire. *Register:* Upon arrival at Visitor Center. *Sites:* Visitor Center, Steuben Memorial, Valley Creek, Redoubts, Conway Huts, Covered Bridge, Varnum's Quarters, Artillery Park, Pennsylvania Columns, Huntington's Quarters, Washington's Headquarters,

Anthony Wayne Statue, Washington Memorial Chapel, Valley Forge Historical Society Museum, National Memorial Arch.

Warrior Trail

Location: Greene County, PA. *Theme:* Recreation. *Sponsor:* Warrior Trail Association, Inc., Rt. 1, Box 35, Spraggs, PA 15362.

Length: 67 miles (straight). *Route:* The trail begins at the Monongahela River in Greensboro and heads westward to the Ohio state line. *Terrain:* Woods, fields and hills. *Cycling:* Not recommended. *Awards:* Patch. *Submit:* No requirement. *Register:* Not required.

Washington Crossing Historic Trail

Location: Washington Crossing State Park, PA. *Theme:* Crossing of the Delaware River by George Washington and troops. *Sponsor:* Bucks County Council, BSA, One Scout Way, P.O. Box 797, Doylestown, PA 18901-4915, (610) 348-9436.

Length: 8.3 miles (loop). *Route:* The route covers areas at and near the Washington Crossing State Park. *Terrain:* Woods. *Cycling:* Not recommended. *Awards:* Medal; Patch. *Submit:* Group leader's certification of completion and 250-word essay. *Register:* In advance. *Sites:* Nature Study Center, Bowman's Hill Wild Flower Preserve, Bird Banding Station, Pennsylvania Canal, Penn's Woods, McConkey Ferry Inn, Durham Boats.

Washington Trail

Location: Cambridge Springs to Waterford, PA. *Theme:* A portion of a 500-mile trail covered by Major George Washington in 1753. *Sponsor:* Langundowi Lodge #46, French Creek Council, BSA, 1815 Robison Rd. W., Erie, PA 16509-4905, (814) 868-5571.

Length: 17 miles (straight). *Route:* The trail begins at the park along French Creek and SR 19 in the borough of Cambridge Springs and follows along the west bank of French Creek northward to the borough of Waterford. *Terrain:* Roads. *Cycling:* Appropriate. *Awards:* Medal $6.00; Patch $2.50. *Submit:* Group leader's certification of completion, plus essay. *Register:* Not required. *Sites:* Washington Statue, LeBoeuf Lake, French Creek.

William Penn Trail

Location: Morrisville, PA. *Theme:* Pennsbury Manor. *Sponsor:* Bucks County Council, BSA, One Scout Way, P.O. Box 797, Doylestown, PA 18901-4915, (610) 348-9436.

Length: 0.5-2 miles (loop). *Route:* This is a compass course at Pennsbury Manor. *Terrain:* Woods and fields. *Cycling:* Not recommended. *Awards:* Medal; Patch. *Submit:* Group leader's certification of completion. *Register:* In advance. *Sites:* Pennsbury Manor, Blacksmith Shop, Bake and Brew House, Ice House, Visitors Center, Smoke House.

York City Historical Trail

Location: York, PA. *Theme:* Local history. *Sponsor:* York-Adams Area Council, BSA, 800 E. King St., York, PA 17403-1797, (717) 843-0901.

Length: 4 miles (loop). *Route:* The trail begins at the York County Court House and takes 3 loops, each beginning and ending there. *Terrain:* City streets. *Cycling:* Appropriate. *Awards:* Medal $3.75; Patch $1.50. *Submit:* Completed 50-item questionnaire. *Register:* Not required. *Sites:* York County Court House, James Smith Grave, Quaker Meeting House, Penn Park, Historical Society Museum, Thomas Hartley Home, Old York County Prison, Currier & Ives Gallery, Christ Lutheran Church, Golden Plough Tavern, William Goodridge Home, Gates House, St. Johns Episcopal Church, Vigilant Fire House, Colonial Court House, James Smith House.

Other Pennsylvania Awards

Colonial Patriot Award—Trip to Washington Crossing or Valley Forge, seven mile hike, 29-point Colonial Philadelphia tour, and an overnight stay at French Creek Park including a visit to Hopewell Village. Medal and certificate. 500-word essay required. Sponsored by Philadelphia Council, BSA, 22nd & Winter Sts., Philadelphia, PA 19103-1085, (215) 988-9811.

Formerly Sponsored Trails

Bald Eagle Scout Trail
Black Hawk Forest Trail
Brandywine Battlefield Trail
Catawba Trail
Doylestown Historic Trail
Fort Pitt Trail

Freedom Shrine Historic Trail
General Forbes Trail
Great Warrior Trail
Honiasont Trail
Northmoreland-Ft. Hand Trail

Oil Creek Historical Trail
Old Trader's Path Trail
Poor Richard's Trail
Wallis Packhorse Trail

RHODE ISLAND

Newport Freedom Trail

Location: Newport, RI. *Theme:* Local history. *Sponsor:* Narragansett Council, BSA, 175 Broad St., Providence, RI 02903-4081, (401) 351-8700.

Length: 20 miles (loop). *Route:* The trail begins and ends at the Newport Historical Society and generally follows Thames, Wellington, Harrison, Ocean and Bellevue Aves. *Terrain:* City streets. *Cycling:* Appropriate. *Awards:* Medal $2.50. *Submit:* Group leader's certification of completion of hike and service project, plus 250-word essay.

Register: Not required. *Sites:* Touro Synagogue, United Baptist Church, Old Colony House, Quaker Meeting House, White Horse Tavern, Governor's Cemetery, Liberty Tree Park, Fort George, Brick Market, Newport Artillery Co., Oliver Hazard Perry House, Redwood Library, Touro Park/Old Stone Mill, Yachting Center, Ida Lewis Yacht Club, Gov. Benedict Arnold Burying Ground, U.S. Coast Guard Station, Belcourt Castle, Cliff Walk, Salve Regina College, The Breakers, Newport Automobile Museum, Forty Steps.

SOUTH CAROLINA

Blue Ridge Railroad Historical Trail

Location: West Union, SC. *Theme:* Route of roadbed of Blue Ridge Railroad. *Sponsor:* Blue Ridge Council, BSA, 2 Ridgeway Ave., P.O. Box 6628, Greenville, SC 29606-6628, (864) 233-8363.

Length: 15 miles (straight). *Route:* The trail begins in West Union and ends at Stumphouse Mountain Tunnel and Park in Oconee County. *Terrain:* Woods. *Cycling:* Not recommended. *Awards:* Medal $6.50; Patch $5.00. *Submit:* Group leader's certification of completion of hike, overnight camp and service project, plus essay. *Register:* At least 2 weeks in advance. *Sites:* Stumphouse Mountain Tunnel, Isaqueena Falls.

Charleston Bicentennial Trail of Freedom

Location: Charleston, SC. *Theme:* Local history. *Sponsor:* American Historical Trails, Inc., P.O. Box 769, Monroe, NC 28111-0769, (704) 289-1604, Carotrader@trellis.net.

Length: Route A—8 miles (loop). Route B—12 miles (loop)

Route: The trail begins at White Point Gardens, loops through the city, and returns to the start. *Terrain:* City streets. *Cycling:* Appropriate. *Awards:* Medal $6.00; Charleston Patch $2.25; National Patch $2.25. *Submit:* Completed 50-item questionnaire. *Register:* Not required. *Sites:* Fort Mechanic Site, Granville Bastion Site, Old Exchange Building, Provost Dungeon, McCrady's Tavern, Huguenot Church, Liberty Tree Site, Old Powder Magazine, Heyward-Washington House, Dubose-Heyward House, Col. W. Washington House, Ramsay House, Gibbs Art Building, Harvey House.

Cowpens Battlefield Historic Trail

Location: Cowpens National Battlefield, Chesnee, SC. *Theme:* Civil War battle. *Sponsor:* Palmetto Council, BSA, 420 S. Church St., P.O. Box 6249, Spartanburg, SC 29304-6249, (864) 585-4391.

Length: 4.1 miles (loop). *Route:* The trail begins and ends at the Cowpens National Battlefield Visitor Center, following the 1.3-mile Battlefield Trail and the 2.8-mile Auto Tour Road. *Terrain:* Roads. *Cycling:* Only on Auto Tour Road. *Awards:* Patch $2.00. *Submit:* Group leader's certification of completion and completed 24-item questionnaire, stamped at park visitor center. *Register:* Not required.

Foothills Trail

Location: Northwest edge of SC. *Theme:* Recreation. *Sponsor:* Foothills Trail Conference, P.O. Box 3041, Greenville, SC 29602.

Length: 43.3 miles (straight). *Route:* The trail begins at Table Rock State Park and proceeds westward to the Whitewater River. *Terrain:* Mountains. *Cycling:* Not recommended. *Awards:* Patch $2.00; Segments $3.00 per set. *Submit:* No requirement. *Register:* Not required.

Kings Mountain Battlefield Trail

Location: Kings Mountain National Military Park, NC, and Kings Mountain State Park, SC. *Theme:* Revolutionary War battle. *Sponsor:* Palmetto Council, BSA, 420 S. Church St., P.O. Box 6249, Spartanburg, SC 29304-6249, (864) 585-4391.

Length: 4.3 miles (straight). *Route:* The trail begins at the state park campground and goes 2.8 miles to the national park visitor center, where an additional 1.5 miles of the trail goes through the battlefield. *Terrain:* Woods. *Cycling:* Not recommended. *Awards:* Patch $1.75. *Submit:* Group leader's certification, stamped by national park ranger and state park ranger, plus completed 17-item questionnaire. *Register:* Upon arrival at state park. *Sites:* National Park Visitor Center, U.S. Monument.

Pine Tree Hill Trail

Location: Camden, SC. *Theme:* Local history. *Sponsor:* Indian Waters Council, BSA, 715 Betsy Dr., P.O. Box 144, Columbia, SC 29202-0144, (803) 765-9070.

Length: 10.5 miles (loop). *Route:* The trail begins at "Historic Camden", loops through the city, and ends at the Lafayette Hall Site. *Terrain:* City streets. *Cycling:* Possible, but does not qualify for awards. *Awards:* Medal $5.00; Patch $1.50. *Submit:* Completed 100-item questionnaire. *Register:* Not required. *Sites:* Quaker Cemetery, Revolutionary Gaol, Grave of Agnes of Glasgow, Mills Court House, Presbyterian Meeting House, Dekalb Monument, Old Methodist Parsonage, Joseph Kershaw-Conwallis House, George Washington House, Hampton Park, King Haiglar and Opera House Site, Lafayette Hall Site, Louise Proctor Hall, Greenleaf Villa, Baruch Birthplace, Monument Square, Kershaw Square, Hobkirk Inn.

Siege of Charleston, S.C., Historical Trail

Location: Charleston, SC. *Theme:* Civil War history. *Sponsor:* American Historical Trails, Inc., P.O. Box 769, Monroe, NC 28111, (704) 289-1604, Carotrader@trellis.net.

Length: Route A, 7 miles (loop). Route B, 11.5 miles (loop). *Route:* The trail begins at White Point Gardens, loops through the city, and returns to the start. *Terrain:* City streets. *Cycling:* Appropriate. *Awards:* Medal $6.00; Patch $2.25. *Submit:* Completed 50-item questionnaire. *Register:* Not required. *Sites:* Old Slave Mart, St. Phillips Churchyard, U.S. Custom House, Federal Officer Prison, Old Manne Hospital, The Old Jail, Wilkinson House, Grace Church, Marion Square, Charleston Museum, Arch Building, City Market, Fireproof Building, Washington Square, First Scots Church, Russell House, Double Breasted House, Bull House.

Swamp Fox Trail

Location: Francis Marion National Forest near Charleston, SC. *Theme:* Francis Marion, Revolutionary War hero. *Sponsor:* E.F. Holcombe, P.O. Box 30156, Charleston, SC 29417, (843) 884-9993.

Length: 27 miles (straight). *Route:* The trail begins at the Huger Recreation Area and ends at Awendan at US 17N. *Terrain:* Woods. *Cycling:* Not recommended, and does not qualify for awards. *Awards:* Medal $2.00; Patch $1.00. *Submit:* Group leader's certification of completion of hike and service project, plus essay. *Register:* Not required. *Sites:* Quemby Bridge, Indian Shell

Mounds, Hampton Plantation, Little Wambaw Swamp Scenic Area, Silk Hope Plantation, Tar Pits, Belle Isle Plantation.

Other South Carolina Awards

U.S.S. Yorktown Overnight Award— Overnight on aircraft carrier, tours of Fort Moultrie and Fort Sumter. Patch included in overnight price. Patriots Point Naval and Maritime Museum, 40 Patriots Point Rd., Mt. Pleasant, SC 29464, (843) 884-2727 or (800) 327-5723 or fax (843) 881-4232.

Formerly Sponsored Trail

Charles Towne Historic Trail

SOUTH DAKOTA

Formerly Sponsored Trails

Mount Rushmore Trails
Silver Arrow Trail

TENNESSEE

Appalachian Trail Award

Location: Great Smoky Mountains National Park, TN. *Theme:* Recreation. *Sponsor:* Great Smoky Mountain Council, BSA, P.O. Box 51885, 6440 Papermill Rd., Knoxville, TN 37950.
Length: 49 miles (straight). *Route:* The trail begins at Sams Gap (US 23) and ends at Waterville (I-40). *Terrain:* Mountains. *Cycling:* Not permitted. *Awards:* Patch $1.00. *Submit:* Group leader's certification of completion. *Register:* Not required.

Battle of Nashville Trail

Location: Nashville, TN. *Theme:* Civil War battle—December 15-16, 1864. *Sponsor:* Nashville Historical Trails, Inc., P.O. Box 299, Madison, TN 37116-0299.
Length: 13.7 miles (loop). *Route:* The trail begins and ends at the Jet Potter Boy Scout Center at 3414 Hillsboro Pike. *Terrain:* City streets. *Cycling:* Appropriate. *Awards:* Patch $3.00. *Submit:* Completed questionnaire. *Register:* Not required. *Sites:* Shy's Hill, Fort Negley, Fort Casino Site.

Bearwaller Gap Hiking Trail

Location: Cordell Hull Lake, Carthage, TN. *Theme:* Recreation. *Sponsor:* Nashville Historical Trails, Inc., P.O. Box 299, Madison, TN 37116-0299.
Length: 6 miles (straight). *Route:* The trail's endpoints are the parking lot at the Defeated Creek Recreation Area and the Tater Knob Overlook near SR 85. *Terrain:* Woods. *Cycling:* Not permitted. *Awards:* Patch $4.00. *Submit:* Awards order form stamped by park ranger. *Register:* Not required. *Sites:* Cordell Hull Lock & Dam, Tater Knob Overlook.

Blue Beaver Trail

Location: Lookout Mountain, TN. *Theme:* Civil War battle—November 24, 1863. *Sponsor:* Blue Beaver Trail, P.O. Box 274, Signal Mountain, TN 37377-0271.
Length: 10.5 miles (straight). *Route:* The trail begins at the Reflection Riding sign on SR 318, and climbs up Lookout Mountain to end at Point Park. *Terrain:* Mountain. *Cycling:* Not recommended. *Awards:* Medal $3.75; Patch $2.50. *Submit:* Group leader's

certification of completion. *Register:* Not required. *Sites:* Reflection Riding, Craven's House, New York Monument, Lookout Creek, Point Park, Sunset Park.

Bowater Hiking Trails

Location: Eastern TN. *Theme:* Recreation. *Sponsor:* Public Relations Department, Bowater Southern Paper Co., 5020 US 11S, Calhoun, TN 37309, (423) 336-2211 or fax (423) 336-7150.

Lengths: Hogskin Branch Loop Trail, 1.5 miles (loop), Honey Creek Pocket Wilderness Trail, 5 miles (loop), Laurel-Snow Pocket Wilderness National Recreation Trails, 5-6 miles (loop), Piney River Trail, 10 miles (straight). Stevenson Trail, 7.8 miles (loop), Stinging Fork Trail, 3 miles (loop), Twin Rocks Nature Trail, 2.5 miles (loop), Virgin Falls Trail, 8 miles (loop). *Routes:* The Hogskin Branch and Stevenson trails begin and end at the parking area on Montlake Rd. in the North Chattanooga Pocket Wilderness in Soddy-Daisy. The Twin Rocks trail begins and ends at the parking area on Shut-In Gap Rd. northwest of Spring City. The Stinging Fork Trail begins at a parking area on Shut-In Gap Rd. five miles west of the Twin Rocks trailhead. The Piney River Trail runs from the Twin Rocks Trail westward to the Newby Branch Forest Camp. The Virgin Falls Trail runs from a parking area 7.9 miles south of Derossett to the Caney Fork River and back. The Honey Creek trail begins at a parking area about 8 miles north of Elgin and circles near the South Fork River. The Laurel-Snow trails are off US 17 just north of Dayton. *Terrain:* Mountains, woods and creek beds. *Cycling:* Not recommended. *Awards:* Main Patch n/c; Segments n/c. *Submit:* No requirement. *Register:* Not required.

The Carter House Trail

Location: Franklin, TN. *Theme:* Local history. *Sponsor:* The Carter House, 1140 Columbia Ave., Franklin, TN 37064, (615) 791-1861.

Length: 5.6 miles (loop). *Route:* The trail begins and ends at The Carter House, with a loop through downtown Franklin. *Terrain:* City streets. *Cycling:* Appropriate. *Awards:* Patch $5.00. *Submit:* No requirement. *Register:* Upon arrival at The Carter House. *Sites:* Osage Hedge Row, Fort Granger, Moran House, Confederate Cemetery, Marshall House, Carnton Mansion, Confederate Monument, White House, First Baptist Church, City Cemetery, Williamson County Courthouse, First Presbyterian Church, St. Paul's Episcopal Church, Pre-Civil War Houses.

Chattanooga Historic Trail

Location: Chattanooga, TN. *Theme:* Local history. *Sponsor:* Blue Beaver Trail, P.O. Box 274, Signal Mountain, TN 37377-0271.

Length: 10 miles (loop). *Route:* The trail begins and ends at Ross' Landing and loops through most of the downtown area. *Terrain:* City streets. *Cycling:* Appropriate. *Awards:* Patch $2.00. *Submit:* Group leader's certification of completion. *Register:* Not required. *Sites:* Old Post Office Building, Walnut Street Bridge, Cameron Hill, National Cemetery, Chattanooga Choo-Choo, Ross' Landing, St. Paul's Episcopal Church, Tivoli Theatre, Second Presbyterian Church, Read House, Hunter Museum, Dome Building, Andrew's Raiders Monument, Old Library Building.

Dogwood Trail

Location: Memphis, TN. *Theme:* Recreation. *Sponsor:* Eugene E. McKenzie, 1345 Hickory Ridge Cove, Memphis, TN 38116.

Length: 7 miles (loop). *Route:* The trail begins and ends at Herb Parson's Lake, east of Memphis. *Terrain:* Woods. *Cycling:* Not recommended. *Awards:* Patch. *Submit:* No requirement. *Register:* Not required.

Exploring the Past Award

Location: Big South Fork National River and Recreation Area, TN. *Theme:* Nature and history. *Sponsor:* Great Smoky Mountain Council, BSA, P.O. Box 51885, 6440 Papermill Rd., Knoxville, TN 37950.

Length: 9.9 miles (loop). *Route:* The trail begins at the Bandy Creek Trailhead and consists of the Oscar Blevins Loop Trail and the Litton/ Slaven Farm Loop Trail. *Terrain:* Woods. *Cycling:* Not recommended. *Awards:* Patch $2.50. *Submit:* Group leader's certification of completion. *Register:* Not required. *Sites:* Clara Sue Blevins Homesite, Litton/Slaven Farm, Oscar Blevins Farm, Visitor Center.

First Chickasaw Bluff Trail

Location: Fort Pillow State Park, Henning,

TN. *Theme:* Recreation. *Sponsor:* Forrest Historical Society, P.O. Box 11141, Memphis, TN 38111.

Length: 5-8 miles (loop or straight). *Routes:* Either (1) start at north end and hike 4 miles to back-packing campsite and return, or (2) start at north end and hike 1 mile past campsite to trail end, or (3) same as (2) but in reverse direction. *Terrain:* Woods and fields. *Cycling:* Not recommended. *Awards:* Patch $2.00; Overnight Backpacker Segment $1.00. *Submit:* Group leader's certification of completion of hike and required reading. *Register:* At least 3 weeks in advance.

Fort Donelson Trail

Location: Fort Donelson National Battlefield, Dover, TN. *Theme:* Civil War battle—February 14, 1862. *Sponsor:* Fort Donelson National Battlefield, P.O. Box 434, Dover, TN 37058-0434, (931) 232-5348.

Length: 4 miles (loop). *Route:* The trail begins at the Visitor Center and loops around the fort, with visits to the National Cemetery and French's Battery. *Terrain:* Woods and fields. *Cycling:* Not recommended. *Awards:* Patch $2.50. *Submit:* No requirement. *Register:* Upon arrival. *Sites:* Confederate Monument, Dover Hotel, Visitor Center, Fort Donelson, National Cemetery, River Batteries, Jackson's Battery, French's Battery.

Fort Pillow Historical Trail

Location: Fort Pillow State Park, Henning, TN. *Theme:* Civil War battles. *Sponsor:* Forrest Historical Society, P.O. Box 11141, Memphis, TN 38111.

Length: 10 miles (loop). *Route:* The trail begins and ends at the Park Museum. *Terrain:* Woods and fields, with many hills. *Cycling:* Not recommended. *Awards:* Patch $1.50. *Submit:* Group leader's certification of completion of hike and required reading. *Register:* At least 3 weeks in advance. *Sites:* Park Museum, Fort Pillow.

Fort Pillow Trek

Location: Fort Pillow State Park, Henning, TN. *Theme:* Civil War battles. *Sponsor:* Forrest Historical Society, P.O. Box 11141, Memphis, TN 38111.

Length: 5 miles (loop). *Route:* The trail begins and end at the Park Museum. *Terrain:* Woods and fields. *Cycling:* Not

recommended. *Awards:* Patch $1.25. *Submit:* Group leader's certification of completion of hike and required reading. *Register:* At least 3 weeks in advance. *Sites:* Park Museum, Fort Pillow.

Great Smoky Mountain Men Hiking Award

Location: Great Smoky Mountains National Park, TN. *Theme:* Recreation. *Sponsor:* Great Smoky Mountain Council, BSA, P.O. Box 51885, 6440 Papermill Rd., Knoxville, TN 37950.

Length: Varies. *Route:* The award is earned by accumulating 100 points for hiking Appalachian side trails, with each trail counting for from 5 to 15 points. *Terrain:* Mountains. *Cycling:* Not recommended. *Awards:* Patch $0.25. *Submit:* Report of experiences on the trails. *Register:* Not required. *Sites:* Mt. Cammerer, Greenbriar Pinnacle, Mt. LeConte, Fighting Creek, Siler's Bald, Gregory Bald, Tricorner Knob, Chimney Tops, Fontana Lake.

Great Smoky Mountains National Park Trails

Location: On north side of TN/NC border, south of Gatlinburg. *Theme:* Recreation. *Sponsor:* Patches available at The Happy Hiker, 905 River Rd., Gatlinburg, TN 37738, (865) 436-6000. About one-third of the patches are also available at the national park headquarters. *Lengths:* Abrams Falls Trail, 5.0 miles (loop), Albright Grove Trail, 7.0 miles (loop), Alum Cave Bluff Trail, 5.0 miles (loop), Andrews Bald Trail, 4.0 miles (loop), Appalachian Trail, 49.0 miles (straight), Boulevard Trail, 8.0 miles (straight), Brushy Mountain Trail, 5.3 miles (straight), Bullhead Trail, 6.0 miles (loop), Cades Cove Vista Trail, 0.33 mile (loop), Cataract Falls Trail, Chimney Tops Trail, 4.0 miles (loop), Cliff Tops Trail, Cosby Trail, 1.0 mile (loop), Cove Mountain Trail, 8.0 miles (loop), Cucumber Gap Trail, 5.5 miles (loop), Elkmont Trail, 0.75 mile (loop), Gatlinburg Trail, 2.0 miles (straight), Greenbrier Pinnacle Trail, 10.0 miles (loop), Gregory Bald Trail, 11.0 miles (loop), Grotto Falls Trail, 3.0 miles (loop), Henwallow Falls Trail, 4.0 miles (loop), Huskey Gap Trail, 4.5 miles (straight), Indian Gap Trail, 5.5 miles (straight), Jake's Creek Trail, 2.9 miles (straight), The Jumpoff Trail, 6.5 miles (loop), Junglebrook (Ogle) Trail,

Laurel Falls Trail, 2.5 miles (loop), Little River Trail, 8.0 miles (straight), Llama Trail, Maddron Bald Trail, 7.2 miles (straight), Mt. Cammerer Trail, 12.0 miles (loop), Mt. Collins Trail, Mt. Kephart Trail, Mt. LeConte Trail, 11.0-16.0 miles (loop), Myrtle Point Trail, Old Settlers Trail, 15.9 miles (straight), Porter Creek Trail, 3.5 miles (loop), Rainbow Falls Trail, 5.5 miles (loop), Ramsey Cascades Trail, 8.0 miles (loop), Rich Mountain Loop Trail, 7.4 miles (loop), Rocky Spur Trail, Russell Field Trail, 5.5 miles (straight), Spence Field Trail, 11.0-14.0 miles (loop), Sugarlands Mountain Trail, 4.5 miles (straight), Thunderhead Trail, 13.0 miles (loop), Trillium Gap Trail, 6.5 miles (straight), Walnut Bottoms Trail. *Routes:* Vary—check park maps for details. *Terrain:* Mountains. *Cycling:* Not permitted. *Awards:* Patches for each trail named above $1.75 each at The Happy Hiker, $1.99 each at park headquarters. *Submit:* No requirement. *Register:* Not required, but check park rules for overnight hikes.

Historic Trail of Tears

Location: Cleveland, TN. *Theme:* Historic route of Indian forced march. *Sponsor:* Carol Crabtree, Red Clay State Historic Area, 1140 Red Clay Park Rd. S.W., Cleveland, TN 37311, (423) 478-0339.

Length: 6.5 miles (straight). *Route:* The trail begins at the John Ross Cabin Site on Red Hill Rd., heads south on Red Hill Valley Rd., east on Johnson Rd., south on Greenbrier Rd., west on Mitchell Rd., south on Dalton Pike, west on Wilson-Caldwell Rd., and north on Red Clay Park Rd. to end at Red Clay State Historical Area. *Terrain:* Roads. *Cycling:* Possible, but does not qualify for awards. *Awards:* Patch $4.50. *Submit:* No requirement. *Register:* Upon arrival; this is an annual hike held on the first Saturday in April.

Knoxville Historic Trail

Location: Knoxville, TN. *Theme:* Local history. *Sponsor:* Great Smoky Mountain Council, BSA, P.O. Box 51885, 6440 Papermill Rd., Knoxville, TN 37950.

Length: 5.7 and 9.4 miles (straight). *Route:* The trail begins at the rear of Calvary Baptist Church, 3200 Kingston Pike. The shorter trail takes a shortcut, and both end at Fort Dickerson Park. *Terrain:* City streets.

Cycling: Appropriate. *Awards:* Patch $3.50. The miles may also be used toward the East Tennessee Heritage Award, a $1.50 patch by the same sponsor. *Submit:* Group leader's certification of completion. *Register:* Not required. *Sites:* Bleak House, City Hall, Old Gray Cemetery, National Cemetery, Confederate Cemetery, James White Fort, Craighead-Jackson Home, Blount Mansion, First Presbyterian Church, Fort Dickerson.

Memphis Historical Trail

Location: Memphis, TN. *Theme:* Local history . *Sponsor:* William Schadrick III, 639 Harwood Cove, Cardova, TN 38018, (901) 767-8768 (home), (901) 393-2110 (work).

Length: 12 miles (loop). *Route:* The trail begins and ends in the public parking lot west and south of the Holiday Inn-Rivermont (west end of Georgia Ave. West). *Terrain:* City streets. *Cycling:* Appropriate. *Awards:* Medal $3.25; Patch $1.50; Repeat Pin $1.25; Neckerchief $2.00; Neckerchief Slide $1.50. *Submit:* Group leader's certification of completion of hike and required reading, plus written report of hike. *Register:* At least 3 weeks in advance. *Sites:* Ashburn Park, Mississippi River, Forrest Park.

Nashville Historical Trail

Location: Nashville, TN. *Theme:* Local history. *Sponsor:* Nashville Historical Trails, Inc., P.O. Box 299, Madison, TN 37116-0299.

Length: 11 miles (loop). *Route:* The trail loops through downtown Nashville, highlighting 27 landmarks. *Terrain:* City streets. *Cycling:* Appropriate. *Awards:* Patch $3.50. *Submit:* Completed questionnaire. *Register:* Not required. *Sites:* Greek Parthenon Replica, Fort Nashborough, Grand Ole Opry House, Music Row, State Capitol.

Nolichucky Jack Trail

Location: Lookout Mountain, TN and GA. *Theme:* Site of Last Battle of the American Revolution. *Sponsor:* Blue Beaver Trail, P.O. Box 274, Signal Mountain, TN 37377-0271.

Length: 20 miles (double loop). *Route:* The trail begins at the Chattanooga Nature Center, follows Lookout Creek southwest to Skyuka Spring, then loops up and down the mountain to return to the start. *Terrain:* Mountain. *Cycling:* Not recommended. *Awards:* Patch $2.50. *Submit:* No requirement. *Register:* Not required. *Sites:*

Reflection Riding, Skyuka Spring,
Chattanooga Nature Center, Lookout
Mountain.

Perimeter Trail

Location: Skymont Scout Reservation,
Altamont, TN. *Theme:* Recreation. *Sponsor:*
Cherokee Area Council, BSA, 6031 Lee Hwy.,
Chattanooga, TN 37421, (423) 892-8323.
Length: 12.2 miles (loop). *Route:* The trail
begins at the reservation's main gate, follows
the perimeter of the reservation along the
edge of the South Cumberland Plateau, and
returns to the start. There are also the
following side trails: Day Loop Trail, 1.0 mile
(loop). Eagle Bluff Trail, 3.0 miles (straight).
Nature Trail, 5.0 miles (loop). Talidanaganu
Trail, 2.0 miles (loop). Van Dykes Cave Trail,
4.0 miles (loop). *Terrain:* Woods. *Cycling:*
Not recommended. *Awards:* Patch $3.50; 5
Segments $1.50 each. *Submit:* No
requirement. *Register:* Upon arrival at
reservation.

Return of the Eternal Flame Trail

Location: Cleveland, TN. *Theme:* Cherokee
history. *Sponsor:* Carol Crabtree, Red Clay
State Historic Area, 1140 Red Clay Park Rd.
S.W., Cleveland, TN 37311, (423) 478-0339.
Length: 4.3 miles (straight). *Route:* The
trail begins at Red Clay State Historical Area,
and goes north on Red Clay Park Rd., east on
Old Weatherly Switch Rd., north on Dalton
Pike, and northeast on Flint Springs Rd. and
Red Hill Rd. to end at the John Ross Cabin
Site. *Terrain:* Roads. *Cycling:* Possible, but
does not qualify for awards. *Awards:* Patch
$4.50. *Submit:* No requirement. *Register:*
Upon arrival; this is an annual hike held on
the first Saturday in April.

Rich Mountain Loop Trail

Location: Cades Cove, Great Smoky
Mountains National Park, TN. *Theme:* Local
history. *Sponsor:* Great Smoky Mountain
Council, BSA, P.O. Box 51885, 6440 Papermill
Rd., Knoxville, TN 37950.
Length: 8.6 miles (loop)(includes 0.6 mile
each way from parking area to loop trail).
Route: The trail begins and ends just west of
the gate to Cades Cove Loop Rd. *Terrain:*
Hilly horse trail. *Cycling:* Not permitted.
Awards: Patch $2.00. *Submit:* Group leader's
certification of completion. *Register:* Not
required. *Sites:* Cades Cove Overlooks, Cades

Cove Entrance Display, John Oliver Cabin.
The above trail is also known as the "Great
Smoky Mountain Cub Scout Hike"

Shiloh Military Trails

Location: Shiloh National Military Park,
Shiloh, TN. *Theme:* Civil War battle—April
6-7, 1862. *Sponsor:* Historical Hiking Trails,
P.O. Box 17507, Memphis, TN 38187-0507,
(901) 323-2739. *Lengths:* Confederate
Advance Trail (#5), 20 miles. Lew Wallace
Approach Trail (#6), 16 miles. Shiloh
Artillery Trail (#2), 14 miles. Shiloh
Battlefield Trek, 2 miles. Shiloh Cannon Trail
(#2A), 12 miles*. Shiloh Compass-Cross
Country Trail (#4 odd years, #4A even), 10
miles each. Shiloh Environmental Trail (#7),
12 miles. Shiloh Historical Trail (#1), 14 miles.
Shiloh Historical Trail (#3), 14 miles. Shiloh
Indian Mounds Trek, 3 miles (loop). *Routes:*
The Indian Mounds Trek begins and ends at
Bloody Pond and includes the Indian
mounds overlooking the Tennessee River.
The Battlefield Trek begins and ends in the
Hornet's Nest area. The Confederate Advance
Trail runs from Mississippi to Pittsburgh
Landing. The Lew Wallace Approach Trail
runs from Crump & Adamsville to Shiloh.
The remaining trails cover various portions
of the battlefield. *Terrain:* Woods and fields.
Cycling: Not recommended. *Awards:*
Battlefield Trek Patch $1.50; Battlefield Trek
Pin $1.50; Historical Medal $3.75; Historical
(#1) Patch $1.50; Historical (#1) Pin $1.50;
Cannon Medal $4.00; Cannon Patch $2.25;
Cannon Pin $1.50; Artillery Patch $1.50;
Artillery Pin $1.50; Historical (#3) Patch
$1.50; Historical (#3) Pin $1.50; Compass
Patch $1.50; Compass Pin $1.50; Confederate
Advance Patch $2.00; Confederate Advance
Pin $1.50; Lew Wallace Patch $2.00; Lew
Wallace Pin $1.50; Environmental Patch
$1.50; Environmental Pin $1.50; Repeat (#1)
Pin $1.50; Repeat (other trails) Pin $1.50;
Neckerchief $4.00; Indian Mounds Patch
$1.50; Indian Mounds Pin $1.50; Neckerchief
Slide $2.25; Veteran Hiker Certificate $1.00;
Veteran Hiker Patch $3.50; Veteran Hiker Pin
$1.50. *Submit:* Group leader's certification of
completion of hike and required reading,
plus completed 112-item questionnaire for
Lew Wallace Approach Trail. *Register:* At
least 3 weeks in advance. *Sites:* Peach
Orchard, War Cabin, Ruggles' Batteries,
U.S.D. Monument, U.D.C. Monument,

Visitor Center, Ohio Zouaves Monument, Illinois Monument, Wisconsin Monument, Tennessee Monument. *Sponsor reported in August 1995 that Shiloh Cannon Trail is closed for an indefinite time.

Stones River National Battlefield Trail

Location: Stones River National Battlefield, Murphreesboro, TN. *Theme:* Civil War battle—December 31, 1862. *Sponsor:* Nashville Historical Trails, Inc., P.O. Box 299, Madison, TN 37116-0299.

Length: 2 and 5 miles (loops). *Route:* The trails begin and end at the Visitor Center and head south. The shorter trail follows the road, while the longer one follows the boundary of the park property. *Terrain:* Woods. *Cycling:* Appropriate only for the 2-mile trail (the award is for the 5-mile trail). *Awards:* Patch $4.00. *Submit:* Completed 19-item questionnaire. *Register:* Not required. *Sites:* Union Infantry Trench, Stones River National Cemetery, Visitor Center, Hazen Monument and Cemetery, Garesche Marker, Cedar Swamp, Nashville & Chattanooga Railroad, Cotton Field, Round Forest, Toll House Site.

Sweetwater Historical Trail

Location: Sweetwater, TN. *Theme:* Local history. *Sponsor:* Andrew McCampbell, 407 Mayes Ave., Sweetwater, TN 37874.

Length: 5 miles (loop). *Route:* The trail begins at the TMG Administration Building, winds through town and returns to the start. *Terrain:* City streets. *Cycling:* Appropriate. *Awards:* Patch $3.50. *Submit:* Group leader's certification of completion. *Register:* In advance. *Sites:* Sweetwater Heritage Museum, First Presbyterian Church, Westview Cemetery, Sweetwater United Methodist Church, Sweetwater Hosiery Mill, First Baptist Church, Southern Railway Depot, Sweetwater Public Library.

Wolf River Trails

Location: Shelby Farms Forest, Memphis, TN. *Theme:* Recreation. *Sponsor:* Eugene E. McKenzie, 1345 Hickory Ridge Cove, Memphis, TN 38116.

Length: 5 miles each (the two form a loop). *Route:* The Yellow Trail begins at the parking area reached by the access road running to the boat ramp from the soccer field on Walnut Grove Rd., and follows the Wolf River eastward to the boat ramp near Germantown Rd. The Blue Trail returns to the start along a slightly different route parallel to the Wolf River. *Terrain:* Woods. *Cycling:* Not recommended; awards are also available for canoeing the Wolf River from one boat ramp to the other. *Awards:* Patch $1.65. *Submit:* No requirement. *Register:* Not required.

Formerly Sponsored Trails

A. Johnson-D. Crockett Trail
Battle of Franklin Hiking Trail
Big Hill Pond Trails
Britton Lane Trail
Chief John Ross Canoe Trek
Chucalissa Discovery Trail
Downtown Nashville Trail
Fort Johnsonville Redoubts Trail
Hernando DeSoto Bridge Trail
Hoot Owl Trail
Longstreet's Crossing Trail
Meeman Compass Trail
Mississippi River Trail
Overton Zoological Trail
Pinson Mounds Trail
Raleigh Historical Trail
Roane Heritage Trail
Shelby Forest Long Trail
Shelby Forest Short Trail
Smoky Mountain Trail
Tennessee Forrest Trail
Tipton County Historical Trail
W.C. Handy Trail
Warrior's Passage Trail
Well's Creek Basin Trail

TEXAS

Bonham Texas Historic Trail

Location: Bonham, TX. *Theme:* Local history. *Sponsor:* Chamber of Commerce, 1 Main St., Bonham, TX 75418, (903) 583-4811.

Length: 5 miles (straight). *Route:* The trail begins at the original site of Fort Inglish and runs 3.5 miles to Willow Wild Cemetery, then 1.5 miles to the Sam Rayburn House and Museum. *Terrain:* City streets. *Cycling:* Appropriate; the sponsor suggests driving the last 1.5 miles because of heavy traffic. *Awards:* Patch $3.00. *Submit:* No requirement. *Register:* Not required. *Sites:* Fort Inglish, Fannin County Museum of History, Willow Wild Cemetery, Inglish Cemetery, Sam Rayburn Veterans Administration Hospital, Carlton College, Sam Rayburn Home and Museum.

Corpus Christi Historical Trail

Location: Corpus Christi, TX. *Theme:* Local history. *Sponsor:* Gulf Coast Council, BSA, P.O. 3159, 1444 Baldwin, Corpus Christi, TX 78463-3159, (361) 882-6126.

Length: 10 miles (loop). *Route:* The trail begins at Bayview Cemetery, and makes a large figure eight through the city before it returns to the start. *Terrain:* City streets. *Cycling:* Appropriate. *Awards:* Patch $1.85. *Submit:* Group leader's certification of completion. *Register:* Not required. *Sites:* Tex-Mex Depot, Sidbury House, Railroad Exhibit, Corpus Christi Museum, Art Museum of South Texas, Early Lighthouse Site, Lone Star Fair, Centennial House, Kinney's Trading Post, Merriman House, F-9-F Cougar Jet, Bayshore Monument, Confederate Memorial Fountain.

Dallas Historical Memorial Trail

Location: Dallas, TX. *Theme:* Local history. *Sponsor:* Boy Scout Troop 771, c/o Tom Covington, Kirkwood United Methodist Church, 1525 W. 7th St., Irving, TX 75060, (972) 253-4580.

Length: 10 miles (straight). *Route:* The trail begins at Sealey Plaza and heads generally north to end on Turtle Creek Blvd. *Terrain:* City streets. *Cycling:* Appropriate. *Awards:* Plaque $24.95; Patch $2.50. *Submit:*

Completed questionnaire. *Register:* In advance. *Sites:* Old City Park, The Sixth Floor, Thanks-Giving Square.

Fort Concho Historical Trail

Location: San Angelo, TX. *Theme:* Historic fort. *Sponsor:* Concho Valley Council, BSA, 104 W. River Dr., P.O. Box 1584, San Angelo, TX 76902-1584, (915) 655-7107.

Length: 2 miles (straight). *Route:* The trail begins at City Park, heads west on Concho, south on Irving, east on Ave. D, and ends at Fort Concho. *Terrain:* City streets. *Cycling:* Appropriate. *Awards:* Patch $2.00. *Submit:* Group leader's certification of completion, plus completed 37-item questionnaire. *Register:* In advance. *Sites:* San Angelo National Bank , Fort Concho, Taylor Dry Goods Store, Carriage Mark Galleries, Concho Saddlers, Ragsdale Auto Company, Santa Fe Freight Station, North Concho River.

Fort McKavett Historical Trail

Location: Menard, TX. *Theme:* Historic fort. *Sponsor:* Concho Valley Council, BSA, 104 W. River Dr., P.O. Box 1584, San Angelo, TX 76902-1584, (915) 655-7107.

Length: 6 miles (straight). *Route:* The trail begins at Camp Sol Mayer and heads north along the San Saba River and Ranch Rd. 864 to Fort McKavett, where the trail winds through the fort. *Terrain:* Road and fort paths. *Cycling:* Not recommended. *Awards:* Medal $4.50; Patch. *Submit:* Group leader's certification of completion of hike, overnight camping and service project, plus essay. *Register:* In advance. *Sites:* San Saba Mission, Lost Bowie Mine, Mud Flats, Fort McKavett, San Saba River, Slaughter Hole.

Fort Stockton Historical Trail

Location: Fort Stockton, TX. *Theme:* Historic fort. *Sponsor:* Concho Valley Council, BSA, 104 W. River Dr., P.O. Box 1584, San Angelo, TX 76902-1584, (915) 655-7107.

Length: 3 miles (straight). *Route:* The trail begins in front of the Annie Riggs Memorial Museum on Callaghan St. *Terrain:* City streets. *Cycling:* Possible, but does not qualify for awards. *Awards:* Patch $1.50. *Submit:* Group leader's certification of completion. *Register:* In advance. *Sites:* Annie Riggs Memorial Museum, Gray Mule Saloon, Young's Store, Koehler Store, Comanche Springs Pavilion, Fort Hospital, Fort Guard House, Powder Magazine, Old Fort Cemetery, Hotel Stockton, Rogers Building, Coleman Drug Store, Old Freight Depot, Pioneer Building.

Ghosts of Nacogdoches Historical Trail

Location: Nacogdoches, TX. *Theme:* Local and state history. *Sponsor:* Clyde McCullough, 4423 White Oak, Nacogdoches, TX 75961, (409) 564-6081, or East Texas Area Council, BSA, 1331 E. Fifth St., Tyler, TX 75701, (903) 597-7201.

Length: 7.5 miles (loop) with an optional 2.5 mile additional section. *Route:* The trail begins and ends at Banita Creek Park, and winds through the city and along two streams on each side of the city. *Terrain:* City streets and wooded trails along streams. *Cycling:* Appropriate, but extreme caution is recommended on city streets. *Awards:* Medal $5.00; Patch $3.00; Pin $2.00; NH (Nacogdoches Historian) Pin $1.50; T-shirt $12.00; Mug $5.00. *Submit:* Completed questionnaires, official awards application, and confirmation of required reading (cost of book is $3.50). *Register:* In advance, if possible.

Heart O' Texas Historic Trail

Location: Waco, TX. *Theme:* Local history. *Sponsor:* Heart O' Texas Council, BSA, P.O. Box 7127, 300 Lake Air Dr., Waco, TX 76714-7127.

Length: 4.5 miles (loop). *Route:* The trail begins and ends at Fort Fisher, and loops through downtown Waco. *Terrain:* City streets. *Cycling:* Possible, but not recommended. *Awards:* Medal; Patch; Hat Pin. *Submit:* Answers to 63-item quiz. *Register:* Notify the sponsor in advance of hiking date. *Sites:* Texas Sports Hall of Fame, First Street Cemetery, The Brazos Queen II, The Indian Spring, Helen Marie Taylor Museum, Hard Bottom Crossing, St. Francis Church, Franciscan Monastery, St. Paul's Episcopal Church, McCulloch House.

Little Ghosts of Nacogdoches Historical Trail

Location: Nacogdoches, TX. *Theme:* Local and state history. *Sponsor:* Clyde McCullough, 4423 White Oak, Nacogdoches, TX 75961, (409) 564-6081, or East Texas Area Council, BSA, 1331 E. Fifth St., Tyler, TX 75701, (903) 597-7201.

Length: 3 miles (loop). *Route:* The trail begins and ends at Bonita Creek Park, and winds through the city and along one stream through the city. *Terrain:* City streets and a wooded trail along a stream. *Cycling:* Not appropriate for younger children. *Awards:* Patch $2.50; Pin $2.00; T-shirt $12.00; Mug $5.00. *Submit:* Official awards application. *Register:* In advance, if possible. *Sites:* Bonita Creek Park, Red House marker, Old String Shop, Oak Grove Cemetery.

Missions Historic Trail

Location: San Antonio, TX. *Theme:* Spanish missions. *Sponsor:* Alamo Area Council, BSA, 2226 NW Military Dr., San Antonio, TX 78213-1894, (210) 341-8611.

Length: 12.6 miles (straight). *Route:* The trail begins at the Alamo and heads southward along Alamo, St. Mary's, Mission, and Espada, to end at Mission Espada. *Terrain:* City streets. *Cycling:* Possible, but does not qualify for awards. *Awards:* Patch $2.75. *Submit:* Completed 12-item questionnaire. *Register:* At least 1 week in advance. *Sites:* Alamo, Hemisfair Park, Mission Concepcion, Mission Espada, San Antonio River, Mission San Jose, Mission County Park, Mission San Juan, Espada Park and Dam, Espada Aqueduct, Mission Najera Site, La Villita.

Rio Grande Valley Historic Trails Award

Location: Rio Grande Valley, TX. *Theme:* Local history. *Sponsor:* Rio Grande Council, BSA, 1301 S. US 77, P.O. Box 2424, Harlingen, TX 78551-2424, (956) 423-0250.

Length: 50 miles. *Route:* The route is to be established by the hiker, totaling 50 miles at a minimum of 15 miles per day, visiting a minimum of 6 historic sites (including 1 of 4 listed areas). *Terrain:* Depends upon route selected. *Cycling:* Appropriate. *Awards:* Patch $4.50. *Submit:* Report on sites visited and book report on local history. *Register:* Not required. *Sites:* Hidalgo County Museum, Starr County Museum, Stillman House and Museum, Sam Houston School, Cameron County Museum, Fort Brown, Brownsville Public Market, Fort Ringgold, Old Hidalgo County Jail, San Francisco Ranch, William Jennings Bryan House.

Sam Houston Historic Trail

Location: Gonzales to Rose Hill, TX. *Theme:* Route followed by General Sam Houston during the Texas Revolution of 1836. *Sponsor:* Sam Houston Area Council, BSA, 1911 Bagby St., P.O. Box 52786, Houston, TX 77052-2786, (713) 659-8111.

Length: 175 miles (straight). *Routes:* Gonzales to Sam Houston Oak, 9.7 miles. Sam Houston Oak to La Vida Ranch, 9.8 miles. Omega Ranch to Lavaca Crossing, 8.9 miles. Lavaca Crossing to Old Cotton Gin Site, 9.7 miles. Old Cotton Gin Site to Navidad River, 10.2 miles. Navidad River to Hill Memorial Park, 11.9 miles. Hill Memorial Park to Burnham's Ferry, 8.2 miles. North Burnham's Ferry to Shaw's Bend, 10.8 miles. Shaw's Bend to Columbus, 8.0 miles. Columbus to Bernardo, 9.6 miles. Bernardo to Farm Road 2187, 11.0 miles. FR 2187 to Stephen F. Austin Park, 11.1 miles. Stephen F. Austin Park to Burleigh, 12.8 miles. Burleigh to Groce's Plantation, 8.1 miles. Groce's Ferry to Bishop Ranch, 9.1 miles. Bishop Ranch to Waller Lions Center, 12.9 miles. Waller Lions Center to New Kentucky Park, 10.4 miles. *Terrain:* Varies. *Cycling:* Not recommended. *Awards:* 10 Patches $1.50 each (1st-5th year, 5 ceremony patches). *Submit:* Group leader's certification of completion of trail section plus attendance at ceremony. *Register:* Upon arrival; this is an annual event, doing sections on 7 weekends each spring. *Sites:* San Jacinto Monument, Sam Houston Oak, Old Jail on the Square, Andrews Chapel Cemetery, St. Rock's Catholic Church, Stephen F. Austin Historical Site, Maigne-Walther House, Papenberg House, Hill Memorial Park, Old Cotton Gin Site, Colorado County Courthouse, Macedonia Baptist Church, St. Thomas Cemetery.

San Jacinto Battlefield Hike

Location: LaPorte, TX. *Theme:* Battle of April 21, 1836. *Sponsor:* Sam Houston Area Council, BSA, 1911 Bagby St., P.O. Box 52786, Houston, TX 77052-2786, (713) 659-8111.

Length: 3 miles (straight). *Route:* The trail begins at the intersection of park roads south of the monument, loops west to the U.S.S. Texas, then back past the monument and east to end at Peggy Lake. *Terrain:* Roads and fields. *Cycling:* Not recommended. *Awards:* Patch $1.50. *Submit:* Group leader's certification of completion. *Register:* Not required. *Sites:* San Jacinto Monument, Museum of History, U.S.S. Texas, Buffalo Bayou, Golden Standard Cannon, Twin Sisters Cannons.

Texas Heritage Trail

Location: Austin, TX. *Theme:* Local history. *Sponsor:* Capitol Area Council, BSA, 7540 Ed Bluestein Blvd., Austin, TX 78723-2399, (512) 926-6363.

Length: 7.25 miles (straight). *Route:* The trail begins at the foot of Congress Ave. on the west side just north of the bridge, and ends at the State Cemetery on Comal St. An optional section begins at the Capitol grounds and ends at the L.B.J. Library. *Terrain:* City streets. *Cycling:* Appropriate. *Awards:* Patch $2.00. *Submit:* Group leader's certification of completion and completed 27-item questionnaire. *Register:* Not required. *Sites:* 1916 Steam Locomotive, Temporary Capitol Site, O. Henry Home and Museum, French Legation, Governor's Mansion, Statue of Liberty, D.R.T. and D.O.C. Museum, Waterloo Park, Moonlight Tower, Symphony Square, Littlefield Fountain, Sam Houston State Office Building, University of Texas, Memorial Stadium, Texas Memorial Museum.

TFA Woodlands Trails

Location: Many in TX. *Theme:* Recreation. *Sponsor:* Texas Forestry Association, P.O. Box 1488, 1903 Atkinson Dr., Lufkin, TX 75902. *Lengths:* Big Creek Trail, 3.55 miles (loop). Bull Creek Trail, 1.5 miles (loop). Dogwood Trail, 1.5 miles (loop). Four-C Trail, 20 miles (straight). Griff Ross Trail, 0.75 mile (loop). Longleaf Pine Trail, 2.0 miles (loop). Moscow Trail, 2.0 miles (loop). Sawmill Trail, 5.5 miles (straight). Sylvan Trail, 0.5 mile (loop). Wild Azalea Canyons Trail. Yellow Poplar Trail, 1.0 mile (loop). *Routes:* Big Creek begins and ends on FR 217 at the Big Creek Scenic Area in the Sam Houston National Forest. Wild Azalea begins and ends northeast of Newton, off FM 1414. Sylvan is southeast of Newton off US 190. Dogwood begins and ends on Dogwood Dr. off US 190 east of Woodville. Longleaf Pine begins and ends on FM 62 east of Camden. Moscow follows Long King Creek south of Moscow. Bull Creek is located west of Corrigan on US 287. Yellow Poplar is located on US 59 north of Jefferson. Four-C begins at the Ratcliff Recreation Area and ends at the overlook at Neches Bluff, all in the Davy Crockett National Forest. Sawmill is located southeast of Zavalla on FS 303 in the Angelina National Forest. Griff Ross is located east of Mt. Enterprise off US 84. *Terrain:* Woods. *Cycling:* Not recommended. *Awards:* Patch for walking 6 trails; Additional Red Star for walking 11. *Submit:* No requirement. *Register:* Not required.

Other Texas Awards

U.S.S. Lexington Live Aboard Award— Overnight on aircraft carrier. Patch included in overnight price. U.S.S. Lexington Museum On The Bay, P.O. Box 23076, Corpus Christi, TX 78403-3076, (361) 888-4873 or fax (361) 883-8361.

Formerly Sponsored Trails

Great Comanche War Trail
Houston Historical Trail
Kingsville Trail
Victoria Trail

UTAH

Black Ridge Historic Trail

Location: Cedar City, UT. *Theme:* Pioneer heritage. *Sponsor:* Utah National Parks Council, BSA, P.O. Box 106, 250 W. 500 N., Provo, UT 84603-0106, (801) 373-4185.

Length: 16-18 miles (straight). *Route:* The trail begins at Ash Creek Dam, goes to Pintura and to Harmony, or may be hiked in the reverse direction. *Terrain:* Early pioneer wagon roads. *Cycling:* Not recommended. *Awards:* Patch $0.75; Trailmaster Strip $0.50. *Submit:* Group leader's certification of completion of hike and overnight camping. *Register:* Not required. *Sites:* Peter's Leap, Old Fort Harmony, Indian Petroglyphs, Sawyers Springs, Ash Creek.

Dominguez-Escalante Trail

Location: Juab and Millard Counties, UT. *Theme:* Route of 1776 expedition of Franciscan friars Francisco Dominguez and Silvestre Velez de Escalante. *Sponsor:* Utah National Parks Council, BSA, P.O. Box 106, 250 W. 500 N., Provo, UT 84603-0106, (801) 373-4185.

Length: 100 miles (approx.)(straight). *Route:* Contact sponsor for details. *Terrain:* Varies. *Cycling:* Not recommended. *Awards:*

Patch. *Submit:* Group leader's certification of completion. *Register:* Not required. *Sites:* Beaver River, Chicken Creek Reservoir, Salt Creek, Sevier River, Yuba Lake, Pahvant Butte, Cricket Mountains, Black Rock.

Golden Spike Trail

Location: Promontory, UT. *Theme:* Location where on May 10, 1869, the Union Pacific and Central Pacific Railroads drove the Golden Spike uniting them. *Sponsor:* Trapper Trails Council, BSA, 1200 E. 5400 S., Ogden, UT 84403-4599, (801) 479-5460.

Length: 7-10 miles (loop or straight). *Route:* Hike Big Fill Walk, then to Visitor Center, or reverse; hike West Grade Tour then to Visitor Center, or reverse; or ten miles along original railroad grade in or out of the park. *Terrain:* Railroad grade. *Cycling:* Not recommended. *Awards:* Medal $3.00; Patch $2.00; Certificate $0.50. *Submit:* Group leader's certification of completion, plus written essay. *Register:* Only required if hike will be on private property. *Sites:* Golden Spike Visitor Center, Big Fill.

Hole in the Rock Historic Trail

Location: Escalante to Bluff, UT. *Theme:*

1879-80 trek to settle near the San Juan River. *Sponsor:* Utah National Parks Council, BSA, P.O. Box 106, 250 W. 500 N., Provo, UT 84603-0106, (801) 373-4185.

Length: 200 miles (straight). *Route:* The trail begins at Escalante, heads southeast through Hole-in-the-Rock, northeast to Grand Flat and Harmony Flat, then southeast to end at Bluff. *Terrain:* Varies. *Cycling:* Not recommended. *Awards:* Medal $8.50; Patch. *Submit:* Group leader's certification of completion of pre-approved conservation project, required reading, and presentation at Edge of the Cedars Museum, Blanding, UT. *Register:* In advance with Bureau of Land Management. *Sites:* Hole-in-the-Rock, Dance Hall Rock, Register Rock, Grey Mesa, Cottonwood Hill, San Juan Hill, Red House Spring, Navajo Hill.

Maple Lake Trail

Location: Mapleton, UT. *Theme:* Recreation. *Sponsor:* Utah National Parks Council, BSA, P.O. Box 106, 250 W. 500 N., Provo, UT 84603-0106, (801) 373-4185.

Length: 5 miles (straight). *Route:* The trail begins at the upper end of Whiting Campground in Mapleton Canyon, passes Maple Lake, and ends at the U.S. Geological Survey marker on the top of Spanish Fort Peak. The Over the Top Award pin is for those hikers who continue on to Little Diamond Rd. in Diamond Fork Canyon. *Terrain:* Rugged. *Cycling:* Not recommended. *Awards:* Patch $1.75; Pin $1.50. *Submit:* Group leader's certification of completion of hike, overnight camping and conservation project. *Register:* Not required. *Sites:* Diamond Fork Canyon, Spanish Fork Peak, Mapleton Canyon, Maple Lake.

Mt. Timpanogos Conservation Award

Location: Mt. Timpanogos Wilderness Area, UT. *Theme:* Conservation. *Sponsor:* Utah National Parks Council, BSA, P.O. Box 106, 250 W. 500 N., Provo, UT 84603-0106, (801) 373-4185.

Length: 7 miles (loop). *Route:* The trail begins at Aspen Grove, goes to the summit of Mt. Timpanogos, and returns to the start. *Terrain:* Mountain. *Cycling:* Not recommended. *Awards:* Patch $2.00. *Submit:* Group leader's certification of completion of hike and service project, plus report on the project. *Register:* Not required.

Old Spanish Trail

Location: Newcastle to Veyo, UT. *Theme:* Local history. *Sponsor:* Utah National Parks Council, BSA, P.O. Box 106, 250 W. 500 N., Provo, UT 84603-0106, (801) 373-4185.

Length: 35 miles (straight). *Route:* The trail begins at the Old Spanish Trail Monument near Newcastle, through Holt Canyon and Mountain Meadows to Rancho Veyo, and along SR 18 to end in Veyo. *Terrain:* Mountainous. *Cycling:* Not recommended. *Awards:* Medal $4.00; Patch $0.75; Powderhorn Pin $0.75. *Submit:* Group leader's certification of completion of hike, overnight camping and required reading, plus written report. *Register:* Not required. *Sites:* Old Spanish Trail Monument, Pilot Peak, Jefferson Hunt Monument, Ox Shoeing Stalls, Mountain Meadows Monument, Santa Clara River.

Otto Fife Zion Narrows Trail

Location: Zion National Park, UT. *Theme:* Recreation. *Sponsor:* Utah National Parks Council, BSA, P.O. Box 106, 250 W. 500 N., Provo, UT 84603-0106, (801) 373-4185.

Length: Varies. *Route:* The award requires two overnight backpacks through the Zion Narrows, camping in the Grotto area. *Terrain:* Woods. *Cycling:* Not recommended. *Awards:* Patch. *Submit:* Group leader's certification of completion of hikes, overnight camping, and pre-approved good turn project. *Register:* In advance.

Pony Express Trail Award

Location: Anywhere along route of historic Pony Express Trail. *Theme:* Historic route. *Sponsor:* Utah National Parks Council, BSA, P.O. Box 106, 250 W. 500 N., Provo, UT 84603-0106, (801) 373-4185.

Length: 30 miles (loop or straight). *Route:* For the award, hikers must travel at least 30 miles along a portion of the historic route (need not be in Utah). *Terrain:* Varies. *Cycling:* Not recommended. *Awards:* Medal and Patch $5.00. *Submit:* Group leader's certification of completion, plus report on history of the Pony Express. *Register:* Not required.

Rainbow Canyon Hiking Award

Location: Zion National Park, UT. *Theme:* Recreation. *Sponsor:* Utah National Parks Council, BSA, P.O. Box 106, 250 W. 500 N., Provo, UT 84603-0106, (801) 373-4185.

Length: 9-20 miles. **Routes:** Three routes—West Rim, Arches, and Narrows, all in Zion National Park. **Terrain:** Rugged. **Cycling:** Not recommended. **Awards:** Patch $1.80; 3 Segments $0.75 each. **Submit:** Group leader's certification of completion. **Register:** Upon arrival at Zion.

U.S. Mormon Battalion Trail

Location: Salt Lake City, UT. **Theme:** Volunteer unit in war with Mexico 1846-1848. **Sponsor:** Mormon Relations Office, 525 Foothill Blvd., Salt Lake City, UT 84113, (801) 582-6000.

Length: 15 miles (straight). **Route:** This trail award may be earned on any section of either the 2,000 mile trail from Council Bluffs, IA, to San Diego and Los Angeles, CA, or several return trails. **Terrain:** Varies. **Cycling:** Not permitted for awards. **Awards:** Patch $2.00. **Submit:** Group leader's certification of hike, overnight backpack, required reading and research, and visits to historic monuments and museums. **Register:** Not required.

Other Utah Awards

Boy Scout Tour Patch—Utah's National Monuments—Tour one of Cedar Breaks, Natural Bridges, Rainbow Natural Bridges, Timpanogos Cave, Dinosaur, Hovenweep or Pipe Spring National Monuments, view the video at the visitors center, report on the plants, geology and wildlife at the monument, and do something to improve the monument. Patch. Utah National Parks Council, BSA, P.O. Box 106, 250 W. 500 N., Provo, UT 84603-0106, (801) 373-4185.

Boy Scout Tour Patch—Utah's National Parks—Tour one of Arches, Bryce Canyon, Capitol Reef, Zion or Canyonlands National Parks, view the video at the visitors center, report on the plants, geology and wildlife in the park, and do something to improve the park. Patch. Utah National Parks Council, BSA, P.O. Box 106, 250 W. 500 N., Provo, UT 84603-0106, (801) 373-4185.

Sons of Utah Pioneers Award—Tour Sons of the Pioneers National Headquarters at 3301 E. 2920 S., Salt Lake City, UT 84109, (801) 484-4441. Patch $3.00. Utah National Parks Council, BSA, P.O. Box 106, 250 W. 500 N., Provo, UT 84603-0106, (801) 373-4185.

Formerly Sponsored Trails

Snake River Canoe Trip
Trail of the Bridgermen

VERMONT

Long Trail

Location: Runs the length of VT. **Theme:** Recreation. **Sponsor:** Green Mountain Club, Inc., Rt. 1, Box 650, Waterbury Center, VT 05677, (802) 244-7037.

Length: 270 miles (straight). **Route:** The trail follows the crest of the Green Mountains, from the junction of the Appalachian Trail and the VT/MA border in the south to the Canadian border near North Troy, VT. **Terrain:** Steep and rugged. **Cycling:** Not recommended. **Awards:** Patch $1.75. **Submit:** Written report of experiences on the trail. **Register:** Not required. **Sites:** Glastenbury Mountain (3748'), Green Mountain National Forest, Stratton Mountain (3936'), Bromley Mountain (3260'), Camel's Hump Forest Preserve, Peru Peak (3429'), Mt. Mansfield State Forest.

VIRGINIA

Appomattox Court House Historical Trail

Location: Appomattox Court House National Historical Park, VA. *Theme:* Location of Lee's surrender, ending the Civil War. *Sponsor:* Blue Ridge Mountain Council, BSA, 2131 Valley View Blvd., N.W., Roanoke, VA 24019-0606, (540) 265-0656.

Length: 6 miles (loop). *Route:* The trail begins and ends at the Visitor Center, and follows the "Appomattox History Trail" in the park. *Terrain:* Woods and roads. *Cycling:* Not recommended. *Awards:* Medal $6.00. *Submit:* Completed 25-item questionnaire. *Register:* Upon arrival at park. *Sites:* Visitor Center, McLean House, Surrender Triangle, Appomattox Wayside, Lee's Headquarters Site, Apple Tree Site, Sweeney Prizery Field, Confederate Cemetery, North Carolina Monument, Raine Monument, Grant's Headquarters Site.

Arlington National Cemetery Trail

Location: Arlington National Cemetery, Washington, DC. *Theme:* Graves of military leaders of the U.S. *Sponsor:* American Historical Trails, Inc., P.O. Box 769, Monroe, NC 28111-0769, (704) 289-1604, Carotrader@trellis.net.

Length: 8.0 miles (loop). *Route:* The trail begins and ends at the Visitor Center and follows the cemetery roads to visit several monuments and gravesites. *Terrain:* Paved roads. *Cycling:* Not recommended. *Awards:* Medal $6.50; Patch $2.25. *Submit:* Completed 24-item questionnaire. *Register:* Not required. *Sites:* Pan Am Flight 103 Marker, Iwo Jima Monument, Graves of the Unknowns, Arlington House, USS Maine Memorial, Iran Rescue Monument, Canadian Cross, Spanish American War Monument, USS Serpens Memorial, John F. Kennedy Grave, Chaplain's Hill.

Chatham and Old Towne Falmouth Historical Trail

Location: Falmouth, VA. *Theme:* Local history. *Sponsor:* Was Troop 849 BSA, P.O. Box 193, Thornburg, VA 22565; maps and patches are available at the visitor center in Fredericksburg.

Length: 8 miles (loop). *Route:* The trail begins at St. Clair Brooks Park, heads north along the Rappahannock River, through Falmouth, south to the park, then south to Chatham Manor, then back to the start. *Terrain:* Roads and woods. *Cycling:* Appropriate. *Awards:* Patch $3.00. *Submit:* Completed 4-item questionnaire. *Register:* Not required. *Sites:* Shelton Cottage, Union Church, Moncure Conway House, Chatham House, Cotton Warehouse, Surveyor's Office, Gordon Green Terrace, Payne House, Dunbar Kitchen, Master Hobby School, Counting House, Stone House, Belmont Estate, Barnes House, Temperance Tavern.

Fredericksburg Historic Trail

Location: Fredericksburg, VA. *Theme:* Local history. *Sponsor:* Boy Scout Troop 847, Tabernacle United Methodist Church, 7310-A Old Plank Rd., Fredericksburg, VA 22407.

Length: 5.0 miles (loop). *Route:* The trail begins at the Fredericksburg Visitor Center, loops through the city and includes the National Park Service Battlefield Visitor Center, and returns to the start. *Terrain:* City streets. *Cycling:* Appropriate. *Awards:* Medal $4.00; Patch $2.00; Cannon Tie Tac $2.00; Cannonball Tie Tac $1.50. *Submit:* Completed 32-item questionnaire. *Register:* Not required. *Sites:* Sentry Box, Wells House, Stone Warehouse, Rising Sun Tavern, James Monroe Museum, Kenmore Mansion, Hugh Mercer Apothecary Shop, Masonic Lodge, Town Hall and Market House, Old Auction Block, Mary Washington House, St. George's Church and Graveyard, Mary Washington Monument, Religious Freedom Monument, Hugh Mercer Monument, Brompton, Fredericksburg United Methodist Church, Martha Stevens House.

Fredericksburg and Spotsylvania National Military Park Trails

Location: Fredericksburg, Chancellorsville and Spotsylvania, VA. *Theme:* Civil War battles. *Sponsor:* Boy Scout Troop 847, Tabernacle United Methodist Church, 7310-A

Old Plank Rd., Fredericksburg, VA 22407. *Lengths:* Chancellorsville History Trail, 4 miles (loop). Gordon Flank Attack Trail, 2 miles (loop). Hazel Grove Trail, 1 mile (loop). Lee Drive Trail, 5 miles (straight). Spotsylvania Battlefield Trail, 7 miles (loop). Sunken Road Trail, 0.2 mile (loop). *Routes:* Sunken Road Trail begins and ends at the back of the Fredericksburg Battlefield Visitor Center. Lee Drive Trail begins 1 mile southwest of the Fredericksburg Battlefield Visitor Center, follows Lee Drive to the southeast, and ends at Prospect Hill. Hazel Grove Trail begins and ends 0.8 mile south of the Chancellorsville Battlefield Visitor Center, where the Chancellorsville History Trail begins and ends. Gordon Flank Attack Trail begins and ends at the Wilderness Battlefield Exhibit Shelter. Spotsylvania Court House Trail begins and ends at the Spotsylvania Battlefield Exhibit Shelter. *Terrain:* Woods and fields. *Cycling:* Not recommended. *Awards:* Patch $3.00. *Submit:* Completed questionnaires for trails aggregating at least 5 miles. *Register:* Not required. *Sites:* Landram House, Harrison House, Fairview Gunpits, Meade Pyramid, McCoull House, Chancellor Cemetery, Chancellorsville Inn, Prospect Hill, Stonewall Jackson Monument, Howison Hill, Lee Hill, Stevens House, Innis House, Kirkland Monument.

James Monroe Historical Trail

Location: Charlottesville, VA. *Theme:* James Monroe. *Sponsor:* American Historical Trails, Inc., P.O. Box 769, Monroe, NC 28111-0769, (704) 289-1604, Carotrader@trellis.net.

Length: 2-4 miles (loop). *Route:* After a guided tour of the Mansion and grounds, the trail begins at the gate across the road from the gift shop and heads toward (or up) Carter's Mountain. *Terrain:* Woods. *Cycling:* Not permitted. *Awards:* Patch $2.25. *Submit:* Completed 12-item questionnaire. *Register:* Not required. *Sites:* Ash Lawn-Highland, Gift Shop, James Monroe Statue, Carter's Mountain, Overseer's Cottage, Smoke House, Well House.

Jamestown Colony Trail

Location: Jamestown Island, VA. *Theme:* Oldest settlement. *Sponsor:* Colonial Virginia Council, BSA, 11725 Jefferson Ave., Newport News, VA 23606-1935, (804) 595-3356.

Length: 5.5 miles (loop). *Route:* The trail begins at the Visitor Center, passes through the Townsite, follows the Island Loop Drive, and returns to the start. *Terrain:* Road and footpath. *Cycling:* Appropriate for Island Loop Drive. *Awards:* Patch $2.25; Completing this and Yorktown Battlefield Trail qualifies the hiker for the Yorktown-Jamestown Trail Medal $4.00 and Patch $2.25. *Submit:* Completed 47-item questionnaire. *Register:* Not required. *Sites:* Long House Ruins, Jacquelin-Ambler Mansion Ruins, Sir George Yeardly Grave, Church Tower, Visitor Center Museum.

Lexington Historic Trail

Location: Lexington, VA. *Theme:* Local history. *Sponsor:* Boy Scout Troop 122, c/o Hebron Presbyterian Church, Rt. 1, Box 58, Staunton, VA 24401.

Length: 4 miles (loop). *Route:* The trail begins and ends at the Lexington Visitor Center, and includes stops in the city, Washington and Lee University, and Virginia Military Institute. *Terrain:* City streets. *Cycling:* Appropriate. *Awards:* Patch $3.00. *Submit:* Group leader's certification of completion, plus completed 105-item questionnaire. *Register:* Not required. *Sites:* Stonewall Jackson Cemetery, Courthouse Square, R.E. Lee Episcopal Chapel, Lee Chapel, VMI Chapel and Museum, Preston Library, Jackson House, George C. Marshall Research Library and Museum, Stonewall Jackson Statue, Lexington Presbyterian Church, Crozet Memorial.

Manassas National Battlefield Historical Trails

Location: Manassas, VA. *Theme:* Civil War battles. *Sponsor:* American Historical Trails, Inc., P.O. Box 769, Monroe, NC 28111-0769, (704) 289-1604, Carotrader@trellis.net. *Lengths:* First Manassas Trail - 9.1 miles (straight). Second Manassas Trail - 7.75 miles (straight)

Routes: The First Manassas Trail begins at the Visitors Center, loops to the northeast, and ends at the picnic area. The Second Manassas Trail begins at the picnic area, loops to the southwest, and ends at the Visitors Center. *Terrain:* Fields and roads. *Cycling:* Not recommended. *Awards:* Medal $6.00; 2 Patches $2.25 each. *Submit:* Completed 50-item questionnaire. *Register:*

Not required. *Sites:* Van Pelt House Ruins, Old Stone Bridge, Barnard E. Bee Monument, Carter House Ruins, Buck Hill Cannons, Old Stone House, First Bull Run Monument, Farm Ford, Second Bull Run Monument, Dogan House, Stonewall Jackson Statue, Hooe Family Cemetery, Col. Bartow Monument, Chinn House Ruins, Groveton Cemetery Monument, Hood's Attack Mural.

Mount Vernon Historical Trail

Location: Mount Vernon, VA. *Theme:* Home of George and Martha Washington. *Sponsor:* The Mount Vernon Ladies' Association, Mount Vernon, VA 22121, (703) 780-2000.
Length: 1.5 miles (loop). *Route:* The trail begins at the fee entrance, circles the home, outbuildings and the grounds, and returns to the start. *Terrain:* Improved walkways. *Cycling:* Not recommended. *Awards:* Patch $2.50; Tomb Pin $2.00; Reading Pin $2.00; Surveying Patch $2.50; GW Pin $2.00. *Submit:* No requirement for Historical Trail Patch; extra requirements for other awards. *Register:* Not required. *Sites:* Washington's Mansion, Stable, Museum and Annex, Smokehouse, Lower and Upper Gardens, Wharf, Slave Burial Ground, Tomb of George and Martha Washington, Mount Vernon Inn.

Old Dominion Trail

Location: Richmond, VA. *Theme:* Local history. *Sponsor:* Robert E. Lee Council, BSA, 4075 Fitzhugh Ave., Richmond, VA 23230-3935, (804) 355-4306.
Length: 7.5 miles (straight). *Route:* The trail begins at St. John's Church at 24th and Broad Sts., and heads westward to end at Maymont Park. *Terrain:* City streets. *Cycling:* Appropriate. *Awards:* Patch $1.25. *Submit:* No requirement. *Register:* Not required. *Sites:* St. John's Church, Old Bell Tower, Egyptian Building, Governor's Mansion, Virginia State Capitol, Monroe Park, George Washington Statue, Hollywood Cemetery, Byrd Park.

"Old Town" Alexandria Historical Trail

Location: Alexandria, VA. *Theme:* Local history. *Sponsor:* American Historical Trails, Inc., P.O. Box 769, Monroe, NC 28111-0769, (704) 289-1604, Carotrader@trellis.net.
Length: 8 miles (loop). *Route:* The trail

begins at the Ramsay House, winds through the streets of Alexandria, and returns to the start. *Terrain:* City streets. *Cycling:* Appropriate. *Awards:* Medal $5.00; Patch $2.00. *Submit:* Completed 50-item questionnaire. *Register:* Not required. *Sites:* Bank of Alexandria, Carlyle House, Lee-Fendall House, Dalton House, E. Jennings Lee House, R.E. Lee House, General Harry Lee House, Flounder House, Anne Lee Memorial Home, Gadsby's Tavern, Friendship Fire House, Anthenaeum, Dr. Elisha Dick House, Old Apothecary Shop.

Petersburg National Battlefield Trail

Location: Petersburg, VA. *Theme:* Civil War Battle. *Sponsor:* Eastern National Bookstore, Petersburg National Battlefield, 1539 Hickory Hill Rd., Petersburg, VA 23803, (804) 732-6094.
Length: 10.0 miles (loop). *Route:* The trail begins at the Visitor Center and follows tour roads south through the battlefield, taking side trails into the woods before returning to the Visitor Center. *Terrain:* Roads and dirt trails. *Cycling:* Not appropriate. *Awards:* Patch $2.50 plus $1.00 S&H. *Submit:* Completed 32-item questionnaire. *Register:* Not required. *Sites:* The Dictator, Fort Haskell, Powder Magazine, The Crater, Fort Stedman, Battery 9, Spring Garden, Gracies Dam.

Washington and Lee Trail

Location: Mount Vernon to Alexandria, VA. *Theme:* George Washington and Robert E. Lee. *Sponsor:* American Historical Trails, Inc., P.O. Box 769, Monroe, NC 28111-0769, (704) 289-1604, Carotrader@trellis.net.
Length: 22 miles (straight). *Route:* The trail begins at Mount Vernon, follows the George Washington Pkwy. northward, passes through Old Town Alexandria (where walkers or cyclists may switch to cars) and ends at Arlington National Cemetery. *Terrain:* City streets and paved bike path. *Cycling:* Appropriate. *Awards:* Patch $2.00. *Submit:* Completed questionnaire. *Register:* Not required. *Sites:* Arlington National Cemetery, Ramsay House, Forts Washington and Hunt, Old Apothecary Shop, Belle Haven Grove, Old Presbyterian Meeting House, Carlyle House, Gadsby's Tavern, Washington's Reconstructed Town House, Christ Church, Fort Ward Park, George

Washington National Masonic Memorial, Friendship Firehouse, Custis-Lee Mansion, Lee Corner.

Waynesboro Historic Trail

Location: Waynesboro, VA. *Theme:* Battle of Waynesboro—March 2, 1865. *Sponsor:* Stonewall Jackson Area Council, BSA, 801 Hopeman Pkwy., P.O. Box 813, Waynesboro, VA 22980, (804) 943-6675.

Length: 3 miles (loop). *Route:* The trail begins and ends at Constitution Park, and passes historic buildings and sites important in the "Last Valley Battle" of the Civil War. *Terrain:* City streets. *Cycling:* Appropriate. *Awards:* Patch $3.00. *Submit:* Completed 11-item questionnaire. *Register:* Not required. *Sites:* Harman Monument, Cook Building, Sharon Bookstore Building, Rose Hall Site, Coiner-Quesenberry House, Howard Plumb House, News-Virginian Building, Old Presbyterian Cemetery, Fishburne Military School.

Williamsburg Colonial Trail

Location: Williamsburg, VA. *Theme:* Colonial-era history. *Sponsor:* Colonial Virginia Council, BSA, 11725 Jefferson Ave., Newport News, VA 23606-1935, (804) 595-3356.

Length: 5 miles (loop). *Route:* The trail begins and ends at the College of William and Mary, and visits many sites in the restored area of Colonial Williamsburg. *Terrain:* City streets. *Cycling:* Not recommended. *Awards:* Patch $2.25. *Submit:* Completed 10-item questionnaire. *Register:* Not required. *Sites:* Bowden-Armistead House, John Blair House, Bruton Parish Church, George Wythe House, McKenzie Apothecary, Courthouse of 1770, Josiah Chowning's Tavern, Governor's Palace, Robertson's Windmill, Brick Kiln and Carpenter's Yard, Raleigh Tavern, King's Arms Tavern, The Capitol, The Public Gaol, Bassett Hall, Christiana Campbell's Tavern, Williamsburg Inn, Magazine and Guardhouse, Providence Hall.

Winchester Historic Trail

Location: Winchester, VA. *Theme:* Local history. *Sponsor:* Stonewall Jackson Area Council, BSA, 4075 Fitzhugh Ave., Richmond, VA 23230-3935, (804) 355-4306.

Length: 2.5-5.5 miles (loop). *Route:* The long version of the trail begins at the Winchester-Frederick County Visitor's Center, loops through the city, and returns to the start. The short version leaves the Visitor's Center by car, and is a walk from the Winchester Auto Park to the Rouss City Hall. *Terrain:* City streets. *Cycling:* Possible, but does not qualify for awards. *Awards:* Patch $3.00. *Submit:* Completed 32-item questionnaire. *Register:* Not required. *Sites:* Abram's Delight Museum, Mt. Hebron Cemetery, National Cemetery, Stonewall Jackson's Headquarters, Sheridan's Headquarters, Old Stone Church, Handley Library, Daniel Morgan's Home, Old Frederick County Courthouse, Rouss Fire Hall, Rouss City Hall, George Washington's Office Museum, Hexagon House.

Yorktown Battlefield Trail

Location: Yorktown, VA. *Theme:* Battle which ended Revolutionary War. *Sponsor:* Colonial Virginia Council, BSA, 11725 Jefferson Ave., Newport News, VA 23606-1935, (804) 595-3356.

Length: 9-12.5 miles (loop). *Route:* The trail begins at the Visitor Center, circles the battlefield, and returns to the start. *Terrain:* Paved roads. *Cycling:* Appropriate. *Awards:* Patch $2.25; Completing this and the Jamestown Colony Trail qualifies the hiker for the Yorktown-Jamestown Trail Medal $4.00 and Patch $2.25. *Submit:* Completed 19-item questionnaire. *Register:* Not required. *Sites:* Visitor Center Museum, Surrender Field, Reconstructed Redoubt, Washington Headquarters Painting, French Artillery Park, Beaver Dam Creek, Grand American Battery, Grand French Battery, National Cemetery.

Formerly Sponsored Trails

Jefferson Historical Trail
Virginia Trail

WASHINGTON

O'Neil Historic Hiking Trail

Location: Olympic National Park, WA. *Theme:* Route of 1890 expedition. *Sponsor:* T'Kope Kwiskwis Lodge No. 502, Chief Seattle Council, BSA, 3120 Rainier Ave. S., Seattle, WA 98144-6095, (206) 725-5200.

Length: 45.4 miles (straight). *Route:* The trail begins at Lake Cushman and heads upstream along the north branch of the Skokomish River, cross-country through the O'Neil Pass, then downstream along the east fork of the Quinault River. *Terrain:* Rugged. *Cycling:* Not recommended. *Awards:* Patch. *Submit:* Journal of trip and essay. *Register:* At least 10 days in advance. *Sites:* Staircase Rapids, Duckabush River, Lake Cushman, Jumbo's Leap, O'Neil Pass, Home Sweet Home, Quinault River.

Formerly Sponsored Trails

Hartford Monte Cristo Gold Mines Trail
Press Expedition Trail

WEST VIRGINIA

Adahi Trail

Location: WV. *Theme:* Recreation. *Sponsor:* Tri-State Area Council, BSA, 733 7th Ave., Huntington, WV 25701-2110, (304) 523-3408; or Charles Dundas, Forest Ranger, (304) 736-2110.

Length: 20.4 miles. *Route:* Available from sponsor. *Terrain:* Hills and ridges. *Cycling:* Not permitted. *Awards:* Medal $3.50, Patch $3.00. *Submit:* Available from sponsor. *Register:* Available from sponsor.

Harpers Ferry Heritage Trail

Location: Downtown Harpers Ferry, WV (the lower city—do not confuse with national park located to the north). *Theme:* Civil War era people and events, with emphasis on abolitionist John Brown. *Sponsor:* Harpers Ferry Historical Association, Inc., P.O. Box 197, Shenandoah St., Harpers Ferry, WV 25425.

Length: 3 miles (loop). *Route:* The trail begins on the green directly across the street from the Information Center on Shenandoah St. After winding through the town, you proceed up steep Fillmore St. to the campus of former Storer College, then down a steep hillside to Virginius Island, then back to the Information Center. *Terrain:* Level city streets while in the lower city, but steep footpath, street and wooded trail for upper portion. *Cycling:* Impossible on footpath between lower city and Jefferson Rock, and between Storer Campus and Virginius Island (this is a portion of the Appalachian Trail that descends the face of a fairly steep cliff). *Awards:* Patch $2.95. *Submit:* Completed 32-item questionnaire. *Register:* Not required. *Sites:* Stagecoach Inn, Information Center, Provost Office, Dry Goods Store, Master Armorer's House, John Brown's Museum, John Brown's Fort, Arsenal Square, Whitehall Tavern, Civil War Story, Storer College, The Stone Steps, Harper House, St. Peter's Catholic Church, St. John's Episcopal Church, Jefferson Rock, Harper Cemetery, Lockwood House, Brackett House, Morrell House, Curtis Freewill Bap. Church, Mather Training Center, Savory Mill Ruins, Virginius Island Trail, Old Bridge, Armory Workers House, Intake Arches, Water Tunnels, Cotton Mill Ruins, Flood Story.

Kanawha Trace

Location: Barboursville to Fraziers Bottom, WV. *Theme:* Recreation. *Sponsor:* Tri-State Area Council, BSA, 733 7th Ave., Huntington, WV 25701-2110, (304) 523-3408; or Charles Dundas, Forest Ranger, (304) 736-2110.

Length: 31.68 miles (straight). *Route:* The trail begins at the junction of Merritts Creek Rd. and Mud River Rd. at the confluence of the Mud and Guyandotte Rivers near Barboursville and ends at the junction of Stave Branch Rd. and US 35 (Sider's Country Store) in Fraziers Bottom. *Terrain:* Hills and ridges, with 5.41 miles on paved roads and 4.93 on unpaved roads. *Cycling:* Not permitted. *Awards:* Medal $3.50; Patch $3.00.

Submit: Available from sponsor. *Register:* Available from sponsor. *Sites:* Newman Cabin, Old Wagon Road, Teays Valley, Blue Sulphur Community, Tag Hollow, Gobbler Knob, Blackjack School, Bear Hollow Creek.

Formerly Sponsored Trails

Mountaineer Capitol Trail
Nitro Historical Trail

WISCONSIN

Circus Heritage Trail

Location: Baraboo, WI. *Theme:* Circus Heritage Weekend. *Sponsor:* Baraboo Circus Heritage, Four Lakes Council, BSA, 34 Schroeder Ct., Madison, WI 53711, (608) 273-1005.

Length: Contact the sponsor for the length for a specific year. *Route:* The trail begins at the county fairgrounds on the edge of town and, after an overnight campout, proceeds to the Circus World Museum. *Terrain:* City streets. *Cycling:* Not recommended. *Awards:* Patch $11.50 (includes fee for camping and other events). *Submit:* No requirement. *Register:* In advance—this is an annual event, held each May. *Sites:* Ringling Brothers Home, Circus World Museum, Sauk County Fairgrounds, Scouting Museum.

Devil's Lake Trail

Location: Baraboo, WI. *Theme:* Recreation. *Sponsor:* Badger Trails, Inc., P.O. Box 210615, Milwaukee, WI 53221, (414) 789-9615, info@badgertrails.org, www.badgertrails.org.

Length: 14.0 miles. *Route:* This follows the route of some of the shorter trails at Devil's Lake State Park. Check with the sponsor to find out which ones. *Terrain:* Woods and open areas. *Cycling:* Some of the trails in the park allow cycling. *Awards:* Patch $1.00. *Submit:* Available from sponsor. *Register:* At least two weeks in advance. *Sites:* Devil's Lake, Balanced Rock, East Bluff Woods, Tumbled Rocks.

Eagle Cave Trails

Location: Eagle Cave Natural Park, Blue River, WI. *Theme:* Recreation, especially caving. *Sponsor:* Eagle Cave Natural Park, Inc., Rt. 2, Box 84, Blue River, WI 53518, (608) 537-2988. *Lengths:* Arrowhead Trail, 4 miles, Blackhawk Trail, 3 miles, 16 Compass Trails, Eagle Cave Trail, 5 miles, Gold Nugget Trail, 2 miles, Mountain Goat Trail, 2.5 miles, Old Stage Line Trail, 10 miles. *Routes:* There are 6 hiking and 16 compass trails, covering various routes. Also available is a Nightmare-a-thon and overnight cave camping. *Terrain:* Mostly woods. *Cycling:* Not recommended. *Awards:* Patches. *Submit:* No requirement. *Register:* In advance for overnight cave camping. *Sites:* Wisconsin's Largest Onyx Cave, Wisconsin River, Little Blackhawk Lake.

Ice Age National Scenic Trail

Location: Winds throughout WI. *Theme:* Recreation. *Sponsor:* National Park Service, Ice Age National Scenic Trail, 700 Rayovac Dr., Suite 100, Madison, WI 53711, (608) 264-5610.

Length: 1,000 miles (straight). *Route:* The trail zigzags across the state from Lake Michigan to the St. Croix River. *Terrain:* Chain of glacial moraine hills. *Cycling:* Not recommended. *Awards:* None. *Submit:* Not applicable. *Register:* Not required. *Sites:* Chequamegon National Forest, Sleeping Bear Dunes National Lakeshore, St. Croix National Scenic River, Lake Michigan.

Kettle Moraine Glacial Trail

Location: Kettle Moraine State Forest Northern Unit, WI. *Theme:* Glacial formations. *Sponsor:* Badger Trails, Inc., P.O. Box 210615, Milwaukee, WI 53221, (414) 789-9615, info@badgertrails.org, www.badgertrails.org.

Length: 18.0 miles. *Route:* The trail begins at the Old Wade House in Greenbush, follows blue and white blazes on trees and posts, and ends at the Mauthe Lake Recreation Area. *Terrain:* Dense woods and open meadows. *Cycling:* Not appropriate. *Awards:* Medal $5.00; Patch $1.75; Segments (Geological, Historical, Backpack) $1.00 each; Repeat Pins (2nd Kettle, 3rd Esker, 4th Kames) $1.50 each; Lapel Pin $1.50; Medalion Slide $3.00. *Submit:* Patch order form and completed 10-item questionnaire. *Register:* Not required, except for annual Glacial Trail Backpack Event. *Sites:* Old Wade House, Moraine Hills, Parnell Esker, Butler Lake, Dundee Hill, Crooked Lake, Forest Lake.

Marquette Trail

Location: Portage, WI. *Theme:* History of the area. *Sponsor:* Joshua A. Halasz, 104 E. Wisconsin St., Portage, WI 53901.

Length: 11.0 miles (straight) or 16.0 miles (loop). *Route:* The trail begins at Governor's Bend Locks, heads to the Indian Agency House, then along an old canal and the Wauona Trail to the site of Fort Winnebago. *Terrain:* Woods and dirt paths. *Cycling:* Not appropriate. *Awards:* Medal; Patch. *Submit:* Request for patches. *Register:* Not required. *Sites:* Governor's Bend Locks, Indian Agency House, Old Surgeons Quarters, Wisconsin River.

Milwaukee History Trail

Location: Milwaukee, WI. *Theme:* Local history. *Sponsor:* Milwaukee History Trail, 9711 W. Metcalf Pl., Milwaukee, WI 53222, (414) 461-7107.

Length: 10 miles (loop). *Route:* The trail begins and ends at the Mitchell Park Domes, and winds through most of the downtown area. *Terrain:* City streets. *Cycling:* Appropriate. *Awards:* Patch $2.00. *Submit:* No requirement. *Register:* Advance registration encouraged. *Sites:* Frederick Pabst Mansion, Marquette University, Joan of Arc Chapel, Journal Building, Brooks Memorial Union, Milwaukee County Historical Society Center, Memorial Clock Tower, Milwaukee Museum, Old St. Mary's Catholic Church, Tower Clock, Milwaukee School of Engineering, Milwaukee County War Memorial Center, Alexander Mitchell Mansion.

Ozaukee Historic "76" Bike Trail

Location: Ozaukee County, WI. *Theme:* Local history. *Sponsor:* Thomas E. Weigend, 11511 N.E. Gate Dr., 52W, Mequon, WI 53092-2002, (414) 242-3759.

Length: 76 miles (loop). *Route:* The trail begins near SR 167, south of Thiensville, heads north through Grafton and Saukville, then west to Port Washington, northwest to Fredonia, southwest to Newburg, then south through Cedarburg back to the start. *Terrain:* Roads. *Cycling:* Appropriate. *Awards:* Discontinued. *Submit:* Not applicable. *Register:* Not required. *Sites:* Milwaukee River, Otto H. Bublitz Home, Old Thiensville Village Hall, Old Firemen's Hall, Van Buren School, Thiensville Park, Mee-Kwon Park, Valentine Hahn House, Erhardt G. Wurthmann Home, Cedar Creek Rapids, Grafton Lime Kilns, Milwaukee River Falls, Grafton Woolen Mill, Union Cemetery, St. Mary's Cemetery Chapel, Ozaukee County Courthouse, Port Washington Harbor, Waubeka Mill, . Stony Hill School House, St. Finbar's Cemetery

Root River Trail

Location: Greendale, WI. *Theme:* Recreation. *Sponsor:* Badger Trails, Inc., P.O. Box 210615, Milwaukee, WI 53221, (414) 789-9615, info@badgertrails.org, www.badgertrails.org.

Length: 12.5 to 15 miles. *Route:* Depends on route chosen. *Terrain:* Bike trail. *Cycling:* Possible, but probably prohibited on annual event. *Awards:* Patch $3.00. *Submit:* Request for patches. *Register:* On the morning of the annual event, no registration required at other times. *Sites:* Scout Lake, Whitnall Park, Greenfield Park.

Sinipee Trail

Location: Kieler to Potosi, WI (1 mile north of Dubuque, IA). *Theme:* Indian Mounds. *Sponsor:* Leonard Ihm, P.O. Box 105, Kieler, WI 53812, (608) 568-7731.

Length: About 15 miles (straight). *Route:* Proceed west past the Kieler water tower for

1/2 mile to find the trail markers and a campsite. Follow the markers roughly north across the Platte River and along the railroad track to the campsite at Engineer Park, southeast of Potosi. *Terrain:* Timbered hills. *Cycling:* Not permitted. *Awards:* Patch $3.25. *Submit:* Request for patches. *Register:* In advance. *Sites:* Upper Mississippi Wildlife and Fish Refuge, Platte River, Indian Creek, Finely's Point, Engineer Park, Mississippi River, Indian Mounds.

Other Wisconsin Awards

Wisconsin Century Club Award—Patch

$3.00 for completion of hikes aggregating 100 miles. Sponsored by Badger Trails, Inc., P.O. Box 210615, Milwaukee, WI 53221, (414) 789-9615, info@badgertrails.org, www.badgertrails.org.

Formerly Sponsored Trails

Good Turn Trail
Grotto Pilgrimage Trail
Rib Mountain Trail
Tomahawk Trail
Trumpeter Trail Hike
Wabeno Lumberjack Trail
Wisconsin River Trail

WYOMING

Formerly Sponsored Trails

Mountain Men Hike
Pony Pack
Snake River Canoe Trek
Teton Trail

INTERSTATE TRAILS

Appalachian National Scenic Trail

Location: GA, NC, TN, VA, WV, PA, NJ, NY, CT, MA, VT, NH, ME. *Theme:* Recreation. *Sponsor:* Appalachian Trail Conference, Inc., P.O. Box 807, Washington & Jackson Sts., Harpers Ferry, WV 25425-0807, (304) 535-6331.

Length: 2,135 miles (straight). *Route:* The trail endpoints are Springer Mountain, GA, and Mt. Katahdin, ME. The trail passes near Asheville, NC, Roanoke, VA, Harpers Ferry, WV, and Harrisburg, PA. *Terrain:* Mountainous. *Cycling:* Not recommended. *Awards:* Patch $1.85. *Submit:* No requirement. *Register:* Not required. *Sites:* Nantahala National Forest, Great Smoky Mountains National Park, Pisgah National Forest, Cherokee National Forest, Chattahoochee National Forest, Jefferson National Forest, Delaware Water Gap National Recreation Area, George Washington National Forest, Green Mountain National Forest, White Mountain National Forest.

Bartram Trail

Location: FL, AL, GA, MS, SC, NC, TN. *Theme:* Travel route of William Bartram 1773–1777. *Sponsor:* The Bartram Trail Conference, 430 E. 50th St., Savannah, GA 31405, (912) 652-5766 or fax (912) 652-5787; or North Carolina Bartram Trail Society, P.O. Box 144, Scaly Moun-tain, NC 28775.

Length: 2,550 miles (straight). *Route:* The actual route is being located and documented within a corridor which reaches south through central North Carolina to the Atlantic Ocean, then south along the coast to Savannah. One branch then heads south along the coast into Florida, splitting near DeLand to go to Melbourne and the Gulf of Mexico. The second branch heads north-west from Savannah along the Savannah River, and branches halfway to Tennessee, with one portion ending near Chattanooga. The other portion heads southwest through central Georgia and Alabama, and west through southern Mississippi to end near Baton Rouge, Louisiana. *Terrain:* Varies. *Cycling:* Not recommended. *Awards:* None. *Submit:* Not applicable. *Register:* Not required

Benton MacKaye Trail

Location: GA and TN. *Theme:* Recreation. *Sponsor:* Benton MacKaye Trail Association, P.O. Box 53271, Atlanta, GA 30355-1271, (404) 641-9819.

Length: 250 miles (straight)—only the GA section is complete. *Route:* The trail begins in Georgia at Springer Mountain, which is also the start of the Appalachian Trail. The Georgia section goes 78.6 miles to Double Spring Gap on the Tennessee border in the Cohutta Wilderness Area. When complete, it will pass through the Cherokee National Forest to rejoin the Appalachian Trail in the Great Smoky Mountains National Park in Tennessee. *Terrain:* Mountainous. *Cycling:* Not recommended. *Awards:* Patch $5.50; Pin $5.00. *Submit:* No requirement. *Register:* Not required. *Sites:* Fowler Mountain, Flat Top Mountain, Brawley Mountain, Rhodes Mountain, Toccoa River, Long Creek.

California National Historic Trail.

Location: MO, KS, NE, WY, UT, ID, NV, CA, OR. *Theme:* Historical pioneer route. *Sponsor:* Oregon-California Trail Association, P.O. Box 1019, Independence, MO 64051, (816) 252-2276.

Length: Not yet determined. *Route:* When complete, it will stretch from Omaha, NE, westward through southern WY and northern UT, and NE, to branch into northern CA and western OR. *Terrain:* Varies. *Cycling:* Not recommended. *Awards:* None. *Submit:* No requirement. *Register:* Not required. *Sites:* Scotts Bluff Fort National Monument, Laramie National Historic Site, Caribou National Forest, Wasatch National Forest, City of Rocks National Reserve, Humboldt National Forest, Eldorado National Forest, Stanislaus National Forest, Plumas National Forest, Lassen Volcanic National Park, Lassen National Forest, Modoc National Forest

Continental Divide National Scenic Trail

Location: MT, ID, WY, CO, NM. *Theme:* Recreation. *Sponsor:* Continental Divide Trail Society, P.O. Box 30002, Bethesda, MD 20824, (410) 235-9610.

Length: 3,000 miles (straight) when completed. *Route:* The trail endpoints are the boundary of southern New Mexico and Mexico, and the boundary of Montana, British Columbia and Alberta in Glacier National Park. *Terrain:* Mountains. *Cycling:* Not recommended. *Awards:* Patch $4.00. *Submit:* No requirement. *Register:* Not required. *Sites:* Glacier National Park, Flathead National Forest, Helena National Forest, Teton National Forest, Routt National Forest, Beaverhead National Forest, Yellowstone National Park, Big Hole National Monument, El Malpais National Monument, White River National Forest, Pike National Forest, Roosevelt National Forest, Gila National Forest, Rocky Mountain National Park, Arapaho National Forest, Targhee National Forest, Lewis and Clark National Forest, Bridger National Forest.

Juan Batista De Anza National Historic Trail

Location: AZ and CA. *Theme:* Local history. *Sponsor:* United States Department of the Interior, National Park Service, Western Region, 600 Harrison St., Suite 600, San Francisco, CA 94107-1372.

Length: In planning stages. *Route:* The trail begins at the Tumacacori National Historic Park at the border of Arizona and Mexico, heads west to the southern border of California, northwest to Los Angeles, and northwest to San Francisco. *Terrain:* Varies. *Cycling:* Not recommended. *Awards:* None. *Submit:* Not applicable. *Register:* Not required. *Sites:* Tumacacori National Historical Park, Anza-Borrego Desert State Park, Tubac Presidio State Historic Park, San Bernardino National Forest, Golden Gate National Recreation Area, Santa Monica Mountains National Recreation Area, Angeles National Forest.

Lewis and Clark National Historic Trail

Location: Wood River, IL to Ecola State Park, OR. *Theme:* Route of Lewis and Clark in 1804-06. *Sponsor:* Lewis and Clark Trail Heritage Foundation, P.O. Box 577, Bozeman, MT 59715.

Length: Being established (original expedition covered more than 8,000 miles). *Route:* The trail heads westward along the following rivers Missouri, Yellowstone, Snake and Columbia. There are also land and motor routes along some portions. *Terrain:* Mostly rivers, some mountain and roads. *Cycling:* Not recommended. *Awards:* None. *Submit:* Not applicable. *Register:* Not required. *Sites:* Pompeys Pillar, Upper Missouri National Wild and Scenic River, North Dakota Heritage Center, Fort Mandan, Fort Union National Historic Site, Rainbow Falls, Fort Clatsop, Arrow Rock State Historic Site, Fort Osage, Ionia Volcano, Calumet Bluff, Four Bears Park, Fort Benton, Square Butte, The Dalles

Metacomet-Monadnock Trail

Location: Southwick, MA to Mt. Monadnock, NH. *Theme:* Recreation. *Sponsor:* Patrick Fletcher, Chairman, AMC Berkshire Trails Committee, 20 Linda Dr., Westfield, MA 01085; or New England Trail Conference, 33 Knollwood Dr., East Longmeadow, MA 01028.

Length: 98 miles (straight). *Route:* The Metacomet Trail enters Massachusetts from Connecticut near Southwick, where it becomes the Metacomet-Monadnock Trail. It heads north, parallel to the Connecticut River to Mt. Tom, then heads east to traverse the Holyoke Range, and turns north to end at Mt. Monadnock to connect with the Monadnock-Sunapee Greenway. *Terrain:* Mountainous. *Cycling:* Not recommended. *Awards:* Patch. *Submit:* No requirement. *Register:* Not required. *Sites:* Mt. Monadnock, Mt. Tom, Mt. Grace State Forest, Skinner State Forest, Holyoke Range State Park, Wendell State Forest, Erving State Forest.

Mormon Pioneer National Historic Trail

Location: IL, IA, NE, WY and UT. *Theme:* Route of Mormon pioneers in the late 1840's. *Sponsor:* National Park Service, Rocky Mountain Regional Office, P.O. Box 25287, 12795 W. Alameda Pkwy., Denver, CO 80225, (303) 969-2828.

Length: 1,300 miles (straight). *Route:* The trail begins in Nauvoo, IL, and heads westward through Council Bluffs, IA, Omaha, Grand Island, North Platte and Scottsbluff, NE, and Casper, WY, to end in Salt Lake City, UT. *Terrain:* Varies. *Cycling:* Appropriate in some sections. *Awards:* None. *Submit:* Not applicable. *Register:* Not required. *Sites:* Lacey-Keosauqua State Park, Ash Hollow State Historical Park, Nauvoo Historic District, Garden Grove, Scotts Bluff National Monument, Register Cliff, Mount Pisgah, Wayne County Historical Museum, Rebecca Winters Grave, Mormon Trail Park, Willie's Handcart Disaster Site, Independence Rock, Little Emigration Church, Donner Hill, Chimney Rock, Split Rock, Ayres Natural Bridge Park, The Needles.

Natchez Trace National Scenic Trail

Location: Natchez, MS to Nashville, TN. *Theme:* Historic Indian route. *Sponsor:* United States Department of the Interior, National Park Service, Southeast Regional Office, 75 Spring St. N.W., Atlanta, GA 30303.

Length: 449 miles (straight). *Route:* The Natchez Trace Parkway, plus 825-foot wide corridor begins in Natchez, MS, and passes by Jackson and Tupelo, MS, on the route to Nashville, TN. *Terrain:* Forests, prairie, paved parkway. *Cycling:* Appropriate on parkway. *Awards:* None. *Submit:* Not applicable. *Register:* Not required. *Sites:* Ross Barnett Reservoir, Water Valley, Gordon House, Butler Ridge, Garrison Creek, Rocky Springs, Emerald Mound, Mount Locust, Coles Creek.

Nez Perce National Historic Trail

Location: Wallowa Lake, OR to Chinook, MT. *Theme:* Route used by nontreaty Nez Perce Indians fleeing U.S. Army in 1877. *Sponsor:* U.S. Department of Agriculture, Forest Service, Federal Bldg., P.O. Box 7669, Missoula, MT 59807.

Length: 1,170 miles (straight). *Route:* The trail begins at Wallowa Lake, follows the Lolo Trail through the Lolo Pass, south to Big Hole and Camas Meadows, north to Canyon Creek, Cow Island Landing and the Bears Paw Mountains, where the Nez Perce surrendered. *Terrain:* Mountains and forests. *Cycling:* Not recommended. *Awards:* None. *Submit:* Not applicable. *Register:* Not required. *Sites:* Yellowstone National Park, Whitebird Battlefield, Nez Perce Indian Reservation, Lolo Pass, Bears Paw Battlefield.

North Country National Scenic Trail

Location: NY, PA, OH, MI, WI, MN and ND. *Theme:* Recreation. *Sponsor:* North Country Trail Association, P.O. Box 311, White Cloud, MI 49349, (231) 689-1912.

Length: Approx. 3,200 miles (straight) when completed. *Route:* The eastern endpoint is Port Henry, in eastern New York. The trail heads westward and southward to follow much of the Buckeye Trail in southern and western Ohio, then northward through western Michigan, westward along the southern shore of Lake Superior, and continuing westward to Lake Sakakawea in Central North Dakota. *Terrain:* Varies. *Cycling:* Not recommended. *Awards:* Patch $3.00; Volunteer Strip $2.50; State Strips (NY, PA, OH, MI, WI, MN, ND) $1.50 each; Distance Strips (5, 10, 15, 20, 25 or 35 miles in one day) $1.50. *Submit:* No requirement. *Register:* Not required. *Sites:* Allegheny National Forest, Fort Stanwix National Monument, Wayne National Forest, Ottawa National Forest, St. Croix National Scenic Riverway, Manistee National Forest, Grand Lake St. Marys National Monument, Mound City Group, Hiawatha National Forest, Chippewa National Forest, Pictured Rocks National Seashore, Fort Ranso, Sheyenne

National Grassland, Father Marquette National Memorial, Fort Totten Historic Site.

Oregon National Historic Trail

Location: Independence, MO to Portland, WA. *Theme:* Approximate route used by nearly 400,000 people in the 1800's. *Sponsor:* Forest Service/National Park Service, Outdoor Recreation Information Center, 915 Second Ave., Rm. 442, Seattle, WA 98174.

Length: 2,170 miles (straight). *Route:* The trail heads northwestward generally along the following rivers Kansas, Little Blue, Platte, North Platte, Sweetwater, Green, Snake, Burnt, Umatilla and Columbia. *Terrain:* Varies. *Cycling:* Not recommended. *Awards:* None. *Submit:* Not appropriate. *Register:* Not required. *Sites:* St. Mary's Mission, Blue Mound, Scott Spring, Wagon Ruts, George Winslow Grave, Susan Hail Grave, Simonton-Smith Grave, Fort Kearny, Fort McPherson, O'Fallons Bluff, Amanda Lamme Grave, Register Cliff, Independence Rock, Scotts Bluff National Monument, Ayres Natural Bridge, South Pass, Chimney Rock National Historic Site, The Dalles, Three Island Crossing, Fort Laramie National Monument, Whitman Mission, Flagstaff Hill, Barlow Pass.

Overmountain Victory National Historic Trail

Location: Abingdon, VA to Kings Mountain National Military Park, SC. *Theme:* Route of American army to Battle of Kings Mountain in 1780. *Sponsor:* United States Department of the Interior, National Park Service, Southeast Regional Office, 75 Spring St. S.W., Atlanta, GA 30303.

Length: 220 miles (straight). *Route:* There are 3 designated routes (1) the true historic route, now often inaccessible, (2) a route used annually by the Overmountain Victory Trail Association, and (3) a commemorative motor route over highways passing through Abingdon and Bristol, VA, Elizabethton, TN, Wilkesboro, Lenoir, Morganton and Rutherfordton, NC, and Chesnee and Gaffney, SC. *Terrain:* Mountains, roads. *Cycling:* Recommended on commemorative motor route only. *Awards:* None. *Submit:* Not applicable. *Register:* Not required. *Sites:* Pemberton Oak, Rocky Mount State Historic Site, Roan Mountain State Park, Dunn's Meadow, Gap Creek Monument, Fort Watauga Monument, Carter Mansion, Wilkes Community College, Tory Oak, Doe River Gorge, Fort Defiance, Yellow Mountain Gap, McDowell House, Alexander's Ford, Gillespie Gap Mineral Museum, Cowpens National Battlefield, Brittain Church, Cherokee Ford.

Pacific Crest National Scenic Trail

Location: CA, OR and WA. *Theme:* Recreation. *Sponsor:* Pacific Crest Trail Association, 5325 Elkhorn Blvd., Suite 256, Sacramento, CA 95842-2526, (800) 817-2243.

Length: 2,638 miles (straight). *Route:* The trail begins at the Mexican border near Campo, CA, and heads north near Bakersfield and Redding, CA, Ashland and Portland, OR, and Seattle, WA, to end at the Canadian border near Glacier Peak. *Terrain:* Mountainous. *Cycling:* Not permitted. *Awards:* Patch $3.00; completion certificate for hiking the entire length. *Submit:* No requirement. *Register:* Not required. *Sites:* Sequoia National Park, Devil's Postpile National Monument, Mt. Rainier National Park, Marble Mountain Wilderness, Desolation Wilderness, Goat Rocks Wilderness, Anza Borrego Desert State Park, San Jacinto National Forest, Yosemite National Park, Lassen National Forest

Pacific Northwest Trail

Location: MT, ID and WA. *Theme:* Recreation. *Sponsor:* Pacific Northwest Trail, P.O. Box 1048, Seattle, WA 98111.

Length: 1,110 miles (straight) when completed. *Route:* The trail's endpoints are Brown Pass, on the MT/BC/AB border, and Cape Alava, in the northwest corner of WA. The route generally follows and is south of the U.S./ Canada border. *Terrain:* Mountains, forests, sagelands, tide pools. *Cycling:* Not recommended. *Awards:* Patch $4.00 (SASE required). *Submit:* No requirement. *Register:* Not required, but purchase of the $15 guidebook on a Wordperfect 6.1 diskette would be helpful. *Sites:* Ten Lakes Scenic Area, Glacier National Park, Salmo-Priest Wilderness, Mt. Henry Wilderness (proposed), North Cascades National Park, Pasayten Wilderness, Olympic National Park.

Pony Express National Historic Trail

Location: MO, KS, NE, CO, WY, UT, NV, CA. *Theme:* Route of original Pony Express. *Sponsor:* National Pony Express Association,

1002 Jenkins St., Marysville, KS 66508, (785) 562-3615.

Length: Not yet determined. **Route:** When complete, it will begin in Omaha, NE, and stretch westward through Casper, WY, to end in Salt Lake City, UT. **Terrain:** Varies. **Cycling:** Not recommended. **Awards:** None. **Submit:** No requirement. **Register:** Not required. **Sites:** Scotts Bluff National Monument, Fort Larned National Historic Site, Wasatch National Forest.

Potomac Heritage National Scenic Trail

Location: Chesapeake Bay, VA to Laurel Highlands, PA. **Theme:** Recreation. **Sponsor:** U.S. Department of the Interior, National Park Service, National Capital Region, 1100 Ohio Dr., SW, Washington, DC 20242.

Length: 704 miles (straight) corridor made up of segments located within the boundaries of federally administered areas. **Route:** As of 1994, the three segments were the C & O Canal Towpath from Georgetown in Washington, DC to Cumberland, MD (184 miles); the Mount Vernon Trail from Washington, DC to Mount Vernon, VA (17 miles); and the Laurel Highlands National Recreation Trail in Pennsylvania (70 miles). **Terrain:** Varies. **Cycling:** Appropriate on some portions (Mount Vernon Trail is a paved bikepath). **Awards:** None. **Submit:** Not applicable. **Register:** Not required. **Sites:** George Washington Memorial Parkway, Chesapeake and Ohio Canal National Historic Park, Harpers Ferry National Historic Park, Potomac River.

Santa Fe National Historic Trail

Location: MO, KS, OK, CO, NM. **Theme:** Route of 19th century westward expansion. **Sponsor:** U.S. Department of the Interior, National Park Service, Southwest Region, P.O. Box 728, Santa Fe, NM 87504-0728.

Length: Approx. 1,200 miles (straight). **Route:** Both the Historic and Auto Tour Routes begin in Old Franklin, MO, and head southwestward through or near Kansas City, Council Grove, McPherson and Dodge City. Shortly thereafter, the trail forks, with the Mountain Route (909 miles) passing by Elkhart, KS, Boise City, OK, and Clayton,

NM, and the Cimarron Route (865 miles) passing Garden City, KS, La Junta, CO, and Cimarron, NM. The two forks reunite at Springer, NM, and head south and west to end at Santa Fe, NM. **Terrain:** Major highways (auto route); varies (historic route). **Cycling:** Appropriate on auto route. **Awards:** None. **Submit:** Not applicable. **Register:** Not required. **Sites:** Pecos National Historic Park, Bent's Old Fort National Historic Site, Fort Union National Monument, Kiowa National Grassland, Fort Larned National Historic Site, Fort Leavenworth, Cimarron National Grassland, Kaw Mission, Comanche National Grassland, Fort Aubry, Fort Mann Site, Fort Atkinson Site, Autograph Rock, Wagon Mound.

Trail of Tears National Historic Trail

Location: AL, AR, GA, IL, KY, MO, NC, OK, TN. **Theme:** Route of forced removal of Cherokees from Southeast in 1838-39. **Sponsor:** National Park Service, Southeast Region, 75 Spring St., SW, Atlanta, GA 30303.

Length: 2,219 miles (straight). **Route:** The Northern Route begins in Charleston, TN, heads north-west through Nashville, Hopkinsville, KY, the southern tip of Illinois, and Rolla, MO, then heads southwest through Springfield, MO, to end at Tahlequah, OK. Hildebrand's Route is the same, except for a bypass of Rolla. Bell's Route heads west from Charleston through Memphis, TN, and Fort Smith, AR, to end at Fort Gibson, OK. Benge's Route begins at Fort Payne, AL, heads northwest to near Cape Girardeau, MO, then south to Batesville, AR, and west to Tahlequah. Taylor's Route goes from Charleston to Chattanooga, TN. The Water Route begins in Chattanooga on the Tennessee River, heads northwest to the Mississippi River, then south to the Arkansas River, and west to OK just west of Fort Payne. **Terrain:** Varies. **Cycling:** Not recommended. **Awards:** None. **Submit:** Not applicable. **Register:** Not required. **Sites:** Andrew Ross Home, Hair Conrad Cabin, Ross's Landing, Fort Gibson, Fort Delaney, Fort Cass, Fort Hembree, Fort Butler, Danforth Farm, Brinker House, Massey Ironworks, McMurtry Spring, Mantle Rock, Fort Lovell, Fort Payne, Park Hill, Fort Montgomery, Tuscumbia Landing.

INDEX